Trial Practice Series

Eyewitness Testimony
Strategies and Tactics

Professor Edward Arnolds
John Marshall Law School
Chicago, Illinois

Professor William Carroll
John Marshall Law School
Chicago, Illinois

Professor Melvin B. Lewis
John Marshall Law School
Chicago, Illinois

Professor Michael Seng
John Marshall Law School
Chicago, Illinois

SHEPARD'S/McGRAW-HILL, INC.
P.O. Box 1235
Colorado Springs, Colorado 80901

McGRAW-HILL INFORMATION SERVICES COMPANY
New York • St. Louis • San Francisco • Auckland • Bogotá
Caracas • Colorado Springs • Hamburg • Lisbon • London
Madrid • Mexico • Milan • Montreal • New Delhi
Oklahoma City • Panama • Paris • San Juan • São Paulo
Singapore • Sydney • Tokyo • Toronto

1234567890 SHHA 893210987654

Library of Congress Cataloging in Publication Data

Main entry under title:

Eyewitness testimony.

(Trial practice series)
Includes index.
1. Witnesses—United States. 2. Crime and criminals
—United States—Identification. 3. Trial practice—United States. I. Lewis, Melvin B. II. Series.
KF9672.E94 1984 347.73'66 84-22121
347.30766

ISBN 0-07-056216-4

EYE2

We dedicate this effort to all those who have received injustice from the hands of those who sought to do justice

Preface

That eyewitnesses are often mistaken is a commonplace—except, it seems, to sitting jurors. The eyewitness continues to be deadly in the courtroom. Ever since the United States Supreme Court in *United States v Wade*[1] took note of Wall's book[2] on eyewitness identification, literature on the subject has come forth in a flood. For the most part, it has reiterated in greater detail the truism that eyewitnesses are fallible and that their testimony should be treated with great caution. Psychologists who study perception have multiplied experiments that confirm earlier ones. Clearly, the observation that witnesses are often deceived by their senses need not be stated again.

This volume attempts to move beyond the common wisdom. It is designed to help the practitioner make use of the accumulated knowledge concerning misperception. It explains the mechanisms of the perceptual processes and points out the stages in those processes where error may easily enter. It suggests the probable direction of that error. Moreover, it suggests ways in which this information can be effectively brought before the jury. It demonstrates how the trial lawyer can draw out a witness so as to expose and underscore those very factors which render eyewitness perceptions and memory prone to error.

In short, this is a practical book, designed to help the trial lawyer alert jurors to what they should already know but often overlook when exposed to the sincere, confident, but mistaken eyewitness who holds the key in an important case. Justice can only be served thereby.

---

[1] United States v Wade, 388 US 218, 229 (1967).

[2] P.M. Wall, Eyewitness Identification in Criminal Cases (1965).

Contents

Summary

Detailed

1 The Scope of the Problem

§1.01 The Role of the Percipient Witness

Facts at issue in a trial may be established in many ways. The parties may stipulate to a given statement of the facts. A party opponent may admit the facts. Such admissions may be elicited from the party on the witness stand at trial or in pretrial discovery. Admissions may also be secured from written documents prepared by the party or from statements made by him or her to third persons. Some facts may be established through mathematical calculations, accounting techniques, or the testimony of experts. Other facts are established circumstantially or by inference.

One of the most persuasive ways to establish a fact is through the testimony of an eyewitness to the event. A witness takes the stand and says, "I saw the defendant rob the bank," or "I observed the car traveling at a speed of 75 miles an hour," or "I saw John Smith approach Jane Doe and heard him call her 'a dirty whore.' " For most persons such statements establish the fact. This event must have happened because an impartial third party witnessed it. Such testimony wins lawsuits.

However, for the party against whom the testimony is being offered, eyewitness testimony presents a serious problem. Assuming the witness is not obviously biased or malicious and assuming the witness is not lying but sincere, how does one deal with such testimony? Especially when there was only one witness to the event and that witness swears that the defendant drove the offending car, how does one show that the witness is mistaken? When Jane Doe says that the defendant raped her, how does one establish that this is a case of mistaken identity?

§1.02 Some Cases in Point

Cases of mistaken identity are legion. In February of 1979, Father Bernard T. Pagano, a Roman Catholic priest, was arrested and charged with the armed robbery of six northern Delaware stores.[1] Seven store clerks identified the clergyman as the *gentleman bandit* who had pointed a chrome-plated handgun at them. Following the unwavering testimony of these seven eyewitnesses, the trial had become what is known at the criminal bar as a *slow plea*. Few persons doubted the outcome would be a guilty verdict—until the trial judge announced to a stunned courtroom that another man had just confessed to the robberies.[2]

Father Pagano was one of the lucky ones. Scarcely a week goes by that the newspapers do not report the release of an innocent person who had been convicted and imprisoned on the basis of eyewitness misidentification. The literature is replete with examples of those who not only have

---

[1] The Pagano case was widely reported in the press, e.g., Chicago Sun-Times, Aug 21, 1979 at 7, col 1; Chicago Tribune, Aug 24, 1979, §2, at 2, col 4.

[2] For a detailed account of the case see Buckhout, *The Mistaken Seven: Eyewitness Identification in the Case of Delaware v Father Bernard T Pagano*, 5 Soc Action & L 35 (1979). Dr. Buckhout, whom Judge Andrew Christie had ruled competent to testify for Fr. Pagano as an expert on eyewitness identification, cites six steps in the identification process which led to the in-court misidentifications. Those were:

1. Composite drawings that led to an anonymous tip
2. A showup (which did not result in an identification)
3. A photo spread using a 10-year-old photo of Fr. Pagano (the man who confessed was 14 years younger than the priest) which was distinctive from the other photos in the spread
4. Use of that photo which all the witnesses saw in a newspaper account of the robberies
5. A second photo spread using a recent photograph of the priest wearing a light coat and a hat with a light band, and photographs of police officers, who were all 21 years younger than the priest and who wore dark coats and hats without bands, and where Fr. Pagano's picture was reverse-printed so as to be the only one with the profile to the left
6. A lineup that Buckhout calls "a redundant process which merely gives witnesses who 'flunked' earlier tests a chance to take it again."

Id 38

been jailed, but also executed, on the basis of erroneous eyewitness testimony.[3]

A story in the *Chicago Tribune* in 1981 reported five recent cases in which persons had been freed after having been wrongfully convicted on the basis of eyewitness testimony:[4] Larry Smith, who had served five years of a life sentence for murder; Smith's cellmate, Floyd Fay, also convicted of murder, freed after serving two and one half years; Douglas Forbes, freed after serving five years for two rapes prosecutors say he did not commit; Keith Hart, who had served two years for rape, abduction and robbery; and Aaron Lee Owens, released from San Quentin after having served nine years of a life term imposed for two erroneous murder convictions. The *Tribune* story missed the case of Francis P. Hemauer, who was freed a few days prior to publication of the article after having served 8 years of a 60-year sentence for a rape he could not have committed.[5]

In the early twentieth century, the cause celebre for those who questioned the validity of eyewitness testimony was the trial of Sacco and Vanzetti. On April 15, 1920, two men robbed and killed a paymaster and a guard in South Braintree, Massachusetts. The crime was similar to several others then being investigated by the Braintree police. Eyewitnesses to the other crimes believed the perpetrators to have been Italians. At the same time that the Braintree police were investigating these crimes, the Department of Justice was hunting and deporting Communists. In the course of one of their raids, the department arrested two Italians; Sacco, a worker in a shoe factory, and Vanzetti, a fish pedder. Eyewitness testimony formed the major part of the prosecution's case. However, eyewitnesses also testified for the defense, and other witnesses supported the defendants' alibi that they were elsewhere when the crime occurred. Both men were convicted and subsequently executed.

In his classic work on the Sacco and Vanzetti case, Felix Frankfurter questioned the worth of identification testimony.[6] Frankfurter identified the elements which intensified the uncertainty of the identifications in that case:

---

[3] E.g., E. Loftus, Eyewitness Testimony 1-8 (1979); P. Wall, Eye-Witness Identifications in Criminal Cases 11-24 (1965).

[4] Chicago Tribune, Apr 12, 1981, §1, at 20, col 1.

[5] Chicago Sun-Times, Apr 9, 1981, at 36, col 4. A collection of other newspaper stories of mistaken identifications appears in 6 Soc Action & L 68-79 (L. Schwed ed 1980). See also T. Sannito, Discrediting Eyewitness Testimony 7-9 (1979).

[6] F. Frankfurter, The Case of Sacco and Vanzetti 30 (1927). Frankfurter's reservations were relied upon by the United States Supreme Court in United States v Wade, 388 US 218, 228 (1967).

> [1] All the identifying witnesses were speaking from casual observation of men they had never seen before, men of foreign race, under circumstances of unusual confusion. . . .
>
> [2] [T]he methods pursued by the police in eliciting identification in this case impair its worth. In England, such methods would have discredited the testimony and nullified a verdict based upon it. The recognized procedure is to line up the suspect with others, and so far as possible with individuals of the same race and class, so as not to provoke identification through accentuation. In defiance of these necessary safeguards, Sacco and Vanzetti after their arrest were shown singly to persons brought there for the purposes of identification, not as part of a "parade." Moreover, Sacco and Vanzetti were not even allowed to be their natural selves; they were compelled to simulate the behavior of the Braintree bandits. Under such conditions identification of foreigners is a farce.[7]

While the given examples all occurred in the context of criminal trials, the problem can be equally troublesome in a civil case. Indeed, in a civil case, it is more likely that an eyewitness' testimony would be accepted by the trier of fact because the civil proponent's case need be proved only by a preponderance of the evidence, rather than beyond a reasonable doubt as in a criminal case.

§1.03 The Problem with Eyewitness Testimony

The scientific community has long viewed eyewitness testimony with skepticism for two basic reasons: the normal and universally acknowledged fallibility of perception and memory, and the susceptibility of the mind to suggestive influences.[8] Professors of psychology regularly stage *mock* crimes to demonstrate to their classes the unreliability of the eyewitness' account.[9]

---

[7] Frankfurter, *supra* note 6, at 31-32.

[8] See P. Wall, Eye-Witness Identifications in Criminal Cases 9 (1965).

[9] E.g., Dr. Buckhout reports that he staged an assault on a professor in front of 141 witnesses and videotaped the occurrence. After the attack, he took a sworn statement from each witness, asking for everything the witness could remember about the attack. The descriptions were quite inaccurate: the elapsed time was overestimated by almost two and one half to one; the attacker's weight was overestimated by an average of 14%; and the attacker's age was underestimated by two years. After seven weeks, 60% of the witnesses, including the professor who had been attacked, chose the wrong man from a group of photographs, 25% choosing an innocent bystander. In a similar incident involving a staged purse snatching, only 7 of 52 witnesses correctly identified the purse

Nonetheless, juries accord enormous weight to eyewitness testimony.[10] It is a rare alibi which will stand up against an unequivocal, positive identification by an eyewitness. Indeed, jurors may be willing to accept the statement of an eyewitness despite the testimony of an expert that scientifically the event could not have happened as the witness related it.

Counsel defending against such testimony thus has a major task to convince the jury that the eyewitness' statement is really only an inference which the witness has drawn from a number of stimuli. The fact that a witness says a car was blue does not in and of itself establish that fact. The validity of that conclusion depends upon the witness' powers of observation and memory, the circumstances surrounding the observation, and the influences which prompted him or her to recall and describe the event.

The validity of the witness' conclusion can be attacked in a number of ways. How strong was the light when the witness saw the car? How far away was the car? How closely was the witness observing the car? Was anything else going on when the car passed by? How concerned was the witness about the car's color when the car passed by? How much time elapsed between the observation and the statement? What prompted the witness to assert that the car was blue? Was there any suggestion made to the witness that the color blue should be important? Was the witness shown any photographs or asked to view any cars before making that statement? These and numerous other questions must be asked and answered prior to making a determination on the accuracy of the simple observation, "The car was blue."

This book goes step by step through the trial process and demonstrates how a lawyer should proceed with a case whose outcome depends upon the simple statement by a witness: "The car was blue," "This is the man who pulled the trigger," or "I heard him say he'd get her."

§1.04 Use of Experts in Eyewitness Cases

The first thing a lawyer should do on entering a case whose outcome depends on eyewitness testimony, is to become familiar with the latest scientific studies on perception, memory, and recall. Many recent studies in these areas will give the attorney valuable leads on how best

---

snatcher out of a videotaped lineup. Buckhout, *Eyewitness Testimony*, 231 Sci Am 23-31 (1974).

[10] See E. Loftus, Eyewitness Testimony 8-19 (1979).

to handle the particular eyewitness testimony under consideration. The attorney is also encouraged to consult the recent literature on this subject.[11]

In a case of great importance and complexity the attorney should consider retaining the services of an expert on perception, memory, and recall. Such an expert should be retained at an early stage, if possible even before formal discovery is begun. The expert can be helpful in investigating and interviewing witnesses, in suggesting possible legal theories and lines of attack, and in preparing the direct and cross-examination of witnesses. The attorney should also give serious consideration to calling the expert as a witness at the trial. Trial judges have been reluctant to allow psychologists to testify in eyewitness cases, and appellate courts have generally upheld the discretion of trial judges who refuse to admit such testimony; nonetheless, counsel should be prepared to urge the admissibility of psychological testimony in appropriate cases.[12]

Historically, the law has been aloof to the findings of empirical psychology. At a time when this discipline was in its infancy, several scholars attempted to gain a hearing in legal circles for the results of research that bore on evidentiary issues.[13] John Henry Wigmore was influential in scotching those attempts.[14] He argued that the findings and theories were insufficiently verified. Moreover, since most of the critical literature on the subject was in foreign languages (mainly German), the American bench and bar were not in a position to evaluate properly the data.[15]

Wigmore's observations undoubtedly had merit at the time. Modern empirical psychology dates back hardly a hundred years to the first

---

[11] See, e.g., E. Loftus, Eyewitness Testimony (1979); A. Yarmey, The Psychology of Eyewitness Testimony (1979); B. Clifford & R. Bull, The Psychology of Person Identification (1978); Psychology in Legal Contexts (S. Lloyd-Bostock ed 1981); see also P. Wall, Eye-Witness Identifications in Criminal Cases (1965); T. Sannito, Discrediting Eyewitness Testimony (1979). See generally the extensive bibliographies in all of the above works. Many of these studies are summarized in **ch 3.**

[12] See **ch 8.** See also Arnolds, Carroll & Seng, *The Admissibility of Expert Testimony on the Issue of Eyewitness Identification in Criminal Trials,* 2 N Ill UL Rev 59 (1981).

[13] J. Ram, A Treatise on Facts (1873); S. Freud, *Psycho-Analysis and the Establishment of Facts in Legal Proceedings,* in 9 The Complete Psychological Works of Sigmund Freud 103 (J. Strachey ed 1959); H. Muensterberg, On The Witness Stand (1908); W. Stern, Beitrage Zur Psychologie Der Aussage (1903).

[14] Wigmore, *Professor Muensterberg and the Psychology of Testimony,* 3 Ill L Rev 399 (1909).

[15] Psychologists were not called to testify in English courts before the Second World War, but after that they were allowed a much wider role than in American courts. Haward, The Psychologist as Expert Witness, in Psychology, Law and Legal Processes 45 (Farrington, Harkins, & Lloyd-Bostock eds 1979).

laboratory at the University of Leipzig, Germany.[16] The early experimentalists had been trained in the physical sciences: physics, chemistry, physiology, neurology, and anatomy. Their early studies in sensory perception reflected the methodology of those sciences. When experimentalists first turned their attention to memory and recall, however, they stepped away from this tradition and adopted a softer methodology, introspection,[17] which was used in the study of memory and recall

---

[16] E. Boring, A History of Experimental Psychology (2d ed 1950).

[17] See *id;* D. Schultz, A History of Modern Psychology (1975). The experimental method came to psychology through physiology. The earlier experimentalists were concerned with the organs of sense and the transmission of information from these organs to the brain via the nervous system. Herman von Helmholtz (1821-1894), trained as a physicist, was concerned with the processes of vision and hearing. He measured the speed of the nervous impulse from the external receptor point to the brain. Before his time, everyone assumed, for example, that light falling on the retina was perceived in the conscious brain instantaneously. Helmholtz demonstrated a time lapse, that the impulse traveled the optic nerve at the rate of 50 meters per second; he also discovered that other, unobserved factors can interfere with this process. Ernst Weber (1795-1878), originally an anatomist and physiologist, determined that measurable differences in the stimulation of the senses would not be consciously detected unless the difference reached a certain magnitude. This discovery came to be known as Weber's Law of the Just Noticeable Difference. Gustav Fechner (1801-1887) introduced *psycho-physics* and turned his attention to color vision and the phenomenon of the afterimage. Wilhelm Wundt (1832-1920), who came to psychology from physiology and medicine, believed that the experimental method could be applied only to perception and not to memory and recall. As a result, he introduced a methodology to study unobservable processes such as memory, which he called *introspection.* In this procedure, the experimental subject was asked to report internal, conscious experiences. This clinical approach, to be followed later in other branches of psychology, was rejected as *unscientific* by others in the field; it was considered too unreliable because no two subjects reported the same thing.

A student of Wundt, Bradford Titchener (1867-1927), brought the introspective method to America. He opened a laboratory at Cornell University and pursued the study of perception and recall after the fashion of his German mentor, Wundt. The methodology was very suspect to pragmatic American psychologists; consequently, research in this area of memory and recall for a time was not highly regarded here in scientific circles. It was against this background that Wigmore made his disparaging comments about expert psychological testimony. See Wigmore, *supra* note 14. By 1920, the introspective method had run its course, and the more rigorous experimental method had come to be applied to the study of perception and recall. Herman Ebbinghaus (1850-1909) had shown in his book, *On Memory* (1885), that complex psychological phenomena such as memory and recall were indeed susceptible to the experimental method. John Watson, then of Johns Hopkins University, published a paper in 1913 in which he showed how the experimental method could be used to measure human behavior under controlled circumstances in such a way that unobservable, conscious processes such as memory could be indirectly but reliably studied. Since then, the experimental method has dominated the study of perception and memory. There is a recognized continuum in the field of psychology that has at one end those subspecialties in which the methodologies are akin to those of physics and chemistry and at the other end those subspecialties for which art is perhaps the more appropriate model. Mitroff & Kilman, *On Evaluating Scientific Research: The Contribution of the Psychology*

at this initial stage and was still dominant at the time Wigmore wrote. The subject was asked to report internal experiences while physical and physiological variables were systematically altered. This, of course, was a highly subjective procedure. By the first decades of this century, however, the empirical study of memory and recall in this country was returning to the methodology of the so-called hard sciences. Objective measurement, mathematical expression, and predictability became norms, and by 1913 Wigmore himself was calling attention to some psychological data.[18]

The proper test for the admission of expert testimony is whether the methodology relied upon by the expert is generally accepted as reliable and valid, not whether the experts in the field agree in their conclusions.[19] The methodology of that subspeciality of experimental psy-

---

of Science, 8 Tech Forecasting & Soc Change 163-74 (1975); B. Kantowitz & H. Roediger, Experimental Psychology: Understanding Psychological Research 14 (1978). At the *soft-shelled* end are found the clinicians and therapists. The experimental psychologists—such as those who work on perception and recall—are generally accepted in the field as being located toward the extreme *hard-shelled* end of the continuum.

[18] J. Wigmore, Science of Judicial Proof (1913). Wigmore himself explained the basis for this shift: "When the psychologist is really ready for the courts, the courts are ready for him." 3 J. Wigmore, Evidence 368 (3d ed 1940).

[19] For example, in United States v Alexander, 526 F2d 161 (8th Cir 1975), the court refused to admit an unstipulated polygraph test, offered by the defendant, on the ground that the scientific community generally found the test to be unreliable and invalid. Reliability refers to the question whether the test will yield substantially the same results if repeated again and again under the same controlled circumstances. See L. Tyler, Tests and Measurements: Foundations of Modern Psychology Series 32 (1963). The *Alexander* court noted that research indicated that a polygraph test could be wrong more than once in four tries. 526 F2d at 165. Validity refers to the question whether the test really does measure what it purports to measure. See L. Tyler, *supra* at 28. Again, the *Alexander* court noted that there were opportunities in the polygraph procedure for the tester's biases to affect the outcome and that the results of the test could also be influenced by other extrinsic and uncontrolled factors. 526 F2d at 165-67. The court did state that polygraph tests might be admissible in the future should they find greater acceptability in the scientific community. *Id* 166. As an additional reason for excluding the polygraph test, the court stated that it feared the test would pervade the fact-finding process and have an exaggerated effect on the jury. *Id* 168. In Ibn-Tamas v United States, 407 A2d 626, 639 (DC 1979), where the court held that the testimony of a psychologist on the battered-wife syndrome should have been admitted, the court explained that those cases which had excluded expert testimony had done so not because the scientific knowledge in itself was deficient, but rather because the method of scientific inquiry was not generally accepted (citing, e.g., Brown v United States, 384 A2d 647 (DC 1978) (voice prints inadmissible); Frye v United States, 293 F 1013 (DC Cir 1910) (polygraph results inadmissible); United States v Hearst, 412 F Supp 893 (ND Cal 1976), *affd,* 563 F2d 1331 (9th Cir 1977) (stylistic comparison of defendant's known writings and utterances with later writings and tape recordings inadmissible)), or because the testimony failed to meet the threshold test of believability in that the state of scientific knowledge was so meager as to reflect the conclusion that no reliable methodology for making the inquiry had been discovered, Tonkovich v Dept

chology which deals with perception and memory is currently accepted as reliable. The experimenter takes control over all the factors which might influence the outcome of the test, so that those factors not under study are neutralized. The one factor which is the focus of the study is thus allowed to exert its influence, and it is then observed and measured—sometimes in relation to another factor under control.[20]

It is ironic that the courts have generally permitted the testimony of clinical psychologists[21] but have shown more skepticism about admitting the testimony of experimental psychologists.[22] Unlike clinical

---

of Labor & Indus, 31 Wash 2d 220, 195 P2d 638 (1948) (testimony that cancer caused by on-the-job injury inadmissible). The court illustrated the comparison by reference to two *Hearst* opinions. In the first, United States v Hearst, 412 F Supp 889 (ND Cal 1976), the qualifications of and the methodology used by a psychologist who testified to the impact of kidnapping and related incarceration on the defendant's mental state when she allegedly committed a crime were not questioned and the testimony was admitted. In the second *Hearst* opinion, United States v Hearst, 412 F Supp 893 (ND Cal 1976), *affd,* 563 F2d 1331 (9th Cir 1977), the methodology utilized in psycholinguistics was challenged and testimony comparing the defendant's earlier writings and utterances with her later writings and tape recordings was not admitted. The court of appeals explained that the different results in the two opinions could not be explained on the ground that the trial judge believed that the psychologist was more knowledgeable than the psycholinguist. Rather, the trial judge had determined that there was a generally accepted methodology in the field of psychology which could be utilized to explain the effects of a kidnapping on one's mental state, but that there was no generally accepted methodology in the field of psycholinguistics to explain differences in a person's writing and voice patterns. This distinction makes good sense. A trial judge can readily determine by objective data whether an expert relied on a generally accepted methodology to formulate his or her opinion. But, realistically, a trial judge is usually not in a position to determine whether a sufficient quantum of knowledge exists in a given field so that an expert's opinion can be said to be generally accepted. See J. Weinstein, Evidence ¶702[02] (1981).

[20] R. Hyman, The Nature of Psychological Inquiry 51 (1964).

[21] For example, clinicians are allowed in court to testify to matters concerning: competency, Blunt v United States, 389 F2d 545 (DC Cir 1967); People v Crawford, 66 Mich App 581, 239 NW2d 670 (1976); disability under insurance policies, Hidden v Mutual Life Ins Co, 217 F2d 818 (4th Cir 1954); disability under workers' compensation acts, Bilbrey v Industrial Commn, 27 Ariz App 473, 556 P2d 27 (1976); the causal connection between tortious action and perceived mental conditions, Reese v Naylor, 222 So 2d 487 (Fla 1969); civil commitment, United States v McNeil, 434 F2d 502 (DC Cir 1970); and responsibility for criminal behavior, Jenkins v United States, 307 F2d 637 (DC Cir 1962); People v Felton, 26 Ill App 3d 395, 325 NE2d 400 (1975).

[22] United States v Brown, 540 F2d 1048, 1054 (10th Cir 1976), *cert denied,* 429 US 1100 (1977); United States v Brown, 501 F2d 146, 150 (9th Cir 1974), *revd on other grounds,* 422 US 225 (1975); United States v Fosher, 449 F Supp 76 (D Mass 1978); People v Brooks, 51 Cal App 3d 1, 7, 112 Cal Rptr 834, 837 (1974); Pankey v Commonwealth, 485 SW2d 513, 522 (Ky 1972); People v Suleski, 58 AD2d 1023, 1027, 397 NYS2d 280, 282 (1977). *But see* United States v Watson, 587 F2d 365, 269 n 6 (7th Cir 1978).

A number of critics have pointed out the methodological weaknesses in clinical procedures. See generally J. Ziskin, Coping With Psychiatric and Psychological Testimony (3d ed 1981); Comment, *The Psychologist as Expert Witness: Science in the*

opinions based on interviews and projective tests, which are so dependent on subjective impressions that testing of their reliability and validity is almost impossible, the findings and methodology of experimental psychological studies are published in technical journals for all to scrutinize. A published report of such a study describes in detail the manner in which the subjects were chosen, how extrinsic factors were identified and controlled, how the tester's biases were eliminated, and how the judgment as to the level of reliability and validity was achieved.[23] An experimental psychologist testifying in a court of law can be closely cross-examined on procedures and inferences, since all the data of the experiments upon which he or she relies are available to the world.

Modern rules of evidence emphasize that trial judges should be liberal in admitting reliable evidence which is relevant and material and not unfairly prejudicial, confusing, or misleading, so as to help the jury ascertain the truth. If the testimony of an expert on perception, memory, and recall would help the jury evaluate the testimony, that testimony should be admitted, at least in cases where the eyewitness' testimony is uncertain and is not supported by corroborative evidence.

§1.05 Handling Eyewitness Testimony at Trial

The old saw that trials are won or lost at the preparation stage is especially true of eyewitness cases. It is therefore crucial that counsel thoroughly investigate the scene and interview all witnesses, and the authors here provide checklists to aid counsel's investigation.[24] Counsel should also take full advantage of discovery techniques to insure that there will be no preventable surprises at trial.

Counsel in criminal cases should be prepared to make timely motions to suppress. Suppression may be allowed when an identification is the

---

Courtroom?, 33 Md L Rev 539 (1979). The psychologists (and psychiatrists) who came to testify as to mental conditions and to forecast future behavior lean heavily upon the clinical interview and projective and nonprojective tests. The Minnesota Multiphasic Personality Inventory (MMPI) is the popular nonprojective test, while the Rorshach (ink blot) and Thematic Apperception Test (TAT) are examples of the projective tests used. Wade & Baker, *Opinions and Use of Psychological Tests: A Survey of Clinical Psychologists,* 32 Am Psychologist 874-75, 879 (1977). The reliability of these techniques has never been properly demonstrated. *The Psychologist as Expert Witness: Science in the Courtroom?*, 38 Md L Rev 539, 572 n 169, 573 n 170 (1979). Clinical practitioners, nonetheless, find these tests extremely helpful in arriving at their admittedly subjective evaluations.

[23] See B. Kantowitz & H. Roediger, *supra* note 17, at ch 4, *How to Read a Journal Article.*

[24] See **§§3.02, 3.03.**

"fruit of an unlawful arrest."[25] Also in *Stovall v Denno*[26] and *Foster v California,*[27] the United States Supreme Court held that identifications produced by confrontations which are unnecessarily suggestive and conducive to irreparable mistaken identification, violate due process. In *Stovall,* the Court held that, under the totality of the circumstances in that case, the showing of the suspect singly to the victim who was recovering in a nearby hospital was reasonable. In *Foster,* however, the Court said that the suggestive elements in the lineup and showup procedures utilized in that case made it all but inevitable that the defendant would be identified, and the Court vacated the conviction.

Nonetheless, recent decisions permit in-court identifications by eyewitnesses even though the initial confrontations were suggestive. In *Mason v Braithwaite,*[28] the Supreme Court held that identification testimony is admissible if under "the totality of the circumstances" the identification is reliable, even though the confrontation procedure was suggestive. Reliability is determined by evaluating the opportunity of the witness to view the criminal at the time of the crime, the witness' degree of attention, the accuracy of his or her prior description of the criminal, the level of certainty demonstrated at the confrontation, and the time interval between the crime and the confrontation. More recently the Supreme Court has emphasized that evaluating the reliability of eyewitness testimony is primarily the function of the jury.[29] The cases in which eyewitness testimony will be vulnerable to a motion to suppress are therefore likely to be rare; nonetheless, a motion to suppress may be a valuable tool for discovery and for testing one's theory of the case.

Efforts to protect against suggestive confrontations in *United States v Wade*[30] and *Gilbert v California,*[31] by allowing defense counsel to view the identification procedure, were emasculated in *Kirby v Illinois,*[32] which held that there is no right to have counsel present if the confrontation occurs before formal charges are filed against the accused. Similar attempts to prevent a conviction based on the uncorroborated testimo-

---

[25] *E.g.,* People v Bean, 121 Ill App 2d 332, 257 NE2d 562 (1970). *Cf* United States v Crews, 445 US 463 (1980).

[26] 388 US 293, 302 (1967).

[27] 394 US 440 (1969).

[28] 432 US 98, 114 (1977). *See also* Neil v Biggers, 409 US 188, 199 (1972).

[29] Watkins v Sowders, 449 US 341, 347 (1981).

[30] 388 US 218 (1967).

[31] 388 US 263 (1967).

[32] 406 US 682 (1972). *But cf* Moore v Illinois, 434 US 220 (1977) (holding that the right to counsel attaches where the first identification is made at a preliminary hearing).

ny of a single witness have likewise been rejected by American judges.[33] Thus, while counsel should be careful to preserve the record with motions to suppress and motions in limine, in most situations the evidence will be admitted for consideration by the trier of fact. The crucial question, then, in any litigation involving eyewitness testimony is how it can be best handled at the trial itself.

Counsel should be mindful of the special pitfalls inherent in eyewitness testimony at every step of the trial. Counsel should see that the jurors are sensitized to the problems of eyewitness testimony during voir dire and the opening statement. The jury should also be carefully instructed by the court not only at the end of trial but at the voir dire and at appropriate times during the trial. Some courts have devised model instructions to be used for such purposes.[34] A few courts also may allow the testimony of experts to inform the jurors on the fallibilities of eyewitness testimony.

Notwithstanding all of these methods of educating the jury on eyewitness problems, the crucial part of any trial will be the direct and cross-examination of the eyewitness. If the witness' testimony is positive and credible, the trier of fact probably will accept it despite all arguments to the contrary. Therefore, counsel's greatest effort and expertise should be focused on the examination of the witness.

Finally, counsel will want to end the trial with a forceful argument which summarizes the testimony and puts the eyewitness' account in the proper perspective.

At all stages, counsel must be mindful of the basic findings of psychologists which mitigate the efficacy of the percipient witness. The following chapters proceed step by step through this process.

---

[33] United States v Holley, 502 F2d 273, 274 (4th Cir 1974); United States v Telfaire, 469 F2d 552, 554 (DC Cir 1972).

[34] See **ch 9**.

2 Psychological and Psychoneurological Factors in Perception and Memory

§2.01 Introduction

The act of perception would seem to be a straightforward, uncomplicated event. Something presents itself to a person's eyes, ears, or touch. These senses, like a camera, imprint an image on the consciousness. The senses would seem to be clear windows through which the consciousness looks out upon the world. However, this is not how the process occurs. The act of perception is a complex event.

An analogy will help. A stone thrown into a still pond creates a symmetrical pattern of ripples which run in ever-widening circles to the shore. Since the pond was perfectly still before the stone was thrown, the effect upon the water is attributable completely to the external forces which acted upon it—i.e., the size of the stone and the force and angle at which it was thrown. Theoretically, a physicist, closely measuring the change of the state of the pond, might deduce the characteristics of whatever stimulated the pond: its size, its force, and the angle at which it entered the pond. There would be a direct, uncluttered relationship between the stimulated pond and the stimulus that acted upon it.

Consider now a quickly running mountain stream. It comes hurtling along, its currents twisted this way and that by the rocky formation of the stream bed and banks. It is thrown up and dashed down by the boulders over and around which it flows. Its rate of flow constantly fluctuates as the force of gravity works upon it differentially. The stone in the above example is now thrown into this body of water with the same force and angle as before. The effect upon the water is quite different. The symmetrical, concentric circles which were stimulated in the quiet pond are now distorted by the multiple other forces which are simultaneously acting upon the running stream. The stimulation of the thrown stone is merged with the other forces acting *within* the stream: the gravitational pull, the turmoil caused by the boulders, the sudden change of plane of the bed, and the twisting direction of the flow. It becomes nearly impossible to isolate which observable condition of the stream is attributable to which particular force of the many that are simultaneously acting upon the stream. All the forces modify one another and merge into the observable end product. The stimulation caused by the stone thrown from without is received into an ongoing, dynamic process. The reaction of the stream to the stone is a function of multiple, interacting events.

Human perception is a phenomenon similar to that involving the stone thrown into the mountain stream. An external object or situation acting upon the senses is thrown into an ongoing, dynamic process. By the time it matures into a conscious perception in the higher centers of the cortex, it has merged with many other forces simultaneously at work. It has acted upon them and has been acted upon in return. The final perception is the product of multiple factors, internal and external. In no way is it a simple mirror image of the external reality. To understand perception and to evaluate its fidelity to objective reality, these multiple influences must be understood. An understanding of their interaction assists enormously in understanding how perceptual errors come about and indicate when to anticipate them in the honest but mistaken eyewitness. As Parmenides remarked: "The eyes and ears are bad witnesses when they are at the service of minds that do not understand their language."[1]

---

[1] Diogenes Laertius, Lives and Opinions of Eminent Philosophers (R. Hicks trans 1925). Helmholtz was one of the first to point out the unconscious inferences which people employ in everyday perceptions. Popular Lectures on Scientific Subjects (E. Atkinson trans ed 1903).

§2.02 The Neurological Basis of Perception

The first consideration here is the basic physiology of the sense perception event.[2] Though treated in summary fashion, the discussion is technical. It is introduced here because it provides the neurological foundation for the interaction among emotions, motives, and perception.

A person's initial contact with the external world is at the nerve endings in the various sense organs and the skin. These nerve endings are called *receptors.* The receptors are activated through electrochemical processes induced by pressure, light, heat, and the like. This stimulation is transported as an impulse over complex neural pathways to the central nervous system—i.e., either to the nervous tissue of the spine or to the brain directly. Of the impulses directed to the spine, some are communicated to another pathway and then make their way to the brain by means of this exchange. Other neural pathways proceed continuously through the spinal cord to the brain without this detour. These pathways carrying information to the brain are known as *afferent neurons.*

The brain is a highly complex structure. For present purposes, it should be noted that there are lower and higher centers in the brain to which stimulation from without is directed. The lower centers are located in growths about the end of the spinal stem, forming the base of the brain. The higher centers are located in the upper surface of the brain, the cerebral cortex. It is thought that the lower centers represent the control centers of the organism in an earlier, prehuman stage of evolutionary development. They are oriented to primitive, life-sustaining reactions such as fear, hunger, and anger. The higher cortical centers, on the other hand, are the site of characteristically human activities such as conscious perception, motivation, understanding, and judgment. Information from the outside world passes first to the lower centers and then is relayed to the cortex. It is only then, in the higher centers, that a human being experiences true perception—i.e., that one "sees", "hears", etc. Orders are then sent back down the neural system to the *effectors* in the muscles which control the way in which a person responds to the perception. The transmission devices which convey these orders to the effectors are called *efferent neurons.*

Such is a crude outline of the system which serves sensory perception. The discussion now turns to factors which highly complicate this transmission system.

---

[2] The following discussion is dependent on V. G. Dethier & E. Stellar, Animal Behavior, its Evolutionary and Neurological Basis (1961); A. J. Carlson & V. Johnson, The Machinery of the Body chs 10 & 11 (1948); Katz, *The Nerve Impulse,* 185 Sci Am 55-64 (1952); C. Levinthal, The Physiological Approach in Psychology 9-64 (1979).

The reaction of the receptor is not in direct proportion to the strength of the external stimulus. Physiologists speak of the *all-or-nothing* law. The force of the external stimulus either does or does not rise to the arousal threshold of the neuron. If it does not, the neuron does not detect the presence of the stimulus *at all.* It is not a matter of only a slight response. There is *no* response. On the other hand, if the threshold is crossed, the neuron responds with the *full* force of which it is then capable. Any increase in the strength of the external stimulus has no added effect. The neuron has already responded with an impulse that is at full potential. The proportional strength of external stimuli have a varying effect on the frequency of impulses, but not on their strength.

A crude analogy to the all-or-nothing principle is seen in the firing of a pistol. The pressure put upon the trigger of the gun need be only of sufficient strength to trip the hammer. This, in turn, strikes the shell and releases whatever explosive power is stored there. It is all or nothing. Slight pressure on the trigger has no effect at all on the powder, while an extremely strong squeeze on the trigger has no more effect on the explosion than does the minimal pressure needed to release the hammer. The resulting explosion is totally dependent on the energy stored in the *powder, not* in the trigger finger. So it is with the impulse in the neuron. The amplitude of the impulse is totally dependent on the *subjective* state of the neuron *at the moment.* The condition of the neuron changes from moment to moment. Any factor in the organism which affects the electrochemical condition of the neuron raises or lowers its firing threshold and determines the force with which the neuron is capable of responding. *Thus, the intensity of the impulse is totally independent of what is happening in the external world.* It is dependent upon the subjective condition of the organism. Variations of intensity occur, but they are determined by *internal* factors. What the organism is biologically ready to do at the moment determines whether and how the external stimulus is received.

Impulses from the receptors do not move to the cortex of the brain along a continuous, uninterrupted neural fiber. The transmission system is made up of discrete but interconnected segments. The points of communication between the segments are called *synapses.* Synapses are narrow gaps forming an electrical field over which the impulse jumps to trigger the adjacent segments. What is relevant to this discussion is that the synapse is not a simple relay station. Especially in the central nervous tissue, a great number of neurons are communicating with one another at a single synapse. Because of this arrangement, it is possible for a single impulse to send off messages in many directions. Impulses from quite diverse areas of the body can influence one another.

An example of the interaction among the nerve pathways is seen in the relatively uncomplicated knee-jerk reflex.[3] It can be influenced by messages coming simultaneously from the arm. If the fist is clenched at the time the knee is tapped, the response of the leg is significantly more violent.[4] Note here that the message which influences this otherwise reflex action of the knee is not a message about something occurring outside the body, but rather something the organism itself is doing—i.e., clenching its fist. What is noteworthy is that the organism's sensitivity to its own internal processes colors the message it receives from the external world. Moreover, messages which the organism received at prior times and stored away may color what it is now receiving from the outside world. For instance, when a person is tapped on the knee several times in succession, he or she will soon respond with the knee jerk even when the tapping doctor merely pretends to tap but holds back at the final instant before contact. There is no need to discuss the theory of conditioned reflexes; it is enough to observe that messages from vision, memory storage areas, and emotions can interact with a message coming from tactile receptors in the leg.

At the points where nerve segments communicate—i.e. the synapse—there exist the same subjective factors that determine whether and how an external sensory receptor is stimulated. The impulse that leaps the gap from one segment and attempts to fire the adjoining segment or segments will or will not be successful in firing them depending on the minimum threshold of the adjoining fibers in relation to the intensity of the impulse.

The level of this threshold, along with the intensity of the impulse that will in turn be generated, is once again dependent on the multiple influences which modify the organic condition of that segment of the system. These influences are most immediately electrical and chemical, but these agents are influenced by glandular secretions and events happening elsewhere in the nervous system. However, there is one event which occurs within the segment itself and determines its readiness to respond. This event is the phenomenon of *adaptation*. A nerve fiber which has been stimulated repeatedly (without opportunity to rebalance its electrical polarization) gradually loses its sensitivity and

---

[3] I.e., the involuntary outward movement of the leg when it is struck just below the kneecap.

[4] W. Vinacke, Foundations of Psychology 32 (1968).

becomes temporarily unable to respond at all. This factor plays a role in color perception under certain conditions.[5]

The other phenomena are relevant here—*summation* and *inhibition.* An impulse crossing the synaptic gap may be of insufficient strength to cross the threshold of the adjoining neuron. Consequently, the message from the outside world would stop right there and never make its way to the cortical center of perception, except for the fact that impulses coming from other neurons, which intercommunicate at this synapse, may join with the initial impulse and fortify it. The result is that the combined intensity may cause the adjoining segment to *fire* and carry an originally weak impulse onwards. This phenomenon is called *summation.* Hence, once again, what arrives at the cortex is attributable not only to stimulation from without but also to complex neural activity within the body.

A contrary reaction may occur as well. An impulse which is quite sufficient to cross the synapse and trigger the postsynaptic neuron may be cancelled out by other impulses simultaneously active in the electrical field at the synapse. The impulse may never reach the cortex, even though it had a strong start. This phenomenon is called *inhibition.* Because of this phenomenon, internal activity is capable of shutting out stimulation from the external world.

§2.03 —Interaction of Impulses in the Brain

The opportunity for nerve impulses to interact with one another is multiplied a thousandfold as the impulses enter the brain. As noted in **§2.02,** there are lower and upper coordinating centers in the brain. It is only when impulses reach the upper centers that a human being experiences conscious perception—i.e., that he or she actually sees, hears, or feels in our normal understanding of these terms.

There are fairly specific locations in the cortex where the different forms of perception occur. For instance, sight registers at a location to the rear of the cortex, while hearing registers at a location on the side. However, the greater part of the cortex is given over to the tasks of pooling and coordinating information arriving from the various senses and interpreting and storing it. In one study (made possible when the vision area of a patient's cortex was exposed to remove a tumor) the primary area of vision was artificially stimulated.[6] The subject *saw* bright light straight in front of him when stimulated at one point, while the light shifted to different parts of his field of vision as the stimulation was

---

[5] See **§§2.12-2.15.**

[6] R. Woodworth, Psychology 261 (1949).

moved about in this area of the cortex. When the stimulus was applied outside the vision area proper and in the association area adjacent to it, the subject reported more meaningful visual appearances; flames, stars, shiny balls, butterflies, various objects, and even persons. Thus, while each sensory system is relatively segregated from the others—e.g., the nerve pathways serving vision are distinct from those serving hearing—each nerve system feeds into that nonspecific, intercommunicating area where data from the other senses, prior learning, and nerve impulses from other parts of the body come together, exchange information, and render an interpretation of the outside world. As the nerve pathway of each specific sense ascends to the cortex, it sends off neural branches which connect to the core of the brain. These collateral branches form a tight web of intercommunicating nerves called the *reticular arousal system.* Impulses fed into this system from the various senses and organs of the body are communicated to all parts of the cortex. Thus, the areas of the brain assigned the function of interpreting sensations are simultaneously influenced by impulses from the several senses as well as by stored prior experience—i.e., memories.

Contributing further to the complexity of the nervous network in the brain is the *autonomic system.* The autonomic system is the neural system which controls and reports the activities of the blood vessels, heart, glands, and viscera. Especially important is the fact that the glands control the secretion of hormones, which strongly influence emotions. The autonomic system feeds into a lower brain center which, as noted in **§2.02,** is the seat of the primitive emotions which safeguard the organism's basic well-being—emotions such as fear, anger, and the drives of hunger, thirst, and sex.[7] It is the site of uncritical, emotional reactions to the outside world. Messages from here are sent on up to the cortex of modern humans where, in the associative areas of the higher brain, humans can exercise some supervision over these emotions. It is significant that this autonomic system is also tied into the reticular system, whereby it communicates with impulses of the sensory system. Thus, one more important set of influences is fed into the cortical process which determines the way people apprehend the world about them.

Even if all this complexity were not enough, there may yet be another factor. This entire nervous system is probably not a passive, reacting system at all. At least as far as the brain is concerned, there is evidence

---

[7] For a schematic presentation, see W. Vinacke, *supra* note 4, at 38. See also J. Olds, *Physiological Mechanisms of Reward,* Nebraska Symposium on Motivation 73 (1955); Cannon, *The James-Lange theory of emotion,* 39 Am J Psychology 106 (1927); but see M. Arnold, Emotion and Personality (1960).

that there is activity which is proper to the brain itself. The brain may independently act upon and modify the messages that are flowing in from the external senses.[8]

The structure and operation of the neural network reveal the enormous possibility of subjectivity in human perception of external reality. A person's goals, hopes, fears, attitudes, and expectations all play a subtle but important role in the way he or she sees things happening about him or her.

§2.04 Behavioral Factors in Perception: Three Stages Vulnerable to Distortion

It is clear that data from the external world is not impressed upon a photographic plate. Rather, the data enters upon an ongoing process, and the data's specific contribution to the final outcome of that process is very difficult to determine. In terms of the analogy in **§2.01,** the data is not a stone thrown into a still pond, but rather a stone cast into a mountain torrent.

Nonetheless, the process in each person tends to be roughly similar since, on the whole, all people agree as to the final product—the preception of reality. People generally agree as to what the external world is like. They agree on the color, height, and width of a specific house to which their attention is directed. So it is with most things. Unfortunately, however, there are times when some see things in a way that is peculiar to themselves. No one else seems to see the thing that way. Sometimes, on further inspection, people agree that an earlier perception, for all its seeming clarity at the time, was in error. Since the external reality has not changed, the conclusion must be that somewhere along the way, the stimuli which greeted the senses became distorted before they matured into a fully conscious perception. Other influences within the perceptual process must have intervened.

Perception proceeds in a series of steps or stages.[9] The potential for distortion exists in any or all of these stages, since there is a continuous interplay of forces throughout the process.

Prior to reception of the stimulus, the person exists in a certain *antecedent context,* consisting of all his or her previous learning, associations, motives, desires, attitudes, and emotional states. In addition, there is a given understanding of the situation in which the person

---

[8] Miller, *Analytical studies of drive and reward,* 16 Am Psychologist 739 (1961).

[9] The following organization of the stages draws on C. Solley & G. Murphy, Development of the Perceptual World (1960).

currently finds himself or herself. This total antecedent context gives rise to a perceptual *set* or *expectancy.* This perceptual set or expectancy is a readiness to perceive the world as consistent with the person's existing apprehension of it. If a person is seeking a banana in the pantry, he or she looks for something greenish yellow. He or she does not expect it to be red and consequently looks right past anything of that color. If a person is at the circus and someone suddenly appears in bizarre clothing and make-up, the viewer readily identifies him or her as a clown and knows what behavior to anticipate from him or her. The situation has defined the performer for the audience. However, should a person meet the same sight while entering a dentist's office, that person would be startled and confused. He or she would find it difficult to *fit the clown in.* The person would be unsure how to behave in the presence of such a sight. Expectancy prepared the viewer to respond in a certain fashion at the circus; without this expectancy, the response is initially chaotic.

In this state of expectancy, then, people *attend* to the field of stimuli presented to them. What they will select, from the general mass of stimuli that impinges upon their senses, to focus attention or awareness upon depends on what the antecedent context has readied them to see or hear. Their attention, consequently, will be selective. They are already predisposed to select and organize the available stimuli in a predetermined way (though certain qualities of the stimuli themselves will also be important determinants).

The next stage in the perceptual process is the actual *reception* of the stimuli in the sense organ. An important factor in this stage is the physiological condition of the receptor at the moment.

As soon as the stimuli are received by the sense organ, a stage of *trial and check* ensues immediately. The data presented the senses is now tested against prior learning, motivation, and other affective states, as well as feedback from any motor activities in progress. There is a general interplay among all parts of the behaving system. Only then does the final, formal perception take place—i.e., the person sees, hears, or smells. Thus, the final perception is not merely a response to an object presented to a person from without; it is an expression of a highly complex system of intrinsic forces.

With this scheme, it is now possible to look more closely at the stages in turn, to note the principles which govern their operation, and to study the conditions under which they may tend to distort perception.

§2.05 Stage One: The Antecedent Context

The various schools of psychology differ in their theoretical explanations of human behavior. No school has a comprehensive theory that explains *all* aspects of behavior with equal clarity and persuasion. Typically, one theory may be more helpful in explaining one area of behavior and less so in explaining others. Consequently, the practicing psychologist tends to be eclectic, choosing his or her theories to fit the particular problem with which he or she is currently occupied.

The gestalt theory seems the most helpful in the area of perception.[10] The gestalt theory is that people tend to perceive patterns, whole structures, or organized forms rather than individual sensory stimuli. For instance, when the "Star Spangled Banner" is heard, the listeners do not attend to the individual notes, but rather to the whole organization of the notes—i.e., the melody. This conclusion is clear from the fact that Americans identify their national anthem in whatever key it is played or whatever instrument is used. This recognition occurs despite the facts that the individual stimuli—the notes—are different in each key, and that the timbre is different for each instrument. What is the same in every rendition is the *relationship* among the various notes. This constancy of relationship is perceived as a melody which is identical. The melody is the structure, form, or organization (in German, *Gestalt*) which encompasses the individual sounds. Despite the fact that the individual sounds in the different renditions are not the

---

[10] Not every student of psychology would agree with this evaluation. A very strong viewpoint in contemporary American psychology is neobehaviorist, which understands perception as an almost mechanical linking of isolated stimuli. Neobehaviorism has been helpful in developing techniques of learning based on this hypothesis. However, there exists overwhelming evidence that the perceiving subject displays a synthesizing process in his or her act of perception for which neobehavioristic theory has no persuasive explanation. The gestaltists, on the other hand, are preoccupied with this organizing ability of the mind and have studied it in detail. Unfortunately, however, they have not been able to unveil the essential nature of the power. Nevertheless, by avoiding the extreme atomism of behaviorism, they have been able to suggest helpful hypotheses and establish descriptive laws. Most observers would agree that both behaviorism and the gestalt theory are pointing to realities and that an adequate understanding of perception probably must draw on both of them.

American empiricism is nervous with the gestalt theory because it fears that the gestaltists wish to attribute an unanalyzable quality to human consciousness. There is, in fact, an historic link between the gestalt theory and the a priori categories of Kant. However, modern gestaltists search for the structuring and organizing tendency of mind in the electrochemical activity of the brain.

For an analysis and critique of competing psychological theories, see B. Wolman, Contemporary Theories and Systems in Psychology (1960); M. Marx, Theories in Contemporary Psychology (1963). For a review and critical analysis of the major theories of perception specifically, see F. Allport, Theories of Perception and the Concept of Structure (1955).

same, the overall organization or pattern remains, and so people are able to identify the melody. Even if one note is omitted and not sounded at all, people will still recognize the melody. They mentally supply the skipped note. The mind recognizes the familiar pattern from the earliest notes and automatically supplies an omitted sound. The person *hears* the *whole* melody.

Another example is seen in the experience of movement. If a vertical line is exposed to a person twice, the second time a little to the right or left of the first, and the time interval between exposures is reduced to one-fifteenth of a second, the person *experiences* the phenomenon of movement.[11] The person sees the same line moving to the right or left. This phenomenon is the principle which underlies the motion picture. The individual stimuli do not register in a viewer's consciousness as such. They are organized into a pattern of movement. Another example involves looking up into a star-filled sky at night. Someone suggests looking for the Big Dipper. Suddenly, a single pattern of stars jumps out of the mass, and the viewers *see* the dipper. A moment ago, they did not see it, although they were *looking* at the same stars.

The readiness of the mind to submit to any suggested organization of the stimuli being received by the senses has been pointed out by Shakespeare:

Hamlet:	Do you see yonder cloud that's almost in shape of a camel?
Polonius:	By the mass, and 'tis like a camel, indeed.
Hamlet:	Me thinks it is like a weasel.
Polonius:	It is backed like a weasel.
Hamlet:	Or like a whale?
Polonius:	Very like a whale.[12]

What is clear from such examples is that between the individual stimulus and the perceptual response, some process of organization takes place which builds the elements into a complex unit. The organized totalities, and not the sensory elements, are the truly perceived phenomena. Much research has gone into identifying the principles that govern this organizing phenomenon.[13] In recent years, there has been an upsurge in interest in general cognitive theory. What

---

[11] Much of the original research in this area was conducted by Max Wertheimer. For a discussion of these experiments, see W. Kohler, Gestalt Psychology (1947).

[12] Hamlet, Act III, scene ii.

[13] For a general discussion of such research see W. E. Vinacke, Foundations of Psychology, 469-511, 550-54 (1968).

clearly emerges is that in each person there is an indomitable drive toward *meaning,* toward perceiving relationships between the items of his or her experience. A person is impelled to make sense of his or her multiple experiences. He or she attempts to fit all new experience into his or her established patterns of understanding. Anything that does not *fit* is left unrelated and meaningless. Just as nature is said to abhor the vacuum, so each person struggles over a new experience to make it fit, to make it conform in some way to his or her current understanding of the world. He or she abhors meaninglessness. When confronted with unfamiliar information or a new experience, he or she undergoes a tension, an anxiety, until the experience can be assimilated into his or her established understanding. Only with the greatest difficulty can he or she readjust a prior understanding to fit that which is new. Where there is conflict between novelty and an established pattern, it is usually the pattern that wins. The new experience is forced to conform to the old structure, even though this may do violence to the reality of the new experience. For example, it took human kind a long time to accept evidence that the world is round.

The tendencies to organize and to preserve established structures serve as the dynamic within the *antecedent context* discussed in **§2.04.** Feelings, desires, attitudes, motives, prior learning, and all such elements subserve the goal of a unified and inwardly consistent world view. It is in such a condition of readiness that people encounter new stimuli.

§2.06 —Principles of Similarity, Proximity, and Continuity

Psychologists have been able to identify certain principles which underlie the organizing tendency in perception.[14] Items with common characteristics (similarity), located close together in space or time (proximity), or so placed in relation to one another that they suggest a continuous series or line (continuity) tend to be seen as the figure or pattern they *form* rather than as the individual elements they *are.* The figure or pattern solicits the attention of the perceiver, and other items in the visual or auditory field form a relatively undifferentiated background for the figure. (See Figure 2-1). Black dots of equal size,

---

[14] A summary discussion of these principles is available in most introductions to general psychology. For a fuller discussion, see e.g., W. N. Dember, The Psychology of Perception (1960).

Figure 2-1

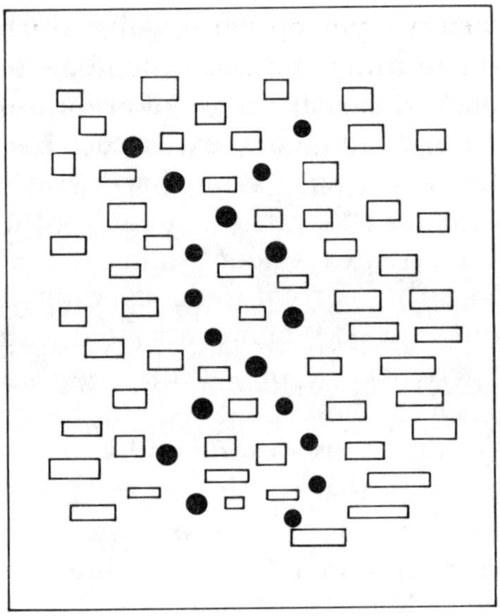

Similarity and Continuity
Dots grouped and seen as line

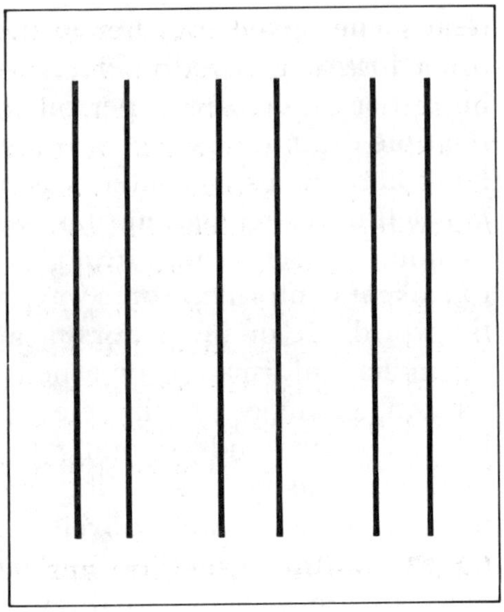

Proximity
Three units are seen rather than six items

interspersed among rectangular shapes in the visual field, tend to be seen as forming a self-contained shape or line in contrast to the rectangular shapes. The similarity and proximity of the black dots allow them to be grouped easily. One dot leads into the other and permits the mind to anticipate yet another which will continue the series.

A similar phenomenon occurs in hearing. Drumbeats interspersed in the orchestration tend to be picked out, especially if they occur in rapid succession—e.g., three short beats together. If the three beats occur together at regular intervals in the piece, they are heard not as three individual beats but as a grouped triad. If the triad recurs at regular intervals in the piece, they are perceived as a series of triads and will be anticipated after the appropriate interval. The rest of the melody is perceived as background to these recurring beats.

A point that is worth emphasizing is that the items which, because of similarity, proximity, and continuity, tend to be grouped into a figure or pattern gather the greater attention in contrast to the other items or stimuli which are also available in the stimulus field. The other items may form so undifferentiated a background that, in some circumstances, they may not be *seen* at all for lack of attention. When a person views a crowded room, those persons whose location, similarity of clothing, expression, movement, or other characteristics lend them to grouping tend to be linked together in the viewer's perception. Events which occur together or follow one another in rapid succession tend to be perceived as somehow related to each other. In fact, the temporal relatedness may be totally fortuitous, but the mind is inclined to link them as tightly as plausibility allows. The medieval philosophers already noted this mental bias and coined an adage as a caution against faulty scientific analysis: "Post hoc non propter hoc" ("*After* does not mean *because of*").[15] The mere fact that one thing follows another in space or time must not immediately lead to the conclusion that the two are causally related. If someone hears a door slam and subsequently sees a person descending a staircase, it does not necessarily mean that the person has just exited an upper room.

§2.07 —Predisposition and Ambiguous Data

Sometimes, items in the external world are so situated that they lend themselves to be organized by the mind in alternative ways with equal ease. These are referred to as *ambiguous figures.* (See Figure 2-2.) A transparent cube allows itself to be perceived as having either of two near edges. Choice of the near edge determines which direction the cube is seen to be facing.

The vase has contours which, when seen as contours of the background rather than contours of the white space, produce a perception of two dark faces confronting one another against a white background. Figure and ground (in psychological terminology) exchange places, depending on how the perceiver organizes the scene.

A descending staircase can be seen equally well as a hanging staircase. Different people can see the same scene in opposite ways, and the same person, if he or she continues to concentrate on the scene, can experience a sudden and almost uncontrollable shift in perception.

Research indicates that when confronted with an ambiguous figure, the observer tends to favor one of the alternative perceptions possible.[16]

---

[15] Merriam-Webster Ninth New Collegiate Dictionary 919 (1983). This was the converse of the logical fallacy "post hoc, *ergo* propter hoc" (after, therefore, *because of*) which David Hume underscored in his famous attack on humankind's assumptions as to causality in A Treatise on Human Nature (1739-40). The philosophic discussion of this fallacy is traceable back to the philosophic school of the Skeptics, *e.g.*, Sextus Empiricus, (CA 200 A.D.). See 14 Encyclopaedia Britannica, Macropaedia 267 (1984) and 1 W. Windelband, A History of Philosophy, 205-06 (1958).

[16] Solley & Santos, *Perceptual learning with partial verbal reinforcement*, 8 Perception &

Figure 2-2

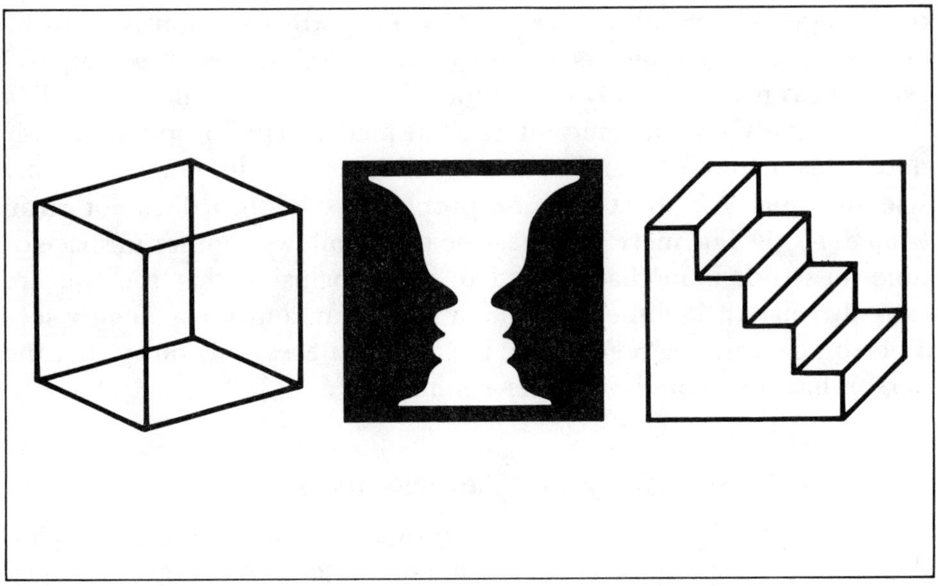

Ambiguous Figures
Perspective shifts automatically after a period of concentrated viewing

It has been suggested that the shift to the less-favored perception occurs when, after a few moments of concentration, the neurons tire and allow the alternative neural pattern to take over.[17] However, higher-level factors also seem to be operating when a choice between the alternative possibilities is being made. Research indicates that emotional and motivational issues are involved. If the less-favored way of perceiving an ambiguous scene is *rewarded,* experimental subjects were found consistently to perceive the rewarded figure on first exposure rather than the normally favored one. In other experiments, it was shown that groups of letters rendered ambiguous by dim illumination are seen as words by those for whom the words are emotionally satisfying, while they cannot be organized into words by those for whom the words to be formed would be emotionally threatening.[18] A person's interpreta-

---

Motor Skills 183 (1958); Shafer & Murphy, *The role of autism in a visual figure-ground relationship,* 32 J. Experimental Psychology 335 (1945); Ayllon & Sommer, *Autism, emphasis, and figure-ground perception,* 41 J. Psychology 163 (1966).

[17] Solley & Santos, *supra* note 16.

[18] McClelland & Liberman, *The effect of need for achievement on recognition of need-related words,* 18 J Personality 236 (1949).

tion of ambiguous stimuli apparently depends on many subjective factors rather than mere physiological adaptation.

§2.08 —Bias toward Symmetry and Closure

The mind's drive toward organization has been found to favor symmetry of figure.[19] A *good figure* is one in which the parts are well harmonized and help to give a clean line to the configuration. (See Figure 2-3) Simplicity, clarity, symmetry, and harmony are characteristics of such a figure. A clear, dominant figure is satisfying to the mind. The mind attends to the clean outlines of such a figure and only secondarily attends to the constituent elements of the pattern. In the gestalt theory, the suggested figure is so controlling that, once it establishes itself, it tends to reorganize its constituent parts into greater and greater harmony and simplicity. Any items that are a bit *out of line* tend to be drawn into a clean contour so as to strengthen the design. An analogy is seen in a cup of milk overturned onto an oilcloth table cover. Fingers of milk run out in all directions at first; then, gradually, the cohesive attraction of the milk for itself pulls the liquid back together and it forms a well-rounded pool or series of such pools. The cohesive action here is chemicophysical dynamism at work within the milk itself. It overcomes the centrifugal movement of the spill as well as the gravitational attraction which tends to keep portions of the milk at the farthest projection they reach. This internal dynamism of the mass of milk distributes the liquid in rounded figures, eliminating all sharp contours and irregularities. In like manner, the dynamism of the mind pulls disharmonious stimuli into line so that they support a good, symmetrical figure.

One of the principles at work in perception which tends to assure a good figure is *closure.* Closure is the magic whereby the mind eliminates discontinuity in the lines of its figure by automatically closing them, making them continuous according to the preconceived notion of what that continuity should be. (See Figure 2-4) An everyday example is seen in the way people read a stenciled sign. Letters printed by the stencil method are necessarily discontinuous, since the pieces of the stencil must be held together with *bridges* which show up in the printed letter as discontinuity of line. Nonetheless, people readily read, for example,

---

[19] W. Kohler, Gestalt Psychology (1947); W. E. Vinacke, Foundations of Psychology 495 (1968).

Figure 2-3

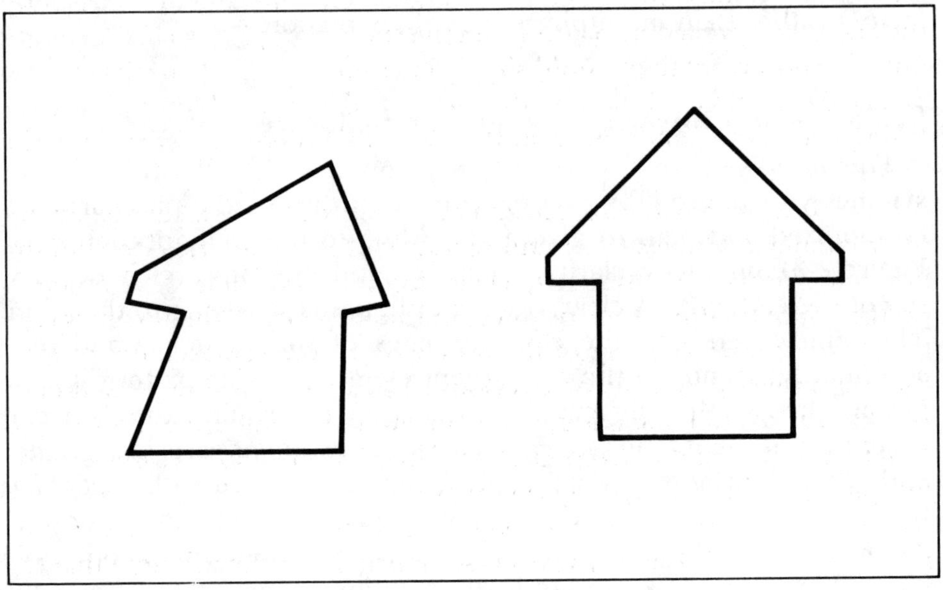

Symmetry of Figure
Movement toward symmetry and good figure

Figure 2-4

Closure

the two curved lines as an *O* in the stenciled word *STOP*. They close the line in their minds. If the two curved lines did not stand in the relation they do to the preceding *S* and *T* and the succeeding *P*, the closure might not have occurred; they would simply have appeared as two curved lines facing each other. However, the organized figure *STOP* had already taken command, and the mind closed all bridges to complete the individual letters.

Line sketches of a house, an animal, or a face may be an arrangement of disconnected lines. The mind readily closes the interruptions in the line and forms a continuous, clean figure. The same phenomenon occurs while reading. For instance, in the sentence "The line forms to he right," the misspelling of the article *the* or the replacement of it by the pronoun *he* can easily be overlooked. A single glace at the sentence reveals its overall meaning. The meaning becomes the figure and dominates the parts. Each part is forced into line, to support the meaning that has been assigned the whole. Thus, *he* is changed into *the* without the conversion ever arising to the level of our awareness. (If the reader rereads the fourth previous sentence, he or she will note that the letter *n* was omitted from *glance.*)

This mechanism of closure is well known to proofreaders. Once they become absorbed in the meaning of what they are reading, they easily overlook items that do not fit that meaning—e.g., dropped letters, missing words, or reversals of position. Once an organizing theme has taken over, the particular parts of the whole are not attended to specifically but are made to serve the whole in perception. This principle is used to advantage in contemporary speed-reading courses. The reader is deliberately encouraged to respond to the theme and ignore the individual words. Gradually, the reader searches out only those words in the sentence which are essential to keeping the theme moving and then quickly moves to the next sentence (or even to the next paragraph).

Closure is an auditory phenomenon as well. Advertising made use of it very dramatically a few years back. Television viewers and radio listeners had drummed into their ears for months jingles like "Winston tastes good like a cigarette should" and "You can take Salem out of the country, BUT—you can't take the country out of Salem." The melody and words formed such strong figures that soon the advertising technique was changed to play half the melody and then pause in silence for the interval it would take to complete the melody. The listener found himself or herself psychologically compelled to complete the melody and words in his or her mind, thus reenforcing the message.

There is considerable research material available regarding the tension that is created when a figure is perceived as incomplete.[20] For emotional relief, a subject is driven to complete the pattern with whatever he or she feels is appropriate. The drive toward a *good figure* is indeed strong.

§2.09 —Bias toward Constancy

A further principle of perceptual organization is *constancy*[21]—the tendency to perceive familiar objects in the size, color, and shape in which the observer normally encounters them. This tendency controls even when a person sees an object at a very unusual angle or perspective so that the stimulation of the retina is quite different from normal. No conscious correction is involved here. The observer actually *sees* the object in its usual size, shape, or color. Thus, when a person who ordinarily wears a white shirt is seen at night in dim light, his or her shirt may be seen by a friend as the customary white, even though the actual reflections of light from the shirt are gray under these conditions. The shirt may not be white at all, but any one of a variety of hues and tones, all of which appear as gray under this illumination. The constancy tendency, however, leads the friend to interpret the very ambiguous stimuli as the familiar white.

The constancy tendency leads to many illusions.[22] People normally estimate the size of various distant objects by comparing them with other objects at the same distance whose size they already know. If the size of the reference object is artificially manipulated, the interpretation of the entire scene may be thrown off. A face in a window may seem of normal size, very small, or enormously large, depending on what one does with the window. A normal house window is what a viewer usually has in mind. By putting the face in an outside window, however, the face can be made to appear unduly small because the relationship of relative sizes has been disturbed. The mind, however, resists abandoning its preconceived notion of the size of a house window, and consequently, the face which fills up but a small portion of the window space is interpreted as tiny. The opposite can also occur. If the face is made to

---

[20] For an interesting instance of this social perception, see Frenkel-Brunswick, *Intolerance of ambiguity as an emotional and perceptual variable,* 18 J Personality 108 (1949); J. J. Gibson, The perception of the visual world (1950); *The reproduction of visually perceived forms,* 12 J Experimental Psychology 1-39 (1929).

[21] W. Vinacke, Foundations of Psychology 498 (1968). For a more extended treatment, see D. Judd, Color in Business, Science, and Industry (1952).

[22] See W. Vinacke, *supra* note 21, at 500, for a discussion of several studies.

fill a window totally by scaling down the window to a very small size, the face, and consequently the person, is seen as enormously large. The normal window size in the viewer's mind remains constant, and since it is the reference object, the face is made to have abnormal proportions. This very illusion was used to dramatic effect by filmmakers in *King Kong*, when Kong discovers Fay Wray in a New York hotel room.

Interesting experiments have been performed to see whether this tendency toward constancy can be consciously resisted. In one experiment,[23] circular and square objects were positioned before the eyes of experimental subjects at such angles that the true shapes were distorted. If photographed from the perspective afforded the subjects, the circles would appear as ellipses and the squares as elongated diamond shapes. The subjects were asked to report what shapes they were *actually* seeing. Instead of reporting the distorted shapes which were actually meeting their eyes, the subjects consistently reported seeing shapes which were truer to the squares and the circles.

The constancy phenomenon occurs also in hearing.[24] Just as known objects tend to be perceived in vision at their true size even when seen at a distance, so also people tend to take account of distance in judging the loudness of a sound. They perceive its intensity not only on the basis of what is vibrating their eardrums, but they perceive the intensity as at its source. The roar of a jet airplane in the distance is perceived as thunderous, even though at the location at which the listener is standing, the sound is not loud enough to disturb a conversation. When a person's voice is heard at a distance, a listener unconsciously draws a conclusion as to what the voice sounds like under closer conditions.

Locating the source of a sound can sometimes be led astray by visual constancy. People are normally quite precise in locating the direction of sound if it comes from the right or left side. This precision is explained by the fact that sound waves from the right reach the right ear before they reach the left ear. However, studies have shown that people are also dependent on visual cues. When there is a conflict between cues, the visual cues tend to be favored and a person *hears* the sound coming from a location from where his or her *sight* indicates it should be coming. In one experiment,[25] the visual environment of subjects was rearranged by use of special glasses. A fireplace was seen on the side of the room opposite to where it actually was located. Nevertheless, subjects heard the fire crackling where the fireplace was

---

[23] Thouless, *Phenomenal regression to the real object,* 21 Brit J Psychology 339 (1931).

[24] R. Woodworth, Psychology 480 (1949).

[25] E. Hilgard & R. Atkinson, Introduction to Psychology 222 (4th ed 1967).

seen, not where it actually was. A similar phenomenon occurs at the drive-in theatre. The conversation of the actors seems to originate on the screen where their lips are moving, whereas it is actually coming from the sound box hooked to the window of the car. Things appear to happen where the observer expects them to happen.

Locating the source of sound is generally difficult without visual cues. As noted above, the direction of sounds to the right or left of the listener can be accurately determined even if the listener is blindfolded or is in the dark. However, beyond these two directions, a listener cannot determine an unseen source. Without further cues, he or she cannot distinguish the direction of a sound coming from above or below, or from the front or the back. When searching for the source of sounds coming from such locations, a listener instinctively twists his or her head so as to present a right-left orientation to the sound.

Perceptual constancy is important, since it allows people to keep their world stable. Things seen at different distances and perspectives register in the consciousness in one familiar way. The bus seen two blocks away appears as the same thing the observer expects to board. The world would seem rather chaotic if people had to register a special conscious shape for every possible perspective in which an object could be seen and then consciously tie all these perspectives to the same object. People are spared this burden by the automatic mechanism of constancy. People are not bothered by the difference in stimuli striking the retina or the eardrum; the images register in the mind as the familiar objects suggested by the stimuli.

This mechanism of constancy is not something a person receives fully developed at birth. Much of it is due to learning and experience.[26] Children gradually learn that the same object may present itself in different ways. In some cultures, where variety of perspective is not available, this tendency is quite undeveloped. The pygmies live in a dense forest where vision is restricted to a couple of yards. When they are introduced to a long view, they cannot recognize familiar objects in the distance. Water buffalo seem like little insects to pygmies. As the buffalo approach the pygmies the animals appear to grow immensely, and it is reported that they terrify the pygmies.[27]

While constancy of perception makes for stability of the perceived world, it can, as noted above, make for inaccuracies of perception. When a familiar object is seen from an unusual perspective, the reason the

---

[26] *Id* 219.

[27] Turnbull, *Some observations regarding the experiences and behavior of Bambuti pygmies*, 74 Am J Psychology 304 (1961).

observer imposes upon the visual stimuli the more familiar shape is that there are usually a number of cues which suggest the familiar object. Returning to the example of waiting for a bus, the color of the distant moving vehicle may be the dominant cue which suggests the bus. There is also the bus's relative size, as well as the fact that the bus is expected at just this time. However, the actual data coming from the distance may be ambiguous. It could be the bus or a truck, but stimulated by these cues and probabilities, the mind leaps ahead to the familiar figure of the bus, and the person *sees* the bus as clearly as though it were right before him or her. Once the organizing figure of the bus is in control of the consciousness, the visual items actually available from the distance are tightly organized into the bus pattern. Unfortunately, sometimes the cues which suggest an object to the mind are misleading. Almost everyone has had the embarrassing experience of waving and gesticulating at a figure in the distance only to discover that the approaching person is not the expected friend at all but a total stranger. So often the expression on such an occasion is: "I would have SWORN that it was my friend!"

In recent years, airplane pilots have occasionally had trouble with gas-powered model airplanes in the sky. A model airplane seen at a certain altitude, devoid of alternative visual cues, is easily interpreted as a full-scale aircraft.

§2.10 Stage Two: Focusing Attention

Attention is the focusing of a person's awareness upon some object or event so that it enjoys a preferred position in that person's consciousness. The object stands out among the mass of competing stimuli impinging upon the senses. Which object or event enjoys this center stage position depends in great part upon the observer's current mental set—i.e., what he or she is *ready* to see or hear. The multiple internal factors which determine the direction of this readiness have been discussed in the previous section. A person's interpretation of the situation he or she is in depends on prior learning, general attitudes, and the tendency to make later experiences consonant with what has gone before; all these factors create a predisposition to focus on some items in the situation rather than on others. As a result, some items immediately stand out like a foreground figure in a painting, while other stimuli receive less attention and recede into a secondary, background position. In psychological terminology, these relative positions are known as the *figure* and *ground* of attention.[28]

When an item enjoys the focus of attention, certain consequences follow in regard to it. The sensation it arouses is more intense. It is sharper and cleaner. The perceptual threshold is lowered for it; for instance, it can be seen under less illumination or heard and distinguished from other sounds at lower volume than things which are not in the focus of attention. Reaction time is changed as well. The perceiver interprets and reacts to it more quickly than he or she would to things to which he or she is not attending. For the most part, these effects increase the accuracy of the perception of things which are the center of attention. However, under some circumstances, they can distort perception.

When a person sits alone in a quiet room with nothing else occupying his or her mind, the ticking of the wall clock can come to sound abnormally loud. Late at night, in a large, empty house, the creaking of the floorboards, the swaying of the trees in the wind, and the crunch of footsteps in the snow outside come through unusually loud and clear. As another example, if the patient is under no anesthetic and the dentist mentions, "Now this is going to hurt a little," the pain will probably be considerably more intense than if the dentist had gone about his or her business without calling attention to the impending sensation. (Thus, some dentists arrange for children to watch cartoons while working on their teeth. Hypnosis and calling attention to something else are also used sometimes in dentistry and local surgery.)

Attention can change the sensory threshold. Subliminal motivation and interest so focus the attention of some subjects that they can make out certain words under very dim illumination or when the words are flashed before them for an extremely brief moment. In one interesting experiment, 160 subjects were divided into two groups.[29] One group was told that words about to be flashed on the screen would have to do with animals and birds. The other group was told the words would have to do with travel and transportation. In fact, the words that were presented had to do with both (and some of the combination of letters formed mere nonsense syllables). The subjects were to write down the words they could make out as they were flashed on the screen. The group with its attention focused on birds and animals was much more successful in accurately perceiving words dealing with birds and animals

---

[28] For a summary discussion of attention as an influential factor in perception, see W. Vinacke, Foundations of Psychology 482 (1968).

[29] E. Siipola, A Group Study of Some Effects of Preparatory Set (Psychological Monographs No 46, 1935).

than was the other group. The other group, in turn, was much more successful with the travel and transportation words.

Attention arising from previous interest or preparation heightens the ability to discriminate among stimuli. The naturalist hears sounds in the woods which the lay person does not. The mother hears the baby stirring in the other room above the buzz of conversation in the parlor. The tightend on the football team hears the change in signals over the roar of the crowd. Experiments have demonstrated the shortening of reaction time on the part of a subject when he or she is expecting and attending to a particular signal.[30]

Unfortunately, attention can also result in a distortion of perception. Later sections discuss the fact that intense stimulation of the visual receptors can cause complementary colors to interchange.[31] It has already been noted that prolonged attention to ambiguous patterns can cause sudden switches in the interpretation of the figure.[32] While attention tends to intensify the sensation and to aid clarity and definition, it also narrows the field of perception. *What* a person sees may be seen very clearly, but the *amount* or *scope* of what he or she sees may be limited. This notion was demonstrated in a classroom experiment.[33] The students, intent upon what they felt would be legally significant in an episode they witnessed, completely missed other simultaneous events which turned out to be more important for purposes of the experiment. The magician depends greatly on this narrowing of perception. He or she calls the audience's attention to his or her right hand. The viewers keep their eyes trained on this hand to detect the deception. Meanwhile, the magician's left hand carries off the trickery, and the viewers are left baffled. To attend to one thing is not to attend to another.

The lowering of the sensory threshold through selective attention can also lead to error. When two things occur simultaneously, the event which was being awaited more intensely will seem to have occurred *before* the unexpected event. The expected event registers in consciousness before the unexpected, even though the two of them actually occurred simultaneously. If a person is avidly awaiting someone's appearance in a window and a gun is fired simultaneously with his or her appearance, it will seem that the shot occurred after he or she appeared. (Perhaps

---

[30] R. S. Woodworth & H. Schlosberg, Experimental Psychology, 10 and following (1958).

[31] See **§§2.12-2.13.**

[32] See **§2.07.**

[33] Otto, *Testimony and Human Nature,* 9 Am Inst Crim L & Criminology 1 (1918). The experiment is described in detail in **§2.40.**

some of the confusion in testimony surrounding the assassination of President Kennedy may be linked to this phenomenon.) Psychologists speak of this phenomenon as the "law of prior entry."[34] When there are two simultaneously competing stimuli, the first to gain entry into consciousness captures the focus of awareness. Experiments with this phenomenon have been done by means of the *complication clock.*[35] While the hand of the clock moves along at its normal rhythm, an electric contact causes a bell to ring at certain points along the hand's progress. The subject is asked to identify the position of the hand on the dial when the bell rings. If the subject has been led to give attention to the clock hand, he or she will err quite significantly in placing the sound of the bell much too late (i.e., after the hand has passed the actual contact point). On the other hand, if the subject is led to attend to the sounding of the bell, he or she consistently judges that it sounded before the hand reached the contact point.

Similar errors occur with ambiguous stimuli. In the experiment described above measuring the threshold of perception, in which subjects whose attention had been selectively aroused to certain categories of words (animals and birds; travel and transportation), a number of nonsense syllables were introduced as well.[36] The interesting result was that the subjects converted meaningless groups of letters into meaningful words of the category to which they were attentive; for example, *pasrrt* was read as *passport.* This perception is another example of a preconceived meaning or pattern imposing itself on the actual sensory data. When a person is *on the look out* for something, the slightest similarity with the object of his or her attention and expectation may trigger a conscious perception of it. The subjects in the experiment felt certain they had seen the words they reported.

How and to what a person attends when confronted with a field of stimuli depends not only on his or her internal predisposition or set, but also, of course, upon the stimuli themselves. Other things being equal, stimuli which distinguish themselves by intensity (e.g., loudness, size, color, brightness, and saturation), by change and movement, by contrast and incongruity, or by repetitiveness tend to capture a person's attention by sheer force of these qualities. A single red marble in a mass of black ones stands out as the figure (focus of attention) against the undifferentiated black background. So also a black person among all whites or a white among blacks appears first in an observer's perception.

---

[34] F. Harmon, Principles of Psychology 269 (1938).

[35] *Id.*

[36] See E. Siipola, *supra* note 29.

A very loud or repetitive sound against other homogeneous sounds or a change or movement against a more static background tends to gain the focus of attention.

An important reservation should be added to the above observations. Sensory *adaptation* may cancel out the attention-getting force of any of these factors. People easily become accustomed to repeated loud noises (e.g., workers in a foundry), strong odors (e.g., workers in a rendering plant), and tactile sensations (e.g., the wristband of a watch). After a while, a person no longer notices their presence.

A further quality of the stimuli themselves which may command attention should be noted. That quality is the ease with which stimuli can be organized into a form or pattern familiar to the perceiver. This factor is discussed above in the treatment of the principles of organization.[37]

§2.11 Stage Three: The Sensory Organs and Lower Order Processes

Some errors of perception are more immediately related to the behavior of lower-order processes—i.e. of the sensory organs—than to the organizing tendencies of the upper brain centers or to selective attention. These errors are discussed in **§§2.12** through **2.15.**

§2.12 —The Afterimage

Errors of color perception are linked to the physiology of the visual receptors. Investigators are not in accord as to a comprehensive theory explaining color perception.[38] However, it is generally agreed that the cone-shaped neurons and rod-shaped neurons in the retina are differentially sensitive. The cones are preferentially adapted to detect wavelengths associated with color, whereas the rods detect achromatic wavelengths—blacks, whites, and grays.

Cones are more abundantly represented in the center of the retina (fovea), while the rods dominate outward toward the periphery of the retina. It is hypothesized that the chemistry of these neurons is such that after intense stimulation by a certain wavelength, the receptor involved *tires* and momentarily ceases to be sensitive to that wavelength in normal white light. This factor results in that wavelength being effectively eliminated from the incoming light, with a resulting color distortion.

---

[37] See **§§2.05-2.09.**

[38] R. Evans, An Introduction to Color (1948).

There are other explanations.[39] Whatever may be the actual reason, it is known that after a person has viewed one color intensively for a time, there is an automatic adaptation or switch to the complementary color. Thus, if a person concentrates upon a red object for a time and then looks away or at some neutral color, that person will see green. In like manner, yellow moves toward blue, black moves toward white, and vice-versa.

One of the writers of this book was once guilty of faulty information because of this color adaptation phenomenon. He witnessed a hit-and-run incident, memorized the license number, and excitedly concentrated on the image of the car as the culprit sped off. He continued to look into the distance as the police arrived. He offered the information and described the car as green and white. Within a few hours, the driver was apprehended. It turned out that the actual colors of the car were red and cream.

§2.13 —Contrast

Another phenomenon associated with the electrochemical principle described in **§2.12** is *contrast.*[40] A colored figure against a colored background may be influenced by adaptation to the background. Since the background is usually stimulating a larger area of the retina than the figure, the retina will tend to tire as to the background color and will *induce* its complementary color into the figure. Thus, a yellow object seen against a green background tends to be perceived as orange (yellow plus the red of the background's complementary color). For similar reasons, gray looks darker against a white background and lighter against a black one.

§2.14 —Twilight Vision (Purkinje Effect)

Another phenomenon in perception is *twilight vision,* also called the *Purkinje effect,* after its discoverer.[41] A certain level of illumination is needed for color wavelengths to be perceived. In low levels of

---

[39] The explanation suggested here is more or less the Young-Helmholtz theory. Competing theories are those of Hering and Ladd-Franklin. While Young-Helmholtz suggest receptors for color (red, green, blue-violet), Hering proposes four. Ladd-Franklin combines both theories. For more see D. McBurney & V. Collings, Introduction to Sensation/Perception 49 (1977).

[40] C.C.D. Shute, The McCollough effect, an indicator of Central Neurotransmitter Activity (1979).

[41] Wald, *Human Vision and the Spectrum,* Sci 653-58 (1945).

illumination, the sensitivity of the human retina shifts toward the shorter wavelengths of the spectrum. Therefore, colored objects seen in dim light, as on a dark evening, appear as variations of blue or gray. If a person perceives such objects as colored under these conditions, it is due to the principle of *constancy,* discussed in **§2.09**—i.e., in the higher centers of the brain, the observer *gives* the object the color he or she thinks it *ought* to have, based upon past experience or expectancy. The perceived color is not always a trustworthy interpretation. Likewise, colored objects seen from the corner of the eye, at the periphery of the visual field, are detected almost exclusively by rods which are not sensitive to color. Thus, they are *gray* as far as the receptors are concerned. If they are perceived in the consciousness as colored, this perception is due to expectation and constancy. Obviously, there is potential for error here.

§2.15 —Light/Dark Adaptation

Another type of adaptation to be noted is the adjustment of the receptors to various levels of illumination. Receptors which have been receiving high illumination and then are suddenly exposed to darkness require considerable time to adjust to this deprived illumination before they can differentiate poorly illuminated objects. A person coming into a dark room from a brightly lighted area may require as much as a half-hour or longer to adjust fully.[42] The adaptation to light after exposure to darkness, in contrast, takes a much shorter time.

§2.16 Aftereffect and Embeddedness

Research indicates that intense concentration on one figure may affect a person's ability to perceive a subsequent figure accurately.[43] For instance, after prolonged concentration on a curved line, it begins to seem less curved. Then, if the observer switches his or her attention to a perfectly straight line, it seems to be curved in a direction opposite to the line he or she had just been viewing. In addition, if a person concentrates upon several items placed at a regular distance to one another and then switches his or her gaze to another set of items, the

---

[42] R. Woodworth, Psychology 443 (1949).

[43] Kohler & Wallech, *Figural after-effects: an investigation of visual processes,* 88 Proceedings, Am Philosophical Socy 269 (1944); Fisher & Lucas, *Illusions in Concrete Situations,* 12 Ergonomics 11-24 (1969).

relative distance between the items in the second pattern are distorted by a *hang over* perception of the first arrangement.

The aftereffect is actually one form of an illusion associated with the phenomenon of *embeddedness*.[44] Objects often appear differently when they are seen in a context. The items with which they are viewed exert an influence on the accurate perception of their attributes—e.g., of their shapes and sizes. What once was known as the Palmolive Building on Michigan Avenue in Chicago (with its Lindberg Beacon) seemed towering to residents until the John Hancock Building was raised beside it. It seems quite small now against *Big John.* Most people are familiar with the impression given by a six-footer on a professional basketball team; the player is known as the *small* guard.

People tend to report heights and weights in relation to some familiar standard, if no other objective standard is available.[45] A person is tall or short in relation to the observer's size. An object is light or heavy depending upon the lifter's strength and what he or she is accustomed to handling; a piano mover has a different standard than a desk clerk.

A related phenomenon is the estimation of space. Filled space seems less extensive than empty space. An empty room seems much larger than one filled with furniture. Architects and interior decorators know that a large blank wall can be made to seem smaller by the addition of some relatively minor decorative item which would break up the visual expanse.

§2.17 Limits of the Perceptual Field

Sometimes, elements in the stimulus field are so arranged that very little help is given to the organizing and relating tendencies of the brain. The perceiver is forced to grasp each item as an individual element. There is a definite limit to the number of individual items which any person can apprehend in a single glance.[46] Again, the span of apprehension differs significantly from person to person. Some can see only six in a single glance while others may see as many as twelve (the average is eight). An individual's ability may vary from day to day. Consequently, if two individuals are given the same amount of time to view the same event, they may be expected to differ as to how much each

---

[44] E. Hilgard & R. Atkinson, Introduction to Psychology 227 (4th ed 1967).

[45] H. Nelson, Adaptation-Level Theory: An Experimental and Systematic Approach to Behavior (1954).

[46] R. Woodworth, Psychology 442 (1949).

saw. Certain items may simply not be present for one witness, while they are fully present to another.

§2.18 Influence of the Affective States

Passing reference to the influence of needs and attitudes upon perception has already been made.[47] The following sections review research in this area.[48]

§2.19 —In the Perception of Objects

Similarity has been shown to be an important organizing principle in the perceptual process. Similar objects tend to be gathered into associative clusters and are perceived as forming a *whole*—a figure differentiated from the rest of the visual background. However, similarity is often a subjective phenomenon.[49] A plumber looking about a well-equipped hardware store mentally categorizes and relates items that appear merely as an undifferentiated mass to someone other than a plumber. The plumber's training, interests, and needs lead him or her to see relationships which do not exist for someone else.

A white person with a lurking fear of dark-skinned people may link blacks, Indians, and Latins under one comprehensive classification, without attending to distinguishing characteristics. The average visitor to the cockpit of a modern airliner sees buttons, knobs, and small, round gauges. A pilot pays little attention to these obvious but superficial bases of organizing the scene. He or she immediately sees clusters of navigation and communication instruments, on the one hand, and clusters of attitude and power control instruments on the other. While some people at a cocktail party may be immediately aware of the different clothing styles that are represented, others may quickly separate the members of the opposite sex into categories of more attractive and less attractive.

Objects with which some people have strong emotional ties look different to them than they do to others. Realtors frequently have a difficult time convincing a homeowner to set a realistic price for his or her house. The homeowner sees the house as practically new and in great condition; a more disinterested observer sees it as rather

---

[47] **§§2.03, 2.04, 2.07.**

[48] See **§§2.19-2.23.**

[49] See W. Vinacke, Foundations of Psychology 592 (1968), for the factors influencing the manner in which people group items.

run-down and in need of considerable renovation. In like manner, the owner of a three-year-old car describes the car differently than the automobile dealer who is considering accepting it as a trade-in.

Considerable research has been conducted over the years into the influence of emotions and attitudes on perception. Subjects who were kept hungry prior to an experiment in interpreting the main theme of pictures tended to interpret the pictures as being related to the preparation or consumption of food.[50] In another test, it was found that poor children tend to overestimate the size of common coins.[51] Rich children estimate more correctly. That this result flows from experienced *need* rather than simple greater or lesser familiarity with coins appears from the fact that the experiment was run with children of equal economic background who were made to *feel* poor or rich through hypnosis.[52] The same kind of test was run with tokens.[53] Tokens were given to two groups of children. One group had to make use of the tokens to get candy from a vending machine; the other group was given candy whether they used the tokens or not. The first group consistently overestimated the size of the tokens while the second group did not.

Experiments with ambiguous figures—i.e., line drawings which can be interpreted in either of two ways—are mentioned in **§2.08.** It has been found that if reward or punishment is associated with one of the interpretations, subjects tend to perceive the figure in just one way—the rewarded way.[54] Similar experiments have been run to test the influence of values and interests on the threshold of perception.[55] Words were presented to the subjects by means of a machine which controls the time a word is exposed to the viewer (a tachistoscope). The investigators measured the time it took a subject to recognize a word. It was found that words which were positively related to an individual's value system (e.g., economics, politics, or religion) were identified much more rapidly than words which were not so valued or were offensive to the individual.

---

[50] Sanford, *The effects of abstinence from food upon imaginal processes,* 2 J Psychology 129 (1936).

[51] Bruner & Goodman, *Value and need as organizing factors in perception,* 42 J Abnormal Soc Psychology 33 (1947).

[52] Ashley, Harper & Runyon, *The perceived size of coins in normal and hypotically induced economic states,* 64 Am J Psychology 564 (1951).

[53] Lambert, Solomon & Watson, *Reinforcement and extinction as factors in size estimation,* 39 J. Experimental Psychology 637 (1949).

[54] Ayllon & Sommer, *Autism, emphasis and figure-ground perception,* 41 J Psychology 163 (1956).

[55] Postman, Bruner & McGinnis, *Personal values as selective factors in perception,* 43 J Abnormal Soc Psychology 142 (1948).

Ingenious experiments have been devised to test the influence of defense mechanisms on perception.[56] A defense mechanism is an unconscious process designed to protect a person from any anxiety-provoking awarenesses. It was discovered that certain pictures could be identified readily under conditions where no anxiety was provoked as to them. However, under conditions which allowed emotions such as sexual fears to be aroused as to them, they could no longer be so readily perceived. In the same way, threatening words are blocked out.

Occupational background is another variable which determines people's perceptions. In experiments with law and medical students, it was found that such words as *cell, administer,* and *complaint* induce quite different conceptual expectations for the two groups.[57] This is one more example of the way in which previous experience, attitudes, interests, and needs color the way people see the world. A young pop singer looks out into an auditorium and sees the adoring teenagers. His or her business manager estimates the number of paying customers. The fire marshall at the same theatre notes the number and locations of exits.

A more dramatic phenomenon is temporary blindness, which can result from emotional trauma or hysteria.[58] It is a blinding of oneself from a scene too horrible to bear. The condition may appear as tubular, restricted vision. The subject sees only those things he or she can presently tolerate in the spectacle before him or her. Total blindness for a short time is another possibility. In the truck-bomb attack on the United States Marine Corps position in Beirut in fall of 1983, a Marine outside the building at the Beirut airport was alerted to the coming explosion a few seconds before the blast. He hit the ground and covered his head. When he looked up again, he was unable to see or hear. Gradually, both his sight and hearing returned.[59] On another occasion, a young man and his younger sister were involved in an automobile accident. The young man was relatively unhurt, but when he turned his sister over and saw her smashed and bloody face, he suddenly cried out, "My God! I can't see! I've gone blind!" As he calmed down and his sister was removed to the hospital, his sight was restored.[60]

---

[56] Blum, *An experimental reunion of psychoanalytic theory with perceptual vigilance and defense,* 49 J Abnormal Soc Psychology 94 (1954).

[57] Foley & MacMillian, *Free association as related to differences in professional training,* 33 J Experimental Psychology 299 (1934).

[58] Grosz & Zimmerman, *Experimental analysis of hysterical blindness,* 13 Archives Gen Psychiatry 255 (1965).

[59] Reported in Chicago Sun Times, Oct 29, 1983, at 1, col 4.

[60] This event was witnessed by one of the authors.

§2.20 —In Perception of Events: Causal Relationships

One important area where habits of thought influence perception is the cause-and-effect relationship. In a new situation, or in an ambiguous one, a person's immediate perception of cause and effect is largely determined by the *proximity* of events in time and space. A person hears a door slam downstairs just as a gust of wind blows against the window, and he or she concludes that the wind blew the door shut. The truth may be that someone just left the house in a rage.

Another factor in perception of cause is *similarity of form* between cause and effect. A person hears a certain rhythm of sounds and looks up to see someone applying a hammer to a nail with a cadence that corresponds to the rhythm of the sounds. The observer interprets the sounds as caused by the hammering. Another person hears heavy footsteps in the corridor marching up to the door and stopping. The person opens the door and finds a large man and a petite young woman. He or she assigns the heavy steps to the man, since heavy things make *heavy* noises and dainty things move daintily.

This principle is used often in the motion pictures where a singing voice is dubbed in while the movie star (who possibly cannot carry a tune) moves his or her lips and sways in rhythm with the melody. It is difficult not to see causal relationships where people would normally anticipate them.

A Belgian researcher has performed a series of laboratory studies of the stimulus conditions which underlie people's perceptions of causality.[61] The researcher projected geometric figures onto a screen and had them move in relation to one another. Viewing subjects were asked to report what they saw.

In the first sequence, a square, A, moved toward another square and stopped, abutting that other square, B, which remained stationary. If A moved rapidly, the subject reported that A *struck* B. If A moved slowly, it was perceived as *gently joining, touching,* or *uniting* with B. In the second sequence, square A reached B and stopped; B immediately began to move. If A's rate of approach was faster than the subsequent motion of B, the moving away of B was seen as *caused* by A. However, when A's approach was slower than B's subsequent motion, B's movement was seen as self-initiated. In the third sequence, if A and B both moved off in the same direction after contact was made, the subjects reported that A was pushing B.

A great many other apparent movements were investigated in this

---

[61] A. Michotte, The Perception of Causality (1963).

way. The findings clearly illustrated people's tendency to impose causal relations under certain conditions of proximity and sequence. The findings have important implications for people's interpretations of others' behavior.

§2.21 —In Perception of People

How a person thinks of and feels toward another individual frequently distorts the perception of his or her physical appearance. Social psychologists have done considerable research on this phenomenon. One study employed the following design.[62] A brief description of the personality and behavior of two fictitious persons was given to the experimental subjects. The subjects were then asked to imagine the facial characteristics of each of the fictitious persons. Person A was described to the subjects in very positive terms regarding personality and behavior. Person B was described very negatively. The subjects subsequently agreed on two quite distinctly different facial patterns for the two persons. They agreed on as many as 25 differing characteristics. For instance, Person A was consistently described by the subjects as having a direct, upward gaze, wide-set eyes, a smooth brow, relaxed nostrils, and a mouth that tended to curve upwards at the corners. Person B, on the other hand, had a furtive, downward gaze, narrow-set eyes, a knitted brow, distended nostrils, and a mouth that tended to curve downwards at the corners.

In another study,[63] subjects were given a personality description of fictitious persons and then asked to pick them out of photographs presented them. Once again, it was clear that certain personality and behavioral characteristics were tied to certain facial features. A similar experiment was conducted with voices.[64] Subjects listened to recordings of voices reciting the same subject matter and then were asked to associate photographs with various voices. Again, the result was that certain voices called up definite facial images.

From such studies as these, social scientists have concluded that the tendency to *stereotype* is very strong in human beings.[65] They see this as yet another instance of the gestalt principle of the whole controlling the

---

[62] Secord, *Facial features and inference processes in interpersonal perception,* in Person, Perception, and Interpersonal Behavior 211 (R. Taguiri & L. Petrullo eds 1958).

[63] *Id.*

[64] Allport & Centril, *Judging personality from voice,* 5 J Soc Psychology 37 (1934).

[65] D. Krech, R. Crutchfield & E. Ballackey, Individual in Society 30, 53 (1962).

parts.[66] Social psychologists employ the terms *balance* and *consonance.* According to this analysis, people have a certain unified cognitive system which they apply to persons in their environment. Certain personality and behavioral traits go with specific facial characteristics, body builds, and voices. When a person is presented with any significant part of the system, the *whole* system is reinstated in his or her imagination. One part of the whole induces the other parts so as to balance out the entire impression. As noted in **§2.05,** a certain dynamic tension holds the whole system together. When one item is presented, the observer becomes *uncomfortable* and relieves the tension by completing the picture. It is very much like hearing the second shoe drop before it actually does. So compelling is this tendency within people that they often block out data that are not consonant with a stereotype. Some psychologists feel that in a person's perception of other people, there are no such things as *objective facts.*[67]

The tendency to stereotype commonly applies to an entire ethnic, religious, or racial group.[68] Once people know that a person belongs to one of these groups, they tend to clothe him or her with certain physical characteristics and personality traits which may, in fact, run counter to the actual experience with *this* individual. This type of generalization occurs particularly when a person's contacts with individual members of a group are limited. Such generalizations have given rise to the familiar line: "They all look the same to me."

This tendency to stereotype was demonstrated in a Harvard study a number of years ago.[69] University students from America, France, and Germany were given brief sketches of fictitious persons which included their occupations and nationalities. They were asked to record their impressions of the personalities of these people. The result was that the subjects came up with strong stereotypical descriptions of the persons based on the given *nationality* of each fictitious person. This stereotyping was true of all nationalities *except their own.* This would seem to indicate that the tendency to stereotype is less the more familiar people are with individuals of a group.

Data are available on people's ability to interpret correctly emotions and personality characteristics from facial expressions and expressive bodily movements. One study presented 100 subjects with photographs

---

[66] See **§2.05.**

[67] See D. Krech, R. Crutchfield & E. Ballackey, *supra* note 65, at 51 and following for subjective processes which filter the objective reality.

[68] *Id* 31.

[69] Bruner & Perlmutter, *Compatriot and foreigner: a study of impression formation in three countries,* 55 J Abnormal & Soc Psychology 253-260 (1957).

of poses by professional actors.[70] While there was fair statistical correlation between the interpretation by the subjects and the emotion intended by the actor, this correlation occurred only if the *correspondence category* was made sufficiently loose. Thus, where the actor intended *love,* if the subject reported *happiness* or *mirth,* he or she was considered to be sufficiently close to love to be scored as a positive correlation. Moreover, a number of subjects reported surprise, fear, and suffering as their interpretation of the pose intended to convey love. A significant number of subjects interpreted love poses as expressing contempt. For other poses, there were such divergent interpretations as fury and hate versus boredom.

A later study,[71] in an attempt to get away from posed expressions, used photographs of people who were put in real-life situations that provoked various emotions which they later described. It was found that, while the emotions actually experienced by the subjects varied greatly for the different situations, the facial expression and muscle tension of each subject tended to remain quite constant for the different emotions. It seems that each individual has a characteristic way of responding to and expressing deep emotions *generally* but does not have a distinguishable expression for each particular emotion, even when they are quite divergent. When the subjects were asked to *pose* for the different emotions they said they had experienced during the experimental situations, they all struck poses which were highly stereotyped and not at all consonant with facial expressions they registered on the candid camera when they were actually experiencing the emotion. Combining these data with those of the earlier experiments with posed actors, psychologists conclude that facial expression of *actual* emotion is very ambiguous; nevertheless, all people have a stereotyped notion of what emotion goes with what expression.

When experiments were run with motion pictures which captured the entire situation confronting the subjects as they expressed their emotions, and which also captured bodily movement, interpretation of emotions by a group of judges correlated highly with the actual emotion experienced by the subjects.[72] It seems, then, that people very readily misinterpret facial expressions unless they have some insight into the total experience of the one expressing the emotion, coupled with an opportunity to check their interpretation against bodily posture and movements.

---

[70] A. Felsky, Feelings and Emotions (1924).

[71] Landis, *Studies of emotional reactions,* 7 J Experimental Psychology 325 (1924).

[72] Sherman, *The differentiation of emotional responses in infants,* 7 J Comp Psychology 265 (1928).

A caution must be added here in regard to the interpretation of bodily movements alone. Studies show that people's ability to judge personality and behavior characteristics from the expressive movements of others is not great; in fact, it is just a bit better than chance.[73] This fact is especially true if the other person is of a different social and cultural background than that of the observer. Movements of the hands, shoulders, and head often are expressive more of cultural habits than an individual's own personality. Forceful gesturing may be indicative of a threatening, excited posture among members of one group, but not at all among members of another. The same caution must be observed with regard to voice interpretation. A cool, controlled voice may be the vehicle of a threat in one social habitat, while in another, much more force is needed to convey that message.

Another way in which the gestalt principle works in people's interpretation of others is seen in what has been called the "implicit personality theory."[74] There are data which suggest that certain prior impressions of a person, whether well founded or not, can induce people to *see* a whole constellation of other personality and behavioral characteristics in that person. It seems that each person has an a priori theory as to what personality factors are always found together. Much research has been done on *warm* versus *cold* traits.[75] In a typical experiment, a lecturer addresses an audience which has been prepared in different ways. One half of the audience has been told prior to the lecture that the lecturer has certain qualities and experience. The other half has been given the same introductory briefing with the following exception: while the first group is told that the lecturer has a *very warm personality,* the second group is told that the lecturer is *rather cold.* After hearing the lecture, the students who had received the *warm* description rated the lecturer as more considerate of others, more informed, more sociable, more popular, better natured, more humorous, and more humane than did the students who had received the *cold* description.

§2.22 —The Halo Effect in Perception of People

A phenomenon related to those discussed in **§2.21** is the "halo

---

[73] D. Krech, R. Crutchfield & E. Ballackey, *supra* note 65, at 65.

[74] *Id* 52.

[75] Asch, *Forming Impressions of Personality,* 41 J Abnormal & Soc Psychology 258 (1946); Kelley, *The warm-cold variable in first impressions of persons,* 18 J Personality 431 (1950); Wishner, *Reanalysis of "Impressions of Personality",* 67 Psychological Rev 96 (1960).

effect."[76] People often come to exaggerate the homogeneity of the personality of an individual in their perception of him or her. If people have a favorable impression of him or her, this impression spreads to all his or her specific traits. People score that person unduly high on all positive traits and unduly low on negative traits. The reverse is true if people think unfavorably of him or her. The following dialogue from Shakespeare's *King Lear* quite clearly illustrates this tendency:

> *Gloucester:* You know the character [in this letter] to be your brother's?
>
> *Edmund:* If the matter were good, my lord, I durst swear it were his; but, in respect of [its unkind remark concerning Gloucester], I would fain think it were not.[77]

An interesting experiment was conducted with a number of children who had been previously analysed for levels of popularity within their group.[78] The children took turns at throwing a ball at a target in a casual setting which suggested that no testing or rating was in progress. In fact, the experimenters recorded the actual performance of each child. Afterwards, the children were asked to rate the performance of their various companions. It was found that the well-liked children were perceived as having performed very well, while the less popular ones were perceived as having done poorly. As a matter of fact, the *actual* performance of the children was in no way related to the *perceived* performance.

In another study, two groups performed calisthenic exercises before an audience.[79] One group was known to be very much disliked by the audience. The other group was well liked. The experimenter had trained the *liked* group to make deliberate mistakes. The *disliked* group was trained to be letter-perfect. At the end of the two performances, the experimenter discovered that the audience had *seen* the disliked group make all the mistakes. Such findings have led one social psychologist to remark:

> A bad act is easily connected with a "bad" person. . . . A crime can be blamed on a person because of a physical similarity: "he looks as if he could have committed this crime." Or he can be held responsible for it because of "spiritual" similarity, that is, a

---

[76] D. Krech, R. Crutchfield & E. Ballackey, Individual in Society 52 (1962).

[77] Act I, scene ii.

[78] Sherif, *Status in experimentally produced groups,* 60 Am J Sociology 370 (1955).

[79] Zillig, *Attitude and Testimony,* 106 Zeitschrift fur Psychologie 58 (1928).

> similarity between the crime as a moral event and the natural disposition of the responsible.[80]

Attitudes people entertain toward a person can cause them to deny the evidence of their eyes.

One consequence of the *halo effect* is that the least accurate judges of another's total personality and behavioral expectations are those who have been associated with that person either a long time or a very short time.[81] Long-time acquaintances come to blind themselves to dissonant, negative qualities of their friend. This effect is the reason that family members often are the last to suspect psychosis in one of their brood. Extreme behavior appears to them as only a little eccentric. On the other hand, a brief acquaintance allows *first impression* dynamics to control one person's evaluation of another. Experimental data confirm the adage that first impressions are lasting.[82]

Psychologists have long been aware of the anxiety-relieving mechanism of *projection.* Projection is the tendency to displace unconsciously an emotion or feeling that a person is experiencing subliminally. It is usually an emotion or awareness that the person cannot handle successfully within himself or herself, and so the person projects it outside himself or herself, into another, where the person can view it and *handle* it from a distance. The officer going into combat gives the soldiers a *pep talk* to settle their fear. In fact, the officer is talking to himself.

Experimental studies support the existence of this mechanism. One study focused on the projection of fear.[83] Two groups of people were shown a film depicting someone performing a number of mechanical tasks. The members of the experimental group were given a series of painful electric shocks at intervals during the showing of the film. The control group was not. Afterwards, the two groups were asked to judge the personality of the person in the film. The experimental group which had dwelt in fear of another shock throughout the film reported the person as generally fearful and anxious to a degree that was not perceived by the control group. Fear in themselves leads people to

---

[80] Heider, *Social perception and phenomenal causality,* 51 Psychological Rev 358 (1944).

[81] D. Krech, R. Crutchfield & E. Ballackey, *supra* note 76, at 65; Backman & Secord, *Liking, selective interaction, and misperception in congruent interpersonal relations,* 25 Sociometry 321 (1962); Berkowitz & Garanson, *Multinational and judgmental determinants of social perception,* 69 J Abnormal & Soc Psychology 296 (1964).

[82] Luchins, *Primacy-recency in impression formation,* in The Order of Presentation in Persuasion (C.I. Hovland ed 1957).

[83] Feshbach & Singer, *The effects of fear arousal and suppression of fear upon social perception,* 55 J Abnormal & Soc Psychology 283 (1957).

perceive another as fearful and anxious. Another experimenter found that people tend to attribute their own traits to others whom they like and to deny them to others whom they dislike.

One study indicates that wants and expectations can distort the way people perceive others.[84] A group of high school students who were very much interested in basketball were offered an opportunity to apply to a three-person board for a free ticket to a highly important basketball game. In their interviews with the students, the members of the board (actually, the experimenters) played different roles. One acted very friendly; another acted in a neutral, nonevaluative manner; and the third was very negative. All three displayed an equal amount of apparent power over the final decision (as judged by neutral observers). The students saw the three as having different levels of influence on the final decision. As they waited for the decision of the board, they reported that the friendly member obviously had the most power and the negative one had the least. Wishful thinking distorts perception.

Finally, the implications of the investigations into the perception of cause-and-effect relationships discussed above[85] should be noted in regard to people's perceptions of personal interactions. In the experiment described in **§2.20,** the investigator was moving geometrical figures about on a screen. The observers interpreted the movements in causal terms. What is of interest here is that they also interpreted the movements of the geometrical shapes as human beings engaged in interpersonal behavior. For instance, when one figure was seen moving away from another which had just approached, the movement (seen as autonomous) was interpreted as *motivated* by fear. When two figures came together and moved off in the same direction, two interpretations were given. When there was a pause after the first figure made contact with the other before they moved off, the interpretation was that they had *gotten together* and *decided* to go off together. When there was no pause, the first figure was interpreted as *carrying off the other by force.*

A similar experiment was undertaken by another researcher.[86] In that researcher's presentation of shapes in movement, the subjects were led to conclude that the figures were fighting, chasing, attacking, and fleeing. Actual human relationships often create such impressions. Two people with their heads together appear to be in intimate conversation. If they move off together, people tend to conclude a joint venture is afoot. If viewers have no other cues, as when they see people moving

---

[84] Pepitone, *Motivational effects in social perception,* 3 Hum Rel 57 (1950).

[85] See **§2.20.**

[86] Heoder & Simmel, *An experimental study of apparent behavior,* 57 Am J Psychology 243 (1944).

in relation to one another at a distance, or when the viewers come upon them suddenly, they tend to impose interpretations that make sense to them in terms of their customary experience.

§2.23 Cross-Cultural Perception

Some studies indicate that a person of one race has more difficulty identifying a member of another race than does another member of that same race.[87] This handicap is not relieved by the witness having had extensive interracial experience; nor is it worsened by prejudice toward that race on the part of the witness.[88] However, the reliability of these studies has been recently challenged.[89]

§2.24 Influences of Age and Sexual Differences

The ability to observe and recall accurately what a person has seen and heard appears to improve up to the age of 20.[90] After age 60, this ability begins to decline. Age begins to affect a person's ability to note and recall details, to discriminate colors, and to adapt to light and darkness changes.

Research results to date do not allow firm conclusions as to whether the sex of the witness is indicative of greater or lesser accuracy in perception and recall. There is some evidence to suggest that women may be better at recalling faces, voices, and events than men.[91] This conclusion supposes normal conditions. When violence and stress are introduced to the scene, however, data suggest that the reverse may be true.[92]

---

[87] Malpass & Kravitz, *Recognition of faces of own and other races,* 13 J Personal & Soc Psychology 330 (1969).

[88] Brigham & Barkowitz, "*Do they all look alike?*" 8 J Applied Psychology 306 (1978).

[89] Lindsay & Wells, *What do we really know about Cross-Race eyewitness identification,* in Evaluating Witness Evidence 219 (S. M. Lloyd-Bostock & B. R. Clifford eds 1983).

[90] Ellis, Shepherd & Bruce, *The effect of age and sex upon adolescents' recognition of races,* 123 J Genetic Psychology 173 (1973).

[91] Clifford & Scott, *Individual and situational factors in eyewitness testimony,* 63 J Applied Psychology 352 (1978); but see Goldstein & Chance, *Visual recognition memory for complex configurations,* 9 Perception & Psycho-Physics 237-41 (1970).

[92] Powers, Andriks & Loftus, *Eyewitness Accounts of Females and Males,* 64 J Applied Psychology 339-47 (1979); Siegel & Loftus, *Impact of anxiety and life stress upon eyewitness testimony,* 12 Bull Psychosomatic Socy 479-80 (1978).

§2.25 Organic and Dysfunctional Factors

Disturbances in color perception, failure to recognize familiar objects (a condition known as *visual agnosia*), distortion of size, shape, and distance, and night blindness can be caused by lesions in that part of the brain which processes visual stimulation (the visual cortex).[93] However, the same impairments of brain function can occur without any physical damage to cortical matter.[94] Emotional disturbances can produce similar results.[95] Hysteria can result in temporary colorblindness.[96] An unconscious aversion to some object may block recognition of it.[97] One person's attitude toward another person may make that person appear larger and spatially closer to the observer than he or she actually is or may make him or her appear more distant and smaller.[98]

§2.26 Three Memory Processes

Memory is a mysterious phenomenon. How is it that people can call back into present consciousness past experiences? Does each experience somehow leave behind a modification of the nervous tissue—some potential energy source which a person can trigger at will? If so, then why is it that some past experiences are beyond a person's power to recall or, when reactivated, return in a garbled way? Is consciousness, present and past, so unique a phenomenon in humans that it is beyond measurement by existing investigative instruments, attuned as those instruments are to mass and energy or space and time? Such questions lead into philosophic anthropology and, indeed, metaphysics. It can suffice for present purposes to review what psychologists have observed about the functioning and malfunctioning of memory and upon what tentative theories and operational *laws* they have thus far agreed.[99]

Although humankind has never had the wisdom or ability to uncover it, there probably exists a single principle which guides all the

---

[93] Teuber, *Alteration of perception and memory in man*, in Analysis of Behavioral Change 1 (L. Weiskrantz ed 1968).

[94] Critchley, *The problem of visual agnosia*, J Neurological Sci 274 (1964).

[95] J. Heaton, The Eye: Phenomenology and Psychology of Functions and Disorder (1968).

[96] Pickford, *Total color blindness of hysterical origin*, 22 Brit J Med Psychology 121 (1949).

[97] Arieti, *The microgeny of thought and perception*, 6 Archives Gen Psychiatry 454 (1962).

[98] W. Ittleson, S. B. Kutash, L. Abramson & B. Seidenberg, Perceptual Changes in Psychopathology (1961); Beloff & Beloff, *The influence of Valence on distance judgment of human faces*, 62 J Abnormal Soc Psychology 720 (1961); Dannenmeier & Thumin, *Authority status as a factor in perceptual distortion of size*, 63 J Soc Psychology 361 (1964).

[99] The classical study on memory is H. Ebbinghaus, Memory (1913). For a summary discussion see E. Hilgard & R. Atkinson, Introduction to Psychology 222 (4th ed 1967).

operations of the memory. However, at the level of present understanding, three distinguishable modes of memory function can be observed: reconstruction, recall, and recognition.

§2.27 —Reconstruction

The reconstructive function is the process whereby the memory reestablishes, with the help of partial cues, an earlier experience.[100] Partial recollections gradually coalesce and call up other ones, and eventually the whole earlier experience is reinstated in consciousness. The distinctive quality about this process is that it reestablishes the *complete* past experience, including its setting in time and place and often charged with the emotional aura that first surrounded the experience. The homecoming game often does this for the former college football player. As he passes familiar spots on the campus, he suddenly becomes filled with memories of how he and his buddies pulled off this prank outside this building, how they ended up on the carpet in the dean's office, etc. Just getting a scent of the peculiar fragrance of the locker room may reinstate a cherished memory of his heroic moment in the *Big Game* of years gone by. The smell of burning leaves brings back past autumns. For other people, a certain melody or a portion of a melody, a sunset, a touch sensation, or a bit of landscape can trigger a recollection that lies just below the threshold of consciousness. Certain qualities of people can do the same. A vocal intonation, a way of walking, a formation of the nose or mouth, or a style of clothes can stir a chain of recollections. We begin to see in our memory an old schoolteacher we liked or disliked very much. She is standing in the classroom. We can see her desk, note the illumination that used to come from the side windows, the sounds of the street outside that used to beckon us on warm spring afternoons, our classmates. If we attend enough, we can begin to call up the feelings we used to have in that setting. What may have precipitated all this was a commuter who passed us as she got off the bus. Sometimes the recollection does not reach the focus of consciousness. A person encounters someone he or she has never met before and is instinctively aware of an attitude toward him or her, such as trust or distrust. The observer has nothing to go on as yet, but already he or she *knows* that he or she will like or dislike the person. Getting to know the person may completely change the preconceived attitude, and the observer may wonder why he or she entertained the initial feeling.

---

[100] Others use the technical term *redintegration, e.g.*, J. Lindworsky, Experimental Psychology 203 (1931).

If the observer bothers to investigate this phenomenon, he or she may discover that this person has a quality about him or her that is in common with that of someone in the observer's past. At the first meeting, a past recollection was stirred which never quite rose to full consciousness. However, it was sufficiently strong to stir emotions that belonged to the past. Unfortunately, since first impressions tend to govern one person's attitude toward another person, people often find themselves setting up a self-fulfilling prophecy. On the basis of subliminal recollections, a person may well communicate his or her dislike to the stranger. Sensing that dislike, the stranger in turn feels hostile and acts accordingly. The first person now has *present* evidence for disliking the stranger and concludes that his or her initial reaction was well justified!

§2.28 —Recall

The process of *recall* is quite different. A person recalls a phone number when he or she must telephone someone. A person picks up a bicycle after many years of not riding one and finds he or she knows how to handle it. The same thing happens with typewriting, swimming, and other various motor skills learned in the past. A person can recite part of the Gettysburg Address after a few drinks at a cocktail party. People rise to sing the "Star Spangled Banner" and can at least get through the first stanza, though it has been many years since last they sang it. People give dates and names in some general information quiz. What distinguishes this process of memory from the reconstruction process discussed in **§2.27** is that people recall these things of the past in an *absolute,* isolated way. They do not reestablish the original setting in which they first learned them. Ordinarily, there is no personal reference. They do not trigger a whole past drama in which the person remembering was a central figure. Psychologists sometimes refer to this process as *active recall,* since no cue has triggered the return of a past learning. The person remembering has purposefully delved into his or her memory and brought out this stored knowledge or skill.

§2.29 —Recognition

Finally, there is the memory process whereby a person *recognizes* a present experience as *familiar.* He or she has met it before. People exercise this memory function every day. In addition, it is the memory activity most operative on multiple-choice examinations.

Upon reflection, it becomes obvious that all three of these processes

—reconstruction, recall, and recognition—actually overlap in any exercise of memory. However, it is helpful to distinguish them, since the malfunctioning of memory—forgetting—seems to affect the three operations in different ways. It is the phenomenon of forgetting that has given rise to various theories of memory.

§2.30 Forgetting

Forgetting occurs basically in two ways: *quantitative forgetting,* in which some past experiences are lost altogether; and *qualitative forgetting,* in which past experiences are remembered in a distorted way. These phenomena are considered in the following two sections.

§2.31 —Forgetting as Loss of Prior Experiences

It is everyday experience that recognition is easier than active recall. Studies confirm this fact.[101] Working with nonsense syllables to standardize the memory task, early researchers found that in tests of recall, subjects forget as much as 50 per cent of what they have learned in the first hour after the learning activity. Sixty per cent is lost in the first 24 hours. In the second 24 hours, the rate of loss slows, and retention of the residual subsequently remains quite constant. Tests of recognition show a loss of only about 5 per cent in the first hour, 20 per cent in the first day, and only a very gradual decline in retention thereafter. The abilities to recall and to recognize are highly correlated. Those who score high on tests of recall do so also on tests of recognition.[102] Intelligence is not a factor in the rate of forgetting.[103] Intellectual differences affect the amount and rate of learning, but once something is learned, intelligence does not seem to give an advantage in retention. Highly intelligent people forget as rapidly as anyone else, other things being equal.

One peculiar phenomenon should be noted. Under some circumstances, retention is found to be *better* after a short interval of time than it is immediately after the learning period. This phenomenon is called *reminiscence.* The process is not understood well. Some have suggested that following the test which concludes the learning activity, subjects

---

[101] H. Ebbinghaus, Memory (1913); C. Lun, The Conditions of Retention (Psychological Monographs No 142, 1922).

[102] W. Morse, Psychology and Teaching 457 (3d ed 1968); Postman & Jenkins, *An experimental comparison of active recall and recognition,* 61 Am J Psychology 511 (1948).

[103] W. Morse, *supra* note 102, at 561.

continue to *practice* mentally for a time.[104] Thus, on retest a short time later, they do better than on the earlier test. However, the same phenomenon is observed in laboratory rats. It seems unlikely they would be given to conscious review. At any rate, this initial improvement is short-lived. The usual forgetting curve sets in thereafter.

Other studies indicate that the rate of forgetting varies quite significantly with the circumstances that surround the original learning task. Meaningful material—i.e., items which can be fitted into a cognitive pattern—is much more readily retained.[105] People often associate a new face and name by anchoring it in a familiar image—e.g., George Stone may be tied to an image of Mount Rushmore. Unfortunately, sometimes the mnemonic devices backfire, and George is given the surname *Rushmore* on next meeting. The associative image replaces what it was meant to suggest. Nevertheless, studies show that subjects faced with a learning task such as the memorization of nonsense syllables or essentially unrelated items attempt to impose some extrinsic meaning or relation upon them so as to fit them into an established world of meaning.[106] The more successful the subjects are at this, the more successful they are at recall. Even their errors tend to be *near misses.*

Motivation affects the rate of forgetting, if it is operating during the initial learning experience. Subjects who are informed *before* a learning experience that they will be tested on the material at some later date or that the material will be very helpful in some future task retain learning much longer than these who are told this *after* the learning period.[107] Apparently, if a person is aware of some long-range advantage to remembering a present experience *while* he or she is experiencing it, he or she is likely to store it in a manner that is not available to another who is told of the advantage of remembering after he or she has finished the experience. The motive must be present when the initial perception and organizing are occurring.

The ability to recognize correctly a previously presented item would seem to depend on what other choices are offered on the recognition test. If a person is at one time presented three pictures, one each of an apple, a peach, and an orange, and then later is presented with another set of pictures and asked to pick out the item which appeared in the previous set, it is clear that the person will have little difficulty in

---

[104] *Id* 457.

[105] Tiedman, *A study of retention of classroom learning,* 41 J Educ Research 516 (1948).

[106] W. Morse, *supra* note 102, at 204.

[107] Jones & Anehansel, *The learning and utilization of contravaluent material,* 53 J Abnormal Psychology 27 (1956); Ausubel, Schpoont & Cukier, *Influence of intention on retention of school materials,* 48 J Educ Psychology 87 (1957).

identifying the peach if the two other choices are a table and a chair. It may be more difficult, however, if the choices are a pear and a tangerine. A person's ability to make discriminating recognitions depends a good deal on the response strengths of the other competing choices.

This common-sense hunch is supported by a study.[108] The experimenters hypothesized that a good deal of *guessing* behavior occurs in recognition testing. A memory association may be too weak to produce active recall, but strong enough to contribute to recognition. This hypothesis was supported by an analysis of *wrong* choices in recognition tests. Items *similar* to the correct one were chosen significantly more often than totally dissimilar ones, with a frequency beyond that expected by chance. Subthreshold association—too weak to identify correct items from similar but incorrect ones—seems to be strong enough to eliminate markedly dissimilar alternatives. Thus, actual choice in such a situation depends on the degree of dissimilarity among the alternative choices.

In a later study, it was found that correct recognitions of items not familiar enough to trigger absolute recall became more difficult as the *number* of alternative choices increased.[109] It is theorized that an item which does not appear sufficiently familiar for a subject to identify it immediately may *gain* response strength when it is compared with another choice which has even less response strength—i.e., which is even less familiar.[110] The correct choice is *relatively* more familiar than the incorrect one and so is chosen (if the subject believes that one of the two must be the correct one). In such a situation, recognition involves a balancing process. As the number of alternative choices is increased, the probability increases that individual incorrect items will each have *some* quality of similarity with the correct item. These individual similarities have a cumulative effect. The subject must now discriminate between the correct item which is not strongly familiar and the *body* of incorrect items whose *cumulative* familiarity approaches that of the correct choice. The differential in response strength between the two is narrowed to a point where the correct choice no longer enjoys a clear, relative superiority. In such a situation, accuracy of choice approaches pure chance, or random choice. The subject no longer feels he or she has any trustworthy cues. The author of the study concluded that for a vaguely familiar correct item to be chosen, it must enjoy a

---

[108] Postman & Jenkins, *supra* note 102.

[109] Postman, *Choice behavior and the process of recognition,* 63 Am J Psychology 576 (1950).

[110] *Id* 581.

minimal differential strength over other possible choices.[111] This differential decreases as the number of alternative choices is increased. It was found that when the number of alternative choices is increased to nine, the efficiency of differential recognition drops steeply. When a subject identifies correctly a previously seen item in a set of nine alternative items, the probability is high that he or she is operating with the firmness of active recall and is not depending on simple differential recognition.[112] He or she is not simply eliminating the less familiar ones.

An earlier study supports the general hypothesis above.[113] It was found that a person's ability to know he or she has *not* seen an object before is stronger than that person's ability to identify correctly what he or she *has* seen. Thus, when a person is required to make a choice among weakly familiar items, he or she employs the process of elimination. It was also found that a recognition not accompanied with a feeling of *absolute certainty* is practically no better than a random guess.

§2.32 —Forgetting as Distortion of Prior Experiences

It is everyday experience that people's memories are not always trustworthy. Not only do memories lose information from the past, but often they report it back in a garbled form. Digits come back in reversed position when a person summons up a telephone number or street address. Letters are dropped or replaced by incorrect ones when a person attempts to spell an old acquaintance's name. A person thinks he or she has met someone before and discovers the meeting was an impossibility. People pick up photographs made in their childhood and are shocked to note the differences between their present memories of people and places in those days and their actual appearance as evidenced by the photographs. People return to the towns of their childhood and discover that the streets are not nearly as broad, the backyards of their old residences not nearly as spacious, and the height of the church steeple not nearly as great as they have remembered all these years. When asked for the date of a friend's death, someone says, "About two years ago," only to discover on confirmation that it was really five years.

Two people describe a movie they have seen or an event they have witnessed. It is hard to believe that the two were at the same movie or

---

[111] *Id* 581-82.

[112] *Id.*

[113] Strong, *The effect of length of series upon recognition,* 19 Psychological Rev 447 (1912).

event, so drastically do their reports differ as to dominant theme and critical details. There is an old poem, song, or quotation which a person has cherished through the years, repeating it many times. How surprised he or she is when the original text changes before his or her eyes. He or she has replaced or dropped words. It is not "Four score and seven years ago our *forefathers* . . .," but rather "*our fathers.*" A person tells someone a story. A month later, the story comes back to the original teller and he or she can hardly recognize it. Memory alters past reality without a person's being aware of the subtle process.

Fortunately, the process of memory distortion has been the subject of considerable study by psychologists.[114] One study attempted to plot the direction of memory distortion.[115] Subjects were presented with geometric figures and then asked to reproduce them from memory over a period of time. The experimenters analysed the gradual distortions of the original figures and concluded that the process has three characteristics, and changes tend to take place in the direction of one of the three. The first is *symmetry.* Irregular figures tend to become more regular and balanced. Nonsymmetrical details are modified or dropped. The second is *accentuation of irregularity.* If the memory seizes on some nonsymmetrical aspect, it may subordinate the rest of the figure to this irregular aspect. The irregular detail now becomes central and is emphasized more and more with succeeding reproductions. The third possible direction is *familiar form.* If the figure resembles in some way a familiar object, in later reproductions it will tend to imitate more and more closely the familiar object rather than the original geometric form. A slightly crescent shape may come to resemble the letter *C* or a moon in early phase, depending on which of the two familiar objects were originally suggested to the subject by the crescent.[116]

These three basic directions were supported in later studies by others.[117] A different terminology is sometimes preferred. The direction of *simplification* occurs when subjects are required to reproduce a story at intervals over a period of two and one-half years. The major

---

[114] F. Bartlett, Remembering: An Experimental and Social Study (1932). Levine & Murphy, *The learning and forgetting of controversial material,* 38 J Abnormal Soc Psychology 507-17 (1943); G.W. Allport & L. Postman, The Psychology of Rumor (1947).

[115] Gibson, *The reproduction of visually perceived forms,* 12 Experimental Psychology 1-39 (1929).

[116] Carmichael, Hogan & Walter, *An experimental study of the effect of language on the reproduction of visually perceived form,* 15 J Experimental Psychology 73 (1932).

[117] Some researchers believe the major distortion actually occurs at the time of the original perception. See Hebb & Foord, *Errors of visual recognition and the nature of the trace,* 35 J Experimental Psychology 335 (1945); D. Riley, *Memory for form,* in Psychology in the Making 402-63 (L. Postman ed 1962).

theme (as interpreted by the subject) is retained, but the whole tale is greatly shortened by omitting details and condensing features. Details are retained which support the subject's original interpretation of the theme of the story. This aspect of simplification is sometimes referred to as *leveling.* If subjects differ as to their original interpretation of the tale, it can be expected that their retention and use of details over time will differ.

What some call *accentuation,* others refer to as *sharpening.*[118] If some detail in the story catches the fancy of a subject, he or she may emphasize it in his or her next reproduction. Thereafter, it receives increasing emphasis and in the end may come to control the entire memory. Probably each succeeding reproduction is influenced more by the memory of the *preceding reproduction* (which has the advantage of recency) than it is by the memory of the original. Thus, the memory is freed bit by bit of its tie to the original and becomes more and more controlled by the intrinsic, creative forces of the subject. Figure 2-5 is a dramatic example of a metamorphosis of an original form over 18 reproductions.[119] Another phenomenon in recalling a story or picture is the movement toward a familiar object or *assimilation.* If the original has a feature or a general outline which suggests a familiar image or meaning, future recollection of the original will be dominated by the previously existing idea to which it has been assimilated. In the experiment relating to Figure 2-5, the original drawing apparently suggested a cat to the subject. One can see that the power of the cat image increased through the 18 reproductions as it gradually solidified itself and became the memory itself.

Gestaltists believe that the three tendencies in memory distortion are best conceptualized as further instances of *closure* and *good figure,* notions discussed at length in the treatment of perception.[120] In each case, the memory has settled upon some principle of organization—some form or pattern—into which the original is fitted or assimilated. The mind goes about its task of dropping details or adding them, modifying here and accentuating there, until a comfortable, clean, good figure emerges which harmonizes with the subject's whole world of meaning.

There is considerable evidence to support the role of *meaning* in

---

[118] G. Allport & L. Postman, The Psychology of Rumor (1947).

[119] Figure 2-5 is adapted with permission from F.C. Bartlett, Remembering: An Experimental and Social Study (Cambridge University Press 1932). Bartlett's creative experiments also demonstrate how details of a story change with each retelling.

[120] See **§§2.05-2.09.**

Figure 2-5

Original

18th Reproduction

memory modification. Experiments have been performed in which the subjects are presented with ambiguous figures.[121] They are asked to note what the figure suggests to them. Later, they are asked to reproduce the figure as exactly as they can. In all cases, the reproduction is in the direction more of the *verbalized interpretation* they have given the design than the original design itself. Thus, when two subjects are presented with an ambiguous figure (see Figure 2-6, upper series), the one who said it looked like a star later reproduced it as *a.* The one who said it looked like an arrow later reproduced it as *b.* Tests have also been conducted with ambiguous figures which are labeled differently for two test groups.[122] The later reproductions move in the direction of the suggested interpretation. Thus, Form X in Figure 2-6, lower series, if labeled *bottle,* is later reproduced *y.* If labeled *stirrup,* it is later reproduced *z.* The role of suggestion is illustrated in Hamlet's exchange with Polonius, quoted in an earlier section.[123]

---

[121] Gibson, *The reproduction of visually perceived forms,* 12 J Experimental Psychology 1 (1929).

[122] Carmichael, Hogan & Walter, *supra* note 116.

[123] See **§2.05.**

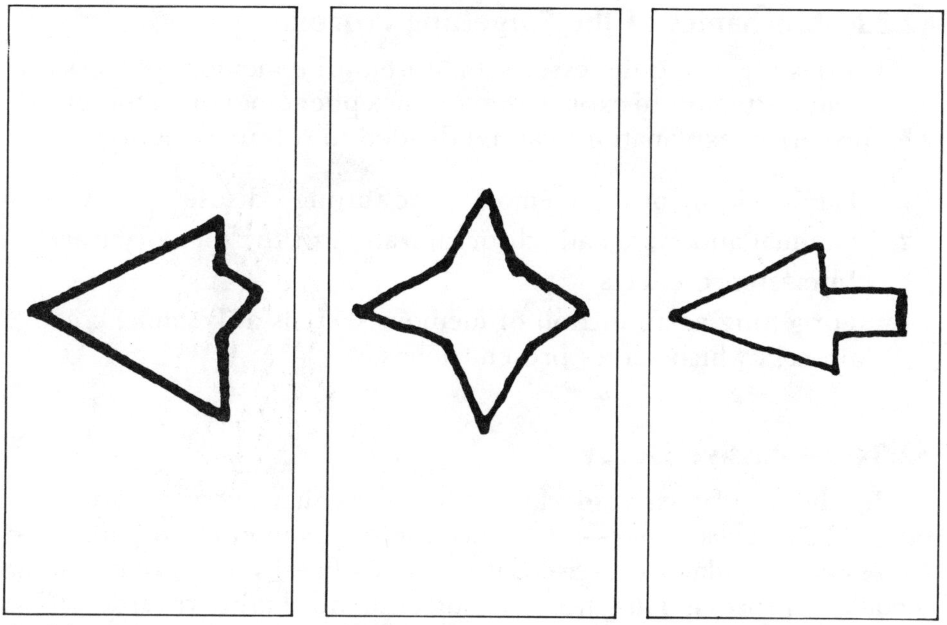

Ambiguous Stimulus Figure — Reproduction a — Reproduction b

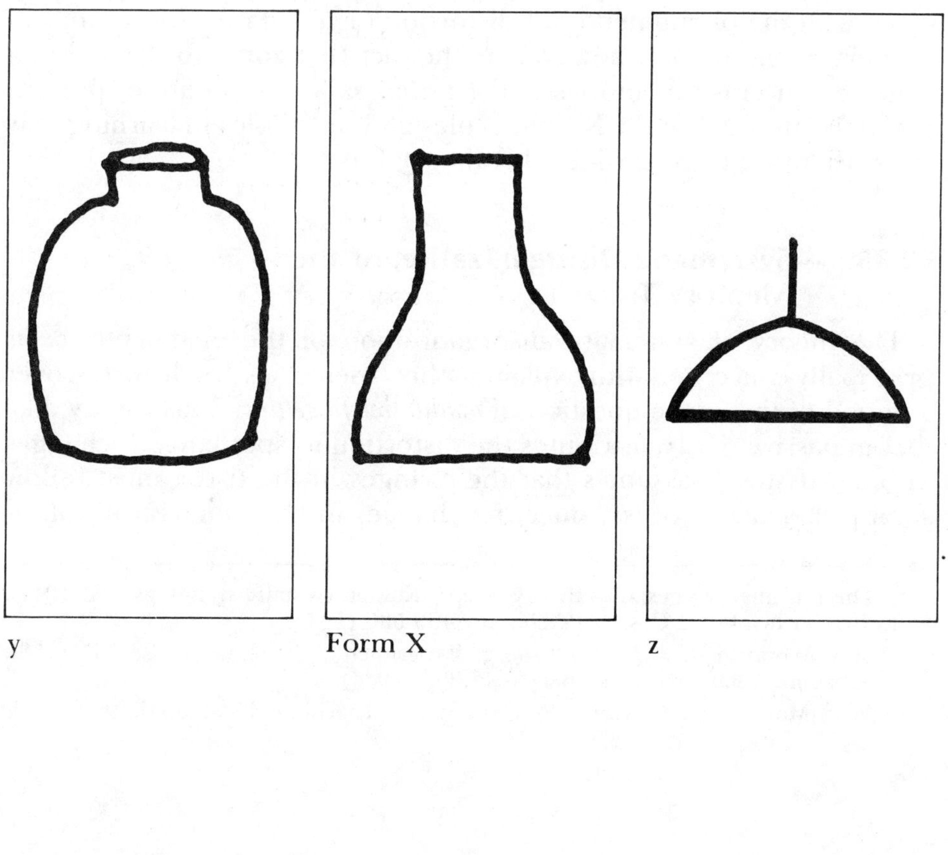

y — Form X — z

§2.33 Mechanics of the Forgetting Process

Theories regarding the essential nature of the memory process are, in the main, attempts to explain the complex phenomenon of forgetting. The proferred explanations can be divided into four categories:

1. Passive decay of the memory trace through disuse
2. Gradual and systematic disorganization of the memory trace
3. Interference effects
4. Forgetting as a function of memory seen as a dynamic, creative process which serves present needs

§2.34 —Passive Decay

The theory of passive decay hypothesizes that every experience a person has leaves a *trace*—a modification of tissue in the organism.[124] Unless it is regularly exercised, it gradually breaks down under some metabolic process. This theory is currently not highly regarded.[125] It fails to explain why some unused memories do not decay. In delirium, in senility, and under hypnosis, childhood memories can be brought back fresh although they have not been activated for decades. It also seems more aimed at explaining quantitative loss but does not help much with the phenomenon of distortion or qualitative forgetting. In support of the theory, however, is the fact that some forms of brain damage can erase memories and learned skills. In addition, present research into DNA and RNA molecules and their roles in learning may force scientists to reconsider this theory.[126]

§2.35 —Systematic Disorganization of the Memory Trace

The theory of systematic disorganization of the memory trace is principally concerned with explaining how memories are distorted over a period of time—the question of *qualitative forgetting.* This theory, like that of passive decay, attributes the distortion to spontaneous changes in brain tissue. It assumes that the changes in the tissue must follow some systematic process, since the changes in conscious recall follow

---

[124] This is primarily a gestaltist theory. See W. Kohler, Gestalt Psychology 177 (1947). K. Koffka, Principles of Gestalt Psychology 493-506 (1935).

[125] R.S. Woodworth & H. Schlosberg, Experimental Psychology 773-76 (1958). Encyclopaedia Britannica, Macropaedia 11,893 (1984).

[126] W.C. Morse & G.M. Wingo, Psychology and Teaching, 458 (3d ed 1969).

a systematic process. Gestaltists modify this theory by suggesting that the trace is really a pattern of dynamic neural forces which tends gradually to become disfigured and realigns itself in another way as other forces interact with the pattern over time.[127]

§2.36 —Interference Effects

The theory of interference holds that mere passage of time and the assumed spontaneous deterioration of tissue are not what affect the forgetting process. Rather, the passage of time exposes people to new experiences, and the new impressions tend to get in the way of what they have already learned. This process is called *retroactive inhibition.* By the time a student has come to the end of a semester studying the plays of Shakespeare, he or she finds it difficult to remember which characters go with what play. He or she tends to interchange subplots. As play follows upon play, it becomes increasingly difficult to keep in proper order what he or she has read earlier. The more recent experience replaces a similar but more distant one. This process is sometimes referred to as the Law of Recency.[128]

In a similar way, once a person has learned something well, he or she finds that it is often more difficult to remember correctly something similar which he or she learned subsequently. Almost everyone has experienced this in attempting to recall a friend's new telephone number. The old one was so well known, so well associated with the friend's name, that it keeps projecting itself into consciousness and interferes with recall whenever a person reaches into his or her memory for the new one. This process is referred to as *proactive inhibition.*

Laboratory experiments support the theory that competing experiences interfere with one another.[129] In some tests, groups of subjects have been given a learning task. Then, one portion of the group is put to sleep or confined to a darkened room for 24 hours, lying as still as possible. A control group is allowed to go about its usual affairs and to report back in 24 hours. The results were that the experimental group retained the original material with almost no significant change. The control group, on the other hand, had suffered a significant decrease in retention. It would seem that the intervening experiences had interfered with what had been learned.

---

[127] R.S. Woodworth & H. Schlosberg, *supra* note 125.

[128] *Id* 696-99, 730, 768.

[129] Grissom, Suedfeld & Vernon, *Memory for verbal material: Effects of sensory deprivation,* 138 Sci 429 (1962).

Educational psychologists have understandably been much interested in this phenomenon of interference and have arrived at some laws in regard to it:

1. Interference increases as the *number* of competing associations increase
2. Interference is greater the more *similar* the material in the two items learned
3. The more *incomplete* the learning, the more it suffers from interference by material experienced later
4. Interference effects are much reduced when the subject matter is *overlearned*—i.e., initially impressed on the memory beyond bare recall—and when the subject matter is meaningful in itself[130]

Educational psychologists are concerned as well with an allied phenomenon, that of *negative transference.* When people are confronted with a new situation that has much in common with a past one, they tend not to discriminate adequately between what is distinctive in the new situation, and they transfer elements of the old into the new. This factor makes attending to the new situation with openness and receptivity difficult. Old understandings and attitudes interfere with present perception.

§2.37 —Forgetting as a Function of a Purposeful Memory

Those who favor a holistic approach to human functioning see memory as an operation integrated into the total response pattern of an individual.[131] They feel it is misleading to treat remembering and forgetting as essentially autonomous dynamisms subject to their own well-defined laws. Rather, memory functions within the individual in the same manner as perception, attitudes, and goals, so as to preserve the individual's unified understanding of himself or herself and the world he or she inhabits. Memory serves the whole. Forgetting and distortions of past experiences are unconsciously *purposeful* in that they serve to preserve this prior understanding of the world.

The fact that what people are consciously able to recall is subject to some selective process is evident from experiments with hypnosis. After

---

[130] W. Morse, Psychology and Teaching 462 (3d ed 1968).

[131] *E.g.*, Alfred Adler, Social Interest: A Challenge to Mankind, ch XII (1938); Practice and Theory of Individual Psychology 4-5 (P. Radin trans 1973). See also K. Goldstein, Human Nature in the Light of Psychopathology (1940).

a subject has attempted to relate all he or she can remember of a past experience, it is found that when put under hypnosis and taken back over the same experience, he or she can often recall many details that earlier escaped him or her.[132]

Effect of Attitudes

The role of affective attitudes in remembering and forgetting has been demonstrated.[133] Pictures of British military personnel were shown to a number of subjects, and their expressed feelings toward each person represented in a photograph were recorded. The investigator then tested their remembrance of the images over a long period of time. Their immediate recollections were already tending toward the conventional images of military personnel of various ranks. For example, the private was recalled as good humored and smiling; the captain was clean shaven and had clear, sharp features and a jutting chin; and the colonel was stern and serious, with a grave expression. With the passage of time, the remembrances became more and more a stereotype of what the subjects felt a military person of a particular rank was probably like. Often, the same distortions took place as had been observed in other studies of forgetting. If a subject was initially impressed with a single characteristic—e.g., a firm chin or deep-set eyes—he or she tended over time to accentuate this feature and gradually *construct a new image* around the one impressive feature. The recall of this fabricated image was surprisingly firm and vivid. Distortion moved in the direction of an image which supported the subject's estimation of the personality of the person pictured.

In a carefully controlled laboratory experiment with word associations, it was found that words having an unpleasant emotional tone for a subject are forgotten much more readily than words neutral in tone.[134] Another study found that people tend to remember things which support their point of view and tend to forget those things which oppose it, even when the time given to learning both is kept constant.[135] In that study, subjects with strong prosegregationist leanings remembered more easily plausible prosegregation and implausible antisegregation statements than they did plausible antisegregation and implausible

[132] R. Reiff & M. Scherrer, *Memory and Hypnotic Age Regression* (1959). But see **ch 11** for discussion of limitations on this process.

[133] F. Bartlett, Remembering: An Experimental and Social Study 53 (1930).

[134] Levinger & Clark, *Emotional factors in forgetting of word associations,* 62 J Abnormal Soc Psychology 99 (1961).

[135] Jones & Kohler, *The effects of plausibility on the learning of controversial statements,* 57 J Abnormal & Soc Psychology 315 (1958).

prosegregation statements. For subjects with strong antisegregation attitudes, the reverse was true. A similar result was obtained in a study using favorable information about Russia.[136] Those having favorable attitudes toward Russia retained the information better than those who held unfavorable views.

The tenacity with which all people tend to preserve their familiar, stable world is illustrated by the following incident.[137] A schoolmaster one day noticed that a medallion which he carried prominently on his watchchain had disappeared. He asked his students in various classes when they had last seen it upon him. Many of them described it in detail and assured him that he had been wearing it earlier that very day. The medallion was eventually found in a restaurant where the schoolmaster had dined *the evening before.*

People tend to remember things the way they think they *ought to be* rather than the way they often actually are. Once, in a classroom lecture, the teacher (one of the writers) spent considerable time giving evidence *contradicting* a popular view on child-rearing practices. Fully half the class reported at the next class meeting that the teacher had offered evidence *supporting* the popular view. (The students who so remembered the lecture confessed that they continued to favor the popular view.)

Defense Mechanisms

Further evidence of the influence of affective states upon memory is seen in psychogenic amnesia cases. Typically, the victim does not forget everything. He or she retains a memory of general information, such as his or her social habits or technical skills. What he or she forgets are items of personal reference (usually painful)—his or her own name, family, and personal biography. Functional amnesia is frequently related to severe emotional stress. Forgetting selected areas of the past provides an escape from those parts of reality that the victim feels he or she is no longer able to handle.[138]

Depth psychology theories have long emphasized the functional role of remembering and forgetting. Selective forgetting is a commonly used method of allaying anxiety. Such forgetting is referred to as *repression.*[139] According to this theory, people drive out of consciousness those memories which are too painful or too threatening to their

---

[136] Garber, Influence of cognitive and affective factors in *learning and retaining attitudinal material,* 51 J Abnormal & Soc Psychology 384 (1955).

[137] G. Williams, The Proof of Guilt 84 (1963).

[138] The situation is different in cases involving brain pathology. In such cases material is truly lost. See J. Coleman, Abnormal Psychology and Modern Life 212 (3d ed 1964).

[139] S. Freud, Interpretation of Dreams (1938).

self-concept to recall. The mechanism whereby repression occurs is itself unconscious. Consequently, people can report in all sincerity that they do not remember such an item. Distortions of past experiences change in the same manner. An unconscious censor is at work deep within each person, monitoring past recollections lest realities too difficult for him or her to bear break through into awareness.

The Adlerian school of thought emphasizes the creative use people make of memories.[140] It sees each individual as developing a lifestyle which dictates the way in which he or she views himself or herself and the world about him or her. The supreme priority of every individual is the maintenance of this lifestyle. All the person's resources, including memory, are bent to this task. As a consequence, memory is a function of a person's *present* attitude toward himself or herself and others. Past events, especially the person's role in them, are recalled in a way that supports his or her present view of himself or herself. Realities of the past which contradict that view are modified so as to support it. As one proponent of Adlerian psychology puts it:

> The memory records all experiences. They are kept, so to say, on file for future reference. In this way they do not interfere with present problems and experiences; but they can always be recalled when we want and need them. We do not always recognize that our memory is entirely at our disposal, unless a brain damage has destroyed the "file." Our conscience often interferes with our realization of the use which we make of our memory. We may be apparently unable to recollect or be plagued by recollections which we cannot forget. In either case the memory functions in accordance with our real intentions, which we do not admit to ourselves. The memory, like emotions, seems to act independently from our intentions and wishes only if our common sense is in conflict with our "private logic." The dynamics of memory explain the fact that we chose to remember from the thousands of experiences of our early childhood, only those which fit our general—and still present—outlook on life. These early recollections, therefore, are indicative of our life style.[141]

Evidence for this theory of memory turns up regularly in therapy

---

[140] Adlerians are followers of Alfred Adler (1870-1937). Adler was one of the earliest associates of Freud. He broke with Freud over the latter's insistence on inherited determinants of behavior. Adler taught that the individual played a purposeful role in the organization of his own experiences. See *supra* note 141.

[141] R. Dreikurs, Fundamentals of Adlerian Psychology 86 n1 (1953).

conducted in the Adlerian manner. At the outset of therapy, the subject is asked to recall his or her earliest memories. These are recorded. They consistently are found to reflect the subject's *present* attitudes toward himself or herself and others. When therapy has progressed satisfactorily, the subject is again asked to recall his or her earliest memories. Frequently, the memories have changed altogether or have been modified in the direction of the new, healthier attitudes the subject has achieved in therapy.

The unconscious monitoring of memories is not a phenomenon reserved for the mentally disturbed. It has been found to be a very general phenomenon.[142] Indeed, laboratory studies with normal subjects have uncovered it.[143]

Conforming Memory to Unified Whole

The dynamic, creative, purposeful functioning of memory can be subsumed under the general gestalt principle that the mind is ever modifying experience so as to effect a unified whole.[144] Each person has his or her own vision of reality, and he or she tends to employ *private logic*—and memory—to keep that vision coherent. *Objective fact* sometimes suffers in consequence. Recognition and recall are especially vulnerable to this unconscious dynamic. People all carry about with them preconceived notions of external reality and the way things are related to one another. Whenever a person encounters an item that might possibly fit one of these preestablished patterns of understanding, it tends to trigger the reinstatement of the entire pattern. This process explains the common error of deja vu—the deceiving impression of having seen something or someone before when, in fact, the person has not. Early philosophers remarked at this phenomenon and inferred that everyone must have enjoyed a previous existence where he or she had encountered this person or object.[145] A more probable explanation is that the present experience has some aspects about it which are similar to a past one, allowing the past experience to reinstate itself. Thus, a pattern of buildings along a street, a row of trees, or a gathering of people is somewhat similar to a significant earlier experience and strong feelings of recognition arise. A certain odor on a spring day, a flight of birds, and the approach of a person with a certain

---

[142] D. Rapaport, Emotions and Memory (1950).

[143] Clemes, *Repression and hypnotic amnesia,* 69 J Abnormal & Soc Psychology 62-69 (1964).

[144] See **§2.05** for discussion of gestalt principles.

[145] E.g., Plato in Timaeus.

gait all may trigger a sense that this very moment has occurred before. A prominent feature on a face, a curve of the mouth, or a way of holding the body may call into consciousness a previously experienced person whose constellation of features included an item very similar to the person presently in view. The viewer has a vivid sense of recognition, but he or she is wrong.

A related error is the confusion of patterns and contexts. It may become difficult for a student studying Shakespeare to assign characters to the proper play when they have similar roles in somewhat similar parts. In such cases, the student is correct in identifying the character as familiar, but he or she experiences *negative transfer.* The student places the character in the wrong context. Most people have had the experience of encountering a familiar face after a long interval and opening the conversation with a reference to the party at which the person met him or her. The speaker is embarrassed to discover that it was not at *that* party, but at another one.

Sometimes, people are vaguely conscious of the process that is going on within them. A person may see a face in a crowd that stirs a feeling of familiarity. It does not harmonize with the present context. The observer knows he or she has not seen the person *here* before—but where? Tension arises within the observer. He or she experiences a drive to establish a new configuration in which this face is a part of the pattern. A search for clues begins. The observer reaches for a past situation in which the face fits. Tension is relieved when a former pattern is reestablished in which this face can merge as part of the whole. Thus, a single clue triggers the reinstatement of an entire constellation of relationships. Unfortunately, the whole process often misfires. There is good reason for people to be cautious about their recollections, given the unconscious mechanism over which they have little control.

§2.38 Witness Confidence

Juries are impressed by the witness who is certain about the accuracy of his or her recollections. Cross-examination cannot sway that witness. He or she *knows* what he or she saw or heard. Research, however, has shown that a witness who is firm about his or her memory is not more likely to be correct than one who is hesitant and tentative.[146] Unfortu-

---

[146] See **§2.39.** See also Hastie, Landsman & Loftus, *Eyewitness testimony: The danger of guessing,* 19 Jurimetrics J 1 (1978); Clifford & Scott, *Individual and situational factors in eyewitness testimony,* 63 J Applied Psychology 352-58 (1978).

nately, most laypersons are not easily persuaded that subjective sincerity does not guarantee objective truth.[147]

§2.39 Specific Inaccuracies of Witnesses

Given the complexity of the processes of perception and memory and their vulnerability to error, it is hardly surprising that percipient witnesses are often mistaken.

Many college psychology classes have included a staged episode, calculated to demonstrate percipient witness fallibility. The standard procedure is to have an otherwise normal class lecture interrupted by some unusual event, such as a fight breaking out among some of the students or an outsider stepping in to consult with the teacher. The class is subsequently asked to report what they saw. The wide differences in the accounts seldom fail to amaze and amuse all. More recent researchers have refined this experiment, subjecting it to controls and statistical analyses of significance. The resulting reports have supplied detailed information as to specific tendencies to err in perception and memory.

§2.40 —Experiments with Elaborate Staged Events

An early experiment was staged at the University of Berlin.[148] A professor had prepared three students to stage a sudden, violent quarrel in the classroom, during which a revolver was to be discharged. All the movements and words of the three actors had been carefully rehearsed and were acted out letter-perfect before an unsuspecting and stunned group of students. The students were then asked to write down what had been said and done. Omissions of significant elements, wrong additions, and alterations were counted as errors. The number of mistakes per observer ranged from 26 per cent of the items in a report to 80 per cent of them. Typical mistakes were: words put in the mouth of actually silent bystanders; actions attributed to the actors which they did not do; and essential elements of the drama overlooked entirely.

Another researcher performed an experiment aimed at studying the role of *closure.*[149] The researcher had four independent events occur nearly simultaneously before a group of university students and then asked the students for an immediate report of what had happened. As

---

[147] Stern, *The Psychology of Testimony,* 34 J Abnormal & Soc Psychology 3 (1939).

[148] H. Muensterberg, On the Witness Stand (1908).

[149] Otto, *Testimony and Human Nature,* 9 J Am Inst Crim L & Criminology 1 (1918). See **§2.08** for a discussion of closure.

anticipated, the students linked the four events together in a causal chain, illustrating the tendency toward structured perception and recall—the movement toward a *good figure*[150] in which all elements of the perceptual field are made to serve the logic of the whole.

The setting for the staged series of events was that while the professor was in the act of returning graded papers to the students, passing down the aisles as he did so, a student in the aisle nearest the door struck the student in front of him with a book, provoking an altercation. Simultaneously, a student at the front of the room threw a coin in the air and allowed it to strike and roll upon the floor. The professor immediately ordered the three students to leave the room, went directly to the board, and wrote something on it, all the while keeping his back to the student body. Simultaneously, a fourth student, located on the other side of the room at the back, rose and calmly walked out of the room through a nearby door. When all this was completed, the professor asked the students to record immediately their observations on what had happened. There was an air of legal testimony about this task, since the university had a student board of discipline and the students believed that their accounts would be used in a subsequent disciplinary hearing. It should be noted that this motivation to be accurate and fair actually came too late to improve accuracy of observation and recall. As mentioned in **§2.31**, the motivation to observe and recall accurately must occur *prior* to the learning experience to be effective.

In the study, the students linked the throwing of the coin with the altercation between the students. A good number of the students reported that no coin was thrown at all but rather that a desk was broken as a result of the altercation and a ball joint in the desk loosened and rolled upon the floor. The professor was seen as rushing to the door and holding it open as he ordered the students out or as rushing to his desk and collapsing there in dismay. In the original reports, most students did not even notice the exit of the fourth student. However, when they were asked why this student left the room, those who had not even seen him leave went on to link him to the disturbance as well. This last factor illustrates the role of suggestion and the tendencies toward logical consistency and simplicity.

The level of vividness of recall and certitude in the reports was studied specifically. The students believed that their reports would be used in a future disciplinary action. Yet there were no *maybe's* or *probably's* in their reports. Those students who had reported the desk as breaking

---

[150] **§§2.08, 2.32.**

were unable to believe that such had not happened even when they later were shown the intact desk.

The role of expectation and mental set is also illustrated by the results of that experiment. When asked where the professor was located when the disturbance broke out, students seated at all points in the room reported that he was close to their seat at the exact moment. The professor was in fact moving around the room and returning graded papers. Each student was anticipating the paper and was emotionally set to receive it. Supposedly, the emotional proximity to receiving the paper translated into physical proximity.

When asked as to the professor's reaction to the incident, the students gave detailed descriptions of the professor's face and volunteered descriptions of his feelings. The actual fact was that the professor had had his back to the students during the episode. It is well established that human beings tend to project their own feelings into others or to assign others feelings which are consistent with an attitude of the observer toward them. In the present case, since the students had no opportunity actually to observe the face of the professor, they were forced to rely on one of these processes. They did so with great confidence. The professor was assigned a range of feelings and responses from helpless timidity and embarrassment to outraged hostility. What is more revealing is that when asked to describe the feelings of the fourth student, the students who reported originally that they did not notice that student leave the room or who were so located that they could not possibly see that a student's face as he left launched into detailed descriptions of the student's facial expression and emotions.

§2.41 —Experiments with Simple Staged Events

Some criticism was raised about staged events such as those discussed in the previous section. It was argued that while they succeed in documenting *closure* and the distortion of reality in favor of a *good figure* and a preestablished logical pattern, they may not test accurately the kinds of situations which figure most commonly in legal testimony.[151] Staged events which present abrupt disturbances and bring together in time causally unrelated elements may invite the errors described. The suddenness and violence of the events arrest attention, but attention tends to focus perception and limits scope. The predisposition to

---

[151] See Morgan, *A study in the psychology of testimony*, 8 J Am Inst Crim L & Criminology 222 (1917).

impose pattern and meaning on simultaneous events then easily leads to distortion. It was argued that most things which witnesses in law are asked to report are things which have occurred within a meaningful framework of their own—a framework to which the witness was properly attuned at the time of the occurrence and therefore was not required to impose some subjective pattern in order to make sense of it all.[152] Consequently, researchers began to study more normal occurrences—those with an easy, internal logic which make no extraordinary demands on attention (and its consequent narrowing) or sudden shifts of mental set.

In one such experiment, a class in psychology was interrupted by a knock at the door.[153] A person entered and gave the professor a note. The professor pretended to read the note and responded: "I will be there at two o'clock." One week later, the class (150 students of both sexes) was asked to report the event and to give descriptions of the intruder and the verbal exchange. The result was that most students could return a fair reconstruction of the event, but with clear evidence of closure and the tendency to fill out the story with fabricated details. There were many errors which might be significant had the incident been of legal importance. For instance, there was a great variation in description of the clothes worn by the intruder. Some had the intruder wearing an overcoat; some did not. Nine different colors were assigned to the intruder's suit. When later asked a direct question whether the suit was brown or black, a large percentage abandoned their original choices and picked one of these colors. The choices were firm, with no qualifications of, e.g., "I think . . ." Actually, the suit was of neither color. The direct question suggested that one of the two was correct, and hazy recollections, not strong enough for absolute recall, seemed to have followed the laws of recognition described above.[154] The students utilized differential recall—i.e., they rejected the color with the least response strength which then firmed up their *recall* of the only alternative left. Seventy-six per cent of the students underestimated the time of day at which the event occurred. This error is interesting in that they had cues working for them—i.e., they knew it occurred during the usual psychology hour.[155]

Errors in estimation of height followed the law of personal reference. The range of heights reported was from four feet to six feet, six inches.

---

[152] *Id.*

[153] *Id.*

[154] See **§2.31.**

[155] Errors in time estimation are discussed in **§2.42.**

The women students almost uniformly underestimated, choosing a height closer to their own. The men students came within closer range of the true height. The same personal reference was at work in their reports on the number of books the intruder was carrying. Actually, he was carrying three. The students reported a number which was in accord with what each was accustomed to carry himself or herself.

Interpretation of feelings supported the findings of other studies. A number of students reported that the intruder stood embarrassed before the class while he awaited the professor's reply. A smaller percentage of the men than women read this into the situation. The Experimenter suggested these women themselves would have felt more self-conscious in such a circumstance, at least at the time the experiment was performed. A further sex difference was the detail offered by the women in respect to clothing and features. We tend to give attention to the things which are of interest to us.

The role of suggestion, triggering a reinstatement of a pattern, was illustrated by a direct question put to the students.[156] Although, in the original free narrative form of their reports, the students had almost uniformly reported that the intruder had stood looking at the class during the episode, when asked why the intruder did *not* look at the class, the students went on to offer explanations which made sense to them—now accepting it as fact that the intruder did *not* look at them. Evidence was found that the free narrative form of report tends to be more accurate, if less complete, than the direct question approach. The direct question suggested a cue around which the subject then built a *recollection.* The students did this with great vividness and certainty.

The normal event was used in another study of the staged episode.[157] During a university lecture, a maintenance worker, appropriately attired, entered the room, crossed in front of the professor's desk, and proceeded to a radiator on the other side of the room. The worker tinkered with the radiator, inquired about the heat, then retraced his steps, and left the room. Sixteen days later, the worker returned with five other men similarly attired and of generally similar appearance. The students were asked to identify the person who had entered the room previously. Three classes of students were represented among the observers. One group were those who had known the event was a test when the worker walked into the room the first time. They were motivated to observe and recall from the beginning of the experience.

---

[156] See Morgan, *supra* note 151, at 226.

[157] Brown, *An Experience in Identification Testimony,* 25 J Am Inst Crim L & Criminology 621 (1935).

In accord with the laws of learning, they were the most successful in identifying the correct person in the line-up; 21 out of the 22 picked the right person. A second group were psychology students who were accustomed to surprise tests from the professor and were somewhat motivated to observe and recall from the beginning of the experience. Seventy-six per cent of these picked out the right person. It should be noted, however, that one of those who was wrong in this group was ready to testify under oath that the person he identified wrongly was the correct one. Of the third group of students, who had had no suspicion at the time that a test was underway, 65 per cent picked the correct person. Several students were presented only the five alternative choices, excluding the correct person. Sixty-five per cent of these positively identified one of the wrong people. Twenty-five per cent said that the correct person was not among the group.

To test the role of suggestion further, an interesting modification was added to this experiment. The line-up was displayed to a group of students who had not even been present for the original episode. The questionnaire which was presented the students, however, presupposed that they had indeed witnessed the episode. On the basis of this supposed experience, they were asked to pick out the person whom they had *seen* on that occasion. Thirty per cent of these students testified that they *recalled* the incident and went on to identify positively one of the people in the line-up. The suggestive capability of the question must have been indeed strong to trigger such an unwarranted recollection. Undoubtedly, at some time in their past, in some setting, they had witnessed this common enough episode of a worker entering a classroom and unceremoniously going about the worker's business. However, it is impressive to note that some people are so susceptible to suggestion as to bring them to link such a vague item of the past with a definite moment and context 16 days prior to the line-up. It would have been interesting to have determined what cues these students used in *identifying* a person whom they had never seen before.

In the context of a wider study, further data were gained on the role of mental set and prior motivation in eyewitness observation and recall.[158] The subjects here were lawyers attending a lecture in legal psychology. The episode involved a stranger knocking on the door soon after the beginning of a lecture. The stranger entered at the lecturer's request, delivered an envelope to the lecturer, and waited for the lecturer to finish reading the contained message. The stranger wore distinctive clothes and carried three books, the color of each being one

---

[158] Marston, *Studies in Testimony*, 15 J Crim L & Criminology 1 (1924).

of the psychological primaries. He carried a long-handled switchblade knife, which he opened and with which he scraped his gloved hand. When the lecturer completed reading the message, he exchanged some remarks with the stranger, and the stranger then left the room. The lawyers were then asked to recall the episode. None of them noticed the knife. They did so poorly in their observations that they argued that if they had been properly motivated to attend to what transpired during the interruption, they would have done much better. To test this hypothesis, the experimenter alerted the next class of lawyers by describing the previous test and the results. In this second group were two of the lawyers who had been present for the first test. Shortly after recounting the entire experiment, there was a knock at the door, and a similar episode was acted out. All the students knew a test was in progress. The result was only a slight gain in completeness of their observations. What was significant was that there was considerable loss in caution—i.e., the second group was firm and confident about *wrong* observations. While the original group had been less complete in the scope of their observations, they had been quite accurate in what they did recall. This second group turned hazy recollections into firm affirmations, perhaps because of their expectations of themselves. This result may indicate that while motivation to recall an event in progress generally makes for better retention, it may also lead to a false sense of confidence in a witness' recollection.

§2.42 The Estimation of Time

The duration of an event or the placing of it in a time sequence is often of importance in law. It is noted in another section that filled space is perceived as smaller than the same space when observed empty.[159] A room filled with furniture seems smaller than when all the furniture is removed. The same is true of temporal space—i.e., time intervals. A number of researchers have studied the accuracy of time estimation and factors affecting it. One study found a general tendency to overestimate periods up to four minutes and to underestimate periods over eight minutes. However, there are wide individual differences. A three-second interval may be estimated within a range of one-half second to fifteen seconds. Twenty seconds are estimated within a range of four seconds to five minutes. One minute is estimated from one second to ten minutes. Two minutes are estimated from thirty seconds to twenty

---

[159] See **§2.46.**

minutes. Nineteen minutes are estimated within a range of five minutes to forty minutes.

Another study compared the estimate of empty time with that of filled time.[160] It found that while there is a general tendency to overestimate time intervals of about a minute under *all* conditions, the overestimation is most exaggerated during idle conditions.[161] The average exaggeration under such conditions is almost 50 per cent.[162] When the interval is filled with intense activity, the increase averages only 13 per cent.[163] It was found that accuracy of estimation is enhanced when an individual has personal time references available—i.e., when he or she knows the approximate time span of certain activities which he or she knows were accomplished within the interval he or she is asked to estimate. Thus, people who live well-regulated lives, filled with recurring activities, tend to be more accurate in their estimation of elapsed time.[164]

Evidence was found in other studies that there is a tendency to equate unequal intervals.[165] Subjects asked to compare two intervals estimated them to be of equal duration even though one was actually fifteen-seconds and the other was a minute and a half. This tendency is not so pronounced when the intervals are of longer duration. Thus, a two-minute interval would not be judged to be equal to an eight-minute interval. The investigators also found that there is a tendency to give estimates in multiples of five minutes when the estimate is demanded of them some time after the test interval—i.e., under conditions of delayed recall. It also seems that a conscious effort to time an interval increases accuracy. It is suggested that under such conditions, the subject unconsciously employs private aids, such as counting the pulse or respiration.

A general tendency to underestimate years has been found when a subject is asked to place an event which has occurred some years previously.[166] The error increases with the number of years involved. In addition, a week was found to be estimated within a range of five to twenty days. Time references can help an individual to better accuracy. If the subject can associate an event with another event whose general date is known, he or she can become quite accurate. It is suggested that

---

[160] Moore, *The Accuracy of Testimony Relative to Time Intervals,* 26 J Crim L & Criminology 210 (1935).

[161] *Id* 212.

[162] *Id.*

[163] *Id.*

[164] *Id* 214-215.

[165] H. Burtt, Legal Psychology (1931).

[166] Unpublished studies cited in Moore, *supra* note 160, at 210-15.

under such conditions, however, he or she is not really depending on a sense of time but on a basically different process—association. People frequently can associate an event with a season of the year more accurately than they can with the year itself. However, under some conditions, a person can overlook the most obvious associations.[167]

Affective states influence the perception of time. An interval spent anxiously awaiting an event seems longer than the same interval spent dreading the occurrence of an approaching event. For most people, Friday seems never to come, whereas the weekend passes all too quickly. A person caught up in a violent, anxiety-provoking situation tends to overestimate the duration of the event when asked to recall it.

§2.43 The Sequence of Events

Numerous studies have shown that witnesses unconsciously rearrange the sequence of events witnessed to fit the meaning or interpretation they have imposed on the incident.[168] This meaning may have arisen simultaneously with the event or may have developed afterwards in accordance with the dynamics discussed above.[169]

Another distinct phenomenon, however, may disturb accurate perception of events. It is the process called *masking.* This process is the erasure of one stimulus by a succeeding one. Research has shown that two events occurring in sufficiently rapid succession may fuse and be perceived as one event; this event, however, may appear more intense than either of the component events individually. Thus, two flashes of light have been perceived as a single flash brighter than either of the actual flashes. The stimuli may address different modalities of perception—e.g., a sound followed rapidly by a sight. The California coroner who investigated the assassination of Robert Kennedy reported that all 50 witnesses to the incident were certain that the victim fell forward before shots were fired. The event had been caught on videotape, and it was possible to determine that all 50 witnesses were wrong as to the sequence.[170] Often, the question of sequence—e.g., whether a screech of brakes preceded the striking of a pedestrian—is crucial to the

---

[167] See **§2.41.** For instance of students overlooking fact that event occured during regularly scheduled class.

[168] See **§§2.39-2.41.** See also G. Allport, L. Postman, The Psychology of Rumor (1947).

[169] See generally the discussion of the influence of the affective states and the memory processes, **§§2.18-2.22, 2.26-2.37.**

[170] T. T. Noguchi, Coroner 103-07 (1983).

outcome of a liability case. The number and sequence of shots fired may be a significant detail in a criminal prosecution.

§2.44 Shapes and Dimensions

Under certain conditions, observers have been found to misjudge the heights of trees, lampposts, and buildings, or the widths of roadways, by 25 per cent or more. This error seems to be the result of the visual distortion that occurs when strong vertical shapes meet a strong horizontal plane in the visual field—for example, a distant horizon.[171] The phenomenon of *embeddedness* has caused other visual errors.[172] The shape and size of an item appears differently depending on the context in which the item is viewed. The path of an aircraft on a radar scope has been misread because of the concentric circles overlaid on the scope. Indicator needles on dials have been misread by several degrees when operating against certain backgrounds and when viewed at angles.[173] Objects seem larger when seen against a background considerably darker than the objects.[174] Because of the phenomenon of the *afterimage,* a *context* can be imposed upon an item even though the item stands isolated in the visual field.[175] For this reason, things can appear to be moving when they are actually still, or they can appear to be moving in a different direction than they actually are. A road ahead may seem to continue straight if a line of trees along the highway continues off into the horizon even though the road itself curves away from the trees before the horizon. A person of moderate height positioned among much taller people seems short, while the same person among very small people seems taller than he or she is. The *positioning* may also occur subjectively. If a witness had been observing very tall people or very short people prior to turning his or her attention to an average-sized person, the immediately prior experience may interfere with the witness' estimate of the average-sized person's true height. Estimates of size and other qualities may also be made in reference to the witness' private standard. What is high, low, thick, smooth, loud, handsome, cold, warm, dark, or bright to one person may not be so in reference to another's standard. People often use their own height as a reference. Affective attitudes can also influence estimates.[176]

---

[171] S. Coren & J. S. Girgus, Seeing is Deceiving: The Psychology of Visual Illusion 43 (1978).

[172] See **§2.16.**

[173] Fisher & Lucas, *Illusions in Concrete Situations,* 12 Ergonomics 11-24 (1969).

[174] Coren & Girgus, *supra* note 171, at 41.

[175] See **§2.12.**

[176] See **§§2.18-2.22.**

Things desired and admired seem bigger and better than they actually are. Things feared tend to become more fearsome than they actually are. The size of a gun or knife may be exaggerated by a victim. The bulk of the attacker may also be enlarged. Vertical things tend to be overestimated in height while the breadth of horizontal things—e.g., the width of a road—tend to be underestimated. Brightly colored objects appear larger than dull things. The tendency to conform reality to a *good figure* is always present.[177] If a witness has definite knowledge of the size of one thing in a scene, he or she may be inferring what the size of other things *ought to be* rather than actually recalling the true size. Because of the many subjective factors involved in estimating dimensions, the true dimension of an object tends to be the average of the reports of several witnesses.[178] Finally, cultural differences may distort the perception of size, and there remains the possibility that distortions may also be related to undetected organic or functional brain disorders.[179]

§2.45 Color Errors

In one experiment, eyewitnesses who had no particular reason to note the color of clothing of a major participant in a staged event firmly reported nine different colors.[180] Color perception and recall are subject to all the factors discussed above: contrast,[181] illumination,[182] afterimage processes,[183] and constancy.[184] Not to be overlooked is simple colorblindness and retinal abnormalities that have organic origins and sometimes develop with age.[185] These deficiencies can go unsuspected by the witness who in good faith testifies that his or her vision is perfect.[186] Moreover, intense emotional disturbance can induce abnormalities in accurate color perception.[187]

---

177 See **§§2.05-2.09.**

178 See **§2.39.**

179 See **§2.25.**

180 See **§2.41.**

181 See **§2.13.**

182 See **§§2.14-2.15.**

183 See **§2.12.**

184 See **§2.09.**

185 J. Davidoff, Differences in Visual Perception 59 (1975); see also Gilbert, *Age changes in Color Matching,* 12 J Gerontology 210 (1957).

186 J. Davidoff, *supra* note 185, at 62.

187 *Id.*

§2.46 Locating the Source of a Sound

A person's ability to determine the direction of a sound is rooted in the time differential as the sound wave strikes first the ear closer to the source of the sound and then the more distant ear.[188] For this reason, people have good discrimination in locating sources of sound positioned to the right or left. However, they have very poor ability to discriminate direction between sounds originating above or below or to the front or back. Even the right-left discrimination often needs the assistance gained by turning the head slightly. If one of the ears is temporarily deafened—e.g., by a cold or by being buried in a pillow or set to a telephone or transistor ear plug—the localizing ability is considerably impaired. A witness may not even suspect that one of his or her ears is less efficient than the other. Such possibility increases with the age of the individual. When binaural cues are inadequate to locate a sound, people unconsciously rely on their higher order strategems for determining location—i.e., they locate the sound where it seems to make the most sense to them in accordance with the processes discussed above.[189] The witness, however, would continue to believe he or she *heard* it coming from the direction he or she identifies.

§2.47 Estimating Speed

While a lay witness is allowed to testify as to his or her estimate of the speed of a vehicle, field research indicates such estimates may be wildly inaccurate. One experiment with United States Air Force personnel revealed that estimates of the speed of a car ranged from 10 miles per hour (m.p.h.) to 50 m.p.h., when the actual speed was 12 m.p.h.[190]

The context in which the moving vehicle is seen and the angle at which it is observed can make the difference.[191] A rider in a vehicle can be influenced by the spacing of posts or trees located sufficiently close to the roadway that they appear in the periphery of his or her vision as he or she passes. They may appear to whip by, even when the speed is quite

---

[188] Woodworth & Schlosberg, Experimental Psychology 350 (1958).

[189] See **§§2.05-2.10**

[190] J. Marshall, Law & Psychology in Conflict 22 (1969).

[191] Denton, *The influence of visual pattern on perceived speed,* Road Research Laboratory Report, *cited in* S. Coren & J. S. Girgus, Seeing is Deceiving: The Psychology of Visual Illusion 43 (1978).

moderate. Finally, the design of a speedometer gauge may encourage false readings when glanced at quickly and from an angle.[192]

§2.48 Estimating Distance

Witnesses tend to underestimate the distance between objects if many other items occupy the space between them. The location of a person in a room seems less distant from an observer also in the room if there are many others present. An observer would estimate himself or herself closer to an automobile accident if there are many cars located between him or her and the site of accident. On the other hand, the tendency is to overestimate distance if the space is relatively empty between objects. The distance between a person observed in an open field and the house or tree toward which he or she is moving would usually appear greater than it actually is.

Affective factors also influence the estimate. Admired and liked persons are estimated to be spatially closer to the observer than is actually the case, while disliked persons are judged to be positioned farther away than is actually true.[193] If the situation is violent, perceived distance tends to be significantly distorted.[194]

§2.49 Voice Identification

Current research indicates that voice identification under all but the most ideal conditions is highly unreliable.[195] Reliability plummets when the voice was originally heard under violent conditions, was partially disguised on first hearing, or was heard unexpectedly and out of context—e.g., when the auditor thought he or she was alone in a room. The length of time a voice is originally heard does not appear to increase the accuracy of identification on a subsequent hearing. The very young and those over 60 years of age tend to be more inaccurate than others. If all other things are equal, females are better than males at voice

---

[192] S. Coren & J. S. Girgus, *supra* note 191, at 24.

[193] W. Ittleson, S. B. Kutash, L. Abrahamson & B. Seidenberg, Perceptual Changes in Psychopathology (1961); Beloff & Beloff, *The influence of valence on distance judgment of human faces,* 62 J Abnormal Soc Psychology 720 (1961); Dannanmeier & Thumin, *Authority Status as factor in perceptual distortion of size,* 63 J Soc Psychology 361 (1964); see also **§2.25.**

[194] Werner & Wagner, *Changes in psychological distance under conditions of danger,* 24 J Personality 153 (1955).

[195] Clifford, *Memory for voices: the feasibility and quality of earwitness evidence,* in Evaluating Witness Evidence 189 (S.M. Lloyd-Bostock & B.R. Clifford eds 1983).

identification, according to recent research.[196] Earlier studies indicated that members of one sex are better at identifying the voice of a member of the opposite sex than that of one of their own sex.[197] Thus, men can identify a woman's voice and women can identify a man's voice more accurately than either can identify the voice of a member of their own sex. Perhaps interest and increased attention play a role in this reported phenomenon.

Racial differences between the speaker and auditor seem to have no effect on accuracy. This conclusion is the finding of both recent and earlier research.[198] In an early experiment, an unfamiliar foreign voice was recognized with the same degree of accuracy as an unfamiliar American voice. The foreign voice was German, and it was picked out of a series of five other foreign voices: Chinese, Greek, Russian, and another German voice. Interestingly, the German voice was most often confused with the Chinese voice rather than the other German voice.

The ability to recognize a voice decreases with an increase in the length of time between the occasions on which it is heard. One study showed that a significant decline in recognition set in after a two-week interval.[199] After three months, only a third of the experimental subjects could correctly identify a voice heard previously. After five months, reliability of identification approached mere chance; only 13 per cent of the subjects correctly identified the voice.

The ability to recognize a specific unfamiliar voice decreases as the number of voices with which it is *originally* heard increases. When a test voice was originally heard with just one other voice, 77 per cent of the subjects were able to identify it two days later when it was heard among a group of four other voices. However, when the test voice was originally heard in a group of five voices, only 46 per cent of the subjects could correctly distinguish it two days later from four other voices. After an interval of a week, a mere 8 per cent were able to identify it.

It should be observed that many of these studies were carried out under laboratory conditions. In settings of more interest in the courtroom, other factors may be present which may affect accuracy. The laws of learning suggest that if an auditor is motivated from the outset to remember a voice with an eye to future identification in a criminal

---

[196] *Id.*

[197] McGhee, *The reliability of the identification of the human voice,* 17 J Gen Psychology 249 (1937).

[198] Werner & Wagner, 24 J Personality 153 (1955); McGhee, *supra* note 197.

[199] McGhee, *supra* note 197.

proceeding, his or her accuracy of retention may be enhanced.[200] On the other hand, there is substantial evidence that voices tend to be associated with faces and body build.[201] The one suggests the other. It would seem there would always be the danger that the memory of an unfamiliar voice would be interfered with when the auditor is supplied with a physical description of the suspected speaker. Following the laws of distortion of memory, there may be a movement toward stereotyping —i.e., the memory of the voice begins to accomodate itself to the type of voice the witness has always associated with the appearance of a particular person.[202] The more the witness is led to believe the accused was the speaker, the greater the accomodation. Stereotyping can move in the other direction as well. A voice tends to call up a facial image. It may be difficult after a considerable interval for a witness to distinguish in his or her memory between the voice he or she actually heard and a face he or she actually never saw. A similar danger arises from the tendency to associate voices and behavioral characteristics. Knowledge of one may modify a memory of the other.

The danger of stereotyping in voice identification would seem to be especially strong in cross-cultural identification. Over a sufficient period of time, a witness not sharing the same dialect, accent, or tonal patterns of a particular person may gradually modify his or her memory of the specific voice in the direction of some generalized characterization. For many Northerners, all Southerners sound alike; for many whites, all blacks sound alike. The findings on foreign voice identification experiments do not nullify this caution. These cautions, of course, are inferences from general psychological laws. Until such inferences are specifically tested, they remain mere cautions.

§2.50 Observing and Recalling Details

What a witness actually saw of an event depends, in great part, on what was the focus of his or her attention at the moment. A driver, late for an appointment and impatiently waiting for a light to turn green, probably sees little of the purse snatching occurring on the sidewalk within his or her view. When the victim screams "Thief!" and the driver sees people scurrying, his or her immediate interpretation of the scene may influence what he or she *sees.* The long-haired, unkempt youth may be seen to have the purse in hand. The well-dressed youth running in

---

[200] See **§2.31.**

[201] See **§2.21.**

[202] See **§2.36.**

the opposite direction may be seen to be hurrying for help. The details of an event *seen* by a witness or recalled as being seen are influenced by what the witness was prepared to see by his or her general expectations of how things normally occur in the world.[203] It behooves the investigator, once he or she has determined the probable focus of the witness' attention at the time of the event, to test the reliability of the details provided by the witness, especially when the details support the meaning and structure the witness gave the event. There is a strong tendency for a witness to impose his or her own private *logic of the situation* on the event. This logic is the product of the witness' own experiences, prejudices, and interests. He or she is inclined unconsciously to bring together details he or she has not actually observed. This factor arose in the staged events discussed earlier.[204]

An experiment is reported in which the subjects viewed a scene of a black man in a business suit on a subway train. The black man was talking to a white man who was dressed in work clothes with a straight razor at his side. Forty of these subjects, when asked to recall the scene, reported that the black man was seen threatening a white businessman with a straight razor.[205] This tendency to *recall* an event in accordance with a person's general theory of how the world works increases with the length of time between the observation and recall of the event.

A witness may also use overly broad categories when asked to describe unfamiliar things. A *pistol shot* may include a shotgun blast for one unfamiliar with firearms. All large, expensive-looking cars may be Cadillacs. Anything less than a 747 may be a Piper Cub to many ground observers. All dark-skinned people may be blacks, and all Orientals, Chinese or Japanese.

Both young children and adults over 60 years of age are more likely than the general population to err in regard to details.[206] There is a dispute in scientific circles as to whether the sex of a witness creates a greater or lesser probability of error in regard to details.[207] Studies have produced conflicting results.[208]

---

[203] See **§§2.07, 2.09, 2.18-2.22.**

[204] See **§§2.39-2.41.**

[205] G. Allport, & L. Postman, The Psychology of Rumor 71 (1947).

[206] Ellis, Shepherd & Bruce, *The effect of age & sex upon adolescents' recognition of races,* 123 J Genetic Psychology 173-74 (1973); A. Goldstein, & Chance, *Recognition of children's faces,* 35 Child Dev 129 (1964).

[207] Powers, Andricks & Loftus, *Eyewitness accounts of females and males,* 64 J Applied Psychology 339-49 (1979).

[208] *Compare* McKelvie, *The effects of verbal labeling on recognition memory for Schematic faces,* 28 J Experimental Psychology 459-74 (1976) *with* Clifford, & Scott, *Individual and situational factors in eyewitness testimony,* 63 J Applied Psychology 352 (1978). The later

Surprisingly, research indicates that the supposedly trained observer is no more accurate than the general population. In one study, police, after viewing a filmed event, were mistaken in identifying criminal behavior more frequently than ordinary citizens.[209]

Violence surrounding the event increases the probability of error by witnesses as to details.[210] Anxiety on the part of the witness, whether caused by the event or not, has the same disruptive effect.[211] Research does not support the theory that intense excitement facilitates perception and assures accurate recall.

The manner of soliciting details from a witness affects the accuracy of recall. What a witness offers in a free narrative style of report tends to be more accurate than his or her replies to direct questions. Direct questions tend to be suggestive, and the witness may weave the suggested items into his or her account. It appears that women are more susceptible to this dynamism than men.[212] What had been a vague and ambiguous perception for the witness may, under direct questions, become very concrete and real. In experiments, subjects encouraged to guess about things they may have seen later become *certain* about these same things when asked to recall what they saw.[213]

§2.51 Causal Relationships

Events which occur close together in time and place tend to be related causally by the mind. If a witness is firm in his or her conviction that he or she *saw* A cause B, while the investigator has strong evidence to the contrary, the investigator may want to inquire into the vantage point of the witness at the time of the occurrence. If possible, it may be helpful to assess the flexibility of the witness' personality. Rigid personalities tend to impose an order on events which is in accordance with their

---

study suggests a female witness may be more accurate as to detail. This finding was not supported in the McKelvie study.

[209] A. Yarmey, The Psychology of Eyewitness Testimony 159 (1979); B. Clifford & R. Bull, The Psychology of Person Identification 183-91 (1978).

[210] Postman & Bruner, 55 Psychology Rev 314 (1948); Johnson & Scott, *Eyewitness testimony and suspect identification as a function of arousal,* paper presented at American Psychology Association meeting, Washington, D.C. (Sept 3, 1976); discussed in K. Deffenbacher, *The Influence of Arousal on Reliability of Testimony* in evaluating witness evidence 235-49 (S. Lloyd-Bostock & B.R. Clifford eds 1983).

[211] Mueller, 11 Bull Psychosomatic Socy 313 (1978).

[212] Clifford & Scott, *Individual and situational factors in eyewitness testimony,* 63 J Applied Psychology 352-58 (1978).

[213] Hastie, Landsman & Loftus, *Eyewitness testimony: The danger of guessing,* 19 Jurimetrics J 1 (1978).

general beliefs as to how reality is put together. These beliefs are often the fruit of private attitudes and prejudices. More flexible personalities leave room for the unexpected and coincidental, and consequently, they are more cautious in their interpretation. As noted in **§2.50,** the *logic of the situation* can overpower the evidence of the senses. Witnesses tend to see and hear what makes sense to them and what supports their preconceptions as to what causes what in this world.

§2.52 Facial Recognition

A person's accuracy in perceiving a face decreases with the violence, anxiety, and stress that accompany the situation in which the face is originally seen.[214] Should the face have features in common with some person known to the witness and whom the witness consciously or unconsciously felt capable of the crime, it would not be surprising if the common features should reinstate the entire gestalt of the familiar face and the witness should *see* the face previously known to him or her.[215]

Error may enter later as the result of the distortion process in delayed recall and recognition. The process moves toward the familiar or the stereotype, or the witness begins to accentuate a single feature and to build a new recollection around this feature.[216] The movement toward the familiar is similar to what is suggested in the preceding paragraph. As the image of the original face becomes more vague with time, it may tend to merge with some familiar or suggested face that has much in common with it, or it may tend toward the private stereotyped face which the witness associates with this kind of crime or event. Finally, some features—such as a prominent nose, a mark on the face, or a hair style—may come to fill the vision of memory, and the witness may begin to build a new face around it. Hence, there is danger in having a witness who gives data to a reconstruction artist view the picture when it is completed. The witness may gradually come to think of the offender in terms of the drawing rather than the original perception he or she had. Anyone who fits the drawing (rather than the original perception) is in danger of being identified by the witness.

Picking a face out of a line-up or a set of pictures runs special hazards. One is the phenomenon of interference discussed above.[217] A face may indeed stir a feeling of familiarity—the deja vu experience. However, the face may be familiar from a different context than the crime itself.

---

[214] Postman & Bruner, *supra* note 210; Siegel & Loftus, *supra* note 209.

[215] See **§2.05** for discussion of gestalt principles.

[216] See **§§2.18-2.22.**

[217] See **§2.36** for discussion of interferences effects.

Not being able to identify the original context from which the face is now breaking into recognition, the witness may place the face in the context of the crime which is now occupying his or her emotions.

Another danger is that of differential recognition. If the alternative choices are markedly different from the witness' vague recollection or the stereotype that is occupying his or her memory, he or she may simply eliminate the others and experience a sense of certitude that the one which stirs some faint sense of recognition is the culprit. In the courtroom, unless a witness accompanies his or her choice with a sense of absolute certitude, the identification is probably worthless. Suggestion is always a danger when differential recognition is operating. Any procedure which suggests to the witness that suspicion already rests upon one of the choices may tip the scale in favor of that choice. Once an identification has been made, whether it is accurate or not, the mechanism of recency[218] may then operate to increase the witness' certitude. What trace of the original face remained in the witness' memory may now fade out completely and be replaced by the face he or she has now identified. Henceforth, that face will be set into the context of the crime in the memory of the witness.

Another problem in identification is the tendency people have to associate certain attitudes, emotions, and behavior with certain physical appearances.[219] There is the danger that a victim of crime may present a description of the offender which is based heavily upon the witness' expectations of what such offenders look like, given the behavior and the emotion provoked in the witness. The witness, who perhaps had an inadequate opportunity to view the offender, may be unable to distinguish what he or she actually saw from what he or she believes he or she saw. If an act were performed by several perpetrators, the witness may be inclined to assign the vilest portion of the deed to the one he or she feels most likely did it. There is also the tendency to associate personality traits and to build a constellation of expected behavior on the basis of very limited knowledge of another. If people have knowledge of one antisocial act of another, they may stand ready to believe that person is the perpetrator of a greater crime, especially if some suspicion already rests upon him or her. In summary, all the objective and subjective dynamics discussed throughout this chapter which tend to distort perception and recall come together in the identification of persons.

---

[218] See **§2.36.**

[219] D. F. Secord & R. Taguiri, Person, Perception and Interpersonal Behavior 300-15 (1958); see **§§2.21-2.22.**

3 Pretrial Considerations

§3.01 Informal Investigation

One needs no particular expertise to know that memory fades with time. The details of an event become less sharp with the progression of weeks and months, and as time goes by events themselves tend to merge one into another. An after-the-fact suggestion may become intimately associated with the real event, and one becomes less able to distinguish between what was an immediate product of the senses and what is a later product of the imagination. Furthermore, the more frequently one repeats a story the greater the reality that the story assumes in one's mind, including the embellishments that may be added in each telling. For these reasons, it is essential that the attorney handling a case which involves the credibility of eyewitness testimony begin as quick as possible to pin down the evidence he or she intends to use in the client's behalf.

This means of course that the attorney must determine precisely what issues are in controversy. If the perception and memory of witnesses is involved, the attorney must become familiar with those factors identified in Chapter 2 which affect perception and memory and must begin immediately to develop the facts to support his or her theory of the case.

If the case is complex, it may be advisable for the attorney to seek the help of an expert. The expert may give the attorney valuable suggestions on what to look for at the scene and in interviewing witnesses and may be able to evaluate witness statements, photographs, and drawings so that the attorney will know from the beginning whether strong arguments are available in support of the client's position. Much time and money may thereby be saved by avoiding fruitless investigations.

While textbooks and manuals frequently emphasize the aspects of fact finding through formal discovery devices, clearly the most basic forms of discovery, at least in the early stages of the investigation, are informal. These include visiting the scene of the occurrence and interviewing witnesses. Informal discovery may involve considerable legwork, but the sooner it is done the better.

§3.02 —The Scene

After interviewing the client thoroughly and reviewing such essential documents as police or insurance investigation reports, the next thing any lawyer should do when handling a case, especially one where eyewitness perception is a crucial element, is to visit the scene of the occurrence. This key element in the preparation of a case is often neglected by attorneys, probably because it means taking time from one's busy schedule and traveling sometimes to out-of-the-way neighborhoods. Thus the attorney will be tempted to rely upon descriptions given by clients or witnesses or on police or insurance investigation reports. While useful, this information is *never* a substitute for the attorney's own immediate observation of the scene of the occurrence. This is true whether the case involves damage to real property, a collision at a busy intersection, living conditions in a jail cell, a robbery in a dark alley, or a shooting in a tavern. No photograph, survey, or diagram and no witness statement will substitute for an on-scene inspection by the attorney, especially if it can be done under conditions similar to those which existed at the time of the occurrence. A visit to the scene gives the attorney first-hand knowledge of the circumstances under which the observation was made so that he or she can use the basic principles of psychology (outlined in Chapter 2) and the rules of evidence to evaluate the case.

The on-the-scene inspection should take place as quick as possible after the attorney has entered the case. The natural tendency is to wait until just before trial before viewing the scene, but that may be too late. Remodeling or reconstruction may completely alter the scene. Also the scene of an event which took place in the winter at 6:00 p.m. may look completely different if viewed at 6:00 p.m. in the summer, when the light is different, foliage is on the trees, and no snow is on the streets.

The lawyer will soon recognize that witnesses frequently disregard the obvious. A prisoner who is complaining about prison conditions may understate the most basic deprivations because he or she takes them for granted. A witness will often overstate or understate such basic facts as the lighting in the hallways of a tenement or on a street corner or the size of a room or the distance traveled on a highway.

Lawyers should take pains to assure the thoroughness of their on-scene investigations. The nature and scope of their examinations will depend largely upon the particular circumstances of the case, but they always should observe the lighting, any obstructions to the witness' view, and any distractions which would have effected the witness' perception. It is also of obvious importance to check distances and any other physical conditions which may have affected the witness' ability to perceive correctly.

When relevant, the attorney may want to take along a photographer, artist, draftsmen, surveyor, or architect who can record the scene. Sometimes he or she will want to observe the scene personally before arranging for a photographer or architect to be present, but sometimes in the interest of time and money the two may go together for the first visit. The attorney should have the photographer record the lighting on a light meter and also keep careful notes showing the position from which each picture was taken, the distances involved, and the types of lenses, films, and settings used. If the attorney knows that the testimony of a third person is needed to verify the conditions, he or she should be accompanied by someone who will be available to testify. This is extremely important because it normally is impractical and undesireable for the lawyer to testify about the conditions at the scene.

Such activities may be viewed by some as a colossal waste of time and money. How can a public defender who handles hundreds of eyewitness cases or an attorney handling a matter on a pro bono or limited-fee arrangement afford to inspect the scene of each occurrence in cases where eyewitness perception is in question? The same question, however, can be asked about interviewing witnesses, researching the law, and every other element of the litigation process. The obvious answer is that these things must be done if the client is to have adequate representation. In the authors' experience, investigation at the scene of the occurrence ranks equally in importance with interviewing witnesses and researching the law in the preparation of a case for trial.

Clearly, not every case warrants the employment of a professional photographer or architect. This is a matter upon which the attorney must exercise sound discretion. If the client lacks funds, a snapshot taken by the attorney on an instant camera and identified as accurate by a witness may be sufficient. Likewise, the attorney or an assistant can take measurements and make a sketch of the scene and this will be admissible in evidence if it is identified as accurate by a witness. Again, however, the attorney must avoid becoming the only one who can testify to the measurement of distances and the like, and therefore it is best to have the actual measuring done by a third party.

The following checklist may be helpful to an attorney inspecting the conditions at the scene of an occurrence:

1. Where were the witnesses or participants positioned? The attorney should stand or sit at each of these positions, if possible, to better perceive the problems in perception
2. What were the lighting conditions? What time of day did the occurrence take place? Were there artificial lights, and if so, where were they placed, and what was their intensity? If the occurrence was out of doors, what were the weather conditions?
3. Were there any obstructions to the witness' view? Was he or she facing the sun or a light so that there was a glare? Were there any shadows which affected the observation?
4. What was the distance between the witness and the event observed?

5. Were there any activities or distractions which might have diverted the witness' attention from the occurrence? Are there any activities or landmarks that the witness, if observant, should have noticed? Is there any other physical evidence at the scene which would help the case?

§3.03 —Witness Interviews

Because of the vagaries of eyewitness testimony, it is important to tie the witnesses down at the earliest time possible. Therefore, no time should be wasted in securing witness statements. Statements can be taken in a number of ways. For instance, the attorney can simply interview the witness informally and take notes of the interview. This is certainly the least desirable method, especially if a subsequent change in the witness' story creates the necessity for impeachment. When witnesses are reluctant or fearful of talking, however, this may be the only way to gain their consent to be interviewed. A better method would be to use a tape recorder to record the interview. Another method is to have the witness sign a written statement. An even more precise method is to interview the witness before a stenographer in much the same way as if the attorney were taking a formal deposition. Selection of method will be determined by the relationship of the witness to the case, the importance of the witness' testimony, the willingness of the witness to cooperate, and the resources available to the attorney. What is important in every case is that the statements of the witness be as pointed and clear as possible, and that they be carefully preserved in case the witness later modifies his or her story.

If the witness is represented by counsel, the attorney should consider carefully whether that counsel should be informed of the proposed interview. In a criminal case, however, the prosecutor cannot instruct the witness not to talk to opposing counsel or require that the witness talk to opposing counsel only in the prosecutor's presence.[1]

It is important that counsel or his or her representative interview every witness to the occurrence. Witness names can be secured from the client, from other witnesses, and from police or other investigative reports, but those sources may not exhaust the list of all potential

---

[1] The right is derived from the free speech provision of the First Amendment, the due process clauses of the Fifth and Fourteenth Amendments, and the Ninth Amendment to the Constitution of the United States, and from Canon 7 of the Code of Professional Responsibility. *See e.g.*, IBM Corp v Edelstein, 526 F2d 37 (2d Cir 1975); Gregory v United States, 369 F2d 185 (DC Cir 1966); Vega v Bloomsburgh, 427 F Supp 593 (D Mass 1977).

witnesses. In some cases it may be necessary to go to the neighborhood which was the site of the occurrence and to go from door to door asking persons if they saw or heard anything related to the event. It is not unusual for such groundwork to uncover helpful testimony.

Frequently, the witnesses who are uncovered will be hostile or uncooperative. This attitude may be present because they do not want to get involved, because of the fear that they will be required to go to court where they will be made to look bad by the attorneys, because of the fear that they will be forced to lose time from work, and sometimes, especially in criminal cases, because they are genuinely fearful of retaliation. The question then is: how does the attorney encourage these persons to talk? Discretion and experience in handling persons are crucial in this area. Sometimes, the attorney can appeal to a sense of civic duty or to the witness' own best interest. If appropriate, the lawyer may refer to the fact that the life of a person hangs in the balance. Rarely will it be successful for the attorney to use threats such as telling the witness he or she will be subpoenaed for a formal deposition. Often the most effective means is to have a friend or neighbor approach the witness to urge him or her to talk. Frequently, when dealing with a hostile or uncooperative witness, attorneys may want to deemphasize the possibility of the witness having to testify and emphasize that the attorney is simply conducting a routine preliminary investigation to see whether their clients' positions are well-grounded. In all cases the witness should be kept at ease and assured that he or she will not be hurt by talking to the attorney.

In conducting the interviews, the attorney normally should begin with open-ended questions and allow the witnesses to tell their stories in their own way. This method may result in rambling narratives, but it may also elicit facts that the attorney would not have learned through narrow, more pointed questioning. After the witness has given his or her narrative, the attorney should follow up with narrow, pointed questions to tie the witness down to the facts, so as to establish precisely what the eyewitness saw and did not see. By the end of the interview the attorney should have committed the witness to a specific answer to each crucial question. The attorney must also be alert to any evidence of bias or lack of credibility and, especially when the witness is hostile, should lay the groundwork for effective impeachment of the witness at trial.

In interviewing the witness, the attorney must be alert to the psychological factors described in Chapter 2. The following checklist may be helpful in this regard.

1. Is the witness relating facts precisely as observed or does he or

she appear in good or in bad faith to be filling in gaps with imagination?

2. Was the witness under any stress, fear, or apprehension when viewing the person or occurrence?
3. Were there any obstructions to the witness' view?
4. Does the witness wear glasses?
5. Could anything else have distracted the witness' attention?
6. What was the precise time frame in which the witness observed the person or event?
7. Has the witness made any statements to anyone?
8. Had the witness ever previously seen the person identified, and if so, when, where, and under what circumstances?
9. Has the witness ever seen the person since the occurrence, and if so, when, where, and under what circumstances?
10. Where the identification is cross-racial, how much contact has the witness had with persons of other races?
11. Did the witness have any personal interest in the outcome of the event?
12. Was the witness ever involved in a similar occurrence either as participant or observer?
13. What is the likelihood that the witness has been influenced by statements of others?

In cases of mistaken identification, an alibi defense may be crucial. Was the defendant somewhere else when the incident occurred, and if so, can this be established through credible witnesses? Therefore, in addition to focusing upon those factors which may have produced an erroneous identification, counsel for the defense will want to interview all alibi witnesses.

§3.04 —A Case in Point

Cases frequently are won or lost based upon the facts which the attorney uncovers by informal investigation, such as the methods described in §§**3.02** and **3.03.** In some instances the facts uncovered by informal investigation may effectively put a stop to the litigation. The following example illustrates the techniques of informal investigation.[2]

On July 27, 1977, at 10:30 p.m., a shooting took place on Evergreen

---

[2] The names have been changed to protect the parties involved in this incident.

Street near the Cabrini-Green Housing Project on the near north side of Chicago. A 21-year-old black man, Henry Williams, was killed. The police report showed that Williams' brother, Ernest Masters, had been walking down Evergreen Street when he was attacked by a group of men who had been sitting on some house steps. The attackers took a radio from Masters and told him to leave the area. Masters returned almost immediately with Williams, and an argument broke out. One of the men on the steps pulled out a gun and shot Williams. Masters ran away. A second man then shot Williams again. One of the group walked to the corner and returned with a yellow Eldorado, and he and the two men who fired the shots drove away. A number of persons were on the street or were looking out of their windows when the shooting occurred. Some of them flagged down a car, and Williams was taken to a hospital. Masters and a 14-year-old youth, Robert Witcomb, who had witnessed the shooting, accompanied him to the hospital. The police canvassed the area but only interviewed a 12-year-old who could not identify any of the perpetrators.

Masters and Witcomb then went to the police station where they were questioned. Masters could not identify any of the perpetrators. Witcomb identified Willie Trent out of a photo album as the man who fired the second shot. Trent, whose mother lived on Evergreen, was arrested, and Witcomb again pointed him out in an eight-man line-up. Trent was then charged with murder, and Witcomb again positively identified him at a preliminary hearing.

Trent was confined in the Cook County Jail because he was unable to provide bail. His alibi was that he was at his home several blocks away from where the shooting occurred with his wife and her friend at the time of the incident. Although his alibi was supported by his wife and her friend, the alibi was weakened by the positive identification of Witcomb. Confident that they had their man, the police pursued the investigation no further.

The shooting had occurred in a high-crime area plagued by gang activity. When Trent's attorney first went to the scene, no one admitted to seeing or knowing anything—no one wanted to get involved. The attorney then asked a local minister to canvass the area. The minister eventually came up with a list of persons who were present when the shooting took place. The minister then accompanied Trent's attorney to interview these persons. At first they refused to sign statements or to be recorded, but after several visits by the attorney to their homes, they made detailed statements describing the incident. Each of these persons stated that he or she knew Taylor and that he or she did not see him on the street that evening.

These statements, some of which were made by persons who were not close friends of Taylor or his family, raised questions about the validity of the state's evidence. Nonetheless, these statements would still be balanced against Watkins' positive identification.

The investigation thus shifted to Watkins himself. His mother and his teacher were interviewed, and his school records were checked. Questions were raised about the boy's powers of perception and his veracity. Then his statement was taken before a stenographer. In sharp contrast to the questioning which occurred at the police station while he was kept incommunicado, his mother was asked to be present to insure that he did not feel pressured or harrassed by defendant's attorney. Watkins first gave a rambling account of what he saw on July 27. The defense attorney made every effort not to appear to be putting words in his mouth. Watkins' account differed from the one he gave the police, and he contradicted himself frequently during the interview. He explained how scared and excited he was at the time of the shooting and how everything happened so fast. His descriptions of the men who fired the shots were general and contradictory, and he admitted that he had never seen either of them before. He then admitted that he had seen Taylor several times prior to July 27. Finally, he specifically stated that Taylor was not one of the men who shot Wallace.

This statement and the statements of the other witnesses were given to the prosecutor prior to trial. On the date of the trial, the prosecutor dismissed all charges against Taylor. Thus, by means of informal discovery, the defendant was saved the trauma and expense of going through a trial, the outcome of which would have been almost entirely dependent upon his attorney's ability successfully to impeach the 14-year-old witness through cross-examination.

§3.05 Formal Discovery: Civil Cases

The alternative or supplement to the informal discovery methods discussed in **§§3.02-3.04** is formal discovery by way of interrogatories, depositions, requests to produce documents, and requests for admissions to the opposing side. Normally the first step in the formal discovery process is the service of written interrogatories on the opposing party.[3] These will be helpful to discover the existence of documents[4] and the names and addresses of witnesses. Because the

---

[3] *See* Fed R Civ P 33. Most states have corresponding provisions in their civil practice acts.

[4] Once the attorney is informed of the existence of documents he or she can then formally request the production of those documents in the possession of the opposing party. *See id* 34.

answers to interrogatories are normally prepared by the attorneys, it is generally not advisable to inquire into the probable testimony of witnesses in interrogatories. This is better done in a deposition where the attorney can carefully examine the witness, and the witness will be forced to answer in his or her own words.[5]

Sample interrogatories might thus include such basic questions as:

1. State the full name and address of each person who witnessed or claims to have witnessed the occurrences alleged in the complaint
2. State the full name and address of each person not named in 1 above who was present or claims to have been present at the scene immediately before, at the time of, or immediately after said occurrences
3. Were any photographs taken of the scene of the occurrence or of the persons or instrumentalities involved? If so, state the date or dates on which such photographs were taken, the subjects thereof, and who now has custody of them
4. Do you have statements from any witness other than yourself? If so, give the name and address of each such witness and the date of said statement, and state whether such statement was written or oral
5. List the names and addresses of all other persons (other than yourself and persons heretofore listed or specifically excluded) who have knowledge of the facts of said occurrence or of the injuries and damages following therefrom

The taking of depositions normally plays a crucial part in the preparation of any civil case when the outcome depends upon the eyewitness testimony of an opposing party or a potentially uncooperative or unfriendly witness. It is generally not advisable to take a witness' deposition until after the attorney has received the answers to written interrogatories and has discovered and inspected all pertinent documents. If the deposition is taken prior to that time, the attorney may not have sufficient facts to confront the witness and to cross-examine him or her effectively. Nonetheless, this general rule may not always apply in eyewitness cases where it may be essential to question the witness while his or her memory is still fresh and before it is unduly influenced by after-the-fact stimuli.

The major objective of a deposition is, of course, to get all the information one can from the witness. However, in doing so, the

---

[5] *See* id 30.

attorney will want to tie the witness down to a specific statement from which he or she cannot with credibility deviate or supplement with additional facts in the future. Second, the attorney will want to secure admissions favorable to his or her side. Before taking the deposition, the attorney should catalog those general psychological factors (described in Chapter 2) which may have influenced the witness and build the framework for discrediting his or her testimony. The attorney will therefore want to focus to some extent on those factors outlined in the checklist at the end of **§3.03.** His or her strategy will be basically the same as when he or she takes informal statements from witnesses. By necessity, the deposition questions will be more structured than is often the case in an informal interview. Nonetheless, the attorney is not limited in his or her inquiry by the rules of evidence as he or she would be at trial. Therefore, he or she should inquire into hearsay matters and freely ask *why* questions so as to get leads into other witnesses and information to aid his or her client.

§3.06 Formal Discovery: Criminal Cases

Formal discovery in criminal cases in both the federal courts and the state courts is generally much more restricted than in civil cases. Under federal practice, the court may permit a party to take the deposition of a prospective witness, but only in "exceptional circumstances" when "it is in the interest of justice" will the testimony be taken and preserved for use at trial.[6]

The federal rules also provide that a defendant may request the government to allow him or her to inspect or copy any relevant written or recorded statements by the defendant, his or her prior criminal record, and any documents or tangible objects, or reports of physical or mental examinations or scientific tests or experiments in the government's possession which are material to the defense.[7] If the defense requests discovery from the government, then the government may request the defendant to allow it to inspect or copy any documents or tangible objects and any reports of examinations and tests which the defendant intends to introduce as evidence in chief at the trial.[8]

The United States Supreme Court has recognized that in some situations due process may require that evidence which is of obvious substantial value to the defendant be disclosed to him or her by the

---

[6] Fed R Crim P 15.

[7] *Id* 16(a).

[8] *Id* 16(b).

prosecution even without a specific request.[9] Thus, the United States Court of Appeals for the Fifth Circuit has granted habeas corpus relief to a prisoner convicted of murder because the state prosecutor failed to disclose to the defense the existence of an eyewitness who would have positively identified the assailant as someone other than the accused.[10] Similarly, the Ninth Circuit has held that fairness requires that the government give the defense adequate notice of a report prepared by an FBI photographic expert so as to enable the defense to obtain an expert to assist in attacking the government's expert.[11]

Attorneys for the defense and for the prosecution should routinely request whatever discovery is allowed them under local rules. Especially in eyewitness cases, the statements and documents and lists of witnesses will normally be crucial to each attorney's preparation of the case. Through discovery, the attorneys will learn what facts they will have to counter by cross-examination or by the introduction of documents or other lay or expert testimony.

A defendant's motion for discovery might well request the state to disclose the following materials relevant to an eyewitness identification:

1. The names and addresses of all identification witnesses and the names of each person whom they identified either tentatively or finally as having participated in the transaction out of which the charge in the case arises
2. All reports, statements, and documents which detail the date, time, place, and circumstances of any police-conducted identifications of the defendant or any other suspect in the case
3. The names and addresses (or badge numbers) of all persons who were present at any police-conducted identifications of the defendant or any other suspect in the case
4. All photographs taken during identification procedures in which the defendant, any coarrestee, or suspect (whether presently or previously accused or charged with the defendant) was identified or exhibited for identification as a participant in the crime underlying the charge in the case—including, but not limited to, photographs of all line-ups, photographs of suspects exhibited either by photograph or in person, and photographs of possible

---

[9] United States v Agurs, 427 US 97 (1976).

[10] Cannon v Alabama, 558 F2d 1211 (5th Cir 1977).

[11] United States v Barrett, 703 F2d 1076, 1081 (9th Cir 1983). The court held that, under the circumstances, the trial court's failure to grant the defense a continuance was harmless error in light of the other overwhelming evidence against the defendant.

suspects or subjects of identification exhibited to an alleged eyewitness in the case

§3.07 —The Right to an Attorney at a Lineup or Showup

Two of the most-used discovery devices available to the prosecution in criminal cases are the lineup and the showup. For our purposes, we will define the showup to include those instances when the accused is exhibited singly to the eyewitness for purposes of identification. The lineup will denote those situations in which the witness is asked to point out the offender from a group of individuals similar in appearance and characteristics.[12] Common sense shows that the lineup offers greater protection for the accused and is more likely to produce an identification free from undue suggestion. Nonetheless, the courts have upheld the use of showups even when it was possible to use a lineup.[13] Because a witness is unlikely at a later date to retract an identification made in a showup or lineup, it is essential that the procedures utilized not be unduly suggestive.

In *United States v Wade,*[14] the United States Supreme Court held that an accused has the right to have counsel present if forced to appear in a lineup or showup after indictment.[15] The Court found that the lineup was a critical stage of the prosecution at which the defendant was as much entitled to counsel as at the trial itself. The Court's conclusion was based on its recognition of the vagaries of eyewitness identifications and the finality of such identifications in determining guilt in the absence of other evidence:

> But the confrontation completed by the State between the accused and the victim or witnesses to a crime to elicit identification evidence is peculiarly riddled with innumerable dangers and

---

[12] The Supreme Court of Georgia upheld the conviction of a man identified in a lineup in which only the hands of those in the lineup were displayed. Wiley v State, 250 Ga 343, 296 SE2d 724 (1982).

[13] *See e.g.,* United States *ex rel* Kirby v Sturges, 510 F2d 397 (7th Cir 1975), *cert denied,* 421 US 1016 (1975). *Cf* Simmons v United States, 390 US 377 (1968).

[14] 388 US 218 (1967). In *Wade,* the Supreme Court rejected the argument that compelling an accused to exhibit his person in a lineup or showup prior to trial violates his rights against self-incrimination. The Court also held that it is proper to require the accused to put on a particular article of clothing and to utter the same words purportedly uttered by the perpetrator of the crime. *Id* 222.

[15] The right applies to live, but not to photographic, identification procedures. *See* United States v Ash, 413 US 300 (1973).

> variable factors which might seriously, even crucially, derogate from a fair trial. The vagaries of eyewitness identification are well-known; the annals of criminal law are rife with instances of mistaken identification. Mr. Justice Frankfurter once said: "What is the worth of identification testimony even when uncontradicted? The identification of strangers is proverbially untrustworthy. The hazards of such testimony are established by a formidable number of instances in the records of English and American trials. These instances are recent—not due to the brutalities of ancient criminal procedure." The Case of Sacco and Vanzetti 30 (1927). A major factor contributing to the high incidence of miscarriage of justice from mistaken identification has been the degree of suggestion inherent in the manner in which the prosecution presents the suspect to witnesses for pretrial identification. A commentator has observed that "[t]he influence of improper suggestion upon identifying witnesses probably accounts for more miscarriages of justice than any other single factor—perhaps it is responsible for more such errors than all other factors combined." Wall, Eye-Witness Identification in Criminal Cases 26. Suggestion can be created intentionally or unintentionally in many subtle ways. And the dangers for the suspect are particularly grave when the witness' opportunity for observation was insubstantial, and thus his susceptibility to suggestion the greatest.
>
> Moreover, "[i]t is a matter of common experience that, once a witness has picked out the accused at the line-up, he is not likely to go back on his word later on, so that in practice the issue of identity may (in the absence of other relevant evidence) for all practical purposes be determined there and then, before the trial."[16]

The Court further recognized that neither the witnesses nor the lineup participants are apt to be alert for conditions prejudicial to the suspect.[17] The Court concluded that the "presence of counsel itself can often avert prejudice and assure a meaningful confrontation at trial."[18]

The efficacy of *Wade* was undercut some four years later in *Kirby v*

---

[16] 388 US at 228-29 (footnotes deleted). The court here quotes Williams & Hammelmann, *Identification Parades,* pt 1 Crim L Rev 479, 482 (1963).

[17] *Id* 230.

[18] *Id* 236. The Court left open the question whether the presence of substitute counsel might not suffice where notification and presence of the suspect's own counsel would result in prejudicial delay. *Id* 237. The use of substitute counsel has been approved by the lower courts. *See e.g.,* United States v Smallwood, 473 F2d 98 (DC Cir 1972). The Court also noted that legislative or other regulations might eliminate the risks of abuse

Illinois,[19] when the Supreme Court held that the right to counsel did not attach to preindictment lineups or showups. The Court resorted to a formalistic inquiry of when a criminal prosecution is commenced. It did not even bother to discuss the dangers and factors which had convinced the *Wade* Court to require the presence of counsel. The Court has continued to adhere to this formalistic approach in determining the right to counsel at lineups and showups.[20]

A number of state courts have rejected the formalism of *Kirby* in interpreting their own state constitutions and have held that counsel is required at investigatory lineups on the ground that as a practical matter they too are crucial stages in the prosecution.[21] These decisions help insure against unduly suggestive lineups and showups at the preliminary stages of a criminal prosecution and thereby help insure the accuracy of all future identifications. If these decisions rely independently upon state law, they are protected against review by the United States Supreme Court.[22]

---

and unintentional suggestions so as to remove the basis for regarding the stage as "critical." 388 US at 239.

[19] 406 US 682 (1972).

[20] Moore v Illinois, 434 US 220 (1977) (right to counsel attaches when the accused is identified by the victim at a preliminary hearing).

[21] *See* People v Bustamante, 30 Cal 3d 88, 177 Cal Rptr 576, 634 P2d 927 (1981); People v Jackson, 391 Mich 323, 217 NW2d 22 (1979); Blue v State, 558 P2d 636 (Alaska 1977). *And see* Commonwealth v Richman, 458 Pa 167, 320 A2d 351 (1974) (holding the right to counsel commences with the arrest). Many states, however, follow the *Kirby* distinction in limiting the right to counsel. *See, e.g.*, People v Hawkins, 55 NY2d 474, 435 NE2d 376 (1982).

[22] See Brennan, *State Constitutions and the Protection of Individual Rights*, 90 Harv L Rev 489 (1977).

If the decision of the state court is to be protected from review by the United States Supreme Court because it rests on "adequate and independent state grounds," the state court must make this clear on the face of its opinion. In *Michigan v Long*, 103 S Ct 3469, 3475 (1983), the Michigan Supreme Court suppressed the "fruit" of what it found to be an illegal search. In its opinion, the state court twice referred to the Michigan Constitution but otherwise relied exclusively on federal law. The United States Supreme Court rejected an ad hoc method of dealing with cases that involve possible adequate and independent state grounds. Instead it held that:

> . . . [W]hen, as in this case, a state court decision fairly appears to rest primarily on federal law, or to be interwoven with the federal law, and when the adequacy and independence of any possible state law ground is not clear from the face of the opinion, we will accept as the most reasonable explanation that the state court decided the case the way it did because it believed that federal law required it to do so. If a state chooses merely to rely on federal precedents as it would on the precedents of all other jurisdictions, then it need only make clear by a plain statement in its judgment or opinion that the federal cases are being used only for the purpose of guidance, and do not themselves compel the result that the court has reached. In this way, both justice and judicial administration will be greatly improved. If the state court decision indicates clearly and expressly that

§3.08 —The Role of an Attorney at a Lineup or Showup

The Supreme Court in *United States v Wade*[23] left open the question of the role of counsel who is allowed to attend a lineup or showup. The Court opined generally that the "presence of counsel itself can often avert prejudice and assure a meaningful confrontation at trial."[24]

The Court also noted that "counsel's presence at the lineup would equip him to attack not only the lineup identification, but the courtroom identification as well."[25] By that statement, the Supreme Court suggested that the presence of counsel would be useful for two purposes: first, to aid in the trial of the case and, second, to avert prejudice at the lineup or showup itself.[26] While the Court seemed to assume that the mere presence of counsel in itself might insure that fair procedures were followed, the Court did not further articulate whether counsel could play an active role in preventing suggestive tactics.

Later in *Moore v Illinois,*[27] the Supreme Court seemed to indicate that counsel had a role to play at the lineup or showup beyond that of a mere observer. The Court noted that "if an accused's counsel is present at the pre-trial identification, he can serve both his client's and the prosecution's interests by objecting to suggestive features of a procedure before they influence a witness' identification."

The Second Circuit appeared to recognize an active role for counsel at lineups and showups in *Solomon v Smith.*[28] The accused had been exhibited to the victim at an uncounseled showup during his arraignment and later in what the Court determined to be a suggestive lineup. The Court noted that "in theory, at least, counsel might have been able either to forestall the prejudicial showup of Solomon at arraignment, or to limit the duration of the witness's observation, or, preferably, to precipitate a proper lineup prior to the arraignment."

Whether counsel can do more than merely make suggestions and raise objections is questionable. In *United States v Allen,*[29] the Court of Appeals for the District of Columbia noted in dicta that:

> it is alternatively bona fide separate, adequate, and independent grounds, we, of course, will not undertake to review the decision.

Id 3476.

[23] 388 US 218 (1967).

[24] *Id* 236.

[25] *Id* 241.

[26] See **§3.07** for the distinction between a lineup and a showup.

[27] 434 US 220, 226 (1977).

[28] 645 F2d 1179, 1187 (2d Cir 1981).

[29] 408 F2d 1287, 1289 (DC Cir 1969).

> It would seem that appellant's counsel might best be able to serve his client's interest and the interest of justice if he is given in advance of the lineup the names of the witnesses who would attend; the time, place and nature of the crimes involved; and the descriptions of the suspect, if any, which the witnesses had given to the police. Counsel also might be allowed to have a role in setting up the lineup and proposing changes to avoid suggestive features.

In *United States v Crouch,*[30] a district court in California reached a different result, holding that counsel's participation is that of an observer only. The court noted that while counsel could make suggestions and raise objections, the prosecution could rightfully ignore them, since "in the final analysis the lineup is a law enforcement tool."[31]

It has been held that counsel has no right to interview witnesses at the time of the lineup.[32] However in *People v Williams,*[33] the Supreme Court of California held that counsel can demand to be present when the identification is made by a witness outside the viewing room immediately after the lineup. The court commented that:

> It is not the moment of viewing alone, but rather the whole "procedure by which [a suspect] is identified" that counsel must be able to effectively reconstruct at trial. . . . If defense counsel is to be able to intelligently cross-examine the witness, he cannot be excluded from the moment of identification any more than he can be excluded from the lineup itself. To hold otherwise would be to reduce counsel's cross-examination "to little more than shooting in the dark," for he would not be fully apprised of what occurred at the identification interview. . . . For example, the defendant would have no way of knowing whether the witness was hesitant or insecure in his identification, and he would not know what language or expressions the witness used. All of these factors could be very significant on cross-examination.[34]

The majority of courts, however, have refused to follow *Williams* and

---

[30] 478 F Supp 867 (ED Cal 1979).

[31] *Id* 890. *Accord* United States v Bierey, 588 F2d 620, 624 (8th Cir 1978), *cert denied,* 439 US 935 (1979).

[32] United States v Callahan, 434 F Supp 1203 (D Minn 1977).

[33] 3 Cal 3d 853, 856, 92 Cal Rptr 6, 8, 478 P2d 942, 944 (1971). *Accord* State v McGee, 350 So 2d 370 (La 1977); Richardson v State, 600 P2d 361 (Okla 1979).

[34] 3 Cal 3d at 856, 92 Cal Rptr at 8, 478 P2d at 944.

hold that there is no right for defense counsel to be present when law enforcement authorities interview witnesses following a lineup or showup.[35]

Because it appears that for all practical purposes counsel's role will be limited to that of an observer, defense counsel may be placed in the awkward position of having to take the witness stand to testify to any irregularities observed at the identification lineup or showup. If this appears likely (and counsel will rarely be in a position, when notified to attend the lineup, to know that it is unlikely) then counsel may be prohibited from participating in the case as the defendant's attorney.[36] This conflict is inherent in the Supreme Court's opinion in *Wade,* although it was never discussed. To avoid this conflict, a substitute attorney,[37] relevant expert, or knowledgeable layman might be delegated to view the identification process.[38]

§3.09 —Compelling a Suspect's Presence at a Lineup

The United States Supreme Court has rejected the argument that compelling a suspect to appear in a lineup prior to trial violates the constitutional privilege against self-incrimination. The Court has also held that it is proper to require a suspect to put on a particular article of clothing and to utter the same words purportedly uttered by the

---

[35] United States v Bierey, 588 F2d 620 (8th Cir 1978), *cert denied,* 439 US 935 (1979); United States v Rich, 580 F2d 929 (9th Cir 1978); United States v Tolliver, 569 F2d 724 (2d Cir 1978); People v Sweeny, 57 Ill App 3d 879, 373 NE2d 663 (1978).

In United States v Daniels, 506 F2d 791 (3d Cir 1974), the accused was shown to witnesses in a lineup, and the witnesses made their identifications by marking paper ballots. Defense counsel asked to see the ballots at the time they were given to the lineup officials but was told they would not be available until the next day at the preliminary examination. Because defense counsel was given the opportunity to view them at the preliminary hearing and because there was no evidence that the ballots had been changed, the court refused to find that the defendant suffered any prejudice.

[36] *See* American Bar Association Model Rules of Professional Conduct Rule 3.7 (Final Draft May 30, 1981). Rule 3.7(a)(3) provides that the lawyer may act as an advocate even though likely to be a witness, if disqualification would work "substantial hardship on the client." The 1980 Model Code contains a similar provision, cast in more restrictive terms. *See* DR5-102(A) and 5-101(B)(4).

[37] *See* United States v Wade, 388 US 218, 237 (1967).

[38] It is certainly possible, although the authors are unaware of any situations where it has occurred, that the prosecution would call the defense counsel or the substitute to testify to the nonsuggestive aspects of the identification procedures utilized by the police.

perpetrator of the crime.[39] It is open to serious question, however, whether the police can require a person to appear in a lineup prior to making a formal arrest.

In *Davis v Mississippi*,[40] the United States Supreme Court held that detentions for the sole purpose of obtaining fingerprints are subject to the constraints of the Fourth Amendment. The Court did note, however, that it did not have to determine in that case "whether the requirements of the Fourth Amendment could be met by narrowly circumscribed procedures for obtaining, during the course of a criminal investigation, the fingerprints of individuals for whom there is no probable cause to arrest."[41]

A recent decision of the Supreme Court of New Jersey considers the applicability of *Davis* to a situation where a suspect is compelled to appear in a lineup.[42] Following a robbery, a witness made a tentative identification of the defendant from a spread of photographs. The prosecution then moved the court for an order to compel the defendant to appear in a lineup. A hearing was held, at which time the defendant and his counsel appeared. The trial judge granted the state's motion. Subsequently, the defendant was identified in the lineup, and he was thereafter formally charged with the crime. On appeal, the New Jersey Supreme Court affirmed this procedure.

The court held that an application to detain a suspect for a lineup was the functional equivalent of an application for a search warrant and hence was governed by the search and seizure standards of the Fourth Amendment and Article 1, ¶7 of the New Jersey Constitution. The court then held that:

> Our reading of *Davis* convinces us that for certain detentions—those that do not entail significant intrusions upon individual privacy or freedom, are productive of reliable evidence, and can be effectuated without abuse, coercion or intimidation—"no probable cause in the traditional sense" is necessary in order to obtain the "authorization of a judicial officer[.]" We conclude that, under a "narrowly defined" set of circumstances, such detentions can be constitutionally permissible. *Davis,* 39 U.S. at 727-28, 89 S.Ct. at 1398, 22 L.Ed.2d at 681.[43]

---

[39] United States v Wade, 388 US 218, 222 (1967).

[40] 388 US 721 (1969).

[41] *Id* 728.

[42] State v Hall, 93 NJ 552, 461 A2d 1155 (1983).

[43] *Id* 1160.

The court proceeded to prescribe the "narrowly defined set of circumstances" under which a trial court could require a suspect to appear for a lineup:

> The court's authorization of an investigatory detention must, first, be based upon sufficient evidence to demonstrate that a particular crime has occurred, that the crime is unsolved and that it is under active investigation. Second, the police must demonstrate a reasonable and well-grounded basis to believe that the individual sought as the subject of the investigative detention may have committed the crime under investigation. Additionally, it must be shown that the results of the detention will significantly advance the criminal investigation and will serve to determine whether or not the suspect probably committed the crime. Further, it must also appear that these investigative results cannot otherwise practicably be obtained.[44]

The court noted that these criteria were substantially the same as those recommended by the American Law Institute.[45] The court recognized that there were a number of reasons why a detention for a lineup on less than probable cause should be allowed:

> [1] The lineup involves no creative or unusual act on the part of the suspect; it involves only a display of evidence that is otherwise publicly visible. . . .
>
> [2] [T]he lineup, when properly conducted, can protect against abuse and insure fairness. . . .
>
> [3] [T]he lineup procedure can be accomplished at a convenient time and need not entail a restraint upon the suspect for an unduly long period of time.[46]

The court also set down procedural guidelines to guard against abuses:

> [1] [The lineup] must be accomplished in a fashion designed to produce the least amount of harassment of, interference with, or prejudice to the suspect. . . .
>
> [2] [I]n most cases, the suspect must be given sufficient notice of the proposed detention. . . .

---

44 *Id.*

45 Model Code of Pre-Arraignment Procedure (1975) §170.2(6).

46 State v Hall, 93 NJ 552, 461 A2d 1155, 1161 (1983).

> [3] [T]he suspect should also be given the opportunity to arrange a convenient time for the detention. . . .
>
> [4] [The suspect should have] the opportunity to have counsel present during the detention. . . .
>
> [5] [U]nusual or untoward consequences to the suspect resulting from the detention should be avoided or minimized.[47]

The court noted that exigent circumstances which require prompt police action might excuse the police from first securing a judicial order, but the court warned that on a motion to suppress, the state would have the burden of showing the exigent circumstances which justified the detention.[48] The court also recommended that the Criminal Practice Committee of the New Jersey Supreme Court give the issue further study.[49]

§3.10 —Appointment of an Expert to Aid the Defense

Because expert testimony may be helpful to the defense at trial or in a motion to suppress, counsel may want to secure the services of a psychologist early on in the preparation of the case. The question thus arises whether counsel for an indigent can force the government to pay the expert's fees.

In federal court, counsel for an indigent may request in an ex parte application such expert services as are necessary for an adequate defense.[50] State laws and decisions vary on whether an indigent defendant may request fees to hire an expert.[51] Whether a defendant

---

[47] *Id.*

[48] *Id* 1162.

[49] *Id* 1163.

[50] 28 USC §3006A(e)(1). Appointed counsel may obtain, subject to later review, expert services without prior authorization if necessary for an adequate defense. The total cost of services which can be obtained without prior authorization is $150. *Id.* §3006A(e)(2). Compensation for an expert may not exceed $300, exclusive of reimbursement for expenses reasonably incurred, unless certified by the court or magistrate. *Id* §3006A(e)(3).

[51] See Annotation, *Right of Indigent Defendant in Criminal Case to Aid of State by Appointment of Investigator or Expert,* 34 ALR3d 1256 (1970).

For instance, in Illinois, the trial court in a capital case may order the county treasurer to pay expert witnesses reasonable compensation not to exceed $250 for each defendant. Ill Rev Stat (1981) ch 38, §113-3(d). Court decisions however have extended the statute to apply to certain noncapital felonies and have allowed reasonable fees in excess of $250 for the purpose of hiring an expert. *See* People v Kinion, 104 Ill App 3d 30, 37, 432 NE2d 363 (1982).

is entitled to an expert as a matter of constitutional right is not fully settled.[52]

In *United States v Sims,*[53] the Ninth Circuit held that neither the federal statute nor the Fifth or Sixth Amendments were violated when the trial

---

[52] In United States *ex rel* Smith v Baldi, 344 US 561, 568 (1953), the Supreme Court held that the Constitution does not mandate that states appoint psychiatrists to make pretrial examinations of those accused of committing crimes. However, since 1953, the Supreme Court has held that the Sixth Amendment requires the states to provide indigents with court-appointed counsel to assist with their defense, Gideon v Wainright, 372 US 335 (1963), and that equal protection requires the states to provide indigents with transcripts and counsel for nondiscretionary appeals. Griffin v Illinois, 351 US 12 (1956) (transcript); Douglas v California, 372 US 353 (1963) (counsel). As a result, some lower courts have held that in appropriate cases states may be required to provide indigents with the assistance of experts. In People v Watson 36 Ill 2d 228, 221 NE2d 645 (1966), the Illinois Supreme Court noted that:

> It has long been a major goal of our entire judicial system to see that all persons charged with a crime "stand on an equality before the bar of justice in every American court." (Chambers v Florida, 309 US 227, 241, 84 L.Ed. 716, 724.) Such cases as Gideon v Wainwright, 372 US 335, 9 L.Ed.2d 799, 83 S.Ct. 792, and Griffin v Illinois, 351 US 12, 100 L.Ed. 891, 76 S.Ct. 585, have gone far to achieve this goal by assuring indigent defendants, even in noncapital cases, the right to counsel and to appellate review. The problem now facing the court concerns the production of witnesses on behalf of indigents. The Illinois constitution provides, in section 9 of article II, that in criminal prosecutions the accused is entitled to have process to compel the attendance of witnesses in his behalf. In almost identical language the sixth amendment to the United States constitution provides that the accused in criminal cases is entitled to have compulsory process for obtaining witnesses in his favor. Thus it is at once apparent that the right to summon witnesses is fundamental to our legal system. It is defendant's contention that a right so fundamental should not be made to depend upon the financial circumstances of the defendant. We share this view.
>
> The court recognizes that there is a distinction between the right to call witnesses and the right to have these witnesses paid for by the government, but in certain instances involving indigents, the lack of funds with which to pay for the witness will often preclude him from calling that witness and occasionally prevent him from offering a defense. Thus, although the defendant is afforded the shadow of the right to call witnesses, he is deprived of the substance.
>
> The value of an expert witness's testimony lies in his experience and, more particularly, in his preparation. Although a subpoena would suffice to compel his appearance at trial, this appearance by itself would be of no value unless he had been able to make findings upon which to base his testimony. It is the cost of making these preparatory findings which the defendant feels should be borne by the government.
>
> . . . .
>
> The opinion of a handwriting expert in this case . . . may have been crucial, and defendant's lack of funds prevented him from presenting to the jury evidence which may have established his innocence. We hold that under the facts presented in this case defendant was entitled to a reasonable fee for the purpose of hiring a questioned document examiner.

36 Ill 2d at 232-34, 221 NE2d at 648-49.

[53] 617 F2d 1371 (9th Cir 1980).

court refused to appoint a psychologist to assist in the defense of an eyewitness identification case. The court doubted whether a reasonable attorney would have engaged an eyewitness expert in this type of case and found that the defendant had not shown any prejudice resulting from the trial court's failure to appoint. Although it noted that the admissibility of this type of expert testimony is strongly disfavored in most courts, the court did state that in the Ninth Circuit, unlike in the First and Seventh Circuits,[54] the test for appointment is not tied to the test of admissibility of the expert's testimony. The court recognized that an expert's services can embrace "pretrial and trial assistance to the defense as well as potential trial testimony" and that to hold the admissibility of testimony to be the only factor in whether to appoint an expert would be inconsistent with the underlying purpose of the Criminal Justice Act.[55] Therefore, if a defendant can show that cross-examination of an eyewitness would be more effective with the help of an expert, a judge may be required to authorize fees to pay the expert.[56]

§3.11 Motions to Suppress in Criminal Cases

Under the Federal Rules of Criminal Procedure and under the rules of most states, motions to suppress evidence should be raised prior to trial.[57] This requirement is designed to promote judicial economy and to provide an orderly procedure for raising suppression issues prior to trial. Because the requirement serves important governmental ends, it must be complied with or the defense may be deemed to have waived its objections.[58]

At the hearing on the motion to suppress, counsel for both sides should be prepared to offer evidence to support their respective positions. Evidence will be elicited in much the same manner as in the trial itself.[59] The defense may have to call police officers as adverse witnesses to establish the facts to support suppression. Also, the defendant may be required to testify as to the facts of the arrest or the conditions which occurred at the identification confrontation. The defendant's testimony at this hearing normally may not be used at trial

---

[54] United States v Fosher, 590 F2d 381, 384 (1st Cir 1979); United States v Penick, 496 F2d 1105, 1110 (7th Cir 1974), *cert denied,* 419 US 897 (1974).

[55] 617 F2d at 1375 n 3.

[56] *Cf* People v Watson, 36 Ill 2d 228, 234, 221 NE2d 645 (1966).

[57] Fed R Crim P 12(b)(3).

[58] *Id* 12(f). *Cf* Henry v Mississippi, 379 US 443 (1965).

[59] See **chs 6** and **7.**

on the issue of guilt.[60] If one of the grounds for suppression is the unduly suggestive procedures utilized by the police to secure an identification, counsel may well consider presenting testimony from an expert in perception and memory.[61] In some cases the court's ruling on the motion to suppress will virtually determine the outcome of the trial itself. Even if the motion is lost however, the hearing will give counsel a valuable opportunity for discovery and for weighing the relative strengths and weaknesses of the motion witnesses and the probable effect of their testimony on the trier of fact. The insights gained from the hearing may thus prove valuable in determining the strategy at the trial.

The grounds for suppression normally will include one or more of the following: the defendant was denied the assistance of counsel at the pretrial identification confrontation, the confrontation was the fruit of an illegal search or seizure, or the confrontation was unduly suggestive. The following example illustrates a typical motion to suppress used in Illinois:

MOTION TO SUPPRESS IDENTIFICATION TESTIMONY OF RONALD WARNER

Defendant, by her attorneys, moves this Court to suppress the identification testimony of Ronald Warner for the following reasons:

1. The identification was induced by the actions of the State. The manner in which the police officers acted directly caused the identification witness to point out the defendant in violation of her Constitutional Rights under the Fifth and Fourteenth Amendments of the Constitution of the United States and Article 1, Sections 1, 2 and 6 of the Constitution of the State of Illinois.

2. Defendant was not advised of her right to the assistance of Counsel at the time of the police confrontation, in violation of her Constitutional Rights under the Sixth and Fourteenth Amendments to the United States Constitution and Article 1, Sections 1 and 2 of the Constitution of the State of Illinois.

3. Defendant was identified during a period of unlawful detention in violation of her rights under the Fourth, Fifth and Fourteenth Amendments to the United States Constitution and Article 1, Sections 1, 2 and 6 of the Constitution of the State of Illinois. *See People v Bean,* 121 Ill App 2d 332 (1st D 1970).

---

[60] Simmons v United States, 390 US 377, 394 (1968).

[61] See **ch 8.**

Although prudential considerations would prefer that a hearing on a motion to suppress identification testimony be held out of the presence of the jury, it is not required by due process. In *Watkins v Sowders,*[62] the Supreme Court rejected a per se rule and held that in the absence of special circumstances a trial court could require defense counsel to present evidence concerning the suggestiveness of an identification confrontation in front of the jury. The Court felt that excusing the jury is the preferable procedure,[63] but that the defendant's due process rights would be adequately protected by cross-examination and closing argument.[64] The petitioners had argued that cross-examination was not effective because it forced counsel to probe in the dark in front of the jury, but the Court noted that this was true with any type of testimony in a criminal case.[65]

The Supreme Court also noted that if the trial court decided that the identification was arrived at improperly, it could always give the jury a proper cautionary instruction.[66] The Court rejected the argument that once the jurors heard the testimony they wouldn't be able to erase it from their minds:

> Where identification evidence is at issue . . . no . . . special considerations justify a departure from the presumption that juries will follow instructions. It is the reliability of identification evidence that primarily determines its admissibility, *Manson v. Brathwaite,* 432 U.S. 98, 113-114, 97 S.Ct. 2243, 2252, 53 L.Ed.2d 140; *United States ex rel. Kirby v. Sturges,* 510 F2d 397, 402-404 (Ca7 1975) (Stevens J.) and the proper evaluation of evidence under the instructions of the trial judge is the very task our system must assume juries can perform. Indeed, as the cases before us demonstrate, the *only* duty of a jury in cases in which identification evidence has been admitted will often be to assess the reliability of that evidence.[67]

The Supreme Court did acknowledge that the better practice, and the

[62] 449 US 341 (1981).

[63] *Id* 345.

[64] *Id* 348-49.

[65] *Id* 349.

[66] *Id* 347.

[67] *Id* 347.

practice followed by virtually all lower courts, is to hold a suppression hearing outside the presence of the jury.[68]

§3.12 —Suppression Because Counsel Was Not Allowed to Be Present at the Pretrial Confrontation

An accused has a right to have counsel present at a pretrial lineup or showup held after formal judicial proceedings have been instituted.[69] Absence of counsel can be established at the suppression hearing in a number of ways. Counsel for the accused may get an admission from the police officer who conducted the lineup or showup that counsel was not allowed to be present. In *United States v Wade,*[70] for instance, defense counsel asked an FBI agent:

Q. Mr. Albert, do your records reflect the date of the line-up which was just discussed and testified to by Mr. Gray?

A. Yes, sir.

Q. What was that date, sir?

A. May the 12th, 1965.

Q. All right, sir.
Was I, Weldon Holcomb, the attorney appointed by the Court, notified of such action by the F.B.I. prior to the line-up?

A. No, sir; you had not been appointed at that time.

Mr. Holcomb: Would you please mark this for identification as Defendant's Exhibit No. 1

(LETTER—(a copy)—dated April 26, 1965, addressed to Honorable Weldon G. Holcomb, signed by Joe W. Sheehy, United States District Court, Eastern District of Texas, was duly marked as:

DEFENDANT'S EXHIBIT NO. 1)

Q. Officer Albert, I hand you, here what has been marked for identification as Defendant's Exhibit No. 1—and would you tell us what it is, sir?
REPORTER'S NOTE: An instrument was then handed to the witness.

(pause)

---

[68] *Id* 345.

[69] See **§§3.07** and **3.08** for discussions on the right to counsel and the role of counsel at a lineup or showup.

[70] 388 US 218 (1967).

A. It's a Court order appointing you to represent Billy Joe Wade.
Q. In what cause number, sir?
A. 6805.
Q. And that is the cause on trial at this time?
A. Yes, sir.
Q. What is the date of that letter, sir?
A. April 26, 1965.
Q. April 26, 1965?
A. Yes.
Q. And by whom is it signed?
A. Judge Sheehy.
Q. And does it reflect on the fact [sic] of it to whom copies of that letter were sent?
A. Yes, sir.
Q. Who are they, sir?
A. Mr. Nicholson and Mr. Reynolds, Mr. Nicholson, the Assistant United States Attorney, and Mr. Reynolds is United States Marshal. Also to James R. Cooney, District Clerk, and to Billy Joe Wade.

Mr. Holcomb: We offer this in evidence, Your Honor. Counsel also asked one of the witnesses who was present at the line-up:

Q. Was I present at the line-up, Ma'am?
A. No.
Q. Was any lawyer representing Mr. Wade present there, as far as you know?
A. No.

In *Kirby v Illinois,*[71] counsel simply asked the accused:

Q. And after you were placed under arrest on February 22d, were you advised of your right to have an attorney present prior to being identified?
A. No.

---

71 406 US 682 (1972).

In *Gilbert v California*,[72] the United States Supreme Court established a per se rule excluding testimony that a witness identified the accused at a postindictment lineup from which defense counsel was excluded. The Court justified this per se exclusionary rule on the ground that:

> [i]n the absence of legislative regulations adequate to avoid the hazards to a fair trial which inhere in lineups as presently conducted, the desirability of deterring the constitutionally objectionable practice must prevail over the undesirability of excluding relevant evidence. Cf. *Mapp v. Ohio,* 367 U.S. 643, 81 S.Ct. 1682, 6 L.Ed.2d 1081.[73]

The Court noted that the defendant was entitled to a new trial unless the Court could declare a belief that the evidence was "harmless beyond a reasonable doubt."[74]

The Court has refused, however, to follow a per se exclusionary rule for identifications which occur *subsequent* to the lineup or showup from which counsel was absent. The Court has held that subsequent identifications, including in-court identifications, are admissible if the prosecution establishes by "clear and convincing evidence that the in-court identifications were based upon observations of the suspect other than the lineup identifications."[75] In determining whether the subsequent identification is independent of the lineup identification, the Court has noted that various factors can be considered, including:

> the prior opportunity to observe the alleged criminal act, the existence of any discrepancy between any pre-lineup description and the defendant's actual description, any identification prior to lineup of another person, the identification by picture of the defendant prior to the lineup, failure to identify the defendant on a prior occasion, and the lapse of time between the alleged act and the lineup identification. It is also relevant to consider those facts which, despite the absence of counsel, are disclosed concerning the conduct of the lineup.[76]

Counsel for the prosecution will thus want to bring out through examination of the state's witnesses, those factors identified by the

---

[72] 388 US 263 (1967).

[73] *Id* 273.

[74] *Id* 274. *And see* Moore v Illinois, 434 US 218 (1977).

[75] United States v Wade, 388 US 218, 240 (1967); Gilbert v California, 388 US 263, 272 (1967).

[76] United States v Wade 388 US 218, 241 (1967).

Court which show that the subsequent identification is independent of the tainted identification.

§3.13 —Suppression Because the Identification Was the Fruit of an Illegal Arrest

Evidence which has come to light through the illegal actions of law enforcement officers will be suppressed as the "fruit of the poisonous tree."[77] The question in each case is "whether, granting establishment of the primary illegality, the evidence to which instant objection is made has been come at by exploitation of that illegality or instead by means sufficiently distinguishable to be purged of the primary taint."[78]

In *Davis v Mississippi,*[79] the United States Supreme Court suppressed evidence of fingerprinting secured during a period of unlawful detention. Relying on *Davis,* the Illinois Appellate Court in *People v Bean*[80] reversed a robbery conviction because the victim identified the defendant at a police station showup following the defendant's invalid search and arrest. The Illinois court found that all subsequent identifications of the defendant by the victim, including the in-court identification, were directly traceable to the unlawful detention of the defendant.

The United States Supreme Court ruled in *United States v Crews*[81] that a victim's in-court identification of a defendant then present because of an unlawful arrest, did not have to be suppressed if the illegal arrest did not affect the victim's ability to give accurate identification testimony. The Supreme Court noted that the illegal arrest had not been the method by which the victim's identity was learned, and that "the trial court had expressly found that the witness' courtroom identification rested on an independent recollection of her initial encounter with the assailant, uninfluenced by the pretrial identifications," and that "this determination finds ample support in the record."[82] The Court did caution, however, that:

> This is not to say that the intervening photographic and lineup

---

[77] Nardone v United States, 308 US 338, 341 (1939).

[78] Wong Sun v United States, 371 US 471, 488 (1963). Recently, the Supreme Court has indicated approval of the so-called "good faith" exception to the exclusionary rule. *See* United States v Leon, 35 Cr L 3273 (US July 1984).

[79] 394 US 721 (1969).

[80] 121 Ill App 2d 332, 335, 257 NE2d 562 (1970); *accord* People v Glover, 64 Ill App 3d 662, 381 NE2d 439 (1978).

[81] 445 US 463 (1980).

[82] *Id* 473.

> identifications—both of which are conceded to be suppressible fruits of the Fourth Amendment violation—could not under some circumstances affect the reliability of the in-court identification and render it inadmissible as well. Indeed, given the vagaries of human memory and the inherent suggestibility of many identification procedures, just the opposite may be true.[83]

At the hearing on the motion to suppress, defense counsel will have to establish that the seizure was made without a warrant and without probable cause. If the identification is the direct fruit of an illegal seizure, the state will be required to produce evidence that the witness' identification was uninfluenced by the tainted confrontation.

§3.14 —Suppression Because the Identification Was Secured through Unduly Suggestive Means

Identification evidence secured by means which are so suggestive and conducive to irreparable mistaken identification as to deny due process of law, is subject to suppression.[84] While the Supreme Court noted in *Stovall v Denno*[85] that the practice of showing suspects singly to persons for the purpose of identification, and not as part of a lineup, has been widely condemned, it upheld the showup in that case due to the exigency of the circumstances. The witness could not leave the hospital and it was questionable how long she might live, so the Court found it was proper for the police to show Stovall to her in her hospital room while he was handcuffed to a police officer.

Similarly in *Simmons v United States,*[86] the Court recognized that improper employment of photographs by the police can cause witnesses to err in identifying prisoners.

> This danger will be increased if the police display to the witness only the picture of a single individual who generally resembles the person he saw, or if they show him the pictures of several persons among which the photograph of a single such individual recurs or is in some way emphasized. The chance of misidentification is also heightened if the police indicate to the witness that they have other

---

[83] *Id* 472. See also Unruh & Nodgaard, *Suppression of In-Court Identification Testimony on the Basis of Fourth Amendment Violation,* 21 Washburn L Rev 219 (1981).

[84] Stovall v Denno, 388 US 293, 302 (1967).

[85] *Id* 302 n 6.

[86] 390 US 377 (1968).

> evidence that one of the persons pictured committed the crime. Regardless of how the initial misidentification comes about, the witness thereafter is apt to retain in his memory the image of the photograph rather than of the person actually seen, reducing the trustworthiness of subsequent lineup or courtroom identification.[87]

Nonetheless, the Court acknowledged that despite the hazards, identification by photograph is effective from the standpoints of apprehending offenders and of sparing innocent suspects the ignominy of arrest.[88] The Court also thought the danger that the use of this technique would result in convictions based on misidentification could be substantially lessened by a course of cross-examination at trial which exposes to the jury the method's potential for error.[89] The Court therefore concluded that:

> each case must be considered on its own facts, and . . . convictions based on eyewitness identification at trial following a pretrial identification by photograph will be set aside on that ground only if the photographic identification procedure was so impermissibly suggestive as to give rise to a very substantial likelihood of irreparable misidentification.[90]

In *Foster v California,*[91] the Supreme Court finally did reverse the conviction of a man who was identified under circumstances which the Court found to be so suggestive and conducive to irreparable mistaken identification as to be a denial of due process. Foster was first exhibited to the witness in a three-man lineup where the other two men were considerably shorter than he. The witness could not positively identify him. Foster was then exhibited to the witness in a one-to-one confrontation, but the witness still could not be sure of his identification. A week later Foster was shown to the witness in a second lineup. This time the lineup included 10 men but Foster was the only man who had also appeared in the earlier lineup. Following the lineup, the witness was "convinced" that Foster was the man whom he saw commit the armed robbery. He subsequently reidentified Foster at trial. The Court noted

---

[87] *Id* 383-384.

[88] *Id* 384.

[89] *Id.*

[90] *Id* 384. The Illinois Supreme Court has ruled that photographic identification procedures should not be used where the suspect is in custody and a lineup is otherwise feasible. People v Holiday, 47 Ill 2d 300, 265 NE2d 634 (1970).

[91] 394 US 440 (1969).

that the suggestive elements in this procedure made it all but inevitable that the witness would identify Foster whether or not he was in fact the offender.[92]

§3.15 —Circumstances Where Courts Have Found an Identification Confrontation to Be Unduly Suggestive

The Supreme Court has expressly recognized the dangers of one-on-one identification showups,[93] and yet the courts have refused to promulgate a per se rule excluding identifications secured by such means.[94] Instead, the courts will look to the circumstances in each case to determine if the confrontation was so unduly suggestive as to deny the accused due process of law.

Showups are generally justified because of exigent circumstances. Thus if the witness is in the hospital or there is a danger that the witness may die soon, showups have been upheld even if they were not entirely free of suggestiveness.[95] Similarly, showups have been justified where prompt identification is necessary for the police to determine whether to continue their search.[96]

To determine whether a show-up is unduly suggestive the courts will frequently look to the following factors:

1. Did the police impermissibly focus the witness' attention on this particular person?[97]

---

[92] *Id* 443.

[93] Stovall v Denno, 388 US 293, 302 (1967).

[94] *See, e.g.*, United States *ex rel* Kirby v Sturges, 510 F2d 397 (7th Cir 1975), *cert denied*, 421 US 1016 (1975). *Cf* Simmons v United States, 390 US 377 (1968).

[95] Stovall v Denno, 388 US 293 (1967); Clark v State, 380 NE2d 550 (Ind 1978).

[96] *E.g.*, Scott v Maggio, 695 F2d 916, 921 (5th Cir 1983); United States v Woody, 690 F2d 678, 680 (8th Cir 1982); People v Manion, 67 Ill 2d 564, 367 NE2d 1313 (1977), *cert denied*, 435 US 937 (1978).

[97] Dickerson v Fogg, 692 F2d 238 (2d Cir 1982) (police focused the witness' attention specifically on two black males and pressured him into taking a second and third look at Dickerson after his first tentative identification; the police thereupon arrested Dickerson in the witness' presence, thereby confirming the correctness of his selection); Rudd v Florida, 477 F2d 805, 809 (5th Cir 1973) (witnesses viewed Rudd as he sat in a small office; Rudd was alone except for two or three police officers who were nearby; he was unaware that he was being exhibited in a showup); Dixon v Hopper, 407 F Supp 58, 61 (MD Ga 1976) (victim viewed a book of mug shots and, upon finding a photograph of Dixon, stated that it "looked like" him, a police officer confirmed the selection by the statement, "yes, that's him;" Dixon was immediately arrested and placed alone in a room, from where, through a two-way mirror, he was identified by the victim); State v Gordon, 441 A2d 119 (Conn 1981), *cert denied*, 455 US 989 (1982)

2. Did the police actually tell the witness that they had captured the perpetrator of the crime?[98]
3. Were the witnesses allowed to confer and to view the suspect as a group?[99]
4. Was the suspect handcuffed?[100]
5. Was the suspect viewed together with persons who had previously been identified by the witness as perpetrators of the crime?[101]

(witness was told by the police that they had taken a man into custody near the scene of the crime and that she must identify him immediately; when she declined to view him, police said she could avoid a face-to-face confrontation by viewing him through a one-way glass; Gordon was the only one in the room who came close to fitting the very general description given by the witness). Each of the above showups was found to have been unduly suggestive.

[98] Styers v Smith, 659 F2d 293 (2d Cir 1981) (witness identified photograph of one of the suspects; police officer then said he was leaving to pick up the suspects, and immediately upon his return the three suspects were displayed to the witness in a showup); People v Lee, 44 Ill 2d 161, 254 NE2d 469, 472 (1970) (witness received phone call from the police to come to the coroner's inquest because the police "had the guys that did it, come on down and identify them," when the witnesses arrived, Lee was handcuffed to a man who had been previously identified as one of the participants in the crime); People v Adams, 53 NY2d 241, 423 NE2d 379 (1981) (police officer informed the witnesses that he thought he had the robbers; Adams and two other suspects were then exhibited in a room with their hands behind their backs with a police officer behind and holding each of them). These identification procedures were each found to be unduly suggestive.

[99] Martin v Donnelly, 391 F Supp 1241, 1248 (D Mass 1974) (witnesses were asked to view arraignment; one of the witnesses had identified one of the suspects the day before in a one-on-one showup; the witnesses all sat together at the arraignment; they saw the suspects in the prisoners' dock; they were present for their arraignment; and they discussed the petitioners with one another); People v Bisogni, 4 Cal 3d 582, 94 Cal Rptr 164, 483 P2d 780 (1971) (after viewing Mrs. Gordon in a lineup, the three witnesses were asked to look through a hole in a door where they observed her alone in a room; the first witness who looked related to the second witness that the lady inside was the one who was involved in the robbery); People v Blumenshine, 42 Ill 2d 508, 513, 250 NE2d 152 (1969) (witnesses to robbery and to other offenses all viewed showup together and identified Blumenshine; the court noted that even though it was unclear whether the other witnesses identified Blumenshine as a participant in the other crimes, "it was improper to have had the appellant viewed for possible identification at the same time and place by witnesses to the robbery and by witnesses to other offenses"); People v Adams, 53 NY2d 241, 423 NE2d 379 (1981) (three witnesses viewed the suspects in a station house showup; when they entered the rooms where the suspects were exhibited, two of the witnesses shouted that these men were the robbers; the third man agreed).

[100] People v Owens, 54 Ill 2d 286, 296 NE2d 728 (1973); People v Blumenshine, 42 Ill 2d 508, 250 NE2d 152 (1969).

[101] Martin v Donnelly, 391 F Supp 1241 (D Mass 1974); People v Lee, 44 Ill 2d 161, 254 NE2d 469 (1970).

6. Did the showup occur after the witness gave only an uncertain identification based on a photograph or lineup?[102]
7. Was the suspect locked up in a jail cell when viewed by the witness?[103]

Lineups are ordinarily less tainted by suggestion than are showups. Nonetheless, under certain circumstances a lineup may also be so unnecessarily suggestive as to violate due process. Factors to which the courts sometimes look are:

1. Did the suspect stand out in the lineup by wearing clothes similar to those worn by the perpetrator of the crime?[104]
2. Did the suspect stand out unduly in the lineup because of physical appearance?[105]
3. Were the witnesses allowed to discuss among themselves their conclusions?[106]
4. Did the police inform the witnesses that the guilty person was in the lineup?[107]

---

[102] Foster v California, 394 US 440 (1969); Dixon v Hopper, 407 F Supp 58 (MD Ga 1976). *And see* United States v Singleton, 702 F2d 1159, 1165 n 20 (DC Cir 1983) ("Furthermore, the police never asked the victims for a description of the robbers before the showup, which they certainly could and should have done . . .").

[103] United States *ex rel* Hudson v Brierton, 699 F2d 917, 924 (7th Cir 1983).

[104] United States *ex rel* Cannon v Smith, 527 F2d 702 (2d Cir 1975) (assailant wore a green shirt; Cannon was directed to wear a green shirt in a pretrial five-man lineup where at least three or four of the other men in the lineup did not wear green shirts); People v Franklin, 22 Ill App 3d 775, 317 NE2d 611 (1974) (police forced Franklin to put on clothing that fit the description given by the witness; he was the only man in the lineup wearing clothing of that description).

[105] Solomon v Smith, 645 F2d 1179 (2d Cir 1981) (witness identified her assailant as 5'7" tall and weighing 145 pounds; Solomon stood 5'6" tall and weighed 130 pounds; The other men in the lineup were, respectively, 5'8" tall and 195 pounds, 6' tall and 165 pounds, and 5'10" tall and 146 pounds; also, the witness' description did not describe her assailant as having a beard or mustache; Solomon has no facial hair, but some of the men in the lineup did); Swicegood v Alabama, 577 F2d 1322 (5th Cir 1978) (Swicegood was only man in lineup over 26 years of age; he was 9 years older than the next-oldest man and 15 years older than the youngest); Royal v Maryland, 529 F2d 1280 (4th Cir 1976) (Royal was only short slight man who limped in the lineup); State v Henderson, 116 Ariz 310, 569 P2d 252 (1977) (other individuals in the lineup were from 12 to 16 years older than the suspect). *But see* United States v Porter, 430 F Supp 208, 211 (WDNY 1977), where the court noted that "there is no requirement that a defendant in a lineup must be surrounded by people nearly identical in appearance, however desirable that may be."

[106] Swicegood v Alabama, 577 F2d 1322, 1327 (5th Cir 1978) (witnesses were given the opportunity to discuss lineup between first and second viewings).

[107] Whitt v State, 361 NE2d 913 (Ind 1977).

5. Did the lineup culminate a series of displays in contexts which could only have induced the witness to identify this suspect?[108]

The courts have generally refused to prescribe how many subjects must be exhibited in order to make the lineup array effective. Wigmore suggested that a lineup contain twelve persons.[109] Wall has suggested that a lineup should contain at least five or six persons to be effective.[110] But courts have sustained lineups with as few as three persons.[111]

The Supreme Court has commented that single-photograph displays should be viewed with suspicion,[112] and most lower courts have held that in the absence of exigent circumstances, single-photograph displays are unnecessarily and impermissibly suggestive.[113] However, displays consisting of as few as five photographs, at least when the subjects are similar in appearance, have been upheld.[114]

Courts have also found photographic displays to be suggestive where:

1. Witnesses are allowed to view the photographs together[115]

---

[108] Foster v California, 394 US 440 (1969) (Foster was first exhibited in a lineup in which the other men were shorter than he; the witness could not positively identify him; Foster was then shown to the witness in a showup, but the witness was still uncertain; a week later the witness identified Foster in a lineup in which Foster was the only man who had participated in the earlier lineup); Solomon v Smith, 645 F2d 1179 (2d Cir 1981) (witness first made uncertain identification of Solomon in an otherwise irreproachable photo array; she then saw that picture on at least four other occasions; she then saw him for about 20 to 30 minutes in a one-person, uncounseled showup at his arraignment; she was finally allowed to see him in a lineup where all the other participants were considerably larger than he).

[109] 3 J. Wigmore, Evidence 164 (3d ed 1940).

[110] Wall, Eyewitness Identification in Criminal Cases 53 (1965).

[111] Patterson v State, 386 NE2d 936 (Ind 1977).

[112] Manson v Brathwaite, 432 US 98, 116 (1977); Simmons v United States, 390 US 377, 383 (1968).

[113] United States v Cueto, 611 F2d 1056 (5th Cir 1980); United States v Kimbrough, 528 F2d 1242 (7th Cir 1976); Carter v Skully, 557 F Supp 626 (SDNY 1981); Dickerson v Fogg, 526 F Supp 1299 (SDNY 1981), *affd*, 692 F2d 238 (2d Cir 1982); United States v Porter, 430 F Supp 208 (WDNY 1977); United States v Barnes, 416 F Supp 1176 (WDNY 1976); People v Rodriguez, 137 Cal Rptr 594 (Cal App 1977).

[114] Nettles v Wainwright, 677 F2d 410 (5th Cir 1982) (five photos not suggestive); United States v Bowie, 515 F2d 3 (7th Cir 1975) (five photos not suggestive); State v Howze, 66 Ohio App 2d 41, 420 NE2d 131 (1979) (six photos not suggestive).

[115] Brown v Blackburn, 625 F2d 35, 37 (5th Cir 1980) (witnesses were in the same room when they picked out the photographs, although they did not know which photograph the other had picked); United States *ex rel* Thomas v New Jersey, 472 F2d 735 (3d Cir 1973) (adult son took his recently injured and dazed father virtually from his hospital bed to the police station; the son picked out a photograph of Thomas, whom he had previously identified, and asked his father if this was one of the men; the father agreed); Martin v Donnelly, 391 F Supp 1241, 1243 (D Mass 1974) (police officer went to bank where robbery occurred and displayed eight or nine photographs to the three witnesses; each one viewed the photograph and passed it on to another; they were where each could see another's selection).

2. One of the photographs stands out because of its color, size, or markings[116]
3. Only one of the subjects in the photographs matches the description of the criminal[117]
4. The police impermissibly focus the witness' attention on a particular photograph[118]

§3.16 —Circumstances Where Courts Have Found Suggestive Procedures Tainted an Identification

Assuming that the pretrial identification procedures were unduly suggestive, the courts then must determine if that identification and any subsequent identifications, normally in-court identifications, are independently reliable.

In *Neil v Biggers,*[119] a rape victim testified that she was attacked in the doorway of her kitchen by a man with a butcher knife. He took her into some woods about two blocks away and raped her. The event took place on a moon-lit night, and the whole incident lasted about 15 to 30 minutes. The victim gave the police what was described as a "very

---

[116] Styers v Smith, 659 F2d 293, 297 (2d Cir 1981) (only 2 photos in array were in color); State v Alexander, 108 Ariz 556, 503 P2d 777 (1972) (of the 17 photos shown the witness only the 2 depicting the defendant were altered to include a mustache and goatee); People v Bryant, 100 Ill App 3d 17, 425 NE2d 1325 (1981) (only 1 photo in array was by Polaroid); People v Levine, 99 Ill App 3d 141, 426 NE2d 215 (1981) (one photo in array was in color); People v Brinson, 80 Ill App 3d 388, 399 NE2d 1010 (1980) (1 photo had markings on it); People v Darlek, 64 Ill App 3d 894, 381 NE2d 1193 (1978) (1 photo had name on it); Commonwealth v Evans, 5 Mass App Ct 843, 363 NE2d 1340 (1977) (only Polaroid picture in array). Other examples of where identifications were found not sufficiently reliable are: Solomon v Smith, 645 F2d 1179 (2d Cir 1981); Green v Loggins, 614 F2d 219 (9th Cir 1980); United States v Ballard, 534 F Supp 749 (MD Ala 1982); Lagana v LeFevre, 493 F Supp 6 (EDNY 1979).

[117] People v Poor, 178 Cal Rptr 375 (1978) (only Asian); Carter v State, 266 Ind 196, 361 NE2d 1208 (1977) (only man with goatee); State v Heald, 120 NH 319, 414 A2d 1288 (1980) (only man in his 40's).

[118] Styers v Smith, 659 F2d 293, 297 (2d Cir 1981) (witness was told by police officer prior to being shown photographs that the officer had just seen at the precinct the fellows who had just robbed the witness' store; the officer then showed the witness a small group of photographs; only the two pictures of the suspects were fresh and in color; the officer then asked the witness, "Are these the two fellows?"; none of the men in the other photographs remotely resembled the general description given by the witness); People v McCoy, 78 Ill App 3d 157, 397 NE2d 79 (1979) (officer showed witness a single photograph accompanied by the statement, "How about this one?").

[119] 409 US 188 (1972).

general description."[120] Some seven months later she was called to the police station where she viewed a showup consisting of two detectives walking the suspect past the victim. The suspect was asked to repeat certain words in front of the victim. The victim testified that she had "no doubt"[121] that this was the man who raped her. The Supreme Court accepted the decision of the lower court that the police had not done all that was necessary to provide an identification confrontation free from unnecessary suggestiveness. But the Court then proceeded to inquire whether "under the 'totality of the circumstances' the identification was reliable even though the confrontation procedure was suggestive."[122] The Court found that the victim had a good opportunity to view her assailant at the time of the crime, that her identification was positive, and that she had resisted making an identification of anyone else at previous lineups, showups, and photographic spreads. The Court did note that in other circumstances the lapse of seven months between the rape and the confrontation would be a serious, negative factor.[123]

In *Manson v Brathwaite,*[124] the Supreme Court specified the factors to be considered in determining whether the corrupting effect of a suggestive identification procedure renders that identification and subsequent identifications inadmissible. A trooper with the Connecticut state police purchased some narcotics from a man whom he was able to describe, but whose identity he did not know. Two days later, based on his description, he was shown a single photograph of a suspect. He subsequently made an in-court identification of the same man. On a petition for writ of habeas corpus, the Second Circuit found the single-photograph examination to be unnecessarily suggestive. The court of appeals employed a per se approach to confrontations occurring subsequent to *Stovall v Denno,*[125] and interpreted *Stoval* as requiring the exclusion of out-of-court identification evidence, without regard to reliability, whenever it has been obtained through unnecessarily suggestive confrontation procedures. The Supreme Court rejected this per se approach, concluding that "reliability is the linchpin in determining the admissibility of identification testimony for both pre- and post-*Stovall* confrontations."[126] The Court relied on *Biggers* in prescribing the factors to determine reliability:

---

[120] *Id* 194.

[121] *Id* 195.

[122] *Id* 199.

[123] *Id* 201.

[124] 432 US 98 (1977).

[125] 388 US 293 (1967).

[126] 432 US at 114.

The Supreme Court of Massachusetts has refused to adopt the *reliability* test as

> These include the opportunity of the witness to view the criminal at the time of the crime, the witness' degree of attention, the accuracy of his prior description of the criminal, the level of certainty demonstrated at the confrontation, and the time between the crime and the confrontation. Against these factors is to be weighed the corrupting effect of the suggestive identification itself.[127]

The Court went through each of these factors and found the identification to be reliable.

1. The witness viewed the suspect for two to three minutes when he was only two feet from him in a well-lighted place[128]
2. The witness was not a casual or passing observer but was a trained police officer of the same race as the suspect[129]
3. The witness gave a detailed description of the physical characteristics as well as the clothing of the suspect[130]
4. The witness was positive in the identification[131]
5. The witness gave the description within minutes of the crime, and the photographic identification took place only two days later[132]

The lower courts generally go through the *Manson* factors seriatim and on occasion have found eyewitness identifications not to be reliable. For instance, in *Dickerson v Fogg,*[133] the Second Circuit found that an accused's right to due process was abridged by the introduction of an eyewitness identification. The victim was robbed on a highway at 4:00 a.m. by four young black men. As the offenders drove off in the victim's automobile, the victim saw one of the men in the backseat stare at him. The man was wearing a hat pulled down to his eyebrows. Forty hours later, when the victim was asked to attend the arraignment of a man

---

enunciated in *Manson* and has held instead that "upon a showing by a defendant by a preponderance of the evidence, the burden falls on the Commonwealth to show that the identification rests on a source independent of the suggestive confrontation." Commonwealth v Moon, 405 NE2d 947, 952-53 (Mass 1980).

[127] 432 US at 114.

[128] *Id.*

[129] *Id* 15.

[130] *Id.*

[131] *Id.*

[132] *Id* 115-116.

[133] 692 F2d 238 (2d Cir 1982).

arrested for driving his automobile, a police officer directed the victim's attention to two men who were sitting together in the visitors' section of the courtroom—one of whom was the cousin of the man being arraigned. The victim tentatively identified him as the man he saw in the backseat wearing a hat. At the officer's urging, he took two more looks and positively identified him. The court found the confrontation to be suggestive and the identification to be unreliable. The court found the victim's description of his assailants as "four young black men," while not inaccurate, to be unduly vague. The court also noted that the victim's hesitancy in making the identification and the extent to which the identification was the product of prodding by the police officer to be significant factors against reliability. Finally, the court noted that although the 40-hour period between the crime and the confrontation may not have decreased the victim's recall facilities, neither did it contribute to the showing that there was an independent basis for the victim's identification.[134]

Nonetheless, as a result of the Supreme Court's decision in *Manson,* the cases in which a trial court suppresses an eyewitness identification are likely to be rare. Indeed, this seems to be the purposeful effect of the most recent Supreme Court decisions. In *Watkins v Sowders*[135] the court emphasized that our system assumes that juries can properly evaluate the reliability of identification evidence. Therefore, while the motion to suppress always merits consideration, counsel should be realistic enough to know that the evidence is likely to come in and that his or her job will be to discredit it in the eyes of the jury.

---

[134] Examples where identifications were found not sufficiently reliable are: Solomon v Smith, 645 F2d 1179, 1186 (2d Cir 1981) (witness' initial descriptions accurately described an alternative candidate and her selection of the defendant was not positive; the finding that the witness had a good opportunity to observe and a high degree of attentiveness "support a conclusion of misidentification rather than suggesting reliability"); Green v Loggins, 614 F2d 219 (9th Cir 1980) (the witness viewed the assailant for only five minutes in a restaurant; he was only a casual observer and did not focus his attention on the assailant; only four hours after the shooting, the witness selected a photograph of a man other than Green, although Green's photograph was in the group; the witness gave no indication he recognized Green in a jailhouse confrontation until after Green's name was mentioned; more than three months had elapsed between the shooting and the witness' identification of Green); United States v Ballard, 534 F Supp 749 (MD Ala 1982) (witness had little opportunity to view the defendant; he was unable to identify him in a lineup immediately after the robbery; there was substantial time between the robbery and the identification); Lagana v LeFevre, 493 F Supp 6 (EDNY 1979) (witness saw assailant for only a split second in a dark area; she was taken to see him in a hospital where he was bandaged which indicated he had just been in a fight).

[135] 449 US 341, 347 (1981).

§3.17 —Examination of the Victim in *Foster v California*

The following are excerpts from the testimony of Joseph E. David, who identified Walter Foster as one of three men who took over $500 from him in an armed robbery at a Western Union office. Foster was tried together with a codefendant named Grice who allegedly remained in the car during the robbery. David testified that the two robbers who came into the office were there about three or four minutes. After establishing the fact of the robbery and identifying Foster as one of the participants, David was asked by the prosecutor:

Q. All right. Have you seen the defendant Foster since this time?
. . .
A. Yes. I saw him twice.
Q. All right. Can you tell the jury when and where?
A. I think that on—it was two or three days. I don't remember the exact date that I was told I was to come down to the police station. There would be a lineup. And in due time there was. So happened in the lineup there were three men and—
Q. How many lineups?
A. Two lineups altogether.
Q. Now at the first lineup did you identify any person; was the defendant Foster in the lineup?
A. I did not at that time say specifically.
Q. Well, let me ask you first, was the defendant Foster in the lineup?
A. Yes, sir, he was.
Q. And did you identify him?
A. I didn't specifically say that is the man. I said I thought it was.
Q. But did you make positive identification at this time?
A. No, I did not specifically positively identify.
Q. All right. Then you were asked to view another lineup later?
A. Yes. At the County Jail there was another lineup.
Q. And about how much time after the robbery?
A. Oh, I—it seems to me at least a week or ten days; now, perhaps longer.
Q. This was the second lineup?
A. Yes, the second time.
Q. Was the defendant Foster in this lineup?

A. Yes, there was five men. They brought five men in for the lineup.

Q. And did you state whether or not Foster was the man who robbed you?

A. Yes, I said I was convinced that he was the man. And I recall I signed some statement to that effect.

MR. QUASCHNICK: All right. I have no further questions.

CROSS EXAMINATION

BY MR. MADDY:

Q. Now, Mr. David, you testified as to these two individuals that came into the Western Union that night, is that correct?

A. (Witness nods head.)

Q. About how long were they in there?

A. It couldn't have been under ten or eleven minutes—total time—it could have been nine minutes total time.

Q. I see. Who entered first, as you testified?

A. Mr. Foster came in first.

Q. All right. And will you tell us how he was dressed?

A. Yes. As I said before I thought he was a garage man because he had coveralls on. I called it a frock at the time, and it seemed to be of a light color, some sort of a large plaid outline on it. And he had some kind of a hat on that—perhaps it was something you would see where they wash cars—the brim was close on his head. It had a brim and when he first came in his face was down, he kept his face down.

Q. What kind of shoes did he have on, do you know that?

A. When he ran I notice—I would like to say he had a sort of a suede gray shoe on his feet like some members of the younger people are wearing now days.

Q. All of these events are distinct in your mind at the present time?

A. Yes, very distinct.

Q. Did you make any notes or any—record your observations after this incident occurred?

A. No, no. It's all pure memory.

Q. Have your reviewed any transcript or any other document before you came to court today?

A. No, not at all, sir.[136]

David then testified that both men who came into the office had guns and that he was fearful he was "going to get hurt real bad."[137] After repeatedly stating that there were two guns involved in the robbery, David was directed to his testimony at the preliminary hearing, where he testified that there was only one gun involved in the robbery. Defense counsel then proceeded to ask the witness if that was his earlier testimony:

> THE WITNESS: Yes, I said there was one gun but I was confused afterwards.
>
> Mr. MADDY:

Q. After when? After the incident was over?

A. Yes.

Q. You were confused as of February 25th, 1966?

A. Yes, sir.

Q. Are these events clearer in your mind today?

A. Yes, sir.

Q. Now about this lineup that you testified that you were at; the first lineup you could not identify Mr. Foster, is that correct?

A. I refused to—to make a positive statement.

Q. All right. Did you see Mr. Foster immediately after that lineup?

Q. I asked if I could see—speak to him.

Q. And they brought him to the office—

A. And—

Q. —and who was in the office?

A. Mr. Kiehl and a gentleman from the District Attorney's Office, I forget his name, a younger man.

Q. And you had some conversation with Mr. Foster at that time, is that correct?

A. Yes. We sat across from each other.

Q. And you still did not identify him at that time, is that correct?

A. Yes—I didn't say.

Q. You were not sure at that time?

---

[136] Transcript at 17-19, Foster v California, 394 US 440 (1969).

[137] *Id* 22.

A. Pardon me?

Q. You were not sure at that time?

A. I—truthfully—I was not sure.

Q. All right. And that was one or two days after this incident occurred, is that correct?

A. Yes, sir.

Q. All right. . . . Do you know who the other two men were in the lineup one or two days after this incident occurred?

A. No.

Q. Had you ever seen either one of them before?

A. No.

Q. Can you describe them for us?

A. You mean the first in the City Hall when there were just three men in the lineup?

Q. That is correct.

A. They were short men, smaller men.

Q. How short would you say?

A. They were maybe five-five, five-six, something in there some place.

Q. Both of the other two men were of that height, is that correct.

A. Very close.

Q. What would you say Mr. Foster was in height?

A. Definite close to six feet.

Q. He was in the lineup with the other two men?

A. Yes, he was on the right side.

Q. Any other description of the two men you can give us, of the other two men that you saw?

A. Well, they seemed to have hats; one a mustache.

Q. And did Mr. Foster have a hat on during the lineup?

A. No, he didn't have a hat on, he had a leather coat on.

Q. Who called you to come down and view the lineup?

A. I couldn't say right now. Probably Mr. Kiehl.

Q. What did he say when he called you?

A. Asked if it was convenient for me to come down. They wanted me to look at some men.

Q. Said they thought they had arrested the man that pulled the robbery?
A. I don't think he made that specific statement. He merely asked me to come down.
Q. That is the entire substance of the conversation that you recall?
A. That I recall.
Q. He didn't say that they had the man?
A. He didn't specifically say that they had the man.
A. I talked with him shortly after the first lineup right after I saw the man in the first lineup.
Q. Do you recall how he was dressed in the second lineup?
A. Yes, sir. I made a mis-statement to you earlier—to you. You asked me at this time if he had a leather coat on and I said, "Yes." He didn't. He had a leather coat at the first lineup. In the second lineup they were five men and they were all dressed in ordinary fatigues.
Q. You mean the blue fatigues?
A. Yes. I have been wanting to correct that all the time.
Q. Anything else you told me that you want to correct?
A. I believe not—Only to the fact that I stated, I saw this same leather coat projecting out from underneath the coveralls—that is the leather coat I saw when he was at the counter when it was open and I observed the zipper teeth, the ring at the bottom and I observed the flange material sticking out from the edge.
Q. That is at the time of the lineup—
A. At the time of the robbery.
Q. You observed the individual that you identified?
A. No—evidence that I added today.
Q. That was added since the preliminary hearing?
A. Today; yes, sir.
Q. Anything else you want to add today that you haven't added or didn't testify to?
A. Yes. I wanted to point out that—Mr. Foster seemed to be—I described him as a ashen gray man as compared to Mr. Clay. Mr. Clay is what you call a coffee brown. Mr. Grice, is of course, quite dark, very dark. Whereas Mr. Foster would—I describe what I call a light complexed man. There is a contributing factor to such a statement because the background when I look out of the office

is absolutely a total darkness there. There are no lights across the street from me.

Q. Okay. Now, since the preliminary hearing we had on February 25th you added the fact there are two guns now; then you added the fact there was a black leather jacket under the coveralls of the man you described as Mr. Foster.

A. Yes.

Q. And you want to change the original description that you gave of Mr. Foster of ashen gray, is that correct?

A. Well, that was my original statement.[138]

The United States Supreme Court held that the identification procedures were so defective as to make the eyewitness identification inadmissible as a matter of law and remanded for consideration whether the error was harmless.[139]

§3.18 —Examination of the Victim in *Moore v Illinois*

James R. Moore was identified by a rape victim at a preliminary hearing in which he was not represented by counsel. At trial the victim of the rape testified that she was awakened in her bed and saw a man standing in her doorway with a knife. The prosecutor asked her:

Q. Now, can you describe the individual that you saw standing in your doorway on that particular day, Miss Miller?

A. Yes.

Q. Would you do that, please, for the ladies and gentlemen.

A. He had on a yellow sweater and dark pants, and he was heavy built. Standing in the doorway, he just filled it up. He was over six feet tall.

Q. Did you notice if the gentleman—Was it a man or a woman that was standing in the door?

A. It was a man.

Q. Did you notice if the individual was Negro or Caucasian?

A. He was Negro.

Q. Do you see that gentleman in the courtroom today, Miss Miller?

---

[138] *Id* 25-30.

[139] Foster v California, 394 US 440, 443 (1969).

A. Yes.
Q. Would you step down from the witness stand and indicate by touching the man on the shoulder that you saw in your room on that day.
A. He didn't have glasses on then.

MR. WALSH: Indicating, for the record, the defendant before this Court, James Moore. Thank you.

Q. Now, at the time you first saw him, what if anything did you do?
A. I screamed.
Q. And then what happened after that, if anything?
A. My feet got tangled in my quilt, and so I couldn't get out of bed as quickly, and he was coming towards me and telling me not to scream, don't scream and don't move, or something. And I was frozen, sort of staring at him and the knife in his hand. . . .
Q. Miss Miller, how long a period of time elapsed from the time you first saw the defendant, James Moore, in the doorway until the time your face was pushed into the pillow?
A. Ten to fifteen seconds. It seemed a lot longer but—
Q. All right. At the time—

MR. COHN: I object to "it seemed a lot longer."
THE COURT: Sustained
MR COHN: She said ten or fifteen seconds.
THE COURT: The latter portion may be stricken. . . .

A. He was on top of me, so I couldn't see him, and he let go of my neck, and I knew he still had the knife or awl. And I don't know what he was doing, but I thought he was going to stab me, so I started screaming again.
Q. Did he make any statement to you at that time?
A. Yes. This was a much longer time. He was choking me, and I felt myself blacking out. And he said, "Don't scream. I'm not going to let go of your throat until you say you won't scream any more."

And I tried to tell him I wouldn't and I couldn't say anything. . . .

I asked him if he was going to kill me, and he said he didn't want to have to.

And then he put his hands under me, I'm still lying on my stomach, and tried to undo the belt. And so I asked him if that was all he wanted, if he wanted to make love, or was he going to kill me. And he said—I don't remember what he said. He made some sort of noise or something. . . .

Q. At the time your pants, your jeans and underpants, were removed, were you still face down on the bed?

A. Yes, I was.

Q. What, if anything happened after that, after part of your clothing was removed?

A. I was turned over and a quilt was put over my face.[140]

The witness then described how the defendant had sexual intercourse with her, how she called the police when he left, and how she identified him from a photo array and at the preliminary hearing.

On cross-examination the following questions were asked and answered:

Q. Now, Miss Miller, at the time you saw your assailant in the room at approximately 12:00—It was approximately 12:00 o'clock, is that correct?

THE WITNESS: To 12:15, yes.

Q. 12:00 to 12:15. And you had been sleeping for approximately a half hour, is that correct?

A. Yes.

Q. And you are presently wearing glasses, is that correct?

A. Yes.

Q. Were you wearing glasses then?

A. No.

Q. Was there a light on in the room?

A. No.

Q. Is there a window in the room?

A. Yes.

Q. Was anything covering the window?

A. Yes.

Q. What was covering the window?

A. A quilt and a bedspread.

---

[140] Transcript at 212-18, Moore v Illinois, 434 US 220 (1977).

Q. And that covered the entire window?
A. Yes.
Q. Prior to the assailant getting on top of you, you saw him for about ten to fifteen seconds??
A. Yes.
Q. And after that time, your face was down in a pillow, is that correct?
A. Yes.
Q. And during the time your face was down in the pillow, on occasion you became dizzy, is that correct?
A. Yes.
Q. And then while you were dizzy you occasionally caught a glimpse of the assailant masked with a bandana, is that correct?
A. No.
Q. Was he wearing a bandana the next time you saw him?
A. Yes.
Q. Was he wearing a bandana after that at all times?
A. Yes. . . .
Q. So you saw the assailant for a total of ten to fifteen seconds having just woken up; and then on five second intervals when he was masked, is that correct?
A. That's true.
Q. Now, the first officer you spoke to, was that Officer Pace?
A. Yes, it was.
Q. Did you tell Officer Pace that the assailant was a male Negro, twenty to twenty-five, 185 pounds, six feet, dark complexion, wearing a yellow sweater?
A. I don't think I would have said 185 pounds. . . .
Q. Did you tell Officer Pace that you had seen the assailant at some prior time?
A. Not at that point, no.
Q. When was the first time you told Officer Pace that you had seen the assailant at some prior time?
A. I told the detectives when we got back from the hospital.
Q. I see. So you never told Officer Pace that?
A. I don't think I did.

Q. How long was it from the time the police arrived until the time you got back from the hospital?

A. I don't know. . . .

Q. Now, on a later occasion, the 21st, you were in Judge Ryan's Court, is that correct?

A. I think it was the 20th.

Q. The 20th or the 21st.

A. Yes.

Q. Who brought you down to Court?

A. Detective Buehler.

Q. Did he tell you, or did you know you were there to view a person?

A. Yes.

Q. Was a name called?

A. Yes.

Q. Was your name called immediately after that name was called?

A. I don't really remember if my name was called or if I was motioned to come up. . . .

Q. And you were called, is that correct?

A. Called or motioned to come up.

Q. Who called and motioned you to come up.

A. I think it was Mr. Neville.

A. He works here. I don't know who he is.

Q. Is he a State's Attorney?

A. I think so, yes.

Q. And you came up, is that correct, to the bench?

A. Yes. . . .

Q. And where was Mr. Moore standing?

A. He was almost right next to me.

Q. Almost right next to you. Was there any other Negroes standing at the bar, the bench of the bar?

A. Yes, there was.

Q. Would you please describe them for me.

A. It was a woman.

Q. Any other Negro men standing there?

A. I don't remember if there was or not.

Q. At that time, did you realize that Mr. Moore had been arrested and charged as being the assailant in the incident which occurred in your apartment?
A. No.
Q. You did not realize that?
A. No.

MR. WALSH: Objection. She answered the question.
MR COHN: Did you think he was just a stranger?
THE WITNESS: I knew I was supposed to look at this man and tell them if he was the one or not.

Q. Right. And was he brought out from the back?
A. Yes, he was.
Q. Was he handcuffed?
A. I don't remember.
Q. Did he come out by himself or did he come out with a Court official next to him?
A. With a Court official.
Q. How long had you sat in the courtroom before Mr. Moore had come out?
A. Quite awhile.
Q. Had you seen other cases called?
A. Yes. . . .
Q. Were people's names called?
A. Yes.
Q. And normally a person came out of the back room and stood here where Mr. Moore had been standing, is that correct?
A. Yes. . . .

MR COHN: Yes or no. Did you believe he was a stranger to the proceedings? Yes or no.
THE WITNESS: No.

Q. . . . . Did you believe he was a police officer?
A. No.
Q. Did you believe he was a State's Attorney?
A. No.
Q. Did you believe he was a defendant?
A. I knew he was the man who raped me. . . .

A. I had signed a complaint, so I recognized the name.

Q. You had signed a complaint charging who with rape?

A. James Moore.

Q. This was before you had come into Court and identified him, is that correct?

A. Right before.

Q. Before you had ever seen him in Court, is that correct?

A. Yes, and I said—I questioned that, and I was told it made no difference.

Q. Ah! Who told you it made no difference?

A. Officer Buehler.

Q. Officer Buehler told you it made no difference, you can—

A. That I would just come up here, and if it is the man, yes, and if it isn't, no.

. . . .

Q. You had been told to sign a complaint against Mr. James R. Moore, is that correct?

A. Yes.

Q. Who told you to sign a complaint against James R. Moore?

A. Officer Buehler.

Q. And Officer Buehler was one of the investigating officers on this case, is that correct?

A. He came in later.

Q. Yes. And when you came to Court and you were called up to the bench of the bar, James R. Moore's name was called out, is that correct?

A. Would you repeat that.

Q. James Moore's name was called out, is that correct?

A. Yes. . . .

REDIRECT EXAMINATION BY MR. WALSH

Q. Was there any light coming in that window even with the bedspread on it?

A. Yes, there's light coming in. And I put a—it was a torn quilt over the top so that no one would be able to look through the thinner material.

Q. And you said there is another window in the bedroom also, is that correct?

A. Yes.
Q. Was there anything covering that window?
A. There were—It's a material you can see right through. It's a gauze, a green colored gauze.

. . . .

Q. Even with this green gauze material on it, there was still light coming through the window?
A. The gauze wouldn't keep any light out. . . .
Q. When you saw James Moore come out of that side door in Judge Ryan's chambers, did you recognize him at that time?
A. Yes.
Q. Did you recognize him at that time as the man who raped you on the 14th of December, 1967?
A. Yes. I'd never forget his face. . . .
MR. WALSH: Are you sure that is the man?
THE WITNESS: I am positive.[141]

Police officers testified that the witness was shown a number of photographs on different occasions and that she had pulled out several, including that of the defendant, which she had said matched the description of the offender.

§3.19 —Subsequent History of *Moore v Illinois*

Based upon the fact that Moore was not represented by counsel at the preliminary hearing in which Ms. Miller identified him, the United States Supreme Court held that the testimony concerning that identification should not have been introduced at trial even if the state could prove that the pretrial identification had an independent basis.[142] The Court remanded for consideration as to whether the failure to exclude the evidence was harmless error.[143] The Court also stated that the court below would be free to examine Moore's other issues presented by the petition upon which it did not pass.[144] These issues included whether the victim's in-court identification was tainted by the prior uncounseled identification and whether the in-court identification was the unreliable product of an unnecessarily suggestive identification procedure and

---

[141] *Id* 263-308.
[142] Moore v Illinois, 434 US 220 (1977).
[143] *Id* 332.
[144] *Id.*

should have been excluded under the due process clause of the Fourteenth Amendment.[145]

On remand, the Seventh Circuit found the error in admitting the pretrial identification to be harmless beyond a reasonable doubt.[146] It found that the pretrial identification added little to the witness' positive identification at trial. The court noted that the jury was exposed to the argument that the pretrial confrontation was suggestive, that the witness was subject to "exhaustive and withering"[147] cross-examination, and that there was extrinsic evidence to link the defendant to the crime. The court also found that the victim's in-court identification was *reliable,* as required by *Manson v Brathwaite,*[148] even though the pretrial confrontation was suggestive, and that the victim's identification at trial was based on observations *independent* of the uncounseled pretrial confrontation, as required by *United States v Wade.*[149]

Considering the *Manson* reliability factors, the court found that the witness had a more than adequate opportunity to observe her assailant at the scene of the crime, even though she had been napping. The court noted that she saw the rapist's face for a full 10 to 15 seconds and then saw brief glimpses of him during the attack. The court found the light to have been adequate and the witness' vision to be good even without glasses.[150] The court also noted that Moore fit the description the witness had given the police immediately after the rape. The court conceded that the description was "somewhat general" but nonetheless found that it "fit Moore to a tee as far as it went and was about as detailed as one might expect from an emotionally distraught, rape victim."[151] The witness' failure to identify Moore positively from photographs was excused either due to the poor quality of the photographs or to the witness' expressed desire to see the suspect in person so that she would be sure she was pointing her finger at the right man.[152] The court admitted that the witness' failure to make a positive identification from the photographs complicated the inquiry but concluded that her certitude was so positive following the confrontation at the preliminary hearing that her testimony could be considered reliable.[153]

Considering the *Wade* factors, the court found that the same facts

---

[145] *Id* n 7.

[146] United States *ex rel* Moore v Illinois, 577 F2d 411 (7th Cir 1978).

[147] *Id* 413.

[148] 432 US 98, 109-14 (1977).

[149] 388 US 218, 239-42 (1967).

[150] 577 F2d at 414.

[151] *Id* 414-15.

[152] *Id* 415.

[153] *Id* 415-16.

which influenced its reliability determination also established that the victim's in-court identification was independent of the tainted preliminary hearing identification.[154]

§3.20 Exhibits

The strength of a case based on the testimony of an eyewitness is determined entirely by the witness' credibility as assessed by the trier of fact. How well was the witness able to observe the person or event? How perceptive is this witness? Has the witness given any contradictory pretrial statements? The attorney proffering the witness will therefore try to bolster the witness' testimony as much as possible through documentary and demonstrative exhibits. The attorney attacking the witness' testimony also will use exhibits, if possible, to cast doubt on the witness' credibility.

Thus, from the beginning of the investigative process, attorneys should be assembling exhibits to be used at trial. If diagrams or blueprints or photographs are going to help the trier of fact to understand a party's theory of the case, they should be prepared. Copies of police and investigative reports should be secured, and opposing parties should be requested to produce all witness statements in their possession.

Once the exhibits are collected, the attorney should determine whether they pose any problems concerning authentication. Frequently, problems of authentication can be solved by obtaining a stipulation from opposing counsel or by serving a request to admit.[155] In appropriate situations, the parties should secure a ruling from the court prior to the time of trial on the admissibility of certain exhibits.

Finally, in the interest of orderly procedure the attorney should carefully catalog all exhibits in such manner as to be able to locate them at a moment's notice during hearing or trial. Also in the interest of time and order, he or she should have those exhibits which he or she intends to use at the trial or hearing marked for identification by the clerk.

§3.21 Preparation of Witnesses

In an eyewitness case, as in any other case, a witness should never be placed on the stand, if at all possible, without thorough preparation. No matter how intelligent, how busy, or how experienced, the witness, like

---

[154] *Id* 416.

[155] *See* Fed R Civ P 36.

the actor, must be carefully prepared for what is truly a *command performance.*

The attorney should first have the witness read and reread all statements he or she has made concerning the case and become familiar with all relevant exhibits. Then the attorney should preview the testimony with the witness, not once but several times, asking questions in the form and order that will be used at trial. The witness should be carefully instructed not to memorize the testimony or to appear to be reciting a script, and should be reassured that anything overlooked by the witness will be raised by the lawyer through appropriate questions. An explanation should normally be given to the witness as to how the testimony fits into the trial as a whole, thus helping the witness to understand the purpose of the questions asked on both direct and cross-examination.

The witness should of course be carefully prepared for cross-examination. Normally, the attorney should actually conduct a mock cross-examination prior to the trial. It is sometimes helpful to get another attorney to act the role of the cross-examiner.

The witness should be told to answer questions directly and narrowly and not to volunteer information. He or she should be cautioned against getting flustered (but reassured that some nervousness will be normal), and to refrain from gratuitous exhibition of personal hostility or animosity, especially toward opposing counsel. The witness must be made to understand that it is important not only to *be* honest but also to *appear* honest.

4 Jury Composition and Voir Dire

§4.01 Introduction

In eyewitness cases, even more than in other cases which go to trial, the most important variable is the psychological make-up of the trier of fact. Normally, it is only close cases which go to trial. In such cases, of course, the trier of fact's view of the evidence is every bit as important as the evidence itself. The trier of fact is, after all, an eyewitness to what goes on in the courtroom. Like all eyewitnesses, triers of fact do not observe, remember, and recall everything that happens in their presence. More importantly, the manner in which triers of fact interpret what they see and hear in the courtroom will produce opinions and conclusions which vary according to their psychological make-up and past experiences. In cases which turn on the testimony of eyewitnesses, then, the trier's views of both the particular eyewitness and eyewitness testimony in general are crucial in determining the outcome.

§4.02 The Dilemma: Waiver or Demand?

All other things being equal, there can be a distinct advantage to choosing a bench trial where eyewitness testimony forms the crux of the opposition's case. The advantage stems from the supposition that most judges are more aware of the fallibility of eyewitness testimony that are most laypersons. Moverover, it is much easier to persuade a judge to hear expert testimony than it is to persuade the judge to allow a jury to hear such testimony; it is easier to educate the judge. Thus, in a weak case—one where there is only one eyewitness, where the witness' observation was made under less than ideal conditions, and where there is no significant corrobrating circumstantial evidence—a jury is probably more likely to be persuaded by the single eyewitness' positive in-court testimony than a knowledgeable judge would be. In other words, if the case hinges solely on the testimony of a single eyewitness, opposing counsel should think seriously about a bench trial.

All other things are not always equal, of course. Unless one is quite sure he or she is dealing with a judge who is not susceptible to extrajudicial influences, it may be unwise to elect a bench trial in what is known at the bar as a heater case—i.e., is one which has received substantial publicity, usually because of the parties involved or the nature of the crime or cause of action. The same caveat applies where there are multiple eyewitnesses, where evidence has been suppressed, where a criminal defendant has prior convictions but will not testify (since the judge probably knows of them anyway), and where the single eyewitness is a law enforcement officer or an important person. Jurors, one must remember, do not take the same heat after returning their verdicts as do judges. On the other hand, a judge who can withstand outside pressures may be preferable to a jury where a client with an impeachable criminal record is going to testify, where the pretrial publicity has made selection of an unprejudiced jury highly unlikely, and where there is a general bias or prejudice in the community for or against the type of client or case.[1]

---

[1] An analysis of data covering a 20-year period, from 1961 through 1980, reveals the following jury conviction rates for various types of crimes: national defense, 82.5%; selective service, 82.1%; immigration, 80.4%; drugs, 79.8%; obscenity, 72.1%; rape 61.4%; antitrust, 38.5%; civil rights, 36.2%; migratory birds, 35.8%. Figures for the

Other factors to be considered include the type of instructions that will be given to the jury and whether extensive voir dire by the attorneys will be permitted. In jurisdictions where detailed instructions are given which set out some of the inherent weaknesses involved in eyewitness identification, juries can be expected to be more open to arguments that an apparently truthful witness was honestly mistaken. Similarly, where the attorneys are allowed to perform an in-depth voir dire of prospective jurors about their attitudes concerning eyewitness testimony, much can be done to offset the popular misconception that eyewitness testimony is the best sort of evidence. Thus, one who must seek to overcome eyewitness testimony may more safely pick a jury if he or she is dealing with a judge who will allow expert testimony on the issue of the reliability of eyewitness testimony, who will instruct the jury about the dangers involved in such testimony, and who will permit extensive voir dire on the matter by the attorneys. If one is dealing with such a judge, however, a bench trial should be considered.

§4.03 General Tactical Considerations

A complete discussion[2] of the law and strategy of voir dire and jury selection is obviously beyond the scope of this chapter.[3] The emphasis placed within this chapter on the selection and conditioning of jurors is in no way meant to minimize the other purposes of voir dire, especially in light of the current restrictions on counsel's role in that process.

---

same years show that a defendant charged with armed robbery was about 20% more likely of being convicted by a jury than was a defendant accused of income tax fraud. The same study shows that juries are more lenient than judges in misdemeanor cases, with juries acquitting about two-thirds of defendants accused of misdemeanors. The opposite is true where felonies are involved. Juries consistently convict those accused of felonies more often than judges do. In addition, in misdemeanor cases, judges, but not jurors, are more lenient to female defendants than to males, while jurors, but not judges, are more lenient to young defendants. See Levine, *Using Jury Verdict Forecasts In Criminal Defense Strategy*, 66 Judicature 449 (1983).

[2] Much of this section appeared in slightly different form in Arnolds & Sannito, *Jury Study Results Part II: Making Use of the Findings*, 5 Trial Dipl J, 13 (Summer 1982) and is published here with permission.

[3] For fuller discussions of the purposes and techniques of voir dire, see generally Jurywork: Systematic Techniques (B. Bonora & E. Krauss eds 1979); A. Ginger, Jury Selection in Criminal Trials: New Techniques and Concepts (1975); W. Jordan, Jury Selection (1980); Fahringer, *"In the Valley of the Blind:" Jury Selection in a Criminal Case*, 3 Trial Dipl J 34 (Summer 1980); see also Auerbach, *Care and Feeding of Prospective Jurors*, 1 Trial Dipl J 16 (Fall 1978); Blinder, *Picking Juries*, 1 Trial Dipl J 8 (Spring 1978); *Overcoming Cultural Bias in Jurors: An Interview with Susan B Jordan*, Trial Dipl J 12 (Spring 1980); Jordan, *Voir Dire: An Interview with the Honorable G Tom Thompson*, 3 Trial Dipl J 40 (Summer 1980).

Any consideration of jury selection must take account of the tendency, most pronounced in the federal court system, to exclude counsel from direct participation in the voir dire questioning of veniremen. Although this restriction precludes the establishment of rapport between counsel and jurors, it may, if properly exploited, confer an unintended benefit: Since all questions appear to originate with the judge, counsel are relieved of any resentment with which a juror might react to a question perceived as impertinent or unnecessarily personal.

In preparation for jury selection in a court which imposes such restrictions, counsel should draw up a set of questions to be asked by the court and should present that list in proper form to the judge prior to the start of the selection procedure. The list should not be burdensome, and the questions submitted in that manner normally should be far less argumentative and leading than those which typically might be asked during lawyer-conducted voir dire. This problem is considered further in **§4.07**.

In addition to affording the opportunity for developing the basis for challenges,[4] direct participation in voir dire also gives the lawyer a chance to tell the jury something about the facts of the case and the applicable law. This information is conveyed through questions which inquire whether certain facts would prejudice the prospective juror or whether he or she could accept certain propositions of law.[5] For example, one might ask: "Mr. Jones, since our defense here is mistaken identification, you would not convict Ms. Smith just because Green was shot and killed, would you?" or, "Mr. Jones, you do not have any quarrel with the proposition of American law that Ms. Smith is presumed innocent of the charge against her, and that that presumption remains with her unless and until the state should prove her guilt beyond a reasonable doubt, do you?" Veniremen almost invariably give acceptable answers to these leading questions. Although such questioning conveys the lawyer's message, it elicits little information about the juror.

Indeed, the most useful function of the traditional voir dire for the

---

[4] This chapter is concerned principally with peremptory challenges. For an excellent example of how to develop challenges for cause, see Minimizing Racism in Jury Trials: The Voir Dire Conducted by Charles R Garry in People of California v Huey P Newton (A. Ginger ed 1969).

[5] In many court systems, reference to propositions of law is forbidden or very narrowly restricted during voir dire. Pretrial preparation should take account of such restrictions while preparing a checklist of the facts and points of law about which one wishes to inform the jury. There is no need to repeat these questions to every juror, since the whole panel will have heard them, unless one wishes to get an individual commitment from each juror on a particular point or believes the repetition is necessary to make the point.

adept practitioner may be that it allows him or her to develop a favorable rapport with the jury. It is not suggested that juries acquit or convict simply because they like one lawyer better than the other, but if the jurors think an attorney is honest, sincere, and open, it is logical to assume that they will be receptive to what he or she says—and perhaps that they will expect that lawyer to be on the side of truth and justice.[6]

Regardless of the importance of the other purposes of voir dire, however, obtaining information upon which to base a challenge is the only one which is judicially recognized as legitimate.[7] The selection of jurors is undeniably the preeminent purpose of the voir dire process.

Actually, most good trial lawyers think about *deselecting* jurors rather than about selecting them. The number of veniremen is limited; more importantly, so is the number of peremptory challenges. The lawyer who selects only "good" jurors normally uses up all of available peremptory challenges long before the panel has been selected. The idea, therefore, is to *deselect* those prospective jurors who are prejudiced against one's self, one's client, or one's case, or who are biased towards the other side.

Ideally, the lawyer has in mind, before voir dire, profiles of favorable and unfavorable jurors in terms of demographic background, life experience, and personality make-up.[8] Relevant personal information then is obtained from each venireman by asking pertinent questions.

Even assuming correct profiles, the task is not easy. For one thing,

---

[6] One study shows that the single factor that best correlated with guilty verdicts was the jurors' perception of the prosecutor as "well-prepared, knowledgeable, persuasive and likeable." Sannito & Arnolds, *Jury Study Results: The Factors at Work,* Trial Dipl J 6 (Spring 1982).

[7] See Suggs & Sales, *Juror Self-Disclosure in the Voir Dire: A Social Science Analysis,* 56 Ind LJ 245, 248-50 (1981) (citing cases).

[8] To construct these profiles, the attorney develops, prior to trial, descriptions of the parties, the important witnesses, and the attorneys. The descriptions include the obvious characteristics such as sex, age, race or nationality, marital status, family history, education, occupation, employment history, residence history, hobbies, and activities and organizations; but one must go further. In a rape case, for example, one will want to reflect on whether older women with sons will be likely to identify with the defendant rather than with the victim. In addition, it is important to include in the profile past experiences which might cause a juror to identify with one side or the other. Again, this means thinking through the facts of the case and listing those related experiences about which to question the prospective jurors.

Generalizations are difficult to make because each case is different. For instance, where expert witnesses are involved, one must be acutely aware of jurors who are apt to identify with the expert. Where the defendant is a police officer or public official accused of graft, a good defense juror profile may be very different from that which applies in an armed robbery case where the defendant is a ghetto teenager. The important thing is to develop profiles of *best* and *worst* jurors and to make a checklist based on the profiles which can be used in the evaluation of each prospective juror.

the formal courtroom setting in which the voir dire takes place and the stringent limitations most judges place on voir dire simply are not conducive to the probing in-depth clinical interview that would be required to ascertain whether a prospective juror is in fact the type of person he or she claims or appears to be.[9] For another thing, it is hard to ask relevant personal questions without sounding impertinent, although, as previously noted, voir dire conducted by the judge can be of benefit to counsel in this respect.

As in other areas of the law, the first rule in questioning potential jurors is not to make things worse. However, to get relevant information about a juror, even assuming the venireman is sufficiently objective to answer truthfully and is willing to do so, requires open-ended, sensitive questions. Even the seemingly innocuous questions can be risky for the novice. For example: "Mr. Jones, what do you think about the idea that a defendant is presumed innocent unless and until proven guilty beyond a reasonable doubt?" or, "Mr. Jones, tell us what books you have read lately." If the venireman has no thoughts about the presumption of innocence or has not read any books lately, the lawyer is in trouble. Even the masters of voir dire cannot inquire innocuously about a potential juror's sex life,[10] although that information might be highly indicative of the juror's unconscious attitudes.

Even the simplest personality is too complex to be adequately understood on the basis of the type of questioning that can usually be done during voir dire. Recognizing the limitation built into the voir dire procedure, one must play the odds. If a juror walks like a policeman, talks like a policeman, and associates with policemen, one must assume that he or she is not an active member of the ACLU. Except in those cases where an overwhelming hunch dictates otherwise, one must rely to a large extent on stereotypes. The question is: what stereotypes? Is it true, for instance, that law-enforcement types vote to convict more often than do other jurors? What type of juror is likely to be skeptical about eyewitness testimony?

---

[9] See Suggs & Sales, supra n 7 (suggesting that voir dire be conducted in the less formal surroundings of the judge's chambers); see also Broeder, *Voir Dire Examinations: An Empirical Study,* 38 S Cal L Rev 503, 528 (1965). Broeder concludes that voir dire is a grossly ineffective screening mechanism, that jurors consciously or unconsciously lie on voir dire, that voir dire is more effective as a forum for indoctrination than as a means of *deselecting* unfavorable jurors, and that jurors prefer *open court* voir dire to in camera proceedings.

[10] But see Morrill, *A Voir Dire Masterpiece,* Trial Dipl J 8 (Fall 1980).

§4.04 Characteristics of the Skeptical Juror

The authors have been unable to find any empirical study that has attempted to correlate jurors' personality types with their inclination to believe or disbelieve eyewitness testimony. Studies do suggest, however, that persons hearing eyewitness testimony seem to ask the question, "Would I have remembered that under those circumstances?"[11] Using this sort of a self-based judgment, a juror tends to believe or not believe eyewitnesses based on whether or not the juror thinks he or she would be able to remember accurately what happened under the same circumstances. It would seem to follow that jurors who are highly confident of their own abilities to perceive, remember, and recall are good jurors for the proponent of eyewitness testimony and bad for the other side.

One way of ascertaining whether or not a prospective juror believes himself or herself to be a good eyewitness is simply to ask—for example, "Mr. Smith, do you consider yourself good at accurately remembering faces or events?" There are two disadvantages with asking that question, though: first, the other veniremen may draw an adverse inference if one attorney strikes everyone who answers in the affirmative; and second, many prospective jurors will simply say they are "about average." A better way to proceed is to ask the prospective jurors about specific instances. For example:

1. Mr. Smith, have you ever had the experience of approaching someone and greeting him only to realize that the person you greeted was not the person you thought he was? [The gender of the salutee should match that of the venireman.]
2. Have you ever deliberately avoided someone on the street, or at a party, or in a store because the person looked like someone you knew but you were not sure?
3. Have you ever been introduced to someone at a party or in business and then failed to recognize the person at a later time?
4. Have you ever seen someone who looked like the double of someone you know?
5. Have you ever been told that you look like someone else's double?
6. Have you ever been greeted by mistake by someone who thought you were another person?
7. Have you ever had the experience of being served a whole meal

---

[11] Wells & Lindsay, *How do People Infer the Accuracy of Eyewitness Memory? Studies of Performance and a Metamemory Analysis*, in Evaluating Witness Evidence 41, 48 (S. Lloyd-Bostock & B. Clifford eds 1983).

by a waiter or waitress and then not being able to tell, when it came time to ask for the check, which waiter or waitress had served you?
8. Have you ever told a friend you saw him or her somewhere only to find out the person had never been there?
9. Have you ever seen a close play at a baseball game where the members and fans of one team were sure a runner was safe and the members and fans of the opposing team were equally sure he was out?

These questions, and others like them, can tell an attorney whether a prospective juror has ever been a mistaken eyewitness or the object of a mistaken identification, or if he or she has ever witnessed situations where confident eyewitnesses were mistaken. These questions also condition the prospective juror to be skeptical about eyewitness testimony.

§4.05 Conditioning Questions

Empirical research bears out what most trial lawyers believe—that the average layperson suffers from serious misconceptions about the reliability of eyewitness testimony.[12] Some scientifically demonstrated propositions that are generally accepted as true by experts but not by many laypersons include:

1. When a person experiences extreme stress as the victim of a crime, he or she will have reduced ability to notice and remember the details of the event
2. Both men and women will remember the details of a nonviolent crime better than the details of a violent crime
3. The victim of an armed robbery will focus on the weapon, which will interfere with his or her ability to remember the robber's face
4. An eyewitness to a crime who is asked to estimate the length of time it took for the crime to take place, probably will overestimate the duration of the the crime
5. White women find it more difficult to identify black men than to identify white men
6. Police officers are no more accurate in making identifications than are civilians

---

[12] See Yarmey & Jones, *Is the Psychology of Eyewitness Identification a Matter of Common Sense,* in Evaluating Witness Evidence 13, 16-37 (S. Lloyd-Bostock & B. Clifford, eds 1983).

7. After a period of several months, a face seen only once becomes indistinguishable from faces never seen before
8. Guilty or not, if the person identified previously in a photograph is present in a lineup, he or she is likely to be identified in the lineup as well
9. A witness who is absolutely positive about his or her ability to identify the perpetrator of a criminal assault committed under poor lighting conditions is no more likely to be correct than a witness who is not absolutely positive
10. The manner in which a question is worded can affect an eyewitness' memory of an event
11. It is unlikely that an elderly eyewitness to a crime will be as accurate in describing what occurred as a younger person would be
12. A question propounded to a child witness is likely to elicit the answer which the child believes the questioner to want

Fortunately, jurors who are exposed to scientific information change their thinking, to some degree, about the reliability of eyewitness testimony.[13] Therefore, in courtrooms where experts are allowed to testify on the issue of eyewitness identification, or in jurisdictions where instructions on eyewitness testimony are given, juror misconceptions can be overcome to some degree. In these jurisdictions, voir dire questions can help condition the juror for the expert's testimony or the judge's instruction. Thus, an attorney in a criminal case might ask:

> Mr. Smith, do you know whether extreme stress reduces or enhances one's ability to notice and remember the details of an event?
> Would you listen to and carefully consider an expert's opinion about that?
> Do you know whether people generally remember the details of a violent event better than the details of a nonviolent one?

To the extent that the court will permit, the attorney should continue with questions covering the points about which the expert will testify.

Even where experts are not allowed to testify on the issue, questions like the above, slightly reworded, can give important information about

---

[13] G. Wells & R. Lindsay, *How do People Infer the Accuracy of Eyewitness Memory? Studies of Performance and a Metamemory Analysis,* in Evaluating Witness Evidence 41, 48 (S. Lloyd-Bostock & B Clifford eds 1983).

what opinions prospective jurors have about the reliability of eyewitness testimony. For instance, "Mr. Smith, do you have an opinion about whether white women generally find it more difficult to identify black men than to identify white men?" However, counsel should be aware that a juror who is forced to state an opinion on voir dire will be committed to that opinion later. Thus, veniremen whose expressed opinions contradict the lawyer's theory are doubly dangerous and should be struck. The number of challenges, however, is often too small to permit disqualification of all such veniremen. One might try a challenge for cause where a juror states an opinion that is at odds with the findings of scientific studies that the lawyer has in hand. The likelihood of the success of such a move, either at trial or on appeal, may not be great. Nevertheless, the graphic illustration of the difference between jurors' opinions and those of the experts might persuade a wavering judge to allow the expert to testify after all.

In courtrooms where experts are not permitted to testify on the issue of identification, an attorney can still condition jurors to some degree on voir dire. In *United States v Telfaire,*[14] the court approved a jury instruction which included the statement, "Identification testimony is an expression of belief or impression of the witness."[15] In jurisdictions where *Telfaire* instructions are given,[16] one might proceed as follows, if local practice permits anticipation of instructions during voir dire.

> Mr. Smith, in this case a witness will identify the defendant as the person who robbed him. Now, if the judge sees fit to instruct you that identification testimony is an expression of belief or impression by a witness, will you be guided by that instruction? In other words, the witness is saying, "In my opinion, the defendant is the person who robbed me." You will not automatically accept that opinion, will you?
>
> You will want to know on what that opinion is based, just as you would any other opinion, isn't that right?
>
> Will you reject the opinion of the state's witness unless you are convinced it is well founded?
>
> Will you reject that opinion if after cross-examination you are not convinced that the witness had the capacity, and an adequate opportunity, to observe the robber?
>
> Will you take into consideration how short a time the witness had to observe the offender?

---

[14] 469 F2d 552 (DC Cir 1972).

[15] *Id* 558-59.

[16] See **ch 9.**

Will you similarly consider how far way the witness was from what he says he saw?

Will you take into account the lighting conditions?

Will you take into consideration what I expect to be the evidence, that the witness had never seen the offender before?

Before accepting the witness' opinion, will you consider whether the observations were made in a fast-moving, chaotic, threatening situation?

Will you consider whether the witness was under extreme stress?

Will you consider the fact that the witness was tired [injured, old, a child, drinking, etc.]?

Before accepting the witness' opinion, will you test it to see if it is the product of personal recollection?

Will you wait for cross-examination to see if the witness was improperly influenced by someone else to identify the defendant?

If you suspected a witness was just accepting the opinion of another witness, you would not credit the testimony, would you?

The judge may also see fit to tell you that if the identification witness may have been influenced by the circumstances under which the defendant was presented for identification, you should scrutinize the identification with great care. Will you do that?

Will you also consider as a factor bearing on the reliability of the identification the length of time that elapsed between the occurrence of the crime and the next opportunity of the witness to see the defendant?

You will hear testimony that prior to this trial the state's witness picked the defendant out of a lineup. Do you understand that the identification that the witness will make here in court is simply a repetition of the lineup identification?

Therefore, you will want to know whether the lineup identification was fair, is that right?

Do you think a lineup would be fair if the other persons in it did not look like the person the victim described as the offender?

Would you take it into consideration in judging the reliability of the identification whether someone pressured the witness to pick someone out of the lineup?

Would you consider whether certain hints or suggestions were made to the witness before the lineup identification?

If it were warranted by the evidence, would you take into consideration that the witness might have wanted to please the police by making an identification?

The testimony will show that prior to viewing the lineup, the witness picked out a photograph of the defendant from a photo-spread. Do you believe that looking at a photograph of the defendant might have influenced the later lineup identification?

In judging the fairness of the photographic identification, will you ask yourself whether the photo-spread was in fact a fair test?

In judging the reliability of the photographic identification, will you take into consideration whether leading and suggestive questions were asked of the witness?

In judging the reliability of an eyewitness identification, will you take into account occasions on which the witness failed to make an identification of the defendant or where the witness made an identification that is inconsistent with the identification in this courtroom at this trial?

Mr. Smith, you indicated earlier that you have had the experience of seeing someone on the street you thought you knew, only to realize when you got closer that it was a stranger. If you had not gotten closer, it would have been your opinion that you knew the person, right?

You would have been honestly mistaken?

Sir, if after examining the opinion of the state's eyewitness you have a reasonable doubt about the accuracy of the identification, how will you find the defendant—guilty or not guilty?

§4.06 The Voir Dire Contract

Before a venireman is accepted as a juror, the attorneys will each attempt to extract a promise. In summation, the attorneys will remind the jurors of their promises.[17] For example:

> Ladies and Gentlemen, during the voir dire each of you promised that you would find my client, Paul Pure, not guilty unless you were convinced beyond a reasonable doubt that it was he who snatched Ms. Good's purse. This whole case boils down, as I told you in my opening statement it would, to whether or not you are convinced beyond a reasonable doubt that Ms. Good's identification of her assailant was accurate. But, as I further promised you, all the evidence points to a faulty, unreliable, inaccurate identification, to a mistake. Is Paul the victim of a mistaken eyewitness identification? The evidence suggests he is! First. . . .

---

[17] Summations are discussed in **ch 10.**

Before voir dire, therefore, it is important to decide what promises one wants the jurors to make. This decision, of course, depends on the variables of the case. It is a bit like deciding what clauses to put into a contract.

Research shows that when the principal disputed issue in a trial is a probabilistic one, such as the identification of the defendant as the perpetrator of the crime, discussion of the standard of proof predominates the jury discussion.[18] Similarly, studies indicate that jurors attempt to disregard stricken evidence, or at least not to discuss it, and otherwise to follow the judge's instructions.[19] Whether or not one believes these results are correct, it is always a good idea to do everything one can to prevent the jury from deciding the case on an impermissible ground. One way to help prevent such an occurrence is to extract a promise from the jurors during voir dire that they will not consider impermissible matters and to remind them of their promise during closing. Such promises can decrease the likelihood of such comments as:

> I don't think we ought to require the state to prove its case beyond a reasonable doubt; that's unfair.
>
> . . . .
>
> The presumption of innocence is the main reason we've got so many criminals on the street today; let's forget it.
>
> . . . .
>
> He was convicted of purse snatching five years ago, so he probably did this one, too.
>
> . . . .
>
> It's the defendant's word against a police officer's. Personally, I'd always believe a police officer in something like this.
>
> . . . .
>
> All right, maybe they sued the wrong guy, but you can bet he's insured for this kind of claim.

Although there is no sure way to prevent a jury from engaging in impermissible considerations, the lawyer must at least attempt to

---

[18] R. Hastie, S. Penrod & N. Pennington, Inside The Jury 87 (1983). These authors also state that when the standard of proof is applied to intuitively less probabilistic issues such as the defendant's state of mind, the juries pay much less attention to the reasonable doubt instruction. *Id.*

[19] *Id.* However, as the authors point out, the studies do not rule out that stricken evidence or other improper considerations do not influence, perhaps even subconsciously, the jury's verdict.

educate the jurors about why certain factors should not affect their deliberations. The first step, of course, is to recognize what impermissible grounds the jury might be tempted to take into consideration. The next step is to get the jurors to promise not to rely on these grounds. Some of them may, of course, not keep their promise, but at least they will probably keep the matter to themselves and not attempt to convince others to consider what they have all promised not to consider. A few examples follow.

> The judge has already mentioned that Paul Pure is presumed innocent of the crime with which he is charged, and that the presumption of innocence remains with him unless and until in your deliberations after hearing all of the evidence you decide that the government has proven every element of the offense beyond a reasonable doubt. This is in the Constitution so I assume that as Americans we all agree with the law that you must give Mr. Pure the benefit of the presumption of innocence. So, considering the presumption of innocence, if you were asked to vote on Mr. Pure now, guilty or not guilty, how would you vote? And unless the state proves beyond a reasonable doubt that it was Paul who snatched Ms. Good's purse, how will you vote after the trial?
>
> . . . .
>
> Paul will tell you when he testifies at trial that he was convicted of stealing a woman's purse five years ago. Now you won't convict him of the crime charged here because he made a mistake half a decade ago, will you? And you won't lower the standard of proof below reasonable doubt because of that prior conviction, will you?
>
> . . . .
>
> One woman whose purse was snatched, and who will testify that Paul was the person who took it, is a police officer. The judge will, I believe, instruct you that you are to judge the credibility of a police officer's testimony the same as you would that of any other witness. You won't believe that the witness was able accurately to perceive, remember, and recall the events in question here just because she is a police officer, will you?

An example of a complete voir dire of a prospective juror is set forth in **§§4.08-4.14.**

§4.07 Submitting Voir Dire Questions to the Court

Unfortunately, in the view of most trial lawyers, there are many jurisdictions in which the voir dire is conducted wholly by the court. Even in those jurisdictions, however, the attorneys are permitted to submit questions for the court to ask. More and more, judges are becoming accustomed simply to ask their own stock questions of the venire, without even amending their stock questions to accommodate those submitted by the attorneys, except in exceptional cases. This practice has prompted many attorneys to stop submitting questions to the court, which is indeed unfortunate. The attorney who fails to submit prepared questions has no real basis for objecting to the judge's manner of proceeding. One finds it somewhat difficult to imagine that an appellate court would sanction a judge's refusal to ask any questions about attitudes towards eyewitness identification in a case involving eyewitness identification. Thus, attorneys must prepare a list of proposed voir dire questions and object strenuously if the judge refuses to ask them.

If the list of questions is too long, especially in simple cases, the feeling might be created that the judge was justified in simply rejecting the whole list. Therefore, it is necessary to tailor the proposed list of voir dire questions to the case, not only in terms of the type of questions proposed but also in terms of the number of questions. However, the prospective jurors' responses must usually be followed up with additional questions. Sometimes a court will follow up without any prompting. Often, however, it becomes necessary for the attorney to submit additional questions. This task is not always easy, especially in the hurried atmosphere which prevails during jury selection in many courts today.

Sometimes, however, the hurried atmosphere can benefit counsel. For instance, it takes quite a bit of time for lawyers to write out proposed additional questions to jurors and to submit those questions to the judge, especially where the responses to the additional written questions invite even further questions. Sometimes a judge can be persuaded to allow the lawyer to ask the follow-up questions in order to save time. In courtrooms where such permission can be obtained, it is usually a good idea to make careful note of each prospective juror's answers to the judge's stock questions in order to have follow-up questions for every juror.

Where the attorneys have no opportunity to question the jurors personally, it becomes especially important that profiles of good and bad jurors be developed prior to jury selection. There are some courtrooms where the jury selection process moves so quickly that there is little time to do much more than write the word *strike* next to the names of those jurors who fit the profile of an undesirable juror.

The judge possesses substantial discretion with respect to the scope of the voir dire questioning. The list of questions which follows almost certainly would transcend the boundaries of a trial judge's willingness to accomodate the curiosity of counsel. It should be regarded as a menu from which selections should be made in a dietary spirit guided by considerations of case specifics and judicial complaisance.

1. After present neighborhood is given:
    a. How long have you lived in your present neighborhood?
    b. Where have you lived before moving to your present neighborhood? Where did you grow up?
    c. With whom do you live?
    d. What are the names and ages of the members of your immediate family? Where do they live?
2. What is your business, profession, or occupation and the business, profession, or occupation of your spouse? Parents? Children? What is your educational background?
3. Have you ever been a member of any police force or employed by any prosecutor's office? If so, please give details.
4. Is there a member of your family or close friend who is a member of any police force or government investigating agency, or who is employed by any prosecutor such as the state's attorney or the United States attorney? If so, please give details. Can and will you judge the credibility of government agents as you would any other witness, and not believe an agent just because of his or her position?
5. Have you ever applied for any job or position with the United States government or any state or municipal government? If so, please give details. Has any relative or close friend applied for any job or position with the federal or a state or municipal government? If so, please give details.
6. Please name any group, club, or organization to which you have belonged during the past five years, whether social, political, civic, or any other kind.
7. What newspapers and/or magazines do you read?
8. Do you regularly watch any television shows of the police story or courtroom drama type? If so, which ones?

9. Have you, any member of your family, or a close friend ever been the victim of any crime, even a minor one? If so, give details.
10. Have you, any member of your family, or a close friend ever been a party to or a witness in a lawsuit, civil or criminal? If so, please give details.
11. Have you ever served on a jury? If so, where? When? What was the nature of the case? Did it go to a verdict? Is there anything about that experience that would cause you to have any feelings about serving as a juror in this case?
12. Without telling me what you may have heard, have you ever heard of this case before?
13. Do you know any of the persons involved in this trial?
14. Have you ever had the experience of seeing someone you thought you knew only to find out either when you got closer or at a later time that you were mistaken about that person's identity?
15. Have you ever had the experience of someone mistaking you for someone else? If so, please explain the circumstances.
16. Have you ever been introduced to someone and later failed to recognize that person when you met later? If so, please explain.
17. Have you ever deliberately avoided talking to someone you thought you knew because you were not sure it was the person you thought?
18. Have you ever been told that you look like someone else's double or have you ever seen someone who looked like the double of someone you know?
19. A psychologist who is an expert in eyewitness identification is expected to testify in this case. Do you have any feelings one way or the other about the field of psychology or about psychologists?
20. Would you consider the opinion of a psychologist on the following issues?
    a. Whether stress such as experienced by the victim of a crime reduces the ability to notice and remember the details of the event.
    b. Whether the details of a nonviolent crime are easier to remember than the details of a violent crime.
    c. Whether the victim of an armed attack will usually focus on the weapon in a way which will interfere with his or her ability to remember the attacker's face.
    d. Whether an eyewitness to a crime is likely to overestimate the time it took for the crime to take place.
    e. Whether white women find it more difficult to identify black

men than to identify white men. [This question should be cast in case-specific gender and racial references.]

f. Whether police officers are more accurate in making eyewitness identifications than are civilians.

g. Whether after a period of several months a face seen only once becomes indistinguishable from faces never seen before as far as most people are concerned.

h. Whether if a person previously identified in a photograph is present in a lineup that same person, guilty or not, is likely to be identified in the line up as well.

i. Whether a witness who is absolutely positive about his or her ability to identify the perpetrator of a criminal assault committed under poor lighting conditions is more likely to be correct in the identification than a witness who is not absolutely positive.

j. Whether the manner in which an eyewitness is questioned can affect what the eyewitness remembers seeing.

k. Whether an elderly eyewitness to a crime is less likely to be accurate in describing what occurred than a younger person would be.

l. Whether a child witness eight years of age or younger is likely to reply to questions in the way he or she thinks the questioner wishes.

21. At the end of the trial you will be instructed that identification testimony is an expression of belief or impression of the witness. In considering whether or not an eyewitness' opinion is well founded in his or her capacity and opportunity to observe, will you consider the following?

a. The time the witness had to observe the event.

b. How far the witness was from what he [or she] claims to have seen. [Use the gender appropriate to the case.]

c. The lighting conditions.

d. Whether the witness had ever seen the offender before.

e. Whether the witness' observations were made in a fast-moving, chaotic, or threatening situation.

f. Whether the witness was under extreme stress.

g. Whether the witness [was tired, was injured, was old, was a child, was drinking, had bad eyesight, had glasses knocked off].

h. Whether the witness' opinion is the product of his [or her] own recollection.

   i. Whether the witness was improperly influenced by someone else.
   j. The time that elapsed between the occurrence of the events observed and the next opportunity the witness had to make an identification.
22. There was a lineup in this case. Will you consider whether the lineup identification made by a state's witness influenced the identification made in court?
23. In regard to the lineup will you consider the following issues?
   a. Whether the lineup identification was fair.
   b. Whether someone pressured the witness to pick the defendant out of the lineup.
   c. Whether certain hints or suggestions were made to the witness before the lineup identification.
24. There was a photographic identification in this case. Will you consider whether the photographic identification might have influenced the lineup identification?
25. In regard to the photographic identification will you consider:
   a. Whether the photographic identification was in fact a fair multiple-choice test.
   b. Whether leading and/or suggestive questions were asked of the witness in relation to the photographic identification.
26. In judging the liability of an eyewitness' opinion, will you take into account the occasions, if any, on which the witness failed to make an identification of the defendant but where he or she made an identification inconsistent with the identification he or she makes in the courtroom at this trial?
27. If after examining the opinion of the government's eyewitnesses you have a reasonable doubt about the accuracy of their identification, how will you find the defendant, guilty or not guilty?
28. Can you accept the proposition of law that [the defendant] is presumed to be innocent of the charge made against him or her in this indictment? Further, can you accept the proposition of law that [the defendant] has no burden to establish his or her innocence, that the burden of proving the defendant guilty beyond a reasonable doubt rests upon the government? Further, can you accept the proposition of law that says the presumption of innocence remains with [the defendant] throughout the trial and unless and until he or she is proven guilty of the crime charged by credible evidence beyond a reasonable doubt?

29. Is there anything else you would like to say or ask about this case or about being a member of this jury?

§4.08 Sample Voir Dire: Introduction

The remaining sections of this chapter present an example of the voir dire of a prospective juror in a hypothetical purse-snatching case, *People of the State of Columbia v Pure.*[20] The *Pure* case, with modifications, is used throughout this volume to illustrate various principles of procedure. The questions are based on the assumption that the judge has made a few brief remarks about the nature of the case to the panel, but that she has not asked any questions of the jurors, either individually or as a group. The state of Columbia is a jurisdiction in which the attorney has no prior knowledge about the individual jurors, even though in many jurisdictions questionnaires containing some often valuable information about each juror are available to the attorneys before jury selection. It should also be noted that in many jurisdictions some of the questions that follow would perhaps not be permitted by every judge, and that in some jurisdictions all or part of the voir dire might be conducted by the judge.[21]

For purposes of the example, all the questions are asked of one juror. In actual practice, many of the questions seeking information would be asked of the panel as a whole; e.g., "Would all of you who have ever been involved in a lawsuit before, either as a party, a witness, a juror, or in any other way, please raise your hand?" Many of the educational questions, in a real case, would be asked of one or another juror, but not of all the jurors, on the theory that all the jurors hear all the questions. Thus, during the questioning of prospective juror Mr. James, the attorney might seek to educate the jury about not giving special credence to the testimony of a police officer, but the attorney might use the voir dire of Ms. Jones to educate the jury about the prior conviction. However, it is a good idea to get all the jurors to commit themselves on every important point. Sometimes it can be done in the following manner, after one prospective juror has promised not to convict the defendant, just because he was found guilty of another purse snatching five years earlier.

---

[20] This fact scenario is based upon the problem "State v. Lawrence," *Problems and Cases in Trial Advocacy, Law School Edition,* 2nd Ed. (1981), which is published by the National Institute for Trial Advocacy (NITA). Adapted and reproduced with the permission of NITA.

[21] *See, e.g.,* Fed R Civ P 47(a); Ill S Ct R 234. For some suggestions about jury selection when it is conducted by the judge, see **§4.07.**

> Ladies and Gentlemen, is there anyone of you who would not presume Paul Pure to be innocent of this charge simply because he was convicted of a similar one five years ago? If so, please raise your hand. Seeing no hands, I take it that you all agree to afford the presumption of innocence in this case in spite of the other one.

For present purposes, assume that Paul Pure is a 22-year-old, black, male college senior who has been charged with theft for allegedly snatching the purse of Joan Good, a 28-year-old, white secretary. Five years earlier, Mr. Pure had pled guilty to theft in a similar case, and he was sentenced to two years' probation. Moreover, after Mr. Pure was arrested in the Good case a police officer spotted him in the jail and identified him as the person who had stolen her purse a week earlier, at 4 a.m. on New Year's Day, when she was off duty and returning home from a party. (These factors may be varied in subsequent chapters in order to emphasize specific propositions.) The trial judge has ruled in response to a motion in limine made by the defendant that the prior conviction is admissible for impeachment purposes if the defendant testifies, and that the police officer's testimony is admissible whether or not the defendant testifies for the purpose of showing common scheme and design, identity, absence of mistake, and modus operandi.

Mr. Pure maintains his innocence and says he was at home asleep during both attacks. He is determined to testify on his own behalf. The prosecution, which believes it has an air-tight case, will press for a maximum sentence if there is a conviction, because the police officer believes Paul is responsible for at least 50 other purse snatchings in the area. The crime charged is a felony, since Ms. Good had more than $100 in her purse when it was taken.

In the following sections, explanatory comments are interspersed throughout the sample voir dire.

§4.09 —Beginning the Voir Dire

After 14 veniremen were seated in the jury box, the prosecutor, Stanley Staat, announced to the court that all of them looked like responsible citizens to him and he was therefore tendering the whole panel to the defense.[22] Thus, the defense begins.

> Ladies, and Gentlemen, my name is Diane DeFene, and I have the privilege of representing Paul Pure, the defendant. It is my duty

---

[22] It should be noted that the prosecutor's announcement facilitates the hypothetical but would seldom occur in an actual case of this type.

to ask you each some questions to enable Paul and me to decide if there is anything in your past experience that might make it difficult for you to be impartial in this case. Some of the questions I ask may sound a bit personal, but I am sure you understand that I am not trying to pry into your personal lives, and I certainly do not want to embarrass anyone in any way. In order not to put anyone on the spot who doesn't want to be, would anyone like to volunteer to go first?

The defense lawyer believes that anyone who volunteers to speak first during voir dire is exhibiting a leadership trait and, if selected, may be a potential jury foreperson or opinion leader. If more than one person responds, the attorney will note all who volunteered.

Q. Yes, juror number four, Mr. Smith, I believe, from my notes. Is it John Smith?
A. Yes.

The following group of questions are designed to elicit demographic information to help the lawyer determine if there is anything in Mr. Smith's background which might make him biased for or prejudiced against any of the important characters in the trial, i.e., the defendant, the police officer, the complaining witness, the prosecutor, the defense lawyer, or the defense expert. However, the lawyer also is trying to educate the jury about the law and the facts in the case, about her client, and about herself.

Q. Where do you live, Mr. Smith?
A. 2650 North Marine Drive.

The lawyer knows that building is a fairly expensive high-rise condominium and that a number of black professionals live there. This fact might indicate that Mr. Smith, who is white, has liberal attitudes. However, purse snatchings are common in the neighborhood, and it is close to the area where Ms. Good's purse was stolen. In addition, the defense lawyer believes that where one grew up is more important than where he or she currently resides.

Q. How long have you lived at 2650 North Marine Drive?
A. About four years.
Q. I believe the building has gone condo, is that right?
A. Yes.

Q. Where did you live before you moved to your current address?

A. In Berwyn.

Q. How long did you live in Berwyn?

A. All my life, except when I was in Korea.

Mr. Smith has mentioned a suburb which has a reputation for being unsympathetic towards minorities. The defense lawyer will have to deal with that problem eventually. However, she feels that to bring up the issue of race prejudice now might alienate the prospective juror because it would indicate that the lawyer associates Berwyn with racial prejudice. Therefore, the attorney decides to pursue the matter of Mr. Smith's apparent military service. The defense lawyer would have asked specifically about military service later in the voir dire, but since Mr. Smith seems to have brought the subject up at this point, the attorney decides to talk about the military service in response to the witness' answer. Voir dire ought to be as spontaneous and unforced as possible.

Q. You mentioned Korea. Were you there in the service?

A. Yes. I was there for 18 months in 1953 and 1954. I was an M.P. in the Army.

The defense lawyer now knows that Mr. Smith is presumably accustomed to giving orders. That fact indicates that he will probably be an opinion leader if selected on the jury and that, as a former military police officer, he may tend to identify with the police officer and the prosecution. Moreover, the prosecutor is a Vietnam veteran and almost always manages to work that fact into his closing statement. The defense attorney now has serious doubts about Mr. Smith. If she thought Mr. Smith would be favorable to the defense, the lawyer might have inquired into his experience in Korea and brought out whatever decorations or awards Mr. Smith had received, to build him up before the jury. As it is, she passes on to another point.

Q. May I ask your age?

A. Fifty-six.

Actually, the lawyer can usually guess a prospective juror's approximate age from looking and from responses to other questions, and precision on this point is unnecessary. Therefore, the question regarding age, embarrassing to some people, will often be omitted.

Q. What is your marital status?

A. I am a widower. My wife died about five years ago.

Q. Do you have any children?

A. Yes, two. A son and a daughter.

Q. What are their ages?

A. John, Jr., is 21. Mary is 28.

Too often questions like these are asked but the lawyer does not know why he or she is asking them. Here, the defense lawyer has obtained useful information. The son is about the same age as the defendant, which may make Mr. Smith identify with the defendant. On the other hand, his daughter is the same age as the victim, which may make him identify with Ms. Good.

Q. Are either of your children married?

A. No.

Q. Mr. Smith, what is your occupation?

A. I am an engineer by profession. I now own my own company.

Q. Tell us, please, a bit about your company and what you do.

A. Well, I am an electrical engineer, but I got into computers early, and about 10 years ago I started my own company. We design computer games, like Pac Man. It's really taken off, if I may say so myself, and we're expanding into other things now. I guess you would say I was in the right place at the right time.

Q. That is undoubtedly part of it, but it certainly must have involved quite a bit of foresight on your part and some risk taking, too. Tell me, how many people do you have working for you now?

A. I think it's about 25 at the moment, 24 to be precise.

Asking prospective jurors to talk about their work is very useful. Since it is a subject most people feel comfortable talking about, the risk of embarrassing the person is slight. While the jurors talk, the attorney learns whether or not they are articulate and verbal, whether others listen to them and appear to be impressed, and whether they are accustomed to exercising responsibility. In addition, the question in this case gives Mr. Smith a chance to show off a bit, which most people appreciate, and it usually gives the lawyer an opportunity to compliment the prospective juror in some way or other. Do not be satisfied simply with finding out what the juror does for a living. It is important to probe a little bit further and find out if the juror is in a supervisory position. If so, that juror would be accustomed to exercising responsibility and therefore might be expected to be an opinion leader on the jury.

Q. What did your wife do before she died?

A. She was a housewife; before we got married she was a teacher.

Q. How about your daughter, Mary?

A. She is a secretary for my company.

Q. And where does she live?

A. In the DePaul area.

Q. What does your son do?

A. He is a student at Circle Campus. He lives near 18th Street and Halsted.

The attorney is not sure how to evaluate this information. Ms. Good and Mary Smith are both the same age, both secretaries, and both live in the same general part of the city. On the other hand, John, Jr., is the same age as Paul, who is also a college student.

Q. Mr. Smith, you mentioned that you are an engineer, how far did you go in school?

A. I have a Ph.D. in engineering from State U.

Earlier responses indicated that Mr. Smith is very likely to be the jury foreperson. The defense attorney decides to inquire further rather than simply to excuse Mr. Smith because he has a military background, grew up in Berwyn, has an exacting profession, and has a daughter who is a lot like the complaining witness. The defense attorney is more interested in Mr. Smith now because she believes the judge will allow a defense psychologist to testify on the issue of eyewitness identification. The expert is about Mr. Smith's age, has a Ph.D., and teaches at State University.

§4.10 —Exploring the Jurors' Attitudes and Preparing Them for Specific Kinds of Evidence

Voir dire offers the attorney an opportunity not only to discover useful information regarding a potential juror's attitudes, but also to prepare those who will serve on the jury for certain types of evidence. The excerpts of the sample voir dire in this section illustrate both these concepts. These excerpts pick up where the excerpts in **§4.09** left off.

Q. Other than your service as an M.P., Mr. Smith, have you or has any member of your family or any close friend ever been employed by any police force, prosecutor's office, government investigating agency, or private security firm?

A. No, I don't think so. I know some policemen, but none are what you would call close friends exactly.

Q. You say none of them are what you would call close friends exactly. Could you tell us, please, a little more in detail how close you are to the police officers? For example, are they neighbors, do you bowl together, are you members of the same church, that sort of thing.

A. There are two police officers who are ushers at my church, and I know them to see them, but we aren't close friends.

Q. I do not mean to pry, but you mention that they are ushers at your church. May I ask what church you attend? The only reason I ask is that some religions have beliefs which make it difficult for persons to serve as jurors.

A. I understand. I am a Catholic.

Q. Again, I do not mean to pry at all, but how often do you go to church? I mean, how often would you have occasion to see the police officers?

A. Well, I go to church almost every Sunday, but I don't see the officers that often because they don't always usher at the same Mass I go to and I don't always go to the same Mass.

The defense lawyer is as interested in the frequency with which the juror attends church as she is about the prospective juror's friendship with police officers. The attorney tends to believe that persons who go to church frequently, especially if they present themselves as otherwise authoritarian, tend to be prosecution jurors. Since the religion question can be touchy, however, the attorney prefaces it with an explanation about how some religious beliefs prevent persons from serving as jurors or make them uncomfortable doing so. The defense lawyer decides to leave the question of religion and pursue the matter of the friendship with police officers.

Q. Sir, I expect one of the state's witnesses in this case will be a policewoman who will testify that someone snatched her purse when she was returning from a New Year's Eve party, at which she had been drinking, and that this crime occurred at about 4 in the morning. A week later, after Mr. Pure had been arrested in this case, the policewoman, who knew that Mr. Pure had been arrested for purse snatching, saw him in the police station lock up and said he was the person who had taken her purse a week previously. Mr. Smith, will you judge the credibility of this policewoman the same as you would that of any other witness and not believe her just because she is a police officer?

A. Yes.

Q. And, sir, if an expert witness were to testify that police officers are no more accurate in making identifications, eyewitness identifications, than are civilians, would you consider that testimony?

A. Yes, I will consider all the testimony.

The defender has done two things here. She has prepared the jury for some evidence that is very unfavorable to the defendant, and she has also instructed the jury about some favorable law. In addition, she has told the jury that a defense expert is going to testify about eyewitness identification. (Many courts, however, will not permit detailed disclosures of anticipated evidence during voir dire.) The lawyer decides to follow up on the question of the eyewitness expert at this point.

Q. Mr. Smith, I mentioned that an expert, a psychologist, is going to testify for the defense. Therefore, I must ask you whether you have any particular scientific knowledge, especially since, as an engineer, you are a scientist yourself, about some of the matters upon which the expert is going to testify. For instance, do you know anything about the studies which have been done on the question of whether extreme stress reduces or enhances one's ability to notice and remember the details of an event?

A. Do I know about those studies? No.

Q. Would you listen to and carefully consider an expert's opinion on those matters?

A. Yes.

Q. By the way, do you have any feelings one way or the other about psychologists or the field of psychology?

A. No.

Q. Okay. If the evidence in this case were to show that the state's witnesses were under stress when they perceived the events about which they are going to testify in this case, would you take into account the expert's opinion?

A. Yes.

Q. Similarly, would you take into account the expert's opinion about whether it is generally more difficult for people to remember the details of an event which involves violence?

A. Yes.

Q. Similarly, would you take into account the expert's testimony or opinion about whether white women find it more difficult to identify black men than they find it to identify white men?

A. As I said, I will take into account all the testimony in the case.

Q. Good. So if the expert testifies, as I believe he will, that if a person who has been previously identified in a photograph is present in a lineup, he or she is likely to be identified in the lineup as well, whether or not he or she is guilty, you will also take into account that opinion?

A. Yes.

Q. And if the expert testifies that in his opinion a witness who is absolutely positive about her ability to identify someone is no more likely to be correct than a witness who is not absolutely positive, you will consider that testimony as well, right?

A. Yes.

Q. Now don't misunderstand me, I am not asking you to accept the opinion of an expert just because he says that it is his opinion. You will want to know on what the expert bases his opinion before you give that opinion too much credence, won't you?

A. Yes, that's what I was about to say.

§4.11 —Educating the Jurors on Aspects of Eyewitness Testimony

In the extracts of the sample voir dire in **§4.10,** the defense attorney prepared prospective juror Mr. Smith, and through him the entire venire, for the expert testimony on eyewitness identification. The next step in the attorney's strategy is to educate the panel on certain aspects of eyewitness testimony. Note that the questions in this section and the preceding section are designed to elicit certain promises from the prospective juror.

It should be remembered, however, that many judges will not permit extensive voir dire questioning concerning details of anticipated evidence. In such situations, counsel should select the strongest favorable fact and ask the juror for a promise to consider all relevant evidence, including the significant fact.

Q. Mr. Smith, in this case, two women are going to testify that Paul here took their purses. They are going to identify him here in court. The judge at the end of the trial is going to instruct you, however, that identification testimony is an expression of belief or impression of the witness. In other words, when a witness makes an identification in court, he or she is saying, "In my opinion the defendant is the person who robbed me." You will not accept that opinion automatically any more than you would accept any other opinion automatically, would you?

A. No, not automatically.

Q. In other words, you will want to know on what an identification opinion is based just as you would want to know upon what any other opinion is based, isn't that right?

A. Yes.

Q. Now, will you reject the opinion of the state's witness about the identification of their attacker unless you are convinced that the identification was well founded?

A. Yes.

Q. And if after hearing all their testimony, including cross-examination, you are not convinced that the witnesses had an adequate opportunity to observe their attacker, will you reject their opinions about his identity?

A. Yes.

Q. Now, in reaching your verdict, will you take into consideration how long or short a time the witnesses had to observe the person who took their purses?

A. Yes.

Q. And, similarly, will you take into account lighting conditions?

A. Yes.

Q. And will you also take into consideration what I expect to be the evidence, that the state's witnesses had never before seen the person who took their purses?

A. Yes.

Q. And before accepting the witnesses' opinions, will you take into account whether their observations were made during a fast-moving, chaotic, threatening event?

A. Yes.

Q. And will you consider the fact, if the evidence shows it, that one of the witnesses was not only tired but also had been drinking prior to the event?

A. I will.

Q. Will you also consider, before reaching a conclusion, that one of the witnesses was not only tired, if the evidence should show that, but also that she wore glasses and that her glasses were knocked off during the event?

A. Yes.

Q. Now, before accepting the state's witnesses' opinion, will you test them to see if they are the products of their own recollections as opposed to the product of somebody else's recollection?

A. Yes.

Q. And will you wait for cross-examination to see if the witness was improperly influenced by someone or some event so as to suggest to her that the defendant was the person who took her purse?

A. I will.

Q. And if you suspect that one or both of the witnesses was just accepting the opinion of another person, you wouldn't give the witnesses' testimony much credit, would you?

A. No.

Q. And will you also consider the factors bearing on the reliability of the identification, including the length of time that elapsed between the occurrence of the crime and the next opportunity that the witness had to make an identification?

A. Yes.

The Prospective Juror's Own Experience

Q. Mr. Smith, as long as we are on the subject of eyewitness identification, let me ask you: Do you consider yourself good at remembering faces?

A. Oh, I don't know, I guess I'm about average.

Q. Okay, Mr. Smith, have you ever had the experience of approaching someone on the street and greeting him or her, only to realize that the person you greeted was not the person you thought he or she was?

A. Well, I know it's happened on occasion, but I can't think of any specific instance at the moment.

Q. All right. Have you ever had the opposite occur?

A. I'm not sure I understand.

Q. I am sorry. Have you ever had anyone come up to you on the street or at a party and act as if he or she knew you, when in fact you did not know each other?

A. Yes, I've had that happen. In fact it happened to me just a day or so ago.

Q. Now have you, Mr. Smith, ever deliberately avoided someone on the street, or at a party, or in a store because the person looked like someone you knew but you were not sure whether that was the person?

A. No, not exactly. I've seen people whom I wasn't sure about, but my style is simply to go up and ask the person. Except, come to think of it, once I was introduced to someone at a party, and there were a lot of people there, and later I didn't remember who he was. There were two people there who looked pretty much alike. So I did just avoid both of them that evening. There were a lot of people there, I remember.

Q. Okay. Now besides that incident at the party, have you ever been introduced to someone at a party, or in business, and later failed to recognize the person when you met him or her at some later date?

A. Yes. It can be quite embarrassing.

Q. Have you ever had the experience in a restaurant of being served a whole meal by a waiter or waitress and then, when it came time to ask for the check, not knowing for sure who your waiter or waitress was?

A. That has happened.

Q. Okay. Now have you ever told a friend or a business acquaintance that you saw him or her somewhere, only to find out that the person had never been at that place—at a ballgame or something, for instance?

A. Why, yes. Once when I was riding in a bus, I could've sworn I saw my wife walking on the street downtown. Later, when I got home, I found out that she never left the house. I knew it couldn't have been her because she was home when I got there and there's no way she could have beat me. It was a strange experience.

Q. All right, if your wife had not been home when you had arrived, it would have been your opinion that she had been downtown, wouldn't it?

A. Yes.

Q. You would have been mistaken, is that right?

A. Yes.

Q. But you would have been honestly mistaken in your opinion, wouldn't you?

A. Yes.

Q. Would you say that the woman you saw in the street that day looked like your wife's double?

A. I suppose I'd have to say that.

Q. But your guess is that if you saw that woman and your wife side by side, they really would not look like doubles, just very similar, right?

A. I'm sure that's true.

Q. Have you ever been greeted by mistake by someone who thought you were another person?

A. Yes.

Q. And then have you ever had the experience of being told by the second person that you look like someone else's double?

A. Yes.

Q. Have you ever had the experience of then later meeting your supposed double and failing to notice much more than just a general similarity?

A. Yes.

Q. So, I guess you would agree that honestly mistaken eyewitness identifications can occur even where exact doubles are not involved, right?

A. Yes.

Q. Sir, if after examining the opinions of the state's eyewitnesses you have a reasonable doubt about the accuracy of their identifications, how will you find the defendant, guilty or not guilty?

A. Not guilty.

This series of questions has been used to educate the juror about eyewitness identification as well as to help the lawyer determine whether or not to accept the person as a juror. A prospective juror who had never been mistaken for someone else and who had never mistakenly identified anyone would be a bad risk for the defendant in this case.

Although the foregoing questions are far more exhaustive than would be permitted in many courts, they are emblematic of the type of inquiry which the lawyer should employ as a conditioning process. If a venireman's answer refers to a relatively dramatic event, such as Mr. Smith's misidentification of a stranger as his wife, the lawyer should question the venireman about the episode at whatever length the court will permit, in order to assure that the significance is appreciated by the other jurors.

§4.12 —Personal Affiliations and Habits

Two areas that are often explored during voir dire are the prospective juror's membership in various clubs or organizations and certain personal habits, such as reading and television viewing. Both items can reveal much about a prospective juror's general attitutes and may even help the attorney determine ways to present evidence or to argue in a manner that would be particularly effective.

In the hypothetical voir dire contained in these sections, the defense attorney explores these topics as her next step.

Q. All right, Mr. Smith, not too many more questions. Have you, or any close friends or relatives, ever applied for any job or position with the United States government or with any state or municipal government?

A. No, not as far as I know; except, of course, when I enlisted.

Q. Okay. Please tell us whether you belong or have belonged to any social, political, or civic organizations such as the American Legion or the VFW, that kind of thing. Again, I am not trying to pry, but sometimes it becomes important. As you can see, Mr. Pure is black and if I did not inquire, someone from the Ku Klux Klan, for example, might be selected, so I have to ask.

A. Only to the Society of American Engineers, the Lions Club, and the Knights of Columbus.

Q. Have you held any positions in those organizations?

A. Yes. I was president of the local Lions Club when I lived in Berwyn.

This last answer suggests that Mr. Smith has some leadership ability. In light of this answer and certain answers contained in the excerpts in the preceding sections, he is very likely, the defense attorney thinks, to become foreperson of the jury if he is selected as a juror.

Q. Again I do not mean to pry, but what newspapers or magazines do you read, if you have any regular ones?

A. I buy the *Tribune* almost every day, and I subscribe to *Time.* Oh, and I get the publication of the National Rifle Association regularly. I forgot to tell you, I belong to the NRA, too.

Q. Are you active in the NRA?

A. No, but I believe in their ideas so I continue to pay my dues.

Q. Do you have any hobbies? The reason I ask is that sometimes we run into jurors who, through their hobbies, have special knowledge about something that pertains to the case.

A. Just music. I play the piano.

Besides the stated one, the attorney has two other reasons for this question. She sometimes uses examples in closing argument taken from a juror's hobby. In addition, the attorney knows that the ability to remember faces is a function of the right hemisphere of the brain. So is music. So is the ability to see spatial relationships. A juror who is an engineer and who has music for a hobby is probably also good at remembering faces, which would be bad for the defense in this case.

Q. Do you watch any television shows of the police story or courtroom drama type? The reason I ask is that sometimes those shows give false ideas about what actually happens in court.

A. Yes, I frequently watch *Perry Mason.*

Q. I do, too. But you realize that real life is different. In *Perry Mason,* the defense lawyer always succeeded, in cross-examination, in having the prosecution witness break down and admit that he or she, and not the defendant, was the guilty party. That is not the way it is in real life. In this case, for instance, I have no doubt that the state's witnesses really believe that they are telling the truth. They will say what they think they saw, so they will not be lying. They will appear unshaken after cross-examination. But the real question will be whether or not their perception, their memory, and their recall are in fact accurate. Will you promise not to allow what you see on *Perry Mason* to enter into your expectations of what will happen in this case?

A. Of course.

Q. For example, consider that day you thought you saw your wife downtown.[23] If you had been cross-examined shortly afterward, before you got home, you would undoubtedly have insisted that it was your wife, and no cross-examiner would have been able to

---

[23] See the excerpt of this sample voir dire in **§4.11.**

make you admit that you were lying because you were not lying. But you would have been mistaken, correct?

A. Yes.

Q. I never expect an eyewitness to admit even that he or she might be mistaken. A witness willing to admit that he or she might be mistaken would not be likely to come in here and say, "That is the man." But will you be able to separate the question of whether the witness thinks she might have been mistaken from whether she in fact might have been mistaken?

A. I'll sure try.

Here the lawyer has again used the answer to a question designed to elicit a fact as an opportunity to educate the prospective juror, this time about cross-examination, so that the juror will have a realistic expectation on cross-examination and not be disappointed when the state's witnesses refuse to change their testimony after being cross-examined. The point might have been kept until later but it fit in naturally here. The attorney did the same thing earlier, in the excerpt in **§4.10,** when Mr. Smith said he had some acquaintances who were police officers. Some courts more easily permit such "education" in response to fact questions. Again, it is important that the voir dire appear as spontaneous and natural as possible.

§4.13 —Prior Experience with Legal and Criminal Justice Systems

An important topic to explore in voir dire is whether the prospective juror has had any prior experience with the legal system. In a criminal case such as the hypothetical purse snatching involved in the sample voir dire in these sections, the prospective juror's prior experience with the criminal justice system or criminal investigations is also very important.

In the following excerpt, the defense attorney discovers and makes use of the fact that the spouse of the prospective juror was once the victim of a crime similar to the one at issue. Later, after learning that the prospective juror had served on a jury in a civil case, the attorney takes the opportunity to explain the difference between the degree of proof required of a civil plaintiff and that required of a criminal prosecutor.

Q. Sir, have you, or has any member of your family or any close friend, ever been the victim of any crime, even a minor one such as having your hubcaps stolen?

A. Yes, just once, as far as I know. My wife had her purse snatched about 10 years ago.

This response is a bit unrealistic. In most major cities, unfortunately, most veniremen, when asked this question, will relate more than just one incident.

Q. Was the offender apprehended?

A. Well, I don't know. The police asked my wife to go down to the station a few days later to look at a lineup, but she was unable to make an identification.

Q. Did you, by any chance, accompany your wife?

A. Yes.

Q. Now, at the lineup, am I right that there were at least five people, all of whom were of similar height and weight and who had similar hair and skin color?

A. Yes, that's right.

Q. Do you know if anyone showed your wife any pictures of one of the men before she looked at the lineup?

A. I was with her all the time; no one showed her any picture.

Q. Did they have her look at any people alone, in what we call a showup, before she viewed the lineup?

A. No.

Q. The testimony in this case will show that there was a lineup in which Mr. Pure was the only person with a beard and that the lineup took place after the identifying witness had been shown two photographs of Mr. Pure and no photographs of anyone else. In reaching your verdict, will you consider those facts as well as all other facts shown by the evidence?

A. Yes.

Q. You will want to know whether the photographic identification was fair, will you not?

A. Yes.

Q. You will want to know whether there was a photo spread, will you not, whether the photographic identification was a fair multiple-choice test, like a lineup?

A. I guess so.

Q. And in judging the reliability of the photographic identification, you will take into consideration, you will want to know, whether there were any leading or suggestive questions asked of the witness, right?

A. Yes.

Q. Now, was your wife's purse taken during the day or after dark?

A. It was in broad daylight.

Q. And was her eyesight good?

A. Yes, I believe she had her glasses on.

In this case, the victim was shown two pictures of the defendant and then asked to view a lineup in which the defendant was the only person with a beard and the only person wearing the same kind of clothing the attacker was wearing during the crime. In addition, the crime in this case occurred at night, and the victim had her glasses knocked off. Although the out-of-court identifications were suppressed by the judge, the judge also ruled that an in-court identification would not be tainted since it rested on an adequate independent foundation. The defense lawyer, therefore, will have to go into the out-of-court identifications on cross-examination. The defense attorney is perplexed because the fact that Mrs. Smith's attacker went unpunished might make Mr. Smith favor the prosecution in this case. On the other hand, Mr. Smith might have some understanding now of how difficult eyewitness identification is.

Q. Mr. Smith, what color was the man who stole your wife's purse?

A. He was a Negro.

Q. Mr. Smith, Paul here is black, as you can see, and two white women, one of them a police officer, are going to identify him positively as the man who took their purses, although the crimes occurred at night, one of them had been drinking, and the other had had her glasses knocked off. Sir, if you have a reasonable doubt about the accuracy of the identification in this case, will you find Paul not guilty?

A. Yes.

Q. Could you do that in spite of the fact that you may understandably still be upset because your wife's attacker went unpunished?

A. Yes. They are two different cases.

Q. Mr. Smith, does it make any difference to you that the defendant in this case is black and the two witnesses against him are white women?

A. No.

Q. Do you think a black man who is accused in this town of attacking a white woman has a right to as fair a trial as a white man would be given?

A. Of course.

Q. But I am sure you would agree that there are some people who would just about automatically convict a black man if there was some evidence against him. If you are selected for this jury, will you do your best to make sure that that kind of thing does not happen to Paul?

A. You bet.

A complete discussion of combating racism on voir dire is beyond the scope of this work.[24]

Q. Now, Paul is going to testify in this case, although he has a constitutional right not to and if he exercised that right you would not be able to consider his silence against him. He is going to tell you that he pled guilty to a purse-snatching charge five years ago. He did it. He pled guilty. He was sentenced to two years' probation. Subsequently, he went to college. He was 17 at the time of the purse snatching. Sir, in this case, Paul has pled not guilty. He will tell you he did not do it, and he will tell you where he was when the crime charged here took place. You will not find Paul guilty in this case simply because of a mistake five years ago, will you?

A. Of course not.

The lawyer has prepared the jury for some more damaging evidence. She has also extracted a promise that may prevent some improper discussion in the jury room.

Q. Mr. Smith, have you or has any member of your family or any close friend or relative ever been involved in a lawsuit before, whether as a party, a witness, a juror, or in any other way?

A. Yes. I was a juror in a case about four years ago.

Q. Was that a civil case or a criminal case?

A. Civil.

---

[24] For further discussion, see A.F. Ginger, Jury Selection in Criminal Trials (1975 & Sup 1977); Fighting Oppression in the Courts (copyright 1978 by Team Defense Project, Inc, 15 Peachtree Street, NE, No 831 Atlanta, GA 30303); A.F. Ginger, Ed, Minimizing Racism in Jury Trials (A.F. Ginger ed 1969); Jury Work: Systematic Techniques (B. Bonora & E. Krauss eds 1979).

Q. Now without telling me what it was, did the jury in that case reach a verdict, actually decide the case?

A. Yes.

Q. Were you, by any chance, the foreperson on that jury?

A. Why, yes, I was.

The odds of Mr. Smith's being foreperson of this jury have just increased.

Q. Is there anything about that experience, that prior jury experience, that would cause you to have any feelings one way or the other about service as a juror in this case?

A. No. As I said, that was a civil case.

Q. In that case, I am sure the judge instructed you that the plaintiff had the burden of proving his or her case by a preponderance of the evidence, is that right?

A. Yes.

Q. And the judge told you that preponderance meant evidence that made something more likely than not, correct?

A. Yes.

Q. In this case, the prosecution has the burden, as the judge has told you, not just of proof by a preponderance of the evidence, or even of proof by clear and convincing evidence, but of proof beyond a reasonable doubt. Sir, can you accept the proposition that proof which might be enough to permit a plaintiff to win a civil case, where the issue is which of two claimants is entitled to some disputed property or was at fault in an accident, might not be enough to support a verdict of guilty in a criminal case?

A. Yes.

Q. In other words, there might be a civil case in which there was enough evidence that the defendant ran a red light, for instance, so that a jury could find that the defendant was liable and had to pay the plaintiff. But on the same evidence, assuming the defendant was charged with a crime, it might be that the same evidence would not support a finding of guilty beyond a reasonable doubt, right?

A. Yes.

Q. Mr. Smith, can you accept the proposition of law that Paul here is presumed to be innocent of the charge against him in this case?

A. Yes.

Q. Can you further accept the proposition of law that Paul has no burden to establish his innocence, that the burden of proving him guilty beyond a reasonable doubt rests upon the government?
A. Yes.
Q. Furthermore, can you accept the proposition of law that says the presumption of innocence remains with Paul throughout this trial unless and until he is proven guilty of the crime charged by credible evidence beyond a reasonable doubt?
A. Yes.
Q. Do you have any hesitation whatsoever about those propositions of law?
A. No.
Q. As you sit there now, having heard no evidence, I take it that if you were asked to vote on this matter now you would vote not guilty?
A. I guess I would have to.
Q. And unless you are persuaded, after all the evidence is in, that Paul has been proven guilty beyond a reasonable doubt, how will you vote?
A. Not guilty.

§4.14 —Prior Knowledge of Case or Parties Involved

Finally, it is imperative during voir dire to determine whether the prospective juror knows anything about the case itself or is acquainted with any of the people involved. The defense attorney in the hypothetical in these sections concludes with this topic. All but one of the characters mentioned in this excerpt are introduced in **§4.08.** The one exception, Dr. Luftholtz, is the expert witness mentioned in the excerpt in **§4.10.**

Q. By the way, this is not a case that has received any publicity, as far as I know. I have been assuming that you have not heard anything about this case. I should not do that. Without telling me what you may have heard, have you ever heard of this case before today?
A. No.

Never ask a prospective juror what he or she has learned in the presence of other prospective jurors. He or she might blurt out that he or she read only yesterday that the notorious northside purse-snatcher was about to go to trial and that the state's attorney had said that he was sure that they had the right man. If the prospective juror has heard something, question him or her in chambers, outside the presence of the venire, about what he or she had heard.

Q. And do you know any of the persons involved in this case, that is, myself or the prosecutor or Mr. Pure or Ms. Good or Officer Justice or Officer Right or Dr. Loftholtz?

A. No.

Q. Now, as you probably remember from your other jury experience, at times it is necessary for attorneys to make objections, and to have conferences with the judge out of the jury's hearing. The rules require us to do this so that the jury can properly focus on the facts of the case without being distracted by discussions about points of law, which are for the judge to decide. The prosecutor and I are not intentionally being rude either to each other or to you when we object or ask for side-bar conferences. Nevertheless, I know it can be annoying to have testimony interrupted or to have to sit and wait for us. If I should do anything during the trial that you find annoying, though, you will not hold that against Mr. Pure, will you?

A. No.

Q. And will you accept my apologies in advance?

A. Sure.

Q. Okay. Is there anything you would like to ask or say about this case or about being a juror on this case?

A. No.

Q. Thank you, Mr. Smith.

§4.15 —Alibis and Alibi Witnesses

If a definite decision has been made that the defendant will testify, the attorney should prepare the jury for the testimony. Often, however, this crucial decision will not be made until the close of the state's case. In addition, the attorney may not want to give away too much of his or her defense or commit himself or herself to definite facts early in the trial. Where the defendant has an alibi and an alibi witnesses, a little preparation is especially helpful.

Q. Mr. Smith, Paul will tell you that he was at home watching television with a friend when the purse snatching occured. That is what is technically called an *alibi,* and his friend, who will also testify, is called an *alibi witness.* Now, sometimes people use the word *alibi* incorrectly to mean a lie. But in the law there is no such connotation attached to the word. It is a technical word for a legal defense. If your wife told you she was at home the day you thought you saw her downtown, that would have been her *alibi,* and it would have been true. If a friend had been with her, the friend would have been her *alibi witness.* So, do you have any questions about what we mean by *alibi?*

A. No.

5 Opening Statements

§5.01 Necessity for Opening Statements

The opening statement is an important and potentially determinative event in almost any type of trial. That importance is underscored when the case involves a challenge to the accuracy of eyewitness identification.

Trial lawyers generally agree that jurors tend to form a tentative impression at an early stage of the trial. Informed estimates, based on reliable data, indicate that 65[1] to 80[2] per cent of all juries decide cases in accordance with an opinion reached at the conclusion of the opening statements.

The reason for that phenomenon is readily apparent in light of the psychological principle of primacy, which dictates that in the resolution of factual questions, the information first received is the information most likely to be believed.[3] Once the jurors have formed a tentative opinion, they tend to welcome evidence and arguments which tend to convey the happy thought that their opinion was correct; correspond-

---

[1] A. Morrill, Trial Diplomacy 22 (1973).

[2] J. Jeans, Trial Advocacy §8.2 (1975).

[3] *Id* §8.3.

ingly, they tend to resist input whose unwelcome message is that he or she was mistaken.

That principle acquires special force when the case turns on the believability of an eyewitness. If opening statements are waived by both sides, the juror's introduction to the facts consists of an apparently straightforward identification by a layperson with whom the juror can identify, followed by a cross-examination whose thrust has not been clarified and which therefore is likely to be viewed as a petulant and nit-picking attack by a hired gun upon a presumptively honest witness who in many cases will receive the sympathy due the victim of a crime or tort. If the proponent of the eyewitness delivers an opening statement, a failure by the opponent to respond to that statement promptly and forcefully is likely to be fatal. In either case, the advantage would lie with the proponent of the eyewitness. One writer on criminal defense tactics prescribes a simple rule: "Never waive an opening statement. It is tantamount to an admission of guilt. . . ."[4]

The same considerations are operative, with substantially the same force, when the respondent, normally a civil or criminal defendant, is given the option to defer the opening statement until the commencement of his or her case in chief. The jury will have received from the plaintiff's or prosecutor's statement an impression which cannot be permitted to pass without prompt rebuttal, lest it become indelible before erasure is attempted. Silence in such a situation is likely to be viewed by the jurors as a "confession of weakness."[5] A criminal defense manual characterizes delay of the defense opening as "a dangerous procedure."[6]

Such admonitions are reinforced by a growing tendency on the part of trial judges to limit or to deny entirely direct participation by counsel in the voir dire examination of veniremen.[7] Strict enforcement of that restriction frequently results in the impaneling of a jury whose members lack all sense of concrete commitment and to whom the litigants and lawyers are unknown and the issues undefined.[8] In that situation, the opening statement may represent the lawyer's only meaningful opportunity to gain credibility in the eyes of the jurors.

---

[4] D. Cohen, How to Win Criminal Cases by Establishing a Reasonable Doubt 506 (1952).

[5] J. Jeans, *supra* note 2, at §8.18.

[6] D. Cohen, *supra* note 4, at 509.

[7] This procedure (or lack of it) is authorized by such provisions as Fed R Civ P 47(a), and Fed R Crim P 24(a). See **§§4.03** and **4.07**

[8] For a clearer picture of the practical impact of that restriction, *see, e.g.*, United States v Banks, 687 F2d 967 (7th Cir 1982).

The only advantage to be derived from waiver or delay of the opening statement is that such action may well conceal the litigant's theory from his or her opponent for a short but critical period during the early stages of the trial.[9] It is at least as likely, however, to have the same effect upon the jury. The soundness of the tactic is further weakened by reflection upon the impact of modern pretrial discovery procedures, which normally eliminate the element of surprise.

§5.02 Tactical Uses of the Opening Statement

In a case which presents a critical issue of credibility of an eyewitness, the proponent's opening statement will inform the jury of facts which tend to buttress the credibility of the witness, while the opponent's statement will present facts calling that credibility into question. For both sides, the case presents the customary opening exercise in "intellectual and emotional salesmanship,"[10] but in a context which involves a stringent test of the lawyer's powers of persuasion.

Any unusual qualifications or impairments of the witness' perceptual or retentive powers should be emphasized as a matter of course. Frequently, however, the case appears likely to turn on the presence or absence of extrinsic corroboration and refutation of the eyewitness' testimony. In that situation, the opening statement provides the advocate with an opportunity to present information of great significance which cannot readily be introduced through testimony and which, if stated for the first time during summation, may come too late.

For example, if only one of several eyewitnesses is available, or if it is impossible to produce corroborative or contradictory evidence which jurors might otherwise expect, the opening statement is the best opportunity to explain that inability.

The proponent might say:

> There were several witnesses to the crime, but there was no opportunity to learn the identity of any of them—except one. They all avoided involvement by hasty departure—except one. That one exception, William Worthy, remained on the scene at considerable risk and inconvenience to himself and performed his duty of citizenship as he saw it by identifying himself to the police when they arrived and giving them information which otherwise might never have come to light.

---

[9] J. Jeans, *supra* note 2, at §8.18; McElhaney, Effective Litigation 117 (1974).

[10] J. McElhaney, Effective Litigation 110 (1974).

The opponent might say:

> There is yet another person who saw the saw the shooting and can provide a first-hand account of everything that happened. Her name is Alice Abscond, and she worked at the check-out counter at the drug store across the street from Pumice Park. I hope that you will hear her testimony. She has given a full written statement concerning the event. Three weeks ago, when the case was set for trial today, I attempted to contact her, but she had moved and taken a different job. I obtained a subpoena for her, but the sheriff was unable to locate her. We are still trying to find her, and, as I say, I hope that you will hear the testimony of that fine young woman. If not, however, there will still be a witness who can tell you everything that happened, and who can confirm that Alice Abscond saw it. That witness is my client, Ben Blackbeard, who will appear before you and given sworn testimony showing everything that happened.

The significance of this tactic lies in the probability that anything disclosed to the jurors is likely to be a factor in their deliberations, even if no formal proofs are offered or if the proofs contain only a sketchy outline of the facts otherwise disclosed.[11] Of course, the authors do not suggest indulgence toward the inexcusable impropriety of making "statements which will not or cannot be supported by proof."[12] The opponent's statement suggested above, however, contains no element of impropriety, provided that competent evidence (in this case, the client's testimony) will indeed prove that Ms. Abscond was present, saw everything, and cannot now be located but is still being sought. That information acquires greater force if disclosed by the lawyer during the opening statement and confirmed by the client in subsequent testimony than if it had come from the client alone.

§5.03 Exploitation of Discovery

Concessions extracted through discovery procedures present a special corollary to the principles advocated in **§5.02.** If information has been produced under compulsion, the party furnishing that information should not be permitted to pose as a volunteer moved by a strong sense of fairness.

As an example, suppose that the lawyer cross-examining Ms. Good,

---

[11] J. Jeans, Trial Advocacy §8.15 (1975).

[12] United States v Dinitz, 424 US 600, 612 (1976) (Burger, CJ, concurring).

the purse-snatching victim in the scenario presented in **§4.08,**[13] had learned through formal discovery procedure that Ms. Good normally wore glasses which were shattered during the attack. That is a dramatic event, but it is a two-edged sword—as likely to evoke sympathy for Ms. Good as to cast doubt upon her power of perception at the scene. Moreover, her candid concession of the cross-examiner's questions will constitute an arguable showing of credibility. These disadvantages can be minimized or avoided by a defense opening statement which includes the following explanation.

> It is normal practice here for a lawyer representing a person in Paul Pure's position to demand certain information from the prosecution for use in defending a client. In almost all cases, obviously, the police, with their immense resources, will acquire much more information than will a person in Paul's position—although I should make it clear that the state frequently demands information from defense lawyers in return.
>
> Knowing that there had to be some logical explanation for the accusation against Paul, I made a formal demand to learn whether glasses had been prescribed for Ms. Good, and if so, whether those glasses were available for testing. It was, as I say, a formal demand under court rules, and any refusal to answer or false statement in that answer would have been a very serious matter indeed. And what I learned, and, in turn, what I will prove to you, is that indeed Ms. Good did wear glasses, but that, unfortunately, they had been shattered during the attack and simply no longer could be tested. It would, of course, have been possible to have new glasses made under the old prescription and tested, but that would have shown nothing concerning the actual quality and condition of the glasses she was wearing at the time. The important thing, however, is that after her glasses were knocked away, she could no longer make a reliable observation of her attacker, or indeed of anything else.

By presenting that statement as a prologue to cross-examination, the lawyer poses credibly as an advocate who believes in his or her cause; deprives his or her opponent of a factitious claim of fairness and honesty; and avoids all suspicion that the concessions extracted from

---

[13] This fact scenario is based upon the problem "State v. Lawrence," *Problems and Cases in Trial Advocacy, Law School Edition,* 2nd Ed. (1981), which is published by the National Institute for Trial Advocacy (NITA). Adapted and reproduced with the permission of NITA.

the witness during cross-examination were produced by tactics which took unfair advantage of a frightened and confused victim.

§5.04 How Much Detail?

As a general proposition, there is no agreement among lawyers concerning the relative desirability of opening statements which contain a wealth of detail describing the anticipated evidence and those which are limited to a minimal and sketchy outline of the litigant's position.[14] One possible reason for this apparent diversity of opinion is that the issue is ill defined. In all probability, no general rule could be useful. There are many cases which, as a tactical matter, demand highly detailed opening statements. There are other cases (a smaller number, in the opinion of the authors) in which the appropriate opening statement is a sketchy outline, giving only a general suggestion of the client's position and designed to excite anticipation of the evidence which will follow. Still other cases are most effectively previewed by a mixture of the two techniques, presenting detail concerning some facts and, as to other aspects of the same case, a tantalizing promise of interesting but unspecified developments to come.

With respect to eyewitness evidence, the authors suggest the following rule of thumb: The degree of detail should be inversely proportional to the on-the-spot persuasiveness of the anticipated trial developments. In those rare cases in which the lawyer is convinced that the eyewitness will be shown conclusively and by readily understandable evidence to be correct (proponent) or mistaken (opponent), the lawyer probably is well advised simply to promise that development to the jury without giving details. In the normal situation, however, trial developments which have only mildly persuasive value can gain additional force through an opening statement in which the lawyer's posture is that of the bearer of highly significant information whose impact on any thoughtful person is not open to doubt.

It is possible, but unlikely, that a detailed opening statement may lead to the coaching of opposing witnesses in an attempt to circumvent the predicted evidentiary developments. The likelihood of such a reaction is in part a function of the character of opposing counsel, agents, and litigants. The chance of such a misfortune may be reduced by such tactics as moving for exclusion of witnesses prior to opening statements

---

[14] *See, e.g.*, R. Keeton, Trial Tactics and Methods §7.11 (2d ed 1973), in which that author summarizes some of the conflicting considerations and concludes by suggesting the adoption of an unspecified "practice between these extremes."

and timing and managing the trial in such manner as to minimize the interval between the opening statement and the examination of the critical witnesses. The safest position, of course, proceeds from reliance upon formal discovery or the transcript of a deposition, preliminary hearing, or related trial testimony of the witnesses in question.

§5.05 Illustration of a Sketchy Opening Statement

Within **§4.08** is presented the scenario of a hypothetical purse-snatching case entitled *People of the State of Columbia v Paul Pure.*[15] The prosecutor, Stanley Staat, might well elect to limit his opening statement to a relatively bare outline of the state's proofs. Essentially, he must ask the jury to accept a direct and conclusory accusation, rather than to draw inferences from minutiae. The state's case, moreover, will be presented through an appealing and unimpeached eyewitness. The prosecutor therefore commences the opening statement with facts which are obvious, uncontested, and monolithically established; he proceeds almost casually to focus on the defendant as the offender as though that fact were equally obvious; he states succinctly and in conclusory fashion several facts tending to support the accusation; and he closes with a confident but oblique suggestion that the defendant must be guilty because the eyewitness is certain of the defendant's identity as the offender.

> MR. STAAT: Good morning, ladies and gentlemen. My name is Stanley Staat. I am an Assistant Flagg County State's Attorney, and I represent the People of the State of Columbia in this case, which is the People of the State of Columbia versus Paul Pure.
>
> The defendant in this case is Paul Pure, the man you see sitting at the table over there next to his attorney.
>
> This case is about a purse snatching. Technically, it is about the crime of theft.
>
> The People of the State of Columbia have the burden of proving to you beyond a reasonable doubt that the defendant, Mr. Pure over there, committed the crime of theft on the date alleged in the indictment, May 4, 1983.
>
> The way the People are going to sustain their burden of proof is by calling a witness to the stand. The witness who you are going

---

[15] This fact scenario is based upon the problem "State v. Lawrence," *Problems and Cases in Trial Advocacy, Law School Edition,* 2nd Ed. (1981), which is published by the National Institute for Trial Advocacy (NITA). Adapted and reproduced with the permission of NITA.

to hear testify is Joan Good. Ms. Good will tell you that she is a legal secretary and that she works downtown in Central City.

On May 4, 1983, she had gone to work, as was her custom, and she was returning home on the bus. At approximately 8:30 in the evening, she got off the bus at the intersection of Diversey Avenue and Clark Street in Central City.

Now, Ms. Good lives on Diversey Avenue about three blocks west of Clark Street; and after she got off the bus, she crossed Clark Street and began to walk west on the south side of Diversey.

After she had walked about a block and a half, that is to say, about halfway home, she heard a noise behind her and she turned; and when she turned, she saw the defendant here, Paul Pure, a few yards from her and running towards her, and Ms. Good was able to get a good look at Mr. Pure because the area on the south side of Diversey Avenue is well lighted with the mercury vapor street lights with which I know some of you may be familiar.

As Ms. Good looked at Mr. Pure, he continued to run towards her; and when he got to where she was standing, he grabbed her purse and he pushed her down, and as he pushed her, Ms. Good fell backwards so that she was looking up and he was looking down at her. And Mr. Pure pushed Ms. Good down at a point on the sidewalk which was directly under one of those mercury vapor street lights; and as she lay there looking up at Mr. Pure, she again got a good look at him.

After Mr. Pure had pushed Ms. Good down, he turned and he ran back towards Clark Street. Miss Good continued to watch him for a few seconds, and then she got up and she went to her home about a block and a half away, where she called the police.

Shortly after she called the police, a police officer named Ronald Right arrived at Ms. Good's home; and Ms. Good gave him a description of the man who had taken her purse and told the officer what had happened.

About a day or two later, Ms. Good received a call from Officer Right, and Officer Right asked her to come down to the police station.

When she got to the police station, she was shown some photographs; and looking at those photographs, she positively identified one of the pictures as a picture of the man who had taken her purse the previous evening, and that picture was a picture of the defendant here, Paul Pure.

After looking at the photographs and making the identification of the picture of Paul Pure, Ms. Good was asked to view a lineup.

Now, a lineup, as many of you know, is a procedure in which a victim of a crime is asked to view a number of people, all of whom more or less resemble one another, to see if the victim can pick out the person who committed the crime.

Ms. Good did look at a lineup. One of the persons in that lineup was Paul Pure, and Ms. Good positively identified him and picked him out of that lineup as the person who had taken her purse the previous evening.

Ladies and gentlemen, Ms. Good is going to testify here in court today; and I fully expect that she will positively identify Mr. Pure over there before you in court today as the person who took her purse on May 4th.

At the close of the evidence in this case, the attorneys, Ms. DeFene and I, are going to have an opportunity to make closing statements. In my closing statement, I am going to ask you to find the defendant, Paul Pure, guilty as charged because the evidence will have proven him guilty beyond a reasonable doubt; and at the close of the case, I am sure you will agree.

Thank you.

§5.06 Illustration of a Detailed Opening Statement

Paul Pure's defense lawyer in the hypothetical case, see **§5.05,** is faced with a more serious challenge than is the prosecutor. The Pure defense must exploit inferences and subtleties, rather than the hard and obvious facts available to the prosecutor. The defense opening must instill an appreciation of the factors which have caused an honest witness to swear to a false accusation.

The difficulty is compounded by the fact that Mr. Pure himself, as an accused purse-snatcher, is unlikely to enjoy the sympathetic acceptance which is the jury's probable initial reaction to Ms. Good, the victim who will accuse him. For that reason, emphasis upon Mr. Pure's anticipated denial is likely to be misplaced.

In framing her opening statement, the defense lawyer, Diane DeFene, reasonably may anticipate a cross-examination of Ms. Good similar to that depicted in **§6.08.** A substantial number of significant points can be made during Ms. Good's cross-examination. If competently presented, those points are likely to be reasonably persuasive. They provide no basis, however, for confidence on the part of the defense lawyer that the jury will perceive the full significance of those points without having been furnished substantial preparatory guidance.

For that reason, the defense lawyer will be likely to deliver an analytical opening statement, designed to condition the jury to understand and accept the defense theory, and to anticipate the factors which blunt the forcefulness of the witness' accusation. The defense attorney also will take pains to minimize the dramatic impact of the victim's anticipated in-court identification of the defendant, by painting that development as both routine and inevitable, produced by influences which long since have warped the witness' recollection with an ineradicable overlay of delusion and misinterpretation.

The defense opening statement which follows is designed to accomodate those requirements. After a forceful initial denial of the accusation, the defense lawyer establishes her claim to no less respect than is accorded to the prosecutor. She then proceeds to develop the evidentiary details tending to minimize the likelihood that Ms. Good's view of her assailant was sufficient to enable her to make a reliable identification several days thereafter. The defense attorney next presents in an unflattering light, treading but not crossing the borderline of argument, the procedures which produced the stationhouse identification and makes the point that the identification, once uttered, was functionally irretrievable. She concludes by reminding the jury that Ms. Good's present belief is relatively unimportant, and that it is only the jury's belief, based on the evidence, that should be determinative.

MS. DEFENE: Ladies and gentlemen, as you know by now, my name is Diane DeFene, and it is my privilege and my responsibility to stand before you protecting Mr. Paul Pure, who is the defendant in this case.

At the outset, let me clarify one point for you just as vigorously, just as forcefully, as is within my power. Paul Pure denies this accusation; he denies it completely. He is not the person who took Ms. Good's purse.

He does not know who that person is, and he pleads and has pleaded and will continue to plead not guilty to every element of this charge, extending to and actually including his very presence at the place at which the crime took place. He was not there.

Now, you have heard a statement as to what Mr. Staat plans to prove in this case; and I'm sure that Mr. Staat, who is a skilled and highly experienced prosecutor, would not say those things if he didn't think he could prove them. And indeed Ms. Good will, I believe, testify that Paul Pure is the man who stole her purse, and I'm sure by this time she really believes it.

In all the circumstances, it might even be somewhat reasonable that she should believe it; but this evidence will show you that she is mistaken, completely mistaken, simply and honestly but completely mistaken, and this evidence also will show you how the mistake occurred.

Paul of course knows nothing about the event. He simply was not there, and he has no information whatever concerning the circumstances under which Ms. Good's purse was snatched.

Based on the things that I have been able to learn, however, from prosecuting agencies and, in a much more limited sense, from Ms. Good herself, I have some information about it; and for that reason, I am able to tell you some things that I believe I will be able to prove to you as this case progresses. In good part, I hope to prove those things through answers which Ms. Good herself is likely to give to questions that I plan to ask of her; but prove them I will. The evidence will show you why Paul was accused by Ms. Good. It is not because he is guilty. I told you that I don't believe Mr. Staat would say things to you if he didn't think he could prove them, and I hope that before we are done here you will have that same opinion about me.

Let me tell you what I propose to prove to you.

The Crime Itself

Ms. Good's purse was snatched at 8:30 at night. The sun had set. It was dark. It was quite literally night.

Mr. Staat has told you that there were mercury vapor street lights in the area. It might also be of interest to you, then, to know that the evidence will show you that those mercury vapor street lights were more than 120 feet apart at that particular point; and on that night, also, between the street lamps and the street itself on the parkway there was an almost continuous row of trees, literally touching each other with their branches, and these trees had sprouted leaves and the leaves created shadows which effectively blocked much of the light that the mercury vapor lamps were intended to cast.

Ms. Good says that she heard a noise behind her as she walked up that shaded street; and as she walked through the shadows cast by those leaves, hearing a noise, she turned around. She was knocked to the ground.

From the time that she turned around until the time that she was knocked to the ground, there intervened a space of no more than four seconds; and during that time, Ms. Good saw a young man running toward her. She was startled by the event.

The one thing that I think we can all be quite confident of from the evidence shown here is that she saw the person moving toward her under circumstances which simply did not lend themselves to a clear view of the features of that individual.

Four seconds from the time she turned around, no more than that, she was knocked to the ground; and in consequence of that startling and very regrettable event, she lay there on the ground stunned and frightened, as any of us would be in that situation, and when she looked up she saw the figure of a man with the light behind him, the light from the street lamps behind him, casting his face into shadow with a darkness accentuated by the trees and the leaves that stood in profusion between the street lamp and the man in question.

The man reached down quickly, took her purse, and ran away from her. The total period of time during which the man was in her presence facing her did not exceed ten seconds, during which time he ran toward her, pushed her down, took her purse, and departed.

Description Provided to Police

Now let me tell you what the evidence will show as to the manner in which Ms. Good first encountered Mr. Pure. After her purse was snatched, and there is no serious question that it was indeed taken, Ms. Good went home and called the police; and after some time, a police investigator arrived, and his name was Ronald Right.

Now, please remember that she was at home. She was in completely familiar and comfortable surroundings. She had had plenty of time to calm down and recover to a large extent from the shock and the excitement of the crime; and no thoughtful person would deny that she had been subjected to very considerable shock and excitement, but Officer Right came to her home more than 45 minutes after the event had occurred.

Now, Officer Right, of course, wanted to solve the crime. That was his job, and Ms. Good wanted to help him. She was in fact the complainant. She was the person who was urging him to catch the perpetrator, as you or I would do, indeed as any thoughtful person would do.

She naturally wanted her attacker to be caught and to be punished; and, furthermore, she had every reason to believe that if he were caught quickly he might still have some of her money, some of her identification, some of her valuables on his person, or at least be able to tell where they were.

So Ms. Good sat down in the comfort of her home with Officer Right and she did everything that she could to help him identify that offender. It was very fresh in her mind. After all, it had happened only some 45 minutes to an hour earlier. She knew right then and there everything that she ever would know about that crime, and she knew it as well as she ever would know it.

Officer Right very naturally asked her to describe the robber; and all that she could say at that time, the only thing she could say, was that he was about six feet tall with medium build, long hair, and a beard, and that he wore white pants and a black T-shirt.

That was all she could say; and really one could not, I think, from this evidence expect her to say a great deal more than that. In a ten-second observation, that is about all that can be done.

As I say, in her eagerness, in her anxiety to see the offender caught as quickly as could be done, drawing on every resource that she had and with a fresh memory of the event, she was able to say that he was about six feet tall, medium build with long hair and a beard, and that he was wearing white pants and a black T-shirt.

She did not, I repeat, she did not say anything about a tattoo; but Paul has a very prominent tattoo indeed on his upper right arm. We can't see it now, but you will see it. You will see it when he removes his jacket, as he will later.

It is an eagle-and-snake design which was etched on his arm by a tattoo artist near Quantico, Virginia, years ago while Paul was serving with the United States Marines.

As you will learn, in fact, as some of you probably already know, it was a very common, accepted thing for young marines to have themselves marked with tattoo designs that suggest manliness and patriotism as viewed through youthful eyes.

We might have advised him against it if we had been there; but in the light of this case, it may be about the best thing that ever happened to him.

You can't see that tattoo now, but it is completely and very prominently visible anytime that Paul wears a T-shirt; and that is exactly what the thief who stole that purse was wearing.

I ask you to look at Paul again, please. Look at him for a moment. Look at the scar above his right eye. Pretty obvious.

Well, you are going to learn from the evidence that Ms. Good said nothing, absolutely nothing, about any scar when she was giving to Officer Right the best description that she possibly could give of her attacker; and the evidence will show to you conclusively that on the day of the theft, on May 4th of 1983, Paul already had that scar and he already had that tattoo, and there simply is no legitimate question about either of those points.

The Identification at the Police Station

Now, in the face of all that, how did Ms. Good come to identify Paul as the thief? I told you that I would give you a preview of the evidence that would show the reason that Paul was brought here. I am going to proceed to that right now, and that evidence I think is going to show you that it really was not Ms. Good's idea in the first instance to have Paul brought here.

Three days or so after the theft, Officer Right arrested Paul, who was, as you can see, six feet tall, medium build, with long hair and a beard. That is a description that, of course, would fit hundreds of thousands of other men; and Officer Right had a great deal of latitude in looking for a man six feet tall, medium build, with long hair and a beard.

He was not restricted to looking for any particular color of hair and beard because Ms. Good had been unable to give him the color of the hair and beard of her attacker.

He was not limited by any age bracket because Ms. Good had been unable to give even an approximation of the age of her attacker.

So he found Paul; and Paul was six feet tall, medium build, with long hair and a beard, and he was wearing white pants.

Now, he wasn't wearing a T-shirt but, for all that Officer Right knew, he might have worn a T-shirt at some time or another in the past; and so Officer Right called Ms. Good and he asked her to come to the police station.

We have no way of knowing, except as they may see fit to tell us, what he told her, what he said to her; but one thing for sure, the evidence will show to you quite conclusively that she came to that police station expecting and hoping that she would find there the man who had stolen her purse.

When she got there, however, Officer Right did not at first show her anyone at all. Instead, he showed her two photographs and he asked her whether the person who stole her purse was pictured there.

Now, again, let me make it very clear, he did not show her a photograph of a lineup. He did not show her a photograph of a group of people. He did not show her a group of pictures, a photo-spread I believe the police call it, and ask her to see whether she could identify anyone in that group.

No. He showed her only two pictures; and both of them, not one but both of them, were pictures of the same man, the defendant, Paul Pure.

Now, the evidence will prove to you conclusively that at that time Officer Right was holding Paul Pure in a jail cell. There were plenty of other people around, police officers, other suspects, employees of the police department, hundreds of people, literally hundreds from whom it would have been possible to have put together a lineup and say, "Can you pick the man who robbed you out of that line-up?" But they chose instead to show her two pictures of Paul Pure.

In that police station, as the evidence will show you, there were literally thousands of photographs that could have been used; and it would have been a very simple thing to have picked out five or six photographs of people with beards and to ask Ms. Good whether the person who stole her purse was depicted in one of those pictures.

In short, the evidence will prove—and it is pretty obvious in any event—that the police had at their disposal, when Ms. Good entered the stationhouse, everything they needed to make a meaningful test of whether Ms. Good could identify her attacker, and more importantly, whether they had the right man. And to be fair, I should say *Officer Right,* not *the police,* because he was the only one involved. The police force as a whole did not make those decisions; he acted on his own. But there were dozens of useful things that he could have done to make the confrontation with Paul reliable, and none of those things was done, not one.

Officer Right simply gave her two pictures and asked something like, "Are either of these the man who stole your purse?" And both of them were pictures of the same man. Both of them were pictures of Paul Pure.

Well, not surprisingly, Miss Good said, "Yes, these photos are photos of the person who stole my purse." They were head-and-shoulders photos, so she couldn't see the tattoo. The scar can hardly be seen there, and we can't blame her for missing it because it barely shows in the photographs.

What she saw essentially were pictures of a man with long hair and a beard who obviously was suspected of the crime, and she did nothing more than what other people would have done in the same circumstances. She said, "Yes, that is the man," or "That looks like the man," which really means the same thing, and which anyone in that position would have said with respect to any photograph that might have been shown her at that time of a person whom she believed to be a suspect and who had long hair and a beard.

Officer Right, of course, was delighted with that response. It was exactly what he wanted to hear, because it meant that he had solved the crime. He was pleased with her, and he showed it. She, for her part, could see immediately that she had done something of which he approved strongly. And in that moment, the die was cast. For her to have changed her mind after that, to disappoint the officer who had worked so hard on her case, to appear erratic and fickle—that would have been very hard to do. For all practical purposes, from the time she was shown two photos of Paul Pure, a man with long hair and a beard, she was committed to the identification. By the time she actually saw the tattoo and the scar, it was easier to rationalize than to back away from the terrible finality of her concession that the photographs looked like the thief.

And it was only after they had done that, only after the leading, suggestive identification by photographs that I have described to you, only then did the police hold the lineup for the first time; and from the evidence, we will never be able to say whether Ms. Good went into that lineup looking for the person who stole her purse or whether she went into the lineup looking for the man whose picture that she had seen or some blurry composite of the two. We really do not know.

Considering the way the lineup was held, it really didn't make a great deal of difference. The offender, you will remember, had been wearing a black T-shirt and white pants. Now, nobody in the lineup wore a T-shirt, but one of them, and only one, was wearing white pants; and by this time, now that you have heard in general the method by which the identification was made, I don't suppose I have to tell you who that one person wearing white pants was. It was Paul, of course.

But as though that weren't enough, you will recall from what I said before that the person who snatched Ms. Good's purse was wearing a beard; and how many people do you suppose there were in that lineup who were wearing beards?

Well, given the procedures adopted in this case, I think perhaps almost instinctively we can all answer that by this point there was one person in that lineup wearing a beard, and of course that one person was Paul Pure. There were two with moustaches and one with long sideburns, but Paul was the only one with a full beard. The evidence will, in short, show circumstances making it completely inevitable that Ms. Good would pick Paul Pure from that lineup.

Any person, any person regardless of whether that person had been present at the scene of the crime, who had received the gross description of the offender as six feet tall, with long hair and a beard, and wearing white pants, any person given that description would have picked Paul Pure out of that lineup because he was the only person there that remotely matched that description. And that on top of the conditioning effect of the two photographs!

In order that there might be no misunderstanding, I want to tell you now that we have no evidence that remotely would suggest that Officer Right or any other police officer was trying to frame Paul Pure. The identification procedure of course was clumsy, even silly; but we have no evidence that it was done corruptly. It is completely understandable that the police would rather list a crime as solved than leave it on their books unsolved, but it is your job and mine to make sure that the bookkeeping adjustments made in this case do not result in an injustice against Paul Pure.

He was identified in consequence of an identification procedure that simply made it inevitable that he would be identified, guilty or innocent.

The Firmness of the Witness' Belief

And one further thing: I believe that Ms. Good on the witness stand will stick to her identification. She will not testify that she was mistaken. She will not testify that there is any possibility that she might be mistaken.

By this time, she is completely committed to her identification of Paul as the thief, and, as I said before, she probably believes it.

I think, however, that she is going to have to admit on that stand the facts that I have just given to you. I believe that I will be able to prove every one of those facts.

I will have to prove it through her, through official records, and, perhaps, through police witnesses, because, you see, during the transaction between Ms. Good and Officer Right, during the time that Ms. Good furnished information to Officer Right, during the time that they met at the police station and he showed her the photographs, during the time that he conducted her to the lineup, just as at the time of the robbery, Paul was not there and he can't tell us anything about it. But the facts are well established by solid records, and I have no hesitancy in telling you that that is indeed what the evidence will show.

Just as Mr. Staat told you, Ms. Good will testify that Paul Pure stole her purse, and she believes that; but that is not why we are here. As Mr. Staat admitted, yours is the only opinion that counts. We are not here to see what she believes. The important thing is what you believe. The important thing is whether this evidence shows beyond all reasonable doubt that Paul Pure stole Ms. Good's purse.

I look forward with some confidence to your answer to that question when the evidence will have been heard fully. When I will have proved to you everything that I have told you now that this evidence will show, I will then ask for your verdict of not guilty; and I believe that that verdict will be amply justified by the evidence that I have described.

Thank you very much.

§5.07 Restrictions on Opening Statements

The basic limitations on opening statements are generally acknowledged and understood: The litigant must "confine himself to a discussion of what he hopes to show"[16] and thereby provide an "outline of proposed proof."[17] As stated by Chief Justice Burger:

> An opening statement has a narrow purpose and scope. It is to state what evidence will be presented, to make it easier for the jurors to understand what is to follow, and to relate parts of the evidence to the testimony as a whole; it is not an occasion for argument.[18]

It seems clear, therefore, that the speaker is not limited to a bare statement of the forthcoming proof. A reasonable amount of analysis, not descending to the level of argument, is well within the bounds of proper advocacy. The special importance of the opening statement as applied to the eyewitness contest, however, warrants the exercise of an unusual degree of caution on the part of the lawyer opposing the eyewitness, in order to avoid furnishing a pretext for being deprived of that crucial trial tool.

During recent years, reviewing courts have been called upon with surprising frequency to consider the question whether the opening

---

[16] United States v Hershenow, 680 F2d 847, 858 (1st Cir 1982).

[17] United States v Escobedo, 430 F2d 14, 20 (7th Cir 1970).

[18] United States v Dinitz, 424 US 600, 612 (1976) (Burger, CJ concurring).

statement is a matter of right,[19] reflecting a tendency on the part of lower courts to adopt draconian measures in expediting the trial process. In recent years, some jurisdictions have denied the existence of such a right,[20] although that remains a minority position. Even where the right is conceded, however, its denial is frequently held to be harmless error if the evidence is strong, or if the issues are readily understandable by the jurors.[21] Moreover, it is generally held that in any case, the trial judge has the right to limit the scope and extent of opening statements.[22]

In order to avoid curtailment or loss of the right to make an opening statement, counsel whose trial posture involves a serious challenge to eyewitness testimony should make a special effort to avoid overt argument. Such restraint normally is justified in any event as a sound persuasive tactic, since lawyers most effectively assume a posture of leadership and reliability in the eyes of the jury if, in the words of Cicero, they contrive "to seem as if [their] sole view was to inform."[23]

The hypothetical opening statement presented in **§5.06** should serve to demonstrate that it is not necessary to argue overtly in order to adopt a strong adversarial posture. Counsel in similar positions would do well to consider carefully whether their statements are objectionably argumentative. It hardly pays to be overly cautious, because almost any statement, no matter how circumspectly crafted, may be vulnerable to an adverse discretionary ruling. Care should be taken, however, to phrase the opening statement in a manner which does not actively invite objection. Carelessness can cause curtailment or loss of the right to make an opening statement, which often is the lawyer's best opportunity to clarify the client's position in the eyes of the jury.

Some portions of the illustrative detailed opening statement for the defense in **§5.06** are arguably improper from a technical standpoint. In general, however, those improprieties are sufficiently innocuous that opposing counsel might well hesitate to object, for fear of appearing hypertechnical and obstructive.

One example is the defense lawyer's reference to Paul Pure's tattoo:

---

[19] Many of these decisions are cited in United States v Salovitz, 701 F2d 17, 19-21 (2d Cir 1983), and Note, *Evidence, Defendant's Right to an Opening Statement,* 34 SCL Rev 145 (1982).

[20] State v Brown, 277 SC 203, 284 SE2d 777 (1981); *see* United States v Salovitz 701 F2d 17, 19-21 (2d Cir 1983); Note, *supra* note 17.

[21] United States v Hershenow, 680 F2d 847, 858 (1st Cir 1982); Hampton v United States, 269 A2d 441 (DC 1970).

[22] United States v Freeman, 514 F2d 1184, 1192 (10th Cir 1975).

[23] Quoted in B. Palmer, Courtroom Strategies, 178 (1959).

"We might have advised him against it if we had been there, but in the light of this case, it may be about the best thing that ever happened to him." The defense lawyer obviously does not plan to call a witness to testify that a more mature person would have argued against the tattooing, or that the tattoo is helpful in proving innocence. Strictly speaking, therefore, the lawyer's comment does not tell the jury what the evidence will show. If an objection is made, however, the defense lawyer can adopt a posture of resigned forbearance and, without waiting for a ruling from the court, state:

> Counsel is, of course, technically correct. I should have said, and herewith do say that *the evidence will show* that Paul bears a tattoo of the type that most mature people would not want, but that *the evidence will show* that he is lucky to have it because the person who attacked Ms. Good did not have such a tattoo. I trust that counsel will forgive me if I follow his example and omit the magic phrase about "the evidence" from time to time.

Other portions of the illustrative statement, however, are essentially argumentative. In referring to the stationhouse identification procedure, the lawyer is depicted as saying "It is completely understandable that [the police] would rather list a crime as solved than leave it on their books unsolved, but it is your job and mine to make sure that the bookkeeping adjustments in this case do not result in an injustice against [my client]." That comment is made more appropriately during summation than in the opening statement. An objection by an experienced prosecutor, however, is unlikely, because it is generally regarded as unwise to object to an isolated remark whose thrust is an affirmation of the seriousness of the jury's responsibility.

The lawyer opposing an eyewitness deals in subtleties, inflections, and inferences. In most cases, therefore, that lawyer's opening loses effectiveness unless it approaches the boundary of argumentativeness more closely than will be necessary for the witness' proponent. At all costs, however, the lawyer must avoid the possibility of summary curtailment. Because the issue is one which involves unusual breadth of judicial discretion, the lawyer is well advised to become familiar with the views and practices of the trial judge before commencing the delivery of the opening statement.

6 Direct Testimony

§6.01 In General

The presentation of the direct testimony of an eyewitness differs little from the presentation of the direct testimony of most other types of witnesses. Obviously, however, since an eyewitness is almost always a very important witness in the case, the attorney must take special care in preparing and presenting the testimony of an eyewitness. It is especially important that a lawyer doing the examination of an eyewitness lay a solid foundation for the crucial testimony by showing that the witness' opportunity to observe was conducive to an accurate observation. The foundation testimony should take into account the psychological factors affecting observation as well as the physical factors.

§6.02 Form of the Question

The general rule for the direct examination of an eyewitness is the same as for the direct examination of any other witness in regard to the form of the question: "Leading questions should not be used on the direct examination of a witness except as may be necessary to develop his testimony."[1] There are, of course, a number of exceptions to this rule. Leading questions are permitted for preliminary matters, for matters not in controversy, for matters that are of no real consequence, and for the introduction of new material. Thus, for example, having established that the victim of a purse snatching is employed downtown as a legal secretary, the attorney eliciting her testimony might properly ask: "Now, Ms. Good, directing your attention to the morning of May 3, 1983, did you go to work that day?"

Leading questions are also permitted where the attorney is questioning a hostile witness, a reluctant witness, an adverse party, a witness identified with an adverse party, or a witness with a limited capacity to communicate. These exceptions recognize that certain witnesses—e.g., those who are antagonistic to an attorney or his or her case—are generally uncooperative if permitted to answer open-ended questions; thus, they must usually be controlled by the use of leading questions. This exception also recognizes that certain other witnesses, whether because of youth or advanced age, speech or hearing disabilities, or unfamilarity with English, are unable to communicate effectively in response to open-ended questions. Before using a leading question where one or more of the exceptions in this second group exists, though, it is advisable to obtain the judge's permission. It is easier to get the judge's permission before asking the leading question than to get him or her to change a ruling. The attorney might proceed as follows.

> The Prosecutor: Your honor, Ms. Good's jaw is wired shut owing to an occurrence which will become clear as her testimony develops. In any event, she currently has great difficulty saying anything but "yes" or "no". I respectfully request, therefore, to be allowed to use leading questions in questioning her.

---

[1] Fed R Evid 611(c).

Finally, leading questions may be used to help a witness remember. Ideally, of course, an eyewitness does not forget his or her testimony. When it happens, however, the attorney may refresh the witness' recollection by use of a document or by using a leading question. Assume that Ms. Good, the victim of the purse snatching, has testified that her purse contained keys, a letter from her boyfriend, her checkbook, and a compact.

Q. Do you recall if there was anything else in your purse when the defendant grabbed it?

[*Note:* Do not ask simply, "Was there anything else in your purse?" The witness might say, "No."]

A. No.

Q. Your memory is exhausted at this point then?

A. Yes.

Q. Is there anything that would refresh your recollection?

A. The police report might. I told the police officer and he wrote it all down.

[*Note:* Anything that will refresh the witness' recollection may be used.]

Q. I show you what has previously been marked as State's Exhibit 1 for identification. Is this the police report you just mentioned?

[*Note:* The exhibit should be marked even if it is not going to be introduced into evidence.]

A. Yes.

Q. Please read it to yourself and return it to me.

[*Note:* The witness should not testify from the document.]

A. I have read the report. You may take it.

Q. Is your memory refreshed so that you have a present recollection of what else was in your purse?

A. Yes.

Q. What else was in your purse?

A. A $20 bill.

If there were no police reports or other documents, the lawyer might proceed as follows.

> The Prosecutor: Your honor, Ms. Good's memory of this matter is obviously exhausted. I request that I be allowed to refresh her recollection with a leading question.
>
> The Judge: Proceed.
>
> The Prosecutor: Would it refresh your recollection if I suggested that you also had a $20 bill in your purse?

A. Yes, that's right; there was a $20 bill, too.

If all else fails, and there is a document available listing the contents of the purse that the witness can testify is accurate even though it does not refresh her present recollection, the past recollection recorded exception to the hearsay rule may be of help. Pursuant to Rule 803(5) of the Federal Rules of Evidence, such a document (a record or memorandum) can be admitted if the witness once had knowledge about a matter as to which he or she now does not have sufficient recollection to enable him or her to testify fully and accurately. The document can be admitted only if the document was made or adopted by the witness when his or her memory was fresh, and if the witness can state that the document was accurate when it was made or adopted by him or her. Such an examination might proceed as follows.

Q. Do you remember the serial number of the $20 bill that was in your purse when the defendant took it?

A. No.

Q. Did you ever record the serial number of that bill?

A. Yes.

Q. When?

A. When I put it in my purse the day before the defendant attacked me.

Q. Did you accurately record the serial number?

A. Yes.

Q. Would it refresh your recollection if I showed you the record you made?

A. No, I couldn't remember the number accurately even looking at my record.

Q. I hand you State's Exhibit 2 for identification. Is that the record you made?

A. Yes.

Q. Is the record you made the day before the defendant robbed you in the same condition now as it was when you made it?

A. Yes.

[*Note:* Under Rule 803(5) of the Federal Rules of Evidence, the record would now be read by the witness but not admitted as an exhibit. In most states, the document would first be admitted into evidence as an exhibit and then shown to the jury.]

Knowing when a leading question may be used in direct examination does not necessarily mean knowing when a question is leading. Probably about 20 per cent of all the questions in the world are clearly leading—for example, "The streetlights were on at 8:30 p.m., were they not?" Similarly, probably about 20 per cent of all the questions in the world are clearly not leading—for example, "What were the lighting conditions like?" With all the rest, it depends on the judge. Who else can say if the following are leading?—"Were the streetlights on?" and "Tell us whether or not the streetlights were on."

The competent direct examiner can rephrase any question so that even the most incompetent judge will find it not to be leading. The competent direct examiner does not use nonleading questions solely because the rules of evidence require him or her to do so, however. Open-ended, nonleading questions allow the witness to do the talking. Because the witness is doing the talking, the jury's attention is focused on the witness. Since the case will be won only if the jury believes that the witness accurately observed and recalls that to which he or she is testifying, it is important that the jury hear the witness, not the lawyer, say what happened. For this reason, the preferred form for asking the key questions of an eyewitness is open-ended and nonleading. For variety, and to avoid boring testimony, the nonleading questions should be interspersed with some leading questions about less important matters.

The key to forming good questions for the direct examination of an eyewitness is the ability to formulate nonleading questions which are, at the same time, specific. Absent a totally *rehearsed* examination—which usually results in a nervous witness who sounds like he or she is telling a fabricated story—there is no other way the examining attorney can control the testimony. The lawyer wants the witness to tell what he or she saw in a particular order, emphasizing some things and skipping over others. The attorney can do this effectively only if he or she knows what the witness is going to say in response to each question, and the questions must be specific. If a lawyer asks the witness simply, "Please describe the intersection of Clark and Diversey," the odds are that neither the witness nor the attorney knows what the response is going to be. The witness might talk about any or all of a thousand different things, which may or may not help the proponent's case. Specific questions, on the other hand, draw the picture deftly in the way the attorney wants it to come out.

Q. Which way does Clark Street run?
Q. How many lanes of traffic are there?
Q. Are there any stoplights at the intersection?
Q. How many?
Q. Where are they located?

The good direct examiner knows precisely what response he or she wants; then, he or she asks a nonleading question which is nevertheless so specific that the witness knows exactly what to talk about. This technique, of course, puts the witness at ease, since he or she knows what the lawyer is leading toward, and since he or she is not struggling to remember a prepared narrative. The effect is that the witness appears more credible and the testimony more coherent. The disadvantage of this method is that the lawyer has to think of a few questions beyond "Please describe what is located there" and "Did anything unusual happen?" But just as a 15-round fight cannot be fought with one punch, or a three-hour movie made with one exposure, a direct examination cannot be conducted with one question.

§6.03 Structuring the Direct Testimony

Assuming the attorney can formulate good, nonleading, specific questions, he or she must decide what to ask about and in what order. What to ask about is determined mostly by the planned closing argument, which in turn is determined by the theory of the case. The purpose of direct examination is to supply ammunition for the closing argument. It follows, therefore, that facts which do not in some way fit into the closing argument should be omitted. Therefore, the closing argument must be prepared before the direct examination questions.

Once the attorney knows what he or she is going to ask the witness to describe, he or she must determine the order in which he or she will ask about different things. In the case of a typical eyewitness, the structure of the direct examination is generally simple and straightforward. The first series of questions develops the witness' background.

The second set of questions sets the scene and lays the foundation for the witness being in a physical place and psychological condition to observe accurately what was happening. Finally, the witness describes what he or she saw.

§6.04 —The Background of the Witness

The proponent of the eyewitness wants to develop the witness' background in order to get the jury to like and trust the witness and to believe the testimony. Ideally, the witness has a background similar in some respects to that of at least some of the jurors. For instance, if the witness is a Girl Scout leader, and if the foreperson of the jury is also a Girl Scout leader, that juror is quite likely to be receptive to the testimony of the witness. In addition, most jurors, like people in general, are interested in other people. The jurors want to know about the witness for the same reason that people read *People* magazine, and they resent the lawyer who does not let them indulge their curiosity. Finally, background questions also give the witness an opportunity to adjust to the courtroom by answering a few easy questions.

As a matter of strategy, the attorney must decide how much background is too much. Too much background is boring no matter who the witness is, but it is more important to develop the backgrounds of some witnesses than of others. It is usually not nearly as important for the prosecution to delve deeply into the background of the complaining witness who is the victim of a purse snatching as it is for the defense to develop the background of the college student who is accused of the crime.

Strategy aside, the extent to which a witness' background can be developed is largely within the trial judge's discretion. The proponent of the witness normally argues that the witness' background is relevant because the jury is charged with deciding whether the witness is credible, and in order to do so they must know something about the witness. The opponent argues that all witnesses are presumed credible until their credibility is attacked, and that therefore the background testimony is irrelevant.

§6.05 —The Scene

The eyewitness testifies to what he or she saw. Therefore, it is important to show the jury that he or she was in a position to see what he or she claims to have seen. Essentially, this involves distance, lighting, and lack of obstruction. The witness must testify how close he or she was to what he or she saw, what the lighting conditions were, and that his or her view was unobstructed. He or she must also testify, of course, that he or she was looking in the right direction, that he or she had enough time to observe what was going on, and that his or her eyesight was adequate.

The good trial lawyer does more than just touch the bases, though. He or she wants the jurors to see a picture in their minds and to remember it. In most cases, the lawyer uses a photograph or a diagram in setting the scene, but he or she must also be able to develop a verbal description. Even when an exhibit is used, it is usually more effective to have a witness describe the scene in purely verbal terms first, and then to introduce the exhibit. This way of proceeding has two advantages. First, the verbal description demonstrates that the witness is familiar with the scene. Second, it assures that the jury both hears and sees the description of the scene. If a photograph or diagram is introduced into evidence before the verbal description, there is a risk that an objection that the photograph or diagram *speaks for itself* will be sustained when the witness is asked to describe the scene. If the attorney fears that a particular witness may give a verbal description which is not consistent with the exhibit, however, the exhibit should be introduced without the prior verbal description.

Any technique used to get a witness to describe the scene effectively requires that the attorney know precisely what he or she wants the witness to describe. It is all right to ask the witness to describe the intersection of Wells and Jackson, as long as the attorney is not content to stop there and be satisfied with whatever the witness happens to say. Even a well-prepared, articulate witness who is accustomed to testifying in court invariably leaves out some important details or does not give the details enough emphasis. The lawyer must be prepared to ask additional questions, such as in the following example.[2]

Q. Officer, are you familiar with the intersection of Wells and Jackson?

A. Yes.

Q. How often have you been there?

A. Hundreds of times.

---

[2] This fact scenario is based upon the problem "NITA Liquor Control Commission v. Jones, et al," *Problems and Cases in Trial Advocacy, Law School Edition,* 2nd Ed. (1981), which is published by the National Institute for Trial Advocacy (NITA). Adapted and reproduced with the permission of NITA.

Q. Are you familiar with how the intersection looked on [the day in question]?

A. Yes, I was there that day.

Q. Please describe the intersection and tell us what is located there.

A. Well, Wells Street runs east and west. It is two lanes. So is Jackson, which runs north and south. There are stoplights at all four corners. On the northwest corner there is a rooming house. On the northeast corner is a parking lot. There is a drug store on the southeast corner. A liquor store is located on the southwest corner.

Q. Are there any crosswalks at the intersection?

A. Yes, at all four corners.

Q. How wide are the crosswalks?

A. Each is about eight feet wide.

Q. Are there any streetlights in the area of Wells and Jackson?

A less articulate witness, especially one who is not accustomed to testifying in court, may well answer a bit differently. For example:

Q. Please describe the intersection of Wells and Jackson.

A. It is busy:

This kind of answer merely requires the attorney to ask more questions.

Q. Which way does Wells Street run?

A. East and west.

Q. Which way does Jackson run?

A direct examination properly setting the scene for subsequent eyewitness testimony by a police officer that he or she saw a drunk walk across a street, enter a tavern, and buy a bottle of wine might go as follows.

Q. Officer, directing your attention to August 1, 1983, at approximately 8:45 p.m., where were you?

A. I was at the intersection of Wells and Jackson.

Q. Were you on foot, or were you in your car?

A. I was in my official Liquor Control Commission vehicle.

Q. Were you alone or with someone else?

A. I was with my partner, Ron Smith.

Q. Where were you located with respect to the intersection of Wells Street and Jackson Avenue?

A. We were parked about a hundred feet south of Wells Street on the east side of Jackson.

Q. From where you were parked, could you see the northwest corner of Wells and Jackson?

A. Yes.

Q. Was there anything that obstructed your view of that corner?

A. No.

Q. Will you tell us what the lighting conditions were like at approximately 8:45 p.m.?

A. It was just turning dusk, but there was enough natural light to see.

Q. Were the streetlights on or off?

A. The streetlights had just come on.

Q. You have testified previously that a liquor store was located on the southwest corner of Wells and Jackson. What was the name of that store?

A. The Gold Seal Liquor Store.

Q. Where were you parked in relation to the Gold Seal Liquor Store?

A. I was parked directly across the street from the Gold Seal Liquor Store.

Q. Were you directly across the street from the east wall of the liquor store?

A. That is correct.

Q. Please tell us whether or not there are any windows on the east side of the Gold Seal Liquor Store.

A. Yes, there is a large plate glass window on that wall.

Q. What were the lighting conditions inside the liquor store at the time you indicated previously, 8:45 p.m.?

A. The lights were on inside the store.

Q. Could you see into the liquor store from where you were located in your car?

A. Yes.

Q. Was anything obstructing your view?

A. No.

Q. Do you know a person by the name of Kendall Walters?

The officer should now be able to testify that he saw Kendall Walters cross the street and go into the liquor store and purchase a bottle of wine.

§6.06 —Psychological and Physiological Factors Affecting Identification

The psychological and physiological factors which affect identification are in general of more concern to the cross-examiner than to the direct examiner. The direct examiner usually simply puts forward testimony that the witness was in a position to see what he or she says he or she saw and leaves the more subtle areas of eyewitness identification to the cross-examiner. One exception, of course, is eyesight. The direct examiner should bring out either that the witness' eyesight is good without glasses or that the witness was wearing glasses at the time he or she observed the event. If the witness wears glasses, the direct examiner should bring out what the witness' eyesight is when wearing glasses and when the witness last had his or her eyes examined.

If there are any special factors which served as a stimulus to observation, the direct examiner should of course bring them out. Similarly, if factors existed which might have caused the witness to be less than fully observant, the direct examiner should be careful to avoid them. For instance, if the police officer in **§6.05** who was parked across the street from the Gold Seal Liquor Store was there for the express purpose of observing activity in the store, it will probably be assumed that his observations are more likely to be accurate than if he just happened to be parked across the street while he was eating a doughnut. Therefore, the direct examiner should bring out why the police officer was present. On the other hand, if the purse-snatching victim in **§6.02** had a spent a particularly long day at the office and was especially tired when she got off the bus to return home, it will probably be assumed that her ability to observe was less than it normally might have been. In this case, the direct examiner should probably omit any testimony about the particularly long day or about the victim being tired.

Some psychological factors are difficult to assess. Psychological experiments tend to show that while a certain level of excitement increases the accuracy of observation, a higher level of excitement, like that caused by viewing violence, actually decreases the accuracy of perception. Many lay persons believe, however, that violent scenes are more likely to be perceived and recalled accurately. Likewise, while psychologists believe that fear decreases the ability to perceive accurately, many laypersons seem to believe that observations made at such a time are particularly reliable because the images have become *etched in the memory*. Thus, it is common for prosecutors to have victims of violent of crimes testify that they will "never forget that face because I was afraid it might be the last face I'd ever see." Whether or not this is a good technique may depend on whether the defense will be permitted to introduce expert testimony on the issue of identification and the type of jury instruction that is given in the jurisdiction on the issue of eyewitness identification.

Although scientific evidence tends to refute the belief, juries seem to believe that witnesses who have professional training or experience in perception, such as police officers, FBI agents, or security guards, are more reliable eyewitnesses than other people. The direct examiner is well advised to stress the eyewitness' professional training or prior experience in making identifications if the witness has such training or experience.

Other factors strengthening the witness' preceptions might include that the witness was in good health at the time of the perception, that he or she had gotten a good night's sleep the night before, that he or she was not under the influence of any drug or medication at the time of his or her observations, and so forth. Since most people believe that perception is enhanced where a person is calm at the time the observation is made, it is a good idea to bring out that fact where it is true. Similarly, although this sometimes can cut both ways, it should be brought out that a witness expected an event to occur and was not surprised by the occurrence where this is true. If the event occurred in a setting with which the witness is familiar, that also should be brought out, because a person is less likely to be mistaken about observations made in familiar circumstances.

In strengthening a witness' observations, it is also helpful to bring out, where applicable, that no distractions competed with the event in question for the witness' attention. If the witness was on the same level as the event which he or she perceived and to which he or she is testifying, that fact also should be brought out, as should the lack of any obstructions to the witness' vision. Where identification of a person is a critical issue, the amount of time that the subject's face was in view should be emphasized. It can be brought out that the witness saw the other person's full face and that, in addition, he or she got profile views. If the witness knew the other person, that fact must be emphasized.

As mentioned in **§6.05,** closeness to the scene is particularly important. Since many witnesses are not adept at estimating distances, however, it is often necessary to demonstrate in the courtroom the distance the witness was from the event. This demonstration can be done by having the direct examiner walk slowly away from the witness stand after having asked the witness to tell him or her to stop walking when the examiner gets to a point equal to the distance the witness was from the occurrence to which he or she is testifying.

A question which almost always arises in regard to the testimony of an eyewitness is how many details should be included in the testimony. The advantage of including details is that the perception of great detail makes the testimony appear highly credible. Thus, if in an identification case, the witness can give not only a general description (including height, weight, age, sex, and build) but can also describe the person's attire (e.g., shoes, pants, jacket, hat, overcoat, belt, and tie), facial characteristics (such as mouth, eyes, forehead, hair, nose, chin, hairline, teeth, and glasses), and, in addition, special identifying features (such as a tattoo), the identification will appear highly credible. The problem is that the use of many details increases the areas in which the witness can be impeached. As psychologists know, the mind or memory tends to fill in details even where those details where not actually perceived. Thus, the use of great detail may in the end discredit the testimony of the witness. For instance, if a purse-snatching victim testifies that the perpetrator had a tattoo on his left hand, and the defendant has no such tattoo, it will probably make little difference to the jury that all the other details of the description match the defendant. In the same way, one must be careful not to overemphasize the opportunity the witness had to observe details. If, for example, the purse-snatching victim were to testify that she looked closely at the face of her assailant, directly under a streetlight, for a period of about two minutes, carefully observing every feature of his clean-shaven face, the jury might be very impressed if the defendant could prove he had a mustache at the time of the robbery.

§6.07 —Dramatizing the Action

Assuming the jury is convinced that the witness was in a good position to observe, that the conditions for observation were propitious, and that the witness' perception, memory, and recall are all functioning properly, it is still necessary that the witness communicate what he or she perceived to the jury in such a way that the jury will itself have a vivid picture of what the witness saw. A good picture is best painted using a number of short strokes. Here, the direct examiner wants to communicate to the jury by using a number of questions about the important event. Usually, where the neophyte will use one question and then go on to some other point, the accomplished trial lawyer will ask about 10 questions, drawing a much more vivid and complete picture. The technique is simply to break the action down into small segments. Assume, for example, that the police officer in **§6.05**[3] is attempting to describe how a subject walked across a street. The direct examiner hopes to convey to the jury that the subject was intoxicated. A beginning trial lawyer might proceed in this manner:

Q. Officer, will you please tell us what Mr. Walters did next?

A. He walked across the street.

Q. Tell us, please, how Mr. Walters was walking.

> The Defense Attorney: Objection. The question calls for a characterization.
>
> The Judge: Sustained

Q. What did you see Mr. Walters do as he walked across the street?

A. He stumbled.

Q. And after Mr. Walters crossed the street, what did he do?

A more experienced trial lawyer might ask the questions a bit differently.

Q. When you first saw Mr. Walters, what was he doing?

A. He was standing on the corner.

Q. Is that the northwest corner of Wells and Jackson?

A. Yes.

Q. Where was Mr. Walters standing in relation to the stoplight on that corner, which you described earlier?

A. He was holding on to the stoplight.

Q. Please describe Mr. Walters' appearance at the time you saw him hanging on to the stoplight.

A. His hair was disheveled, his shirt was completely unbuttoned, he had on only one shoe, and his pants appeared to be ripped at the knee.

Q. At the time you first saw Mr. Walters hanging on to the stoplight, what was he doing?

---

[3] This fact scenario is based upon the problem "NITA Liquor Control Commission v. Jones, et al," *Problems and Cases in Trial Advocacy, Law School Edition,* 2nd Ed. (1981), which is published by the National Institute for Trial Advocacy (NITA). Adapted and reproduced with the permission of NITA.

A. Vomiting.
Q. What did Mr. Walters do next?
A. He walked across Wells Street and went into the Gold Seal Liquor Store.
Q. Did you see Mr. Walters walk from the stoplight to the curb at Wells Street?
A. Yes.
Q. Would you describe for us how Mr. Walters was walking as he went from the stoplight to the curb?
A. He was staggering.

The Defense Attorney: Objection. That is a characterization, and I ask that the answer be struck.
The Judge: Well, the objection is sustained, even if it came a bit late. And the jury is instructed to disregard the answer.

Q. Tell us whether or not Mr. Walters walked directly from the stoplight to the curb?
A. No, it wasn't direct; he zigzagged.
Q. When Mr. Walters got to the curb at the northside of Wells Street, did he proceed directly across the street?
A. He did not.
Q. What did he do?
A. He stood on the curb and appeared to be swaying.
Q. How long did he stay there like that?
A. About five or ten seconds.
Q. Then what happened?
A. He lost his balance, and he fell.
Q. What did he do next?
A. He crawled back up to the curb on the north side of Wells Street.
Q. At that time, where were you located in relation to the stoplight at the northwest corner of Wells and Jackson?
A. I was southeast of it.
Q. Could you see the color of the light from where you were located?
A. Yes.
Q. What color was the light for pedestrians crossing Wells Street?
A. It was red.

Q. What did Mr. Walters do after he crawled back up on the curb at Wells and Jackson?

A. He stood up.

Q. Then what happened?

A. He fell over backward.

Q. What happened after that?

A. He picked himself up and proceeded to walk across the street.

Q. What color was the stoplight for pedestrians crossing Wells Street at this point?

A. It was still red.

Q. As Mr. Walters walked across Wells Street, where was he walking in relation to the lines of the crosswalk, which you previously described?

A. He stayed mostly within the crosswalk.

Q. Will you tell us how he was walking in relation to each of the lines that formed the crosswalk on Wells Street?

A. He was zigzagging. He would walk from the line on one side of the crosswalk to the line on the other side of the crosswalk.

Q. If you know, how wide is the crosswalk at Wells Street?

A. It is about eight feet wide.

Q. And Wells is a four-lane street?

A. Yes.

Q. In walking across Wells Street in the crosswalk, approximately how many times, to the best of your recollection, did Mr. Walters walk from the line on one side of the crosswalk to the other line of the crosswalk?

A. I would say about three times.

Q. Were you still watching Mr. Walters when he got to the other side of the street?

A. Yes.

Q. What happened when he reached the curb on the south side of Wells Street?

A. He again stumbled.

Q. What did he do then?

A. He crawled up on to the sidewalk.

Q. What did he do next?

A. He stood up, and he walked into the Gold Seal Liquor Store.

Q. Did he walk directly into the liquor store?

The use of a series of short questions can also create the impression that an event took a long time to occur and that the witness had a length opportunity to observe what was happening. This factor may be especially important where the principal issue is the identification of a person. A neophyte prosecutor questioning the purse-snatching victim from **§6.02**[4] might proceed like this:

Q. After you got off the bus and had walked about two blocks toward your home, what, if anything, unusual happened?

A. I heard a noise, and when I turned around, I saw a man who ran up from behind me, pushed me down, grabbed my purse, and ran away.

Q. What did you do next?

A. I went home and called the police.

A more accomplished prosecutor might proceed somewhat differently.

Q. After you got off the bus and had walked about two blocks toward your home, what happened?

A. I heard a noise and turned around. I saw a man running toward me. He grabbed my purse, pulled me down, and ran away.

Q. What was the noise you heard that made you turn around?

A. The sound of a man running.

Q. When you turned around, what did you see?

A. I saw a man.

Q. Approximately how far from you was the man when you first turned around?

A. I would say he was about as far away from me as you are from me now.

Q. Let the record reflect that she has indicated a distance of approximately 30 feet.

The Judge: The record may so reflect.

---

[4] This fact scenario is based upon the problem "State v. Lawrence," *Problems and Cases in Trial Advocacy, Law School Edition,* 2nd Ed. (1981), which is published by the National Institute for Trial Advocacy (NITA). Adapted and reproduced with the permission of NITA.

Q. Where was the man at that time in relation to the nearest street light?

A. There was a streetlight on the same side of the street we were on, approximately halfway between him and me.

Q. Did you have any difficulty seeing the man at that time?

A. No.

Q. Was the lighting such that you could see what the person looked like and what he was wearing?

A. Yes.

Q. Please describe the man who was coming toward you.

A. He had long hair and a beard; he was about six feet tall, and he was wearing a black T-shirt and white pants. He was of medium build.

Q. Do you see that man in court today?

A. Yes.

Q. Would you point him out, please?

A. He is the person in the three-piece suit sitting at the counsel table next to the defense lawyer.

Q. May the record reflect that the witness has identified the defendant, Paul Pure?

The Court: It may.

Q. Now, when you first saw Mr. Pure, Ms. Good, which way was he facing?

A. Well, he was facing west.

Q. And which way were you facing at that time?

A. I was facing east.

Q. So you and Mr. Pure were facing each other at this time, is that correct?

A. Yes.

Q. Now what did Mr. Pure do after you first saw him?

A. He came toward me.

Q. And which way was he facing as he came toward you?

A. He was still facing west.

Q. And which way were you facing?

A. I was facing east.

Q. Was there anything between you and Mr. Pure at this time which would obstruct your vision of him?
A. No.
Q. What did Mr. Pure do next?
A. He grabbed my purse.
Q. When he grabbed your purse, approximately how far away from you was he?
A. About a foot; I'd say about 12 inches.
Q. How far, at this time, was his face from your face?
A. I would say about the same.
Q. At the point when he grabbed your purse, which way were you facing in relation to him?
A. I was facing him.
Q. Which way was he facing in relation to you?
A. He was facing me.
Q. At this time, were you standing up, or were you on the ground?
A. I was standing up.
Q. Is it correct to say that you were standing face to face with Mr. Pure at that point?
A. Yes.
Q. Now at the time when he grabbed your purse and you were standing face to face, how far were the two of you from the nearest streetlight?
A. Approximately 15 feet.
Q. After Mr. Pure grabbed your purse, what happened?
A. He pushed me down.
Q. Would you describe for us, please, how you fell?
A. I fell backward.
Q. Immediately after you fell, which way were you looking?
A. I was looking up.
Q. And where was Mr. Pure at this time?
A. He was standing over me.
Q. And which way was Mr. Pure looking at this time?
A. He was looking down at me.
Q. What did Mr. Pure do next?
A. He turned and ran away.

Q. Which way did he run?

A. He ran back east, toward Clark Street.

Q. What did you do?

A. I watched him until I was sure he was gone, and then I got up and ran home and called the police.

§6.08 Corroboration

Assume the following facts are true in the hypothetical purse-snatching case described in **§§6.02** and **6.07.** Immediately after getting to her house, the victim, Ms. Good, called the police, and shortly thereafter a police officer came to her house and asked her to relate what had happened and to describe her assailant. The description given by Ms. Good of her assailant was that he had long hair and a beard, that he was about six feet tall, that he was wearing a black T-shirt and white pants, and that he was of medium build. The police officer dutifully copied down the description and incorporated it into his police report, which is available under the rules of discovery to both sides. Assume, further, that the defendant in the hypothetical case was caught red-handed three days later snatching another woman's purse. The investigating officer in the Good case called Ms. Good the following day, told her of the apprehension of the defendant, and asked her to come down to the police station to see if she could identify him as her assailant as well. Once at the police station, the investigating officer showed Ms. Good two mug shots of the defendant. After that, the investigating officer had Ms. Good look at a lineup in which the only person who had a beard and was wearing a black T-shirt and white pants was the defendant. Ms. Good picked the defendant out of the lineup as the man who stole her purse.

Assume that all the above facts, except the second purse snatching, are admissible into evidence. From the standpoint of strategy alone, does the prosecution want to bring out the corroborative description and identifications? Most lawyers who are unaccustomed to trying eyewitness identification cases would initially answer in the affirmative. Thinking, as they should, in terms of their closing argument, these attorneys want to be able to say to the jury:

> Ladies and gentlemen, not only do we have Ms. Good's description and identification of the defendant here in court today, but we also have the description which she gave to the police officer only moments after this crime occurred. That description, ladies and gentlemen, matches the defendant exactly. Moreover, we have

the photographic identification. Not only did Ms. Good identify the defendant here in court and accurately describe him to a police officer, but three days after this crime occurred, she accurately and unhesitatingly identified not one but two pictures of the defendant that she saw at the police station. And, ladies and gentlemen, not only did Ms. Good accurately identify two pictures of the defendant, she also picked him out of a lineup at the police station. Thus, what we have here is not just the identification in court today; we have a whole history of accurate descriptions and accurate identifications of the defendant as the perpetrator of this dastardly crime.

A more experienced prosecutor, however, may well hesitate before introducing evidence of the description to the police officer, the photographic identification, and the lineup. Each of these elements opens up vast areas for cross-examination. The description made to the police officer shortly after the event may be accurate, but it is also very sparse. The cross-examiner will, undoubtedly, proceed something like this:

Q. When the investigating officer arrived at your house, Ms. Good, were the recent events still very fresh in your memory?

A. Yes.

Q. And this includes the description of your assailant, correct?

A. Yes.

Q. Did Officer Right ask you to describe your assailant to him?

A. Yes.

Q. At this point, you and the officer were sitting down, is that right?

A. Yes.

Q. And the officer was taking notes?

A. Yes.

Q. You knew he was asking for a description in order that the police might be able to catch the person who took your purse, right?

A. Yes.

Q. And you wanted to see that person caught?

A. Yes.

Q. Therefore, you were careful to give Officer Right a full and accurate description of your assailant to the best of your ability, right?

A. Yes.
Q. And did you describe your assailant to the best of your ability?
A. Yes.
Q. But you did not tell Officer Right anything about the shape of your assailant's mouth, did you?
A. No.
Q. You did not tell the officer anything about the color of your assailant's eyes, did you?
A. No.
Q. You did not tell the officer about the shape of his eyes or how far apart they were, did you?
A. No.
Q. You did not tell the officer about the shape of your assailant's forehead, did you?
A. No.
Q. You did not tell the officer anything about the color of your assailant's hair?
A. No.
Q. You did not tell the officer anything about the shape of your assailant's nose?
A. No.
Q. You did not tell the officer anything about the shape of his chin, did you?
A. No.
Q. You did not tell the officer anything about your assailant's teeth, did you?
A. No.
Q. You did not say anything about your assailant's age when you described him to the officer, did you?
A. No.
Q. And you did not describe anything about the shoes the man was wearing?
A. No.
Q. You did not say whether or not he was wearing a belt, did you?
A. No.
Q. And you did not describe to the officer any tattoo on the assailant, did you?

A. No.

Q. You did not say anything about his having a scar over his right eye, did you?

A. No.

Q. Now, in the neighborhood of Clark and Diversey, there is nothing unusual about seeing a six-foot-tall male of medium build who has long hair and a beard, is there?

A. No.

Q. And there is nothing unusual about seeing males in that neighborhood wearing black T-shirts and white pants, is there?

A. No.

Similarly, the cross-examination about the photographic identification may also weaken the prosecution's case.

Q. Now, Ms. Good, when you received a call from the investigating officer three days after you were attacked and he asked you to come down to the police station, you still wanted to see the person who took your purse get caught, didn't you?

A. Yes.

Q. And you were hoping that when you got to the police station, you would see the person who took your purse, weren't you?

A. Yes.

Q. Now, when you got to the police station, the first things the investigating officer showed you were two photographs, right?

A. Yes.

Q. They were photographs of the same person, correct?

A. Yes.

Q. The officer didn't show you a book of photographs containing pictures of different people, did he?

A. No.

Q. He didn't put a spread of various photographs of different people on a desk in front of you, did he?

A. No.

Q. He did not even give you a pile of photographs of different people and ask you to look through them and see if you could identify anyone, did he?

A. No.

Q. What he did was give you two photographs of a person who looked like the man who had taken your purse, right?
A. Yes.
Q. Those two photographs were photographs of the defendant, correct?
A. Yes.
Q. And at this point you were still hoping they had caught the man who took your purse, were you not?
A. Yes.

Similarly, the testimony about the lineup can also backfire a bit.

Q. You say that after you looked at the two photographs you were shown a lineup?
A. Yes.
Q. And you saw in the lineup the man whose photograph you had just seen?
A. Yes.
Q. You were expecting to see him there, were you not?
A. Not especially.
Q. Well you were hoping to see him there, were you not?
A. I guess so.
Q. How many people were in the lineup?
A. Five.
Q. And of the five people in the lineup, how many had on white pants?
A. One.
Q. And of the five men in the lineup how many had on black T-shirts?
A. One.
Q. And of the five men in the lineup how many had beards?
A. Only one.
Q. Isn't it fair to say, then, that only one of the five people matched the description of the assailant that you had given the investigating officer?
A. Well, to that extent.

It may be, of course, that cross-examination on the points mentioned above will be conducted whether or not the material is brought out on direct examination, but the defense attorney may feel that it is the safer course not to get into things that have not been brought up on direct examination. Some judges have even been known to sustain objections of *beyond the scope of direct examination* to lines of questioning such as those outlined above, although such rulings are incorrect in light of the witness' identification of the defendant. Similarly, it is unfortunate, but true, that not all defense lawyers recognize that the corroborative description, the photographic identification, and the lineup identification may be explored in cross-examination, even if they are not brought out on direct, because they are extremely relevant to the accuracy of the identification. In addition, the defense lawyer faces a dilemma if he or she has previously won motions to suppress the photographic and lineup identifications, but not the in-court identification, and then has to decide whether or not to bring up on cross-examination what he or she has previously managed to keep the prosecutor from developing.

Thus, in the example of the purse snatching, it may be that if the complaining witness' identification is quite strong, the prosecutor would gladly forgo getting into the subsequent corroborative description and identifications. However, the victim's identification testimony is often weak. For example, in the case of Ms. Good, the cross-examiner may well bring out these facts: that Ms. Good had spent a long day at the office and was tired; that she had just gotten off a bus in which the lighting inside was much brighter than the lighting on the street, requiring her eyes to adjust to the difference in lighting; that trees along the street cast deep shadows over the sidewalk; that the whole event occurred very quickly; and that Ms. Good, who was quite shaken by the whole event, had her glasses knocked off as soon as she turned around to confront her assailant. Such a cross-examination, in abbreviated form, might go something like this:

Q. Now, Ms. Good, you said you went to work about 8:00 in the morning, correct?

A. Yes.

Q. And you say you were returning from work about 9:00 at night, is that correct?

A. Yes.

Q. Is it fair to say that you worked approximately 12 hours that day?

A. Yes.

Q. And the work you do as a secretary is fairly demanding, right?

A. Yes, I guess so.

Q. Would it be fair to say that you had a long day at the office and were tired when you got on the bus?

A. Yes.
Q. Now, when you got on the bus, it was light inside the bus, was it not?
A. Yes.
Q. It was light enough for people to read on the bus, right?
A. Yes.
Q. Did you actually see people reading newspapers or books on the bus?
A. Yes.
Q. And you were on that lighted bus for at least 20 minutes, weren't you?
A. Yes.
Q. So your eyes had become accustomed to the light inside the bus, isn't that correct?
A. Yes.
Q. Now, when you got off the bus at the corner of Clark and Diversey, it was darker outside the bus than it was inside the bus, correct?
A. Well, there were lights on outside the bus too.
Q. Well, you crossed Clark Street and started to walk west on Diversey immediately after getting off the bus, didn't you?
A. Yes.
Q. You cannot read a newspaper at night on the sidewalk at the place where your purse was snatched with the light that is cast by the streetlight there, can you?
A. No, I don't think so.
Q. Isn't it true that there are trees along the south side of Diversey between the sidewalk and the street?
A. Yes.
Q. At the time of this event there were leaves on the trees, were there not?
A. Yes.
Q. The branches of those trees are lower than the top of the streetlights you described, are they not?
A. Yes.
Q. Isn't it fair to say that the trees cast shadows on the street?
A. Yes.
Q. Now, let me see if I understand what happened. Isn't it true that after you got about two blocks from Clark Street, west of Clark

Street, a man ran up behind you and grabbed your purse, pushed you over, and ran away?

A. Yes.

[*Note:* By stating all the action in one sentence, the cross-examiner has made it appear that the incident occurred very quickly. It is just the opposite of what the direct examiner did.]

Q. Now, you say your vision is 20-20 when you are wearing your glasses, is that right?

A. Yes.

Q. But is it not true that your glasses were knocked off as soon as your assailant struck you?

A. Yes.

Q. And that was right after you turned around, wasn't it?

A. Yes.

Q. Will you tell us what your vision is without your glasses?

A. 20-400.

Q. That means, does it not, that what a person with normal vision sees at a distance of 400 feet you cannot see until you are 20 feet away?

A. Yes.

If the prosecutor anticipates such cross-examination, he or she may well decide that it is necessary to corroborate the direct testimony. One should always try to corroborate the testimony of an eyewitness with circumstantial evidence such as fingerprints. Generally, one should also corroborate the testimony of an eyewitness with the testimony of another eyewitness, if one is available. One would usually hesitate to use a second or even a third eyewitness only when there is a substantial likelihood that their stories will be materially different from one another. In the latter case, it is probably preferable to use only one eyewitness, although when stories which differ in substantial detail nevertheless coincide on the important points, it may be preferable to use the additional witnesses.

§6.09 —The Hearsay Rule and the Confrontation Clause

In the United States, many criminal cases proceed to trial on the basis of the uncorroborated testimony of a single eyewitness. In such cases, prosecutors often attempt to bolster the testimony of the single eyewitness in two ways: by having the eyewitness testify that he or she had previously identified the defendant out of court; and by having other witnesses testify to prior identifications by the eyewitness. Although under the common definition of hearsay[5]—an out-of-court statement offered for the truth of the matter asserted—such bolstering testimony is hearsay, Rule 801(d)(1)(C) of the Federal Rules of Evidence states that a statement is not hearsay if "[t]he declarant testifies at the trial or hearing and is subject to cross-examination concerning the statement, and the statement is . . . one of identification of a person made after perceiving him." Similarly, the law of most states permits bolstering by the eyewitness himself or herself. Where the bolstering testimony—the evidence of the prior identification—is from a third party, not from the testifying eyewitness, the rules differ in different states. Some states totally prohibit third-party bolstering.[6] Other states permit it under limited conditions, such as where it is being offered for the purpose of rehabilitating a discredited eyewitness.[7]

The questions of whether or not bolstering is permitted, under what circumstances, and by whom are important issues because prosecutors generally resort to bolstering only where there is a single eyewitness and that eyewitness' in-court identification is weak. It is in those situations, where the eyewitness' testimony has not been impressive and where the in-court identification appears tentative, that the prosecutor would attempt to have the witness himself or herself and other persons testify to previous identifications by the eyewitness. In the normal case, where the eyewitness' testimony in court appears solid and where the in-court identification is made unhesitatingly and positively, the prosecutor would probably avoid any mention of prior identifications. Indeed, it is usually the defense which brings up the prior identifications in these cases, because the defense can then argue that the prior identifications were suggestive and influenced the in-court identification, accounting for the positive and unhesitating manner in which the in-court identification was made. However, where the in-court identification is weak, the defense would like the jury to believe that it is the only identification, the only real evidence in the case, and therefore the defense would attempt to prevent any testimony about prior identifications.

Another form of bolstering is the composite police sketch created by an artist, sometimes using a commercial kit, based on the eyewitness'

---

[5] Fed R Evid 801(c).

[6] *E.g.*, People v Simpson, 39 Ill App 3d 318, 349 NE2d 441 (4th Dist 1976); State v Degraffenreid, 477 SW2d 57 (Mo 1972); People v Malloy, 22 NY2d 559, 240 NE2d 37 (1968); Towning v State, 521 P2d 415 (Okla 1974); Lyons v State, 388 SW 950 (Tx 1965).

[7] *E.g.*, Fisher v State, 642 SW2d 257 (Tx Crim App 1982).

description. The artist's sketch is technical hearsay because its accuracy rests not so much on the accuracy of the artist as on the perceptions of the eyewitness. Nevertheless, some courts permit the introduction of such sketches into evidence where the victim testifies at trial under oath as to the description of the perpetrator and where the artist also testifies.[8] Other courts exclude the sketches when they are offered to corroborate identification testimony[9] but admit them under the prior consistent statement exception to the hearsay rule[10] where the eyewitness testimony has been impeached.[11] In any event, the prosecutor should be aware that the defense may well turn the use of a composite sketch to its advantage by arguing that the police artist's sketch was itself suggestive. Sometimes, the argument can be made that the police artist had a particular person in mind and sketched that person, thereby suggesting to the eyewitness that the suspect was the perpetrator. In other cases, the artist may have no one in particular in mind, but his or her drawing creates an image in the eyewitness' mind which becomes the basis of the eyewitness' subsequent identification.

Another way in which eyewitness testimony can sometimes be bolstered is by introducing a police report, other public record, or transcript containing the identification testimony of an eyewitness who is not available to testify at trial. While it is difficult to conceive that any prosecutor would attempt to proceed with a case where the only eyewitness was not available and there was no strong circumstantial evidence, it is not inconceivable that a prosecutor might attempt to bolster the testimony of a single eyewitness with the statement of another eyewitness who is currently unavailable, and which statement is contained in a police report, other public report, or transcript. Although, traditionally, such statements would be considered hearsay, Rule 803(8) of the Federal Rules of Evidence makes an exception for public records, and Rule 803(6) makes an exception for records of regularly conducted activities. Moreover, under Rule 804(b)(1), former testimony is not excluded by the hearsay rule if the declarant is unavailable as a witness and if the testimony was given at a hearing at which the party against whom the testimony is being offered had an opportunity and motive to cross-examine the witness.

In addition to the hearsay problem with such bolstering, however,

---

[8] *E.g.*, People v Rogers, 81 Ill 2d 571, 44 Ill Dec 254, 411 NE2d 223 (1980); Commonwealth v Joseph III, 421 NE2d 105 (Mass App Ct 1980).

[9] *E.g.*, People v Jennings, 23 AD2d 621, 257 NYS2d 456 (1965); Commonwealth v Rothlisberger, 197 Pa Super 451, 178 A2d 853 (Pa Super Ct 1962).

[10] *See e.g.*, Fed R Evid 801(d)(1)(B).

[11] *E.g.*, People v Peterson, 25 AD2d 437, 266 NYS2d 884 (1966).

there is a constitutional problem created by the confrontation clause of the Sixth Amendment.[12] Recognizing this problem, Rule 803(8) of the Federal Rules of Evidence excludes from the public record exception to the hearsay rule, in criminal prosecutions, reports of "matters observed by police officers and other law enforcement personnel" and "factual findings resulting from an investigation made pursuant to authority granted by the law." It has been held, however, that this exclusion applies only to the prosecution and does not apply when it is the defendant who seeks to have the police report admitted.[13] The reason for the exclusion when the government seeks to offer a report prepared by its agents against a defendant in a criminal prosecution is that the adversarial posture of the parties causes serious questions about the reliability of the report. Rule 803(6) of the Federal Rules of Evidence does not contain any similar exclusion; however, that rule does exclude records where "the source of information or the method or circumstances of preparation indicate lack of trustworthiness." It can be strongly argued that this portion of Rule 803(6) incorporates the Rule 803(8) exclusion of police reports. The same argument can be made for the catch-all exception, Rule 803(24), which excepts from the hearsay rule, in certain circumstances, statements not specifically covered by "any of the foregoing exceptions but having equivalent circumstantial guarantees of truthworthiness. . . ." Some states, such as Illinois, exclude medical records or police accident reports from the business record exception to the hearsay rule.[14]

In *California v Green*[15] and *Dutton v Evans,*[16] the Supreme Court of the United States rejected the argument that the rule against hearsay and the confrontation clause were coextensive. In *Roberts v Ohio,*[17] the Court explained that the competing interest of an accused's right to confront and cross-examine witnesses against him or her and the state's interest in effective law enforcement could in general be accomodated by a two-part test. First, the prosecution must demonstrate that the out-of-court declarant, whose statement the government seeks to use against the defendant, is in fact unavailable at trial. Second, the government must show that the out-of-court statement bears adequate "indicia of reliability." The Court indicated in a footnote, however, that such

---

[12] The confrontation clause guarantees the accused in all criminal prosecutions the right "to be confronted with the witness against him." US Const amend VI.

[13] *E.g.*, United States v Smith, 521 F2d 957 (DC Cir 1975).

[14] *See, e.g.*, Ill Sup Ct R 236.

[15] 399 US 149 (1970).

[16] 400 US 74 (1970).

[17] 448 US 58 (1980).

indicia of reliability could be inferred where the out-of-court statement fell within a traditional hearsay exception.[18]

In an old case, the Supreme Court of the United States approved the dying declaration exception to the rule against hearsay as unobjectionable under the Sixth Amendment's confrontation clause.[19] Subsequently, the Court held that it was error to admit against the defendant at trial testimony taken during a preliminary hearing at which the defendant was not represented by an attorney and did not cross-examine the witness.[20] Similarly, the Court held that it was reversible error under the confrontation clause to permit a prosecutor to bring into evidence against a defendant at trial an accomplice's confession which implicated the defendant, when the accomplice appeared at trial but invoked the privilege against self-incrimination when on the stand, so that the defendant could not cross-examine the accomplice.[21] In another case, the Court held that it was error to use against a defendant at trial a witness' preliminary hearing testimony where the state had not made a diligent effort to have its witness in attendance at the trial.[22] Then, in *California v Green,* the Court approved the use of a prior inconsistent statement which was given at a preliminary hearing at which the defendant's counsel cross-examined the witness where the witness had a convenient memory lapse when called to testify at trial.[23] Finally, in *Dutton v Evans,* the Court held that it did not violate the defendant's Sixth Amendment right to admit into evidence against him a nontestifying coconspirator's out-of-court statement, at least where: the out-of-court statement was of peripheral significance; the in-court declarant was fully cross-examined; the out-of-court declarant had no apparent motive to lie and made the statement spontaneously; the statement was against penal interest, did not make any express assertion about a past fact, and was so ambiguous that the jury was not likely to give it great weight; and where the out-of-court declarant clearly had personal knowledge about which he was speaking, the possibility of his having a faulty recollection was extremely unlikely, and the possibility that

---

[18] *Id* 66 n 8.

[19] Mattox v United States, 156 US 237 (1895).

[20] Pointer v Texas, 380 US 400 (1965).

[21] Douglas v Alabama, 380 US 415 (1965).

[22] Barber v Page, 390 US 719 (1968).

[23] 399 US at 170. The credibility of a witness may be attacked by any party, including the party calling him or her, under Fed R Evid 607. The rule is the same in many states. *See e.g.,* Ill Sup Ct R 238.

cross-examination of the out-of-court declarant would reveal unreliability was wholly unreal.[24]

Although, as noted above, the Court in *Roberts v Ohio* attempted some sort of workable solution, the problem of the interrelationship of the hearsay rule and the confrontation clause has hardly been satisfactorily resolved. What must be kept in mind is that all attempts to use out-of-court statements of declarants who are unavailable at trial to bolster the testimony of an eyewitness will be met with two objections: the first objection will be hearsay; the second will be that the hearsay, even if it comes within some exception to the rule against hearsay, violates the confrontation clause of the Sixth Amendment.

§6.10 Anticipating Defenses

It is always necessary to anticipate cross-examination as much as possible. The attorney anticipates cross-examination primarily by bringing forth a good foundation for the witness' perceptions.[25] Second, the attorney anticipates cross-examination by anticipating what the defense is likely to be and closing the loopholes. For example, in the case of the drunk[26] who staggered across the street, entered the liquor store, and emerged carrying a bag in which the investigating officer found a bottle of liquor, where the officer subsequently gave the liquor store propietor a citation for knowingly selling liquor to a person whom the proprietor knew to be intoxicated, there are three possible defenses. The first is that the buyer was not intoxicated. The second is that while the buyer may have been intoxicated, the proprietor did not know that he was intoxicated. The third is, of course, that the proprietor did not sell the liquor to the drunk. Anticipating the first defense, the prosecutor took pains to show that the person who crossed the street and entered the liquor store was acting in a very peculiar way.[27] He or she would probably go on to show that the police officer gave the drunk some form of sobriety test. That testimony may be such as what follows.

Q. Officer, after Mr. Walters emerged from the liquor store, what did you do?

A. I got out of my car[28] and crossed the street and confronted him.

---

[24] 400 US at 87-90.

[25] See **§§6.04-6.06.**

[26] The hypothetical is set forth in **§§6.05-6.07.**

[27] This testimony is set forth in **§6.07.**

[28] As an aside, it should be noted that a police officer would probably prefer to say something like "I exited my official vehicle," rather than "I got out of my car." It is very important for all witnesses to testify in plain, simple English, and law enforcement officers in particular need to be coached to avoid the peculiar jargon of their profession.

Q. At this time, approximately how far were you from Mr. Walters?
A. I would say I was approximately three feet away when I first spoke with him.
Q. At that time, did you notice his eyes?
A. Yes.
Q. Would you describe them?
A. They were bloodshot.
Q. Did you notice his breath?
A. Yes.
Q. At this time, approximately how far were you from Mr. Walters?
A. About three feet.
Q. And what, if anything, unusual did you notice about his breath?
A. It smelled of alcohol.
Q. Now, were you watching Mr. Walters from the time he left the store until the time you confronted him on the sidewalk?
A. Yes.
Q. Would you describe how he was walking?
A. He was walking in the same manner as when he entered the store.
Q. Did you have occasion to speak with Mr. Walters?
A. Yes.
Q. What did you say to him and what did he say to you?

The Defense Attorney: Objection, hearsay.
The Prosecutor: It is not offered for the truth of the matter asserted.
The Judge: Objection is overruled.

A. I said, "What is your name? I am a police officer."
Q. And how did Mr. Walters respond?
A. He started singing the Star Spangled Banner.
Q. What, if anything, did you notice about his manner of singing?
A. His words were very slurred.
Q. What did you do next?
A. I administered what we call a field sobriety test.
Q. What is a field sobriety test?

A. It is a way of determining whether or not someone is intoxicated. I ask a subject to perform five simple acts.

Q. What are those acts?

A. I asked him to touch his nose with each index finger. I asked him to walk a straight line. I asked him to pick up three coins from the sidewalk. I asked him to count backward from 10. And I asked him to stand on one foot with his eyes closed and jump up and down.

Q. Did you ask Mr. Walters to count backward from 10?

A. Yes.

Q. Would you describe what he did?

A. He started singing *Ninety-Nine Bottles of Beer on the Wall,* but he only got to 98, and then he fell over.

Q. Did you ask him to pick up three coins from the sidewalk?

A. Yes. After we picked him up.

Q. What did he do?

A. When he bent down, he again fell over.

Q. And then what did you do?

A. I asked him to walk along a chalk line I drew on the sidewalk.

Q. And what did he do?

A. He turned around and started to walk into the middle of the street.

Q. Is that the way you had drawn the chalk line?

A. No.

Q. Then what did you do?

A. I asked him to close his eyes, stand on one foot, and jump up and down.

Q. What did he do?

A. As soon as he closed his eyes, he started to fall, and we had to catch him.

Q. Based on the sobriety test that you gave to Mr. Walters, and on your observations of him, and on your training and experience as a Liquor Control Commission investigator, do you have an opinion as to whether he was intoxicated?

The Defense Attorney: Objection!
The Judge: Overruled.

A. Yes.

Q. And what is that opinion?

A. In my opinion, he was intoxicated.

It should be noted that it is possible for a direct examiner to *overprove* his or her case. For example, if the direct examiner in the liquor case above has overemphasized the observations which lead the investigating officer to conclude that Mr. Walters was intoxicated, the cross-examiner whose defense is that the proprietor did not know Mr. Walters was intoxicated might proceed as follows.

Q. Now, Officer, as I understand it, one of the reasons you concluded Mr. Walters was intoxicated was because you saw him stumble and fall as he crossed Wells Street. Is that correct?

A. Yes.

Q. But you did not arrest him at that time for being intoxicated, did you?

A. No.

Q. And then after Mr. Walters emerged from the liquor store, you walked up to him, and you say that when you were approximately three feet away, you smelled alcohol on his breath, right?

A. Yes.

Q. But you did not arrest him at that point, did you?

A. No.

Q. Is it not true that many people smell of alcohol who are not intoxicated?

A. Yes.

Q. You also stated that one of the bases for your conclusion that Mr. Walters was intoxicated was that his eyes were bloodshot?

A. Yes.

Q. Sir, is it not true that many persons whose eyes are bloodshot are not intoxicated?

A. Well, not everyone whose eyes are bloodshot is intoxicated. Yes, that's true.

Q. Sir, did you not also testify that one the bases upon which you concluded that Mr. Walters was intoxicated was the fact that when he spoke to you his speech was slurred?

A. Yes, that's correct.

Q. Is it not a fact, Officer, that there are other reasons besides intoxication why one's speech might be impaired?

A. Yes.

Q. Now, Officer, is it not also true that you did not hear the conversation that Mr. Walters had with the proprietor when he was in the liquor store?

A. That is correct; I could not hear it.

Q. Officer, you did not observe how Mr. Walters walked in the liquor store because you could only see him from the shoulders up, correct?

A. Yes.

Q. So you do not know whether he stumbled or fell in the liquor store, do you?

A. No.

Q. Now, Officer, even after you observed Mr. Walters stumble and sway, and after you smelled liquor on his breath, and after you observed he had bloodshot eyes, and after you heard him speak in a slurring way, you still did not arrest him immediately at that point, did you?

A. No, I gave him a field sobriety test first.

Q. Yes, of course, and that field sobriety test consisted of having him touch his nose with his index finger, pick up three coins from the sidewalk, walk a straight line, jump up and down on one foot with his eyes closed, and count backward from 10. Is that correct?

A. Yes.

Q. Now, Officer, you did not see the defendant in this case ask Mr. Walters to touch his nose with his index finger in the store, did you?

A. No.

Q. And you did not see the defendant in this case ask Mr. Walters to pick up three coins from the store floor, did you?

A. No.

Q. And you did not see the defendant ask Mr. Walters to stand on one leg and jump up and down with his eyes closed, did you?

A. No.

Q. And you did not see the defendant ask Mr. Walters to walk a straight line in the store, did you?

A. No.

Q. But it was only after you had given Mr. Walters this sobriety test that you arrested him for public intoxication, right?

A. Yes.

Q. By the way, Officer, when you were watching Mr. Walters cross the street, stumble, and zigzag and so forth, you were not looking into the store at that time, were you?

A. No.

Q. So, Officer, you do not know whether or not the defendant saw Mr. Walters stumble while he was walking across the street, do you?

A. No.

In order to anticipate the defense that the proprietor of the store did not know that Mr. Walters was intoxicated, the direct examiner is going to have to show that the proprietor had a good opportunity to observe Mr. Walters in the store. If the prosecutor does not do this, the defense may elect not to touch the matter on cross-examination—and then argue in closing that the element was never sufficiently proved. A direct examination, anticipating the defense, may go something like this:

Q. Officer, approximately how long was Mr. Walters in the store?

A. I would say he was in the store about three or four minutes.

Q. From where you were parked in your car, were you able to see Mr. Walters in the store?

A. Yes. I could see him from about the shoulders up.

Q. What did you see Mr. Walters do after he entered the store?

A. I saw him walk over to the counter at about the middle of the store.

Q. And approximately how wide would you say the counter is?

The Defense Lawyer: Objection, improper foundation.
The Judge: Sustained.

Q. Officer, have you ever been inside the Gold Seal Liquor Store?

A. Yes, immediately after I arrested Mr. Walters, I went into the store.

Q. When you were in the store, did you observe the counter?

A. Yes.

Q. Would you describe the counter for us?

A. It extends the length of the store.

Q. How wide is the counter, if you remember?

A. It is about two feet wide.

Q. How wide is the counter at the point to which Mr. Walters walked when he first entered the store?

A. It is about two feet wide.

Q. At the time Mr. Walters entered the store, did you see anyone else in the store?

A. Yes.

Q. And who was that?

A. The defendant.

Q. Do you see the defendant in the courtroom today?

A. Yes, I do.

Q. Will you point him out?

A. He is sitting there at the defense table.

The Prosecutor: May the record reflect that the officer has correctly identified the proprietor of the Gold Seal Liquor Store.

The Judge: It may so reflect.

Q. Where was the defendant at the time Mr. Walters entered the store?

A. He was standing at the cash register.

Q. And what did you see him do, if anything, after Mr. Walters entered the store?

A. He walked from the cash register to a point directly across from Mr. Walters, but on the other side of the counter.

Q. So, approximately how far from Mr. Walters was the proprietor at this point?

A. Approximately two feet.

Q. And what happened next?

A. They appeared to have a conversation.

Q. Could you hear the conversation?

A. No, but I could see the proprietor's lips moving.

Q. For approximately what period of time was Mr. Walters standing across from the proprietor at this point?

A. I would say for approximately 20 seconds.

Q. And then what happened?

Note that the direct examiner has at this point established that the defendant was in close proximity to Mr. Walters, closer than the arresting officer testified he was when he made observations indicating intoxication.

The direct examiner must also anticipate the defense that there was no sale. In doing so, he or she might ask questions such as this:

Q. Officer, after you observed what appeared to be a conversation between Mr. Walters and the defendant, what happened?
A. Mr. Walters pointed to something directly in front of him.
Q. In which way was Mr. Walters pointing; toward what was he pointing?
A. He was pointing toward the shelves directly in front of him and behind the defendant.
Q. What, if anything, was on those shelves that you could observe?
A. There were bottles on the shelves.
Q. What happened next?
A. The proprietor turned around and reached up and took a bottle from the shelf.
Q. Then what happened?
A. Mr. Walters walked over to the cash register.
Q. What did the defendant do, if you saw?
A. He also walked over to the cash register, but they were on different sides of the counter.
Q. Then what happened?
A. They stood facing each other at the cash register for about 10 seconds.
Q. Then what did you observe?
A. Mr. Walters then left the store.
Q. When Mr. Walters left the store, what, if anything, was he carrying?
A. He was carrying a brown paper bag.
Q. Officer, when you observed Mr. Walters enter the store, were you able to see his hands?
A. Yes.
Q. Was he carrying anything at the time that he entered the store?
A. No.
Q. Now, after you confronted Mr. Walters, did you place him under arrest?
A. Yes.
Q. After you placed him under arrest, did you search the brown paper bag which he was carrying?

A. Yes.

Q. What, if anything, did you find in the bag?

A. A bottle of Thunderbird wine and a receipt from the Gold Seal Liquor Store.

§6.11 Anticipating Impeachment

Aside from the question of anticipating possible defenses,[29] the attorney must decide whether or not to anticipate other forms of cross-examination, especially impeachment. Some forms of impeachment are so obvious that the attorney can be certain that they will not be missed by the other side. When the area of impeachment is both obvious and quite damaging, it ought to be anticipated. On direct examination, for example, where the eyewitness has been convicted of a felony, that fact should usually be brought out by the direct examiner. Even in such a case, however, it may sometimes be better for the direct examiner not to anticipate impeachment. For example, let us assume that Ms. Good, the purse-snatching victim,[30] had been convicted of the felony of possessing marijuana nine years before the purse-snatching case. Unless the prosecutor brings up the matter, the defense attorney may feel that the jury will resent the defense attempting to bring out such irrelevant *dirty laundry,* even though the Rule 609 of the Federal Rules of Evidence would permit him or her to do so. In any event, the direct examiner must be careful, in anticipating impeachment, not to do such a thorough job of discrediting his or her witness that he or she actually destroys the testimony. For example, if the prosecutor decides to bring out Ms. Good's previous marijuana conviction, he or she should be content with establishing that she was convicted of possessing marijuana nine years previously rather than bringing out additional facts regarding the conviction, although under the federal rules, the cross-examiner can, if he or she wishes, elicit any facts about the conviction which are contained in the judgment of conviction, including the amount of marijuana involved.[31]

In most instances, the direct examiner is perhaps better advised to leave impeachment to the cross-examiner. It happens often enough that the cross-examiner fails to go into some area which one anticipates he or she would develop. In addition, the cross-examiner may go into an area but develop it so poorly that no harm is done. Of course, the direct

---

[29] See **§6.10.**

[30] The hypothetical is set forth in **§§6.02** and **6.06-6.08.**

[31] *See, e.g.*, United States v Harding, 525 F2d 24 (7th Cir 1975).

examiner always has redirect examination in which to repair whatever damage may done by the cross-examiner. Rather than detract from one's own case, therefore, it may be generally better not to anticipate most forms of impeachment in the direct examination.

It is especially important not to undermine the eyewitness' testimony where the anticipated impeachment of an eyewitness is not that the witness is lying, that his or her perception was impaired, or that his or her memory is faulty, rather than the more subtle area of subsequent suggestion which has influenced recall. It may well be that Ms. Good identified the purse snatcher because she did not wish to look foolish in front of the investigating officer; that she thought of herself as a neighborhood *crime stopper* and identified with the police and law enforcement in general, whom she tried always to please; that being a witness in court made her feel important; that she expected to observe the person who had taken her purse when she was called down to the police station; or that her identification had been suggested by police conduct or by some newspaper account of the second purse snatching. All of these areas of impeachment are quite difficult to develop on cross-examination. The direct examiner, therefore, is probably better advised not to try to anticipate such attacks; there is no point in giving the jurors any ideas which might not otherwise enter their minds. Rather, the attorney would prefer to have his or her witness tell a simple, straightforward story, with a positive in-court identification based on an accurate perception following a good opportunity to observe. Anticipating the cross-examination always weakens the effect of such testimony and should be done only where absolutely necessary.

§6.12 Exhibits

Exhibits, of course, are not peculiar to eyewitness cases. Nevertheless, exhibits are very frequently used in the course of an eyewitness' testimony. While exhibits are often used in the cross-examination of an eyewitness, they are more commonly used in the direct examination.

In discussing exhibits, it is perhaps best to begin by asking why an attorney should use exhibits at all. The new trial lawyer, or the law student who is learning to try cases, often fails to make the maximum use of exhibits. Perhaps the reason is that the neophyte thinks in terms of the minimum he or she is required to prove in order to make a prima facie case, rather than in terms of producing the maximum evidence in order to persuade the jury to decide the case in favor of his or her client and against the other side. For example, a new prosecutor trying a murder case may well think that there is no real reason to put the murder weapon into evidence where there is an eyewitness who can testify that he or she saw the defendant shoot the victim. Why, after all, is the murder gun necessary?

The gun may not be necessary, but it is evidence; and evidence is what persuades juries. Moreover, the evidence of the murder weapon corroborates the testimony of the eyewitness. The witness said he or she saw someone shoot someone else with a gun, and the prosecution has produced the gun. In addition, during the course of the direct examination of the witness, the prosecutor can have the witness use the weapon to demonstrate exactly what he or she saw. In closing argument, the attorney can use the weapon, often very effectively, to rivet the jury's attention on him or her while he or she is talking. When the jurors go to the jury room to deliberate, they can take the weapon with them. The presence of the gun should induce the jury to recall the testimony of the witness who testified when the weapon was introduced into evidence. Moreover, the jurors can actually handle the weapon and decide for themselves, for instance, whether they believe the defendant's story that the gun went off accidentally. Having the exhibit in the jury room is almost like having a witness present in the jury room. In even simpler terms, the weight of the evidence is what wins cases, and the gun is evidence. In a certain sense, the side which has more exhibits has more evidence.

Of course, there are times when one should not use an exhibit. In some criminal cases, the principal defense is that the stories of the various eyewitnesses do not coincide, and that therefore none of them can be believed to the point of proving guilt beyond a reasonable doubt. In such a case, it would be a mistake for the prosecution to make use of a chart or diagram which would graphically demonstrate to the jury inconsistencies in the stories of the prosecution witnesses about where witnesses were located and who did what. The defense in such a case, on the other hand, might well make use of a diagram, perhaps using separate cellulose acetate overlays for the cross-examination of each prosecution witness to demonstrate the inconsistencies. The point is that the attorney should not use an exhibit for the sake of using an exhibit. In the purse-snatching case discussed earlier,[32] it would be a mistake for the prosecutor to use photographs which showed that trees on the street blocked the light from the streetlights. In the same way, it would be a mistake in the Liquor Control Commission case[33] for the plaintiff to make use of a diagram showing that the police officer's view from his car into the liquor store was obstructed by trees and bushes.

---

[32] See **§§6.02, 6.06-6.08,** and **6.11.**

[33] See **§§6.05-6.07** and **6.10.**

§6.13 —Introducing Exhibits

Assuming that the attorney has decided that an exhibit will help his or her case, the exhibit must be put into evidence and shown to the jury. A number of treatises exist which can help the trial lawyer in this regard.[34] What follows is only a brief synopsis of the area.

It is perhaps helpful to think of exhibits as falling into classes. The first class can be referred to as the *real thing*. In the Liquor Control Commission case[35] for instance, the receipt from the Gold Seal Liquor Store, which was found inside the bag, and the bottle of wine itself are real evidence. In order to introduce such items into evidence, it is necessary only to have a witness who can testify that each item is relevant to the case, that it is authentic, and that its condition is the same at the time of trial as it was at the relevant time.

Real thing exhibits can be further divided into two subdivisions. There are those items which can be identified as authentic by a witness who simply looks at the object, and there are those which require the proof of a chain of custody. In the liquor case, for example, the investigating officer may be used as the witness who lays the foundation for the introduction into evidence of the receipt which was found in the paper bag. Questioning of the officer would probably proceed something like this:

Q. Officer, I hand you what has been previously marked as State's Exhibit 1 for identification, and I ask you to look at it. Do you recognize State's Exhibit 1?

A. Yes.

Q. Will you please tell us what it is?

A. It is the receipt which I recovered from the paper bag Mr. Walters was carrying when I arrested him.

Q. Tell us, please, how you know that this is the receipt which you took from Mr. Walters' bag?

A. For one thing, I recognize the writing on the front of the receipt—that is, the name of the store, the date, and the amount. For another thing, on the back of the receipt I wrote my name, the date, and Mr. Walters' name.

The Prosecutor: Your honor, I move that State's Exhibit 1 for

---

[34] Two which are well known are the American Jurisprudence multivolume treatises Trials and Proof of Facts.

[35] See **§§6.05-6.07** and **6.10.**

identification be admitted as evidence and ask that the identifying symbols be struck.

It should be noted that the officer was able to identify the receipt simply by looking at it.

The second subdivision of *real thing* evidence comprises those articles which cannot be identified simply by looking at them. For example, if it were necessary for the state to prove in the liquor case that the liquid contained in the wine bottle was in fact alcohol, the state might call a chemist to testify that he or she analyzed the contents of the bottle. Especially if the bottle had been opened, it would be necessary for the state to prove a chain of custody—that is, the state would be required to account for the bottle from the time it was taken from Mr. Walters until it was received by the chemist, and from the time the chemist made his or her analysis until the bottle was moved into evidence. Although the bottle itself might be an object which could be marked or otherwise recognized by a witness as the bottle taken from Walters, no one can testify that the liquid in the bottle was the same liquid which was in it when it was taken from Walters. Thus, the chain of custody must be proved. It is beyond the scope of this chapter, however, to go into more detail about the proof of chain of custody.[36]

The second division of exhibits can be termed *replicas of the real thing.* Often, the real thing—for example, an intersection or a locomotive—simply cannot be brought into the courtroom. It is often possible, however, to have a scale model, a photograph, a scale diagram, or a blueprint brought into the courtroom. These types of exhibits are accurate representations of the real thing and ought to be received into evidence as exhibits.

This second division of exhibits can also be divided into two subdivisions. The first subdivision comprises those replicas which can be identified as accurate by a layperson. A photograph is a good example. In most jurisdictions, it is not necessary for the witness who is answering questions designed to lay the foundation for the admission into evidence of a photograph to have taken the picture himself or herself. Neither is it necessary that he or she know who took the picture, what kind of a camera was used, what kind of lens was used, or anything about the developing process. It is enough if the witness testifies that he or she has seen the object in the picture in real life—for example, the intersection of Wells and Jackson in the liquor case—and that he or

---

[36] For an excellent example of how to prove the chain of custody, see T. Mauet, Fundamentals of Trial Techniques 186 (1980).

she can tell by looking that the photograph accurately portrays the intersection. Such an examination might proceed as follows.

Q. Officer, you have testified that you have been at the intersection of Wells and Jackson numerous times. I hand you what has been previously marked as State's Exhibit 2 for identification, and I ask you to look at it and tell us what State's Exhibit 2 for identification is.

A. It is a photograph of the intersection of Wells and Jackson.

Q. Does State's Exhibit 2 for identification fairly and accurately portray the intersection as it appeared to you on [the day in question]?

A. Yes.

The Prosecutor: Your honor, I move that State's Exhibit 2 for identification be admitted as evidence.

A scale diagram of the intersection, on the other hand, may require the testimony of an expert witness. If the prosecution wishes to put such a diagram into evidence, it might call an engineer or an architect to testify that he or she measured the intersection, and that based on his or her measurement, he or she drew the diagram contained in the exhibit, or that he or she compared his or her measurements with the diagram and found the diagram to be accurate. Especially where the scale diagram or model contains measurements, a lay witness, or at least one who had not checked the measurements, would probably be unqualified to testify that the diagram was accurate. In most eyewitness cases, it is probably a good idea to take the time and effort to prepare, or to have prepared, diagrams drawn to scale. In that way, witnesses can accurately indicate on the diagram where different things were located, and the jury can get an idea of exactly how the events occurred.

The third class or division of exhibits are *demonstrative aids.* These include the ever-present blackboard, slides which can be projected by means of an overhead projector, butcher paper and felt-tip pen, a plastic skeleton that a doctor would use to describe to the jury what a femur looks like, and so forth. The principal difference between the first two classes of exhibits—the real thing and the replicas—and demonstrative aids is that the exhibits in the first two classes generally go back to the jury room, whereas demonstrative aids should probably be before the jury only while the witness is testifying. The key questions in laying the foundation for the use of a demonstrative aid is whether the exhibit will help the witness explain his or her testimony to the jury and whether it will help the jury understand the testimony. In introducing a diagram in this category in the Liquor Control Commission case, a lawyer might proceed as follows.

Q. Officer, is there anything that would help you describe to the jury what the intersection of Wells and Jackson looked like on the night in question and where you were located in relation to the Gold Seal Liquor Store?

A. Yes, in the course of making my report in this case, I prepared a diagram.

Q. Officer, I hand you what has been previously marked as State's Exhibit 2 for identification, and I ask you to look at it. Will you tell us what that is?

A. That is my diagram.

Q. Does State's Exhibit 2 for identification fairly and accurately portray the intersection of Wells and Jackson as it was on the night in question?

A. It is not drawn to the scale, but it is otherwise accurate, at least insofar as what it portrays. Not everything is on the diagram.

The Prosecutor: Your honor, I move that State's Exhibit 2 for identification be admitted as evidence.

The Defense Attorney: Objection, your honor. It is not to scale and not complete.

The Prosecutor: Your honor, I offer State's Exhibit 2 for identification only for the limited purposes of helping the officer to testify and of aiding the jury in understanding his testimony.

The Judge: State's Exhibit 2 will be received for that limited purpose. I suspect, however, that I will not send it back to the jury room.

The Prosecutor: Your honor, may State's Exhibit 2 be shown to the jury at this time?

The Judge: Yes.

§6.14 —Using Exhibits

An important point to remember with regard to most exhibits is that they should generally be *used* in the course of the witness' testimony. All too often, attorneys admit exhibits into evidence and then fail to maximize them by having the witnesses testify about the exhibits. For example, it is one thing to have a diagram of the intersection of Wells and Jackson admitted into evidence.[37] That diagram will undoubtedly help the jury understand what the intersection looked like at the time of the event in question. However, it is more effective to have the investigating officer testify as to the path Mr. Walters took when he walked across the street and entered the liquor store by indicating that path on the diagram.[38]

The question arises as to who should actually make marks on the diagram. Should the witness go to the blackboard or to the diagram and draw on it, or should the attorney be the one who makes the marks? In the opinion of many trial lawyers, it is better for the attorney to do the marking. While it is true that having the witness himself or herself mark the diagram lends a certain spontaneity and credibility to the testimony, the danger is too great that the witness will make a mark in the wrong place or become confused. It is much better if the trial lawyer asks questions of the witness and then has the witness confirm that his or her markings on the diagram are accurate. This technique may be carried out in the following manner.

Q. Officer, you have indicated that Mr. Walters was standing on the northwest corner of Jackson and Wells when you first saw him. I am going to point with a red marker to an area on the diagram which has been admitted into evidence as State's Exhibit 2, and I ask you to tell me when I am pointing to the place where Mr. Walters was when you first observed him.

A. That is it right there.

Q. Have I correctly indicated on the diagram with this red marker where Mr. Walters was when you first observed him?

A. Yes.

The Prosecutor: Your honor, may the record reflect that I have drawn with a red grease pencil a stick man on State's Exhibit 2 in the place where the witness has testified that Mr. Walters was when the witness first observed him.

The Judge: The record may so reflect.

In regard to witnesses drawing diagrams, perhaps a word should be said about blackboards. Generally, their use ought to be discouraged. If a diagram is drawn on a blackboard beforehand, it is vulnerable to being erased at any time. If the witness is asked to draw on a blackboard,

---

[37] See **§6.13.**

[38] The hypothetical is set forth in **§§6.05-6.07** and **6.10.**

it is very likely that the diagram will be less than perfect. If the attorney, on the other hand, in response to the witness' answers, attempts to draw a diagram on the blackboard, he or she has a relatively difficult task. First, the attorney must ask the witness what the intersection looked like. Then, he or she must draw on the blackboard something that corresponds to what the witness said, and then he or she must ask the judge to let the record reflect that what he or she has drawn on the blackboard corresponds to what the witness said. The process is tedious and time consuming. Moreover, a good cross-examiner in the course of his or her cross-examination may well erase things on the blackboard and move marks to other positions. In the end, the blackboard has not served any purpose very well. Any case worth trying is probably worth the time and effort expended in constructing or obtaining professional diagrams, charts, and other demonstrative aides.[39]

Where there are insufficient funds available to make large blow-ups of photographs, diagrams, charts, and the like, it is often possible to achieve a perfectly acceptable result using an overhead projector.[40] Slides for such projectors can usually be made quite inexpensively. Once the foundation for the slide has been laid, the slide can be introduced into evidence, and then it can be projected on a screen. The advantage of such a slide, besides the fact that it is inexpensive to produce, is that when the lights go out and the projector projects a large image on the wall, the jury's attention is almost always fixed on the exhibit, perhaps even more than when a large, expensive enlargement of a diagram or photograph is used.

The steps for introducing an exhibit into evidence are the same regardless of the type of exhibit. First, the exhibit is marked for identification. In some jurisdictions, this marking is still done by the court reporter, but the more common practice today is to have the attorney mark his or her own exhibits. Most judges prefer that the exhibits be marked prior to trial. Second, after the exhibit has been marked, it is customary in most jurisdictions to show the exhibit to opposing counsel. It should be noted that the fact that opposing counsel may have seen all the exhibits prior to trial is no reason for omitting this step. Some lawyers object to having an exhibit shown to a witness without first seeing it themselves, even when they have received the exhibits prior to trial. The ground for their objection is that they do not know that what is being shown the witness on the stand is what was

---

[39] One way of preventing the cross-examiner from making marks on a permanent exhibit is simply to provide the cross-examiner with an unmarked copy of the exhibit.

[40] An interesting discussion of the use of overhead projectors at trial appears in Chipman, *The Overhead Projector in the Courtroom,* 2 Trial Dipl J. 14 (Summer 1979).

shown to them previously. The third step is to show the exhibit to the witness, indicating for the record what it is the lawyer has shown the witness by using the identifying symbol. Fourth, the witness is asked the questions necessary to lay the foundation for the admission of the exhibit. Fifth, the lawyer moves that the exhibit be admitted into evidence. Sixth, the exhibit is shown, or *published,* to the jury.

Publication of the exhibit to the jury can take place in a number of ways. If the exhibit is a document, the witness can simply read the document to the jury, or copies of the document may be distributed to the jury. It should be noted that if this latter method is chosen, it is a good idea to have a copy of each document for the judge and each juror. That way, each juror is able to look at a document without worrying about holding up the proceedings. Where a single document is passed among the jurors, usually no one actually reads the document.

Exhibits can also be published to the jury by means of overhead projectors or enlargements, or simply by showing objects to the jury or allowing the objects to be passed among the jurors. In some cases, a number of ways of publication are combined. For example, a copy of a document may be given to each juror so that the jurors can follow the document as the witness reads from the original. The important thing is that the jury see the exhibit. However, some judges do not like to take the time to publish exhibits to the jury and simply indicate that the jurors will see the exhibits at the end of the trial. If that is the case, it is doubly important that the attorney who is the proponent of an exhibit make sure that the exhibit actually is sent back to the jury room during the deliberations.

§6.15 —Objections to Exhibits

Although a whole treatise could be written on the subject of objections to exhibits, space permits only a couple of points to be made here. It is usually best to make an initial objection to the introduction of exhibits as general as possible. For example:

> The Prosecutor: Your honor, at this point we move that State's Exhibit 2 for identification, the diagram of the intersection of Wells and Jackson,[41] be admitted as evidence.
>
> The Defense Attorney: Objection, your honor. Improper foundation.

---

[41] The hypothetical is set forth in **§§6.05-6.07** and **6.10.**

By making his or her objection in general terms, the opponent of the exhibit has not educated the other side as to what he or she believes is improper about the foundation. In addition, the judge may well sustain the objection made in general terms on grounds known only to the judge and of which the opponent would never have thought. If the judge sustains the objection, the proponent of the exhibit is put in the uncomfortable position of having to guess what it is that he or she has missed, or having to ask the judge. If the judge overrules the objection, the opponent of the exhibit can ask to be heard and can make a specific record of his or her objection.

Assume, however, that the judge responds by asking the attorney to be more specific in the objection. At this point, the opponent can ask the judge to be allowed to conduct voir dire of the witness regarding the exhibit. If the judge permits voir dire, the opponent will have an opportunity to cross-examine the witness, in the middle of the other side's direct examination, without having indicated to the witness or anyone else what it is that he or she feels is lacking in the foundation. Thus, if the opponent requests such voir dire, the proponent is well advised to ask the court to require the opponent to make specific objections before being permitted to break up the direct examination. The court should usually comply. An exchange might go something like this:

> The Prosecutor: Your honor, at this point we move that State's Exhibit 2 for identification, the diagram of the intersection, be admitted into evidence.
>
> The Defense Attorney: Objection, your honor. Improper foundation.
>
> The Judge: Counsel, will you please be more specific in your objections?
>
> The Defense Attorney: Your honor, may I be allowed to conduct voir dire of the witness about this exhibit? I think I can develop my objection that way.
>
> The Prosecutor: Your honor, we object to voir dire at this time. The defense is simply trying to disrupt the direct examination. If she has a valid basis for objecting to the introduction of this exhibit, let her state it now, so that we may have an opportunity to perfect our foundation by supplying whatever it is that may be missing.
>
> The Judge: Yes. Counsel, I think you should state the basis for your objection more specifically.
>
> The Defense Attorney: The prosecution has failed to show that the engineer who prepared the diagram was familiar with the

intersection on the day in question. The engineer merely testified that, at some subsequent date, he went out there and took some measurements and drew the diagram.

The Judge: Mr. Prosecutor, can you clear that up?

The Prosecutor: Yes, your honor, of course.

§6.16 —Discrepancies in the Exhibit

A photograph or diagram must be fair and accurate in its representation of those things which are relevant to the purpose for which the photograph or diagram is being offered, although the photograph or diagram need not be complete and fully accurate in every detail. For example, in a photograph of an intersection taken sometime after an event occurred, it is almost certain that some things would have changed. The traffic would undoubtedly be different. It is very possible that the trees or shrubbery in the picture would have different foliage or lack foliage. Weather conditions, like snow or rain, may be different. However, unless those differences are somehow prejudicial to the other side, the photograph ought to be admitted into evidence if it fairly and accurately portrays that which it is being offered to show—for example, the relative positions of the two streets, the crosswalks, the stoplight, the streetlight, and the entrance to the liquor store.[42] It is good idea, however, for the direct examiner to have his or her witness testify to these differences rather than simply to have the witness say that the photograph fairly and accurately represents the intersection as he or she saw it on the day of the event in question.

If the direct examiner simply has the witness say that the photograph or diagram is a fair and accurate representation, the cross-examiner can make unearned points by showing that there are inaccuracies. The cross-examination may go something like this:

Q. Now, Officer, you just testified, did you not, that State's Exhibit 2, a photograph of the intersection of Jackson and Wells, is a fair and accurate representation of that intersection as you saw it on the day in question?

A. Yes, that is correct.

Q. Officer, is it true that the events that we are talking about here occurred in August?

A. Yes, that is right.

---

[42] The liquor store hypothetical is set forth in **§§6.05-6.07** and **6.10.**

Q. And, in August, there were leaves on the trees and bushes that are in front of the parking lot, which is cater-cornered from the gas station, is that right?

A. Yes.

Q. But, Officer, there are no leaves on the bushes and trees in State's Exhibit 2, are there?

A. Well, no; that picture was taken in November.

Q. Similarly, Officer, there is a truck parked in front of the rooming house in the photograph marked as State's Exhibit 2, is that right?

A. Yes.

Q. Officer, that truck was not there on the day you were observing the liquor store, was it?

A. No.

Q. And in the photograph marked State's Exhibit 2, there is snow on the sidewalk and the street, is that right?

A. Yes.

Q. Now, in August, when these events occurred, there was no snow on the street or sidewalk was there?

A. No, of course not.

Q. So, in fact, State's Exhibit 2 does not fairly and accurately portray the intersection of Wells and Jackson as you observed it on August 3rd, does it?

A. Well, ah . . . ah . . . ah.

This kind of cross-examination could be avoided if the direct examiner simply has the witness bring out the differences in the scene between the time when the photograph was taken and the time of the events. The same thing, of course, is true of prepared diagrams. Diagrams, unlike photographs, seldom contain everything that exists in real life. The diagram of an intersection rarely contains all of the street signs, street markings, and so forth. In fact, quite often, such a diagram may contain only what is essential for the purpose for which the diagram is being offered. Unless this fact is brought out on direct examination, however, the cross-examiner can spend time pointing out that the diagram does not show the parking lot which was located on the northeast corner, or the rooming house that was located on the northwest corner, or the gas station that was located on the southeast corner, or the electric lines and telephone lines. Again, this type of cross-examination can be avoided if the direct examiner has the witness indicate what is lacking.

Of course, if there is some serious discrepancy between the photograph, or the diagram, and the actual scene that prejudices the other side's case, the opponent should object and the diagram or photograph ought not to be admitted into evidence unless a limiting instruction can cure the problem. For example, in a case involving a collision at an intersection, if a bush appears in the photograph which is sought to be introduced into evidence that partially obscures the stop sign at the intersection, such a photograph should not be admitted into evidence without a limiting instruction if, at the time of the accident, the bush did not obscure the stop sign. Similarly, if the weather conditions are relevant to the case, a photograph showing snow and ice probably should not be admitted into evidence without an instruction, even for the purpose of showing where the stop sign was located, if the accident occurred on a day when the pavement was dry. The question, as with all evidence, is whether the prejudicial effect outweighs the probative value.

7 Cross-Examination

§7.01 Scope of the Chapter

Like the remainder of this volume, this chapter deals with the eyewitness as distinguished from other types of witnesses. However, that distinction is both unnecessary and inappropriate if the witness is a deliberate liar. The lawyer attempting to discredit a perjurer almost certainly employs techniques tailored to the character of the witness rather than to the circumstances surrounding an observation which, after all, the witness never made. This chapter, therefore, deals only with the cross-examiner's approach to a witness who claims to have observed an event and whose testimony, according to the trial theory of the cross-examiner, simply is mistaken or overstated as a result of error, reasonable bias, or suggestive influences.

§7.02 The State of the Art

The available literature and research provide little useful guidance concerning the impact upon the trier of fact of various techniques which might be adopted by the cross-examiner. That void may well lie beyond the capabilities of lawyers, social scientists, and statisticians to fill, at least in significant part. The heterogeneous personalities of witnesses, cross-examiners, and jurors compound the wide diversity of factual scenarios, presenting an infinite number of variables which defy classification.

Legal literature includes many efforts to prescribe guidelines and techniques for cross-examination. Some of those writings address the specific problems posed by the cross-examination of eyewitnesses. To the extent that those authors rely upon interviews with witnesses, jurors, and other participants, they may call to mind the allegory of the three sightless men who encounter their first elephant and attempt to determine its shape by feeling, respectively, its tail, leg, and trunk. To the extent that published advice for cross-examiners relies upon the personal experiences of a practitioner, it can be no more than intuitive. Rarely, if ever, will a lawyer's courtroom experiences produce a series of questions which may be translated with confidence to a different case involving different facts with different people on both sides of the witness stand.

Therefore, this chapter is not based upon existing research or writings. In general, those writings may be interesting and in some cases helpful—but only to the lawyer seeking guidance in the formulation of an individualized technique, and not to the lawyer seeking a model.

This chapter cites little authority because there is little which would be authoritative in the sense of guidance for the adoption of a questioning format for cross-examination of the mistaken percipient witness. Instead, this chapter presents information which the authors consider highly reliable and which has received inadequate consideration in the existing literature. The judgments contained here are concededly subjective and therefore may be regarded as no less deserving of skepticism than other writings in this field. Even so (and perhaps in ironic emulation of those predecessors), the authors strongly believe that the reader will find this chapter useful.

§7.03 The Realist's View of the Jury

Cross-examination does not cause the eyewitness to admit that he or she, rather than the cross-examiner's client, is the guilty party. Perry Mason achieved a protracted string of spectacular victories by accomplishing exactly that result—but only because the cases were "fixed" by Erle Stanley Gardner.

In spite of that truth, or perhaps because of it, many jurors bring to a trial a high sense of expectation of a real-life drama not radically different from that which they have observed for years through electronic voyeurism. Professor James Jeans, a preeminent analyst of the trial dynamic, employs a picturesque simile in describing the popular notion of cross-examination: "It is to a trial what a fist fight is to a hockey game."[1]

As a natural consequence of that attitude, jurors tend to be disappointed by any cross-examination which does not produce visible sparks. Frequently, a cross-examiner scores very meaningful points which fail to impress the jurors because the dialogue between the witness and the lawyer contained none of the obvious melodramatic responses which the jurors had come to associate with significant trial developments.

Consider the cross-examinations of the victims in *Foster v California*[2] and *Moore v Illinois.*[3] Both those transcripts contain completely competent cross-examinations whose effects, as an abstract proposition, are a substantial weakening of the reliability of the identifications made by those witnesses. In both cases, however, the defendants were convicted at trial. Although it is impossible to say that any single factor produced either of those convictions, it must be presumed that each jury believed the eyewitness testimony, in theory beyond reasonable doubt, notwithstanding a cross-examination which established a serious possibility that the witness was mistaken. One almost can hear the prosecutor in each of the cases arguing during summation that the eyewitness' story

---

[1] J. Jeans, Trial Advocacy §13.1 (1975).

[2] Foster v California, 394 US 440 (1969). See **§3.17.**

[3] Moore v Illinois, 434 US 220 (1977). See **§3.18.**

remained unshaken after extensive and grueling cross-examination. One can likewise almost see the jurors nodding sagely, reflecting that (by their standards) no weakness in the witness' testimony was revealed during cross-examination.

§7.04 The Realist's View of the Eyewitness

A witness does not withdraw his or her accusation during cross-examination, regardless of whether he or she fits the Erle Stanley Gardner paradigm of having performed the crime of which the cross-examiner's client stands accused. The authors of this book, unlike Perry Mason's patron, assume that the reader is most likely to confront eyewitnesses who are guilty only of erroneous identification. From time to time, however, that error may be the functional equivalent of a capital crime, all the more serious because it is not subject to punishment. Sincere but mistaken eyewitnesses tend to reject the suggestion that they could be mistaken. Their reactions, therefore, are likely to be vastly different from the self-denunciation characteristic of the witnesses pilloried by Mr. Mason. They are, however, no less readily predictable.

Whatever may have been the witnesses' initial uncertainty, they will be completely committed to the essentials of their stories by the time they commence to testify. They will not change sides on the witness stand. They may well be mistaken but they will not admit their mistake. Indeed, they are most unlikely to admit, in any useful context, the serious possibility that they *might* be mistaken. They will hold to their accusations. A question asked on cross-examination which, if answered with a *yes,* would cause the villain of a Mason plot to writhe in a near-orgasmic paroxysm of grandiloquent and unregenerate guilt will be answered in the real world with a *no.*

It is likewise poor strategy to rely upon obviously trick questions. Many jurors enter upon their duties with a preconception, unfortunately pandemic to the public as a whole, that lawyers are inclined by nature toward tricks. Opposing counsel would embark on a relatively easy task in attempting to persuade the jury during summation that the cross-examination reflected nothing more than a lawyer's trained cleverness exploiting the simple honesty of a victim or passerby. If, as normally must be done, the lawyer's strategy is based on the theory that the witness is sincere, the lawyer will have little prospect for favorable consideration unless he or she achieves a comparable posture of sincerity in the eyes of the jury.

On a more practical level, it is very likely that the direct examiner will have prepared the witness to respond in a convincing manner to any stock question. The cross-examiner who inquires, for example, whether the witness ever has made a mistake or is capable of making a mistake forces the client to assume the risk that the witness may respond softly: "Yes, but not this time. I could never say these things about a fellow human being under oath in a criminal trial if I were not morally certain that what I am saying is the truth." During the inevitable pause following that answer, for all practical purposes the jury may well reach its verdict.

§7.05 Correlation to Voir Dire and Opening Statement

A cross-examination for which the jury has been given inadequate preparation would probably fail to inspire skepticism concerning the accuracy of the witness' observations, regardless of the materiality of any substantive concessions which the questioning may elicit from that witness. As noted in **§7.03,** the cross-examinations in *Foster v California*[4] and *Moore v Illinois*[5] produced facts of far greater substance than those available to the cross-examiner in most typical trials. Notwithstanding that colorable success, both trials resulted in convictions. So much for the numerous purveyors of infallible cross-examination techniques! Any writer who might prescribe a series of questions guaranteed to produce admissions by eyewitnesses that on first view they had been unable to identify the client as the offender undoubtedly would receive a substantial bonus from his or her publisher and extravagant praise from the legal profession—and would richly deserve it. Yet, the cross-examiners in both *Foster* and *Moore* extracted exactly that admission from the respective eyewitnesses, with no apparent effect on the juries.

These comments are certainly not intended to suggest that either of those cross-examinations was inadequate in any degree. The transcripts would refute any such contention. It may, however, be surmised that the juries in those cases may not have been *prepared* for the cross-examinations which they observed.

It seems only reasonable that jurors who are offered less than they have come to expect will react as would most people in that situation by holding the offering in low esteem. A failure by the witness to have identified the client at the first opportunity is unlikely to make a strong impression upon a juror who is waiting for that which never arrives: a concession that the witness was, or at the least may have been, mistaken.

---

[4] Foster v California, 394 US 440 (1969). See **§3.17.**

[5] Moore v Illinois, 434 US 220 (1977). See **§3.18.**

The lawyer contemplating cross-examination of an eyewitness would be well advised to give serious consideration to instilling a realistic set of expectations in the jury.

During voir dire, if permitted under local procedure, the questioning should impress upon the jurors that it is *their* opinions, and not those of the eyewitness, which must determine the outcome of the trial, and that they must not let anyone else form their opinions for them. The lawyer should attempt to obtain a promise that the jurors will give careful consideration to the circumstances under which the witness' observations were made. That treatment can return handsome dividends during summation.[6]

The lawyer may well find it useful to advise the jurors during the opening statement that the witness will not recant, no matter what questions might be asked, and is completely committed to his or her story. Assuming that the lawyer is dealing with a witness who is not a deliberate liar, the jury should be informed of that proposition as well. A jury conditioned to the job of passing judgment on a sincere but mistaken witness is unlikely to base its judgment upon the obvious fact that the witness is honest.

These considerations would seem to militate in favor of the type of detailed opening statement of which a sample is presented in **§5.04.** By advising the jurors in some detail concerning the facts upon which the lawyer bases his or her contention that the witness is mistaken, the opening statement conveys the implied message that those facts are sufficient to have created an erroneous impression on the part of the witness. The jurors, accordingly, are likely to expect only that which they will receive, and they are likely to be better disposed toward according proper respect to those facts.

The lawyer who is denied *both* voir dire and an opening statement may well question the objectivity of the court. Such reflections, however, are of little practical help to a client. The lawyer's initial response must be a motion for mistrial, supported by a vigorous argument showing that the restraints thus imposed have denied his or her client the "opportunity to make the elements of his defense [or, less probably, his or her case as plaintiff] clear to the jury,"[7] and that the restraints will likely "substantially impair his defense."[8]

That argument probably would fail to persuade the court and would provide only a marginal predicate for appellate review. If the law of the

---

[6] See **§10.10** for amplification of this proposition.

[7] See Comment, *Defendant's Right to an Opening Statement,* 34 SC L Rev 145, 147 (1982).

[8] *Id.*

jurisdiction confers a clear right to an opening statement, the trial judge is unlikely to deny it. If, on the other hand, the right is not clearly established, the preclusion frequently is found to be a matter of discretion.[9] Forceful objection at that juncture, however, is the best strategy for palliation of the impact of the impairment, because it enhances the likelihood that the trial judge may extend greater latitude during cross-examination, lest he or she be rendered vulnerable to reversal on the ground of effective denial of due process.

The difficulties besetting counsel in that situation are very real, but that fact should not inspire hopelessness. The *guiding hand of counsel* loses much of its effectiveness if it merely grasps a white flag.

When a lawyer is thus deprived, the first opportunity to clarify his or her position for the jury comes at the start of the cross-examination of the eyewitness. Normally, the disadvantaged lawyer will represent the defense, and the questioning will take the form of cross-examination. In that situation, the following format of opening questions is suggested.

Q. [Mr. or Ms. Witness], you are, of course, just as willing to answer my questions as you were to answer [opposing counsel's] questions, aren't you?

Q. And if I behave fairly toward you, will you promise to behave fairly toward me and [client]?

Q. In fairness, I do not expect you to change your story, and I never did. Does that fact make you feel more at ease in answering my questions?

Q. I understand that by this time you are completely committed to your [identification, or version of the event], but notwithstanding that, are you completely willing to give me full and fair answers to my questions?

Q. And are you willing to do that even if I suggest that you are mistaken and ask questions designed to show that you are?

In some respects, these questions may be vulnerable to technical objections in that they constitute assertions by the cross-examiner rather than questions. An attempt has been made to frame them in terms designed for legitimate probing of the witness' attitude and possible bias. They should be asked, in any event, for their effect in conditioning the jury, even if objections are sustained. Even in some cases in which

---

[9] United States v Salovitz, 701 F2d 17, 20 (2d Cir 1983).

an opening statement has been made, such introductory questioning may provide a useful supplement.

§7.06 Preparation and Objective

The cross-examination of an eyewitness, like all features of a well-conducted trial, must be planned carefully. As far as reasonably possible, the diligent lawyer must attempt to anticipate trial developments and to devise a strategy to enhance the apparent significance of favorable evidence and circumstances, while minimizing the impact of facts tending to support the opponent.

In contemplating the cross-examination of an eyewitness, the suggested starting point is a review of the psychological and psychoneurological factors involved in perception.[10] The purpose of that review is to attempt to construct a list of factors applicable to the case which might have caused the witness to reach a mistaken conclusion.

The most attainable objective of cross-examination of the sincere but mistaken eyewitness is the establishment of solid points in a self-assured and composed manner. The case ordinarily should not be permitted to turn on a dramatic encounter with the witness. The cross-examination should instead be conducted as an important but integral part of a coherent trial in which the opening statement and the summation play equally important roles.

The preparation, therefore, consists in compiling a list of facts which tend to detract from the reliability of the witness' testimonial recollection, and in assuring that the propositions suggested by the cross-examiner's questions can be sustained extrinsically if the witness refuses to concede their validity. It is that list which forms the predicate for the opening statement, and which guides the conduct of all elements of the case toward a summation which exploits fully the inferences to be drawn from the listed propositions.

§7.07 Analysis of Influences: The Scene Revisited

To the extent warranted by the facts and significance of the case, every reasonable possibility of a distracting or distorting influence should be considered. The scene should be visited under circumstances of weather, traffic, season, and time of day which resemble as closely as possible the conditions which existed at the time of the questioned

---

[10] See **ch 2**, especially **§§2.39-2.52.**

event.[11] In the specific aspect of an inspection in preparation for cross-examination, a few suggestions are offered here.

The prospective cross-examiner should bear constantly in mind the necessity to preserve proof of those matters which the witness might not be willing to concede—and for that purpose, the cautious lawyer assumes that every proposition tending to weaken the identification will be disputed by the witness. Few experiences produce greater frustration than a witness' denial of a fact known to the cross-examiner to be true, but which the cross-examiner is not prepared to prove by competent evidence. The lawyer's testimony is barred by both practical and ethical considerations, and frequently he or she has no means to tell the jury that the witness is wrong. The best answer to the problem is to visit the scene in the company of a credible person who can prove any relevant fact which the witness may deny. Such persons frequently are referred to as *provers*. For this purpose, the authors recommend that a law student be used as the prover if available. The student probably will welcome the opportunity. His or her participation may be explained to the jury quite properly in terms of an interest in trial practice. He or she is likely to present a good appearance, to be articulate, and to respond intelligently as a witness. A law student carries an aura of presumptive credibility far superior to that of a private investigator and is relatively free from the suggestion of bias which might attach to the lawyer's secretary or office associate.

If it becomes necessary to prove points which the eyewitness will not concede, the prover should be questioned in a manner which makes it clear that he or she was in the presence of the lawyer every step of the way. The prover should be asked to tell what "we" saw. The dialogue between the prover and the lawyer would make it clear to the jury that the prover's testimony carries the imprimatur of the lawyer's personal knowledge, and that if the lawyer were to testify, he or she would swear to the same facts. It is wise, however, to tell the jury during summation that ethical considerations prevented the lawyer from testifying. Otherwise, an uninformed juror might draw an adverse inference from the lawyer's testimonial silence.

In the final analysis, the purpose of visiting the scene is not merely to learn facts, but to acquire proof. The lawyer must attempt to attain a position of strength, such that the witness is forced to choose between acknowledging facts tending to weaken his or her accusatory testimony or being subjected to embarrassing contradiction by unimpeachable evidence. The lawyer must not permit the witness to dissemble with

---

[11] See **§3.02**.

respect to provable facts such as the distance between two points or the number of stairs between two landings. Tape measures and cameras are available as tools for the resolution of such issues, and they should be employed accordingly.

A frequently contested issue is the lighting conditions at the scene of the event. As long as the issue is treated as a subjective matter, the cross-examiner cannot expect agreement from the witness. Lighting intensity which appears dim to a defense lawyer may seem to approximate sunshine in the recollection of a witness bent upon avoiding a suggestion of mistaken identification. A common and relatively cheap photographer's light meter can serve to quantify the light available to the witness at the scene. A second reading can be taken at a dim point in the courtroom or at some other place familiar to the jurors. The prover may then be able to testify that the light at the scene had only one-third the intensity of the light at a place to which the jurors can readily relate. Two predicates for that testimony, of course, would be calibration of the light meter before each reading and at least a rudimentary knowledge of photographic data.[12] Readings should be taken at both the witness' claimed position and the point at which the event occurred. The difference may be very significant, since it is hard to observe a dark scene from a lighted position.

Photographs used during the examination of witnesses should be large enough to enable the jurors to follow the action. Gross enlargements can be very expensive, particularly if color is used. It is possible to use smaller photographs with copies for each juror, but that method does not enable the jurors to see the items to which the witness points while testifying. Consideration should be given to the use of a slide projector. Effective employment of that instrument involves reduction of the courtroom lighting intensity, which may not be practical; to do so, on the other hand, may furnish a dramatic basis for the testimony of comparative light meter readings. Another option is to copy a black-and-white photograph onto an overhead projector transparency. That transfer may be done at very reasonable cost, using transparency sheets which can be imprinted through an ordinary flat-sheet copier.

In summary, the important thing is to assure that the eyewitness will be unable to quarrel credibly with the facts suggested by the cross-examiner's questions. For present purposes, the word *scene* must be used in its broadest sense. The investigation must not be limited to the place at which the crime or tort occurred. It should extend to the location of

---

[12] For example, a light meter indication of f 5.6 means that the light striking the meter is one-fourth as intense as would be the case if the reading had been f 11. The witness should be prepared to discuss such matters knowledgeably.

every event concerning which the eyewitness is to testify—including, where relevant, the place at which the initial identification was made.

§7.08 Analysis of Influences: The Event Reconstructed

Complete familiarity with the places to which the eyewitness will refer is essential to a proper understanding of the strengths and weaknesses of his or her story. Once that familiarity has been achieved, all available statements and prior testimony of the eyewitness and persons who may offer supporting or contradictory testimony should be reviewed thoroughly. Careful notes should be made of any aspects in which the physical layout and environmental influences tend to cast doubt on the likelihood that the witness might have made clear observations of the event. That comparison between the witness' story and the objective facts shown by the lawyer's examination of the scene forms the basis of the lawyer's cross-examination plan.

§7.09 —Impediments and Distractions

In those cases in which it can be suggested credibly that the presence of some physical obstacle would have prevented or seriously impeded the observations which the witness claims to have made, the lawyer would be able to make a forceful impression upon the jury. The case in which the lawyer can demonstrate that it would have been physically impossible for the witness to have observed the events concerning which he or she has testified is, obviously, quite rate. However, that possibility, remote though it may be, underscores the importance of a careful investigation at the scene of the event in all cases. In many cases, moreover, the lawyer's investigation discloses a basis for the contention that the layout of the scene presented obstacles to the claimed observation in some degree.

Impediments and distractions may be very meaningful even though they may fall far short of an impenetrable barrier to the witness' claimed observations. Subtle influences such as passing traffic, reflections of sunlight from the windows of a building across the street, physical discomfort arising from weather or other circumstances, and the annoyance created by loud noises or even by the unwelcome persistence of softer sounds—all these and many more can prevent a full focus of attention on an event.

Another class of distractions is generated internally by the witness. Almost always, he or she had arrived at the scene in pursuit of an objective which did not involve close attention, if any at all, to the event in question. Such influences can be much more powerful than any physical distraction. It becomes important, therefore, to learn what brought the witness to the scene, and to treat the possible preoccupation thus created as a significant factor, if that may be done convincingly. The lawyer should proceed to list every factor which may have caused the witness to react to the questioned event with anything less than total concentration.

It should not be overlooked that events contain their own potential for distraction. The witness who can describe in detail the gun carried by the offender, did not devote the entire period of observation to a study of the facial features of the person who carried that gun. The greater the number of details which the witness is prepared to offer, the less likely it becomes that any one of those details is as accurately recounted as would be the case if that detail had been the primary focus of the witness' attention.

As an example, Ms. Good, the hypothetical purse-snatching victim whose testimony is set forth in **§6.06**,[13] claimed that she had an unobstructed view of the robber from a distance of approximately 12 inches when her purse was forcibly taken from her. A cross-examiner would almost certainly be able to phrase questions so that Ms. Good would claim to have seen the offender seize the purse strap with his hand. Quite likely, if challenged to do so, she would attempt to demonstrate the actual seizure, complete with hand positions. She could not, however, have made those observations while looking at the robber's face, a fact which can be pointed out to good effect during the defense summation.

§7.10 —Time Frame

The passage of time has several dimensions of importance in planning the cross-examination. The length of time available for the witness' observations is a matter of obvious significance. Hardly less important, however, is the length of time which elapsed between the making of those observations and the witness' identification of the supposed actor. Another factor which must not be overlooked is that a *short* lapse between a suggestive influence and an identification tends to point up a causal connection between the two events, so that the identification

---

[13] This fact scenario is based upon the problem "State v. Lawrence," *Problems and Cases in Trial Advocacy, Law School Edition,* 2nd Ed. (1981), which is published by the National Institute for Trial Advocacy (NITA). Adapted and reproduced with the permission of NITA.

can more readily be pictured as a reaction induced by the suggestive tactic.

The impact of a lapse of time can be accentuated in some cases by showing that there was no particular reason for the witness to have remembered the event. A point more frequently available, but frequently overlooked, is the absence of any means by which a witness could have kept the event fresh in his or her mind during the interval between impression and recall. If, as usually is true, the witness made no notes at the time and was totally dependent upon his or her power of recollection in the face of a large number of unrelated intervening events, that fact should be emphasized.

§7.11 —Familiarity

Eyewitness testimony acquires enhanced reliability if the witness has an established familiarity with the person or event in question. That fact has a corollary of no lesser significance: If the testimony relates to an unfamiliar individual, object, or event, its reliability is weakened.

The lawyer's inquiry should not be limited to the witness' prior familiarity with the person identified by that witness. Most events which give rise to litigation of the type involving a challenge to the credibility of an eyewitness are of an unusual and startling nature. The witness probably had never before seen anything quite like it. That fact in itself creates sensations of confusion and excitement which tend to detract from the reliability of the ensuing observations. The lawyer should lose no opportunity to point out that the witness' observations involved unfamiliar persons, events, or circumstances.

§7.12 Predisposition and Bias

At this point, the discussion approaches but does not cross the line which separates the sincere but mistaken witness from the deliberate liar. As every experienced lawyer is aware, bias is more likely to produce exaggeration than outright falsehood. Sympathy for the victim, a desire to be a factor in the solution of the case, the hope of participation in a possible reward, and many similar factors can cause a witness to suppress doubts concerning the accuracy of his or her recollection. For example, if it is shown that the witness entered a lineup room with a strong desire to find the offender it can be argued with good effect during summation that the witness' predisposition made it more likely that he or she would pick someone from the lineup than that he or she would admit an inability to do so.

Frequently, bias is implanted rather than ingrained. The suggestive tactics described in **§§3.14** through **3.16** are offensive principally because they create bias. If a witness has been subjected to such tactics, the lawyer should suggest during cross-examination and argue during summation that the intent was to implant bias, that the officials are skilled and experienced in that tactic, and that they succeeded. The witness who has been told that strong extrinsic evidence inculpates the prisoner and that the prisoner has an unsavory background is most unlikely to view that prisoner objectively.

§7.13 The Prior Inconsistency

An eyewitness behaves inconsistently with his or her accusatory trial testimony whenever that witness:

1. Fails during a pretrial or investigatory encounter to make the questioned identification with the same degree of certitude which he or she displays on the witness stand
2. Omits from a recorded statement a relevant detail to which he or she testifies at trial
3. Changes his or her story in respect to a matter which a person in the witness' claimed position should reasonably be expected to remember with clarity

If there is no record of the witness' prior statements, that absence should in itself be treated as a fact tending to cast doubt on the accuracy of the accusatory testimony. A failure to record carefully the witness' initial impression should be viewed during cross-examination and summation as a suggestion of skepticism or dissatisfaction on the part of the investigators. Any sketch made under the direction of the witness should be examined carefully for significant deviations from the appearance of the accused. In that connection, it is worthy of note that some police agencies deliberately fail to ask the witness whether the final version of the sketch is accurate, in order to prevent the establishment of a predicate for later impeachment if the witness has adopted a sketch which turns out not to resemble the accused. A failure overtly to adopt the sketch, however, is not a basis upon which impeachment may logically be interdicted. The important thing is the use made of the sketch after its completion. If it has been published in the police bulletin or otherwise disseminated in furtherance of the effort to apprehend the offender, it is a defiance of logic to imagine that the police had not been told by the witness that the sketch is accurate.[14]

§7.14 Multiple Eyewitnesses

The larger the number of accusatory eyewitnesses, the grimmer the prospects for the person accused by their testimony. There is no easy answer to this problem. The lawyer should explore every lead suggesting that a conference may have been held among the eyewitnesses, since the most probable purpose of such a conference is the reconciliation of differences in their stories. All pretrial statements should be scrutinized carefully in order to extract every inconsistency. If the inconsistencies are repeated on the stand, the cross-examination should be minimal, with primary reliance placed upon the discrepancies. If the inconsistencies are disavowed at trial, the cross-examination should suggest, and the subsequent summation should charge, that the change demonstrates the employment of suggestive and even coercive tactics against the witnesses in order to distort their stories into an artificial state of mutual conformity.

If the circumstances described by each witness are somewhat different, the cross-examiner should address each of them as a discrete challenge, avoiding as far as practicable repetitive questioning which is likely to cause the jury to lose interest. If their stories are identical, the cross-examiner should consider concentrating his or her fire upon the least attractive or most suggestible of the witnesses, while treating the others in a manner which suggests that there is no point in retracing the same path. The order in which the witnesses appear affects the strategy of the cross-examiner to some degree, but it need not dictate basic tactics. If, for example, the target witness is the fourth one to be called, it may be wise to conduct a restrained cross-examination of the first three. The lawyer is thus enabled to close on a high note, and to explain during summation that "I had to hear that story three times before I realized that something was very wrong."

One innovative lawyer has devised a technique which should be reserved for cases in which the relative physical locations of the participants at the scene is subject to some possible uncertainty, and in which there is no clear cooperation among the witnesses. A diagram of

---

[14] The line of cases admitting published statements as hearsay exceptions where the publication is made by a responsible agency and publication of a falsehood would have been self-defeating, derives from Dallas County v Commercial Union Assurance Co, 286 F2d 388 (5th Cir 1961). When offered against the prosecution, police bulletins describing wanted offenders clearly are nonhearsay within the meaning of Fed R Evid 801(d)(2)(B), (C), and (D).

the scene is placed on an easel, and a separate transparent overlay is used for each witness. Each is asked to point out the specific positions of the participants, and the points are duly marked. A comparison of the several overlays is likely to demonstrate to the jury a substantial disparity among the stories of the witnesses. The lawyer must choose carefully the cases in which that technique is to be employed, for obvious reasons. If the tactic fails, the thud is very audible.

§7.15 Illustrative Cross-Examinations

The effectiveness of a cross-examination cannot be appreciated unless it is considered in the light of the direct examination. The direct and cross-examinations of eyewitnesses, taken from two actual cases, are reprinted in **§§3.17** and **3.18.** A reading of those partial transcripts will be useful preparation for consideration of the questioning demonstrated within the remainder of this chapter.

It is never wise, of course, to rely blindly upon emulation of techniques which may appear, from the perspective of the reader of a transcript, to have been employed by the questioner. Each cross-examination is unique and can be evaluated only in the light of the courtroom ambience, the influences imparted by preceding events, and the ammunition available to the cross-examiner. One question propounded by the cross-examiner in the *Foster* case[15] is a facial violation of every accepted precept of cross-examination: "Anything else you want to add today . . .?" The answer to such an open-ended question can inundate the cross-examiner with a fearful volume of adverse information, including much that otherwise would be inadmissible. The witness in the *Foster* case, however, gave an answer which was very helpful to the cross-examiner. It is impossible to say whether that result was obtained through sheer good fortune or whether it was the product of preparation so very thorough as to preclude the possibility of an adverse consequence.

In general, the cross-examiner of an eyewitness should take special pains to ask only questions which properly are to be answered with a yes or a no. The eyewitness normally should not be given any opportunity to offer embellishments or explanations, because such offerings almost always will tend to reinforce the challenged identification. The cross-examiner in *Foster,* however, violated that rule to good effect. In commenting upon a cross-examination, as with all other

[15] Foster v California, 394 US 440 (1969). See **§3.17.**

aspects of trial practice, it is difficult to express credible disapproval of anything that proves effective.

The eyewitness in *Foster* also provided an illustration of the type of evasive answer which, because it is in the nature of a negative pregnant, is likely to be appreciated by the jury only if properly emphasized. The emphasis, however, must not take a form which enables the witness to change his or her statement. When Foster's counsel pressed for a concession that a police officer had told the witness that the offender was one of the persons in the lineup, the witness answered: "He didn't specifically say that they had the man." A useful response in that situation is for the lawyer to call upon the witness to reaffirm that answer, without permitting him to vary it. One technique which frequently is employed for that purpose is to ask immediately: " 'He didn't *specifically* say that,' is that what you just said?" with appropriate emphasis on the key word. Another procedure is simply to rejoin, "Not *specifically*. I see." Yet a third procedure is to base further questions on the witness' reference to the police officer's failure to have made the crucial statement *specifically:*

Q. Now, Mr. David, in normal conversation you're smart enough to understand what people mean when they talk to you, even when they don't say things specifically, isn't that right?

A. Yes.

Q. And you were able to do that when you were talking to Mr. Kiehl, weren't you?

A. Yes.

Q. So even when he didn't spell things out *specifically*, you were able to understand him, weren't you?

In the transcript of the eyewitness testimony in the *Moore* case,[16] the cross-examination opens with a series of short, incisive questions which reasonably must be answered simply yes or no. Many of the questions are interrogatory rather than leading—e.g., "Was there a light on in the room?"—but the answers supported the cross-examiner's theory, and one must suppose that the questioning was based upon an earlier transcript (possibly that of the preliminary hearing) which the witness could not have disavowed with credibility. The apparent noncoercive quality of such questions tends to minimize the likelihood that a jury might believe that the witness' favorable answers had been the products of unfairness or mistake.

---

[16] Moore v Illinois, 434 US 220 (1977). See **§3.18.**

Those two transcripts, like most others, can be used by the aspiring cross-examiner with good effect. Persons in that position are advised to read each question, and to consider why it was asked, why the questioner adopted the particular form, and whether the questioning might have been improved. The transcript should be reviewed a second time for the purpose of determining whether additional questions should have been asked, and a third time to plan a sample summation based on those questions.

§7.16 Illustrations: The Scenario

The majority of the practical demonstrations contained within this volume are based upon the hypothetical case of *People of the State of Columbia v Paul Pure,* a scenario portrayed within **§4.08.**[17]

The postulated facts of that case provide a reasonable amount of ammunition for the cross-examiner, including darkness, a fleeting observational opportunity, and an ambiguous earlier description of the offender. An example of the direct and cross-examination of the complainant based upon those facts appears within **§§6.07** and **6.08.**

The next few sections present cross-examination vignettes based upon facts much more supportive of the eyewitness' identification. For purposes of the illustrations which follow, assume that Ms. Good has testified that her purse was stolen in clear daylight by a person whom she had the opportunity to observe (but whose appearance she had no reason to scrutinize) for several minutes preceding the theft. Assume further that no suggestive practices influenced her subsequent identification of the defendant. There is, in short, nothing in the assumed facts which enables the cross-examiner to base an attack upon an inherent weakness in the eyewitness' testimony.

The purpose here is to show that the principles enunciated within this chapter can be exploited reasonably to challenge eyewitness testimony in many situations where the observations have been made under circumstances lending substantial presumptive credibility to the accuser's story.

---

[17] This fact scenario is based upon the problem "State v. Lawrence," *Problems and Cases in Trial Advocacy, Law School Edition,* 2nd Ed. (1981), which is published by the National Institute for Trial Advocacy (NITA). Adapted and reproduced with the permission of NITA.

§7.17 —Exploiting Knowledge of the Scene

The importance of familiarity with the scene of the event is considered in **§7.07**. The following examination exemplifies the manner in which routine facts may sometimes be employed to weaken the force of the witness' identification.

The cross-examiner here proceeds to demonstrate complete familiarity with the scene, including a mastery of details which have escaped the notice of the witness. Ultimately, having employed her knowledge of the scene to lead the witness into a condition of general acquiescence in the attorney's suggestions, she extracts a concession which might well have been refused if the ultimate question had not been preceded by that conditioning process.

It should be noted that this cross-examination does not suggest that the scene itself presents some obstacle to the witness' claimed observations. Commonplace facts, instead, are employed in such a manner as to suggest an alternative theory to the defendant's guilt, consistent with the general circumstances surrounding the identification.

It must be noted that this examination, and those presented in the following sections of this chapter, are only segments of the questioning which normally would be conducted in a case of this type. They are not intended to illustrate the totality of a useful cross-examination.

Q. (BY MS. DE FENE). Now, Ms. Good, you have testified that at the time your purse was stolen, you were on your way from work to your home on Diversey Avenue, isn't that right?

A. That's right.

Q. Now, you actually live about three blocks down from Clark Street, west of Clark Street, isn't that true?

A. Yes.

Q. And so you get off the bus at Clark and Diversey, isn't that right?

A. Yes.

Q. You cross to the south side of the street, then, don't you?

A. Yes.

Q. And then you begin to walk.

A. Of course.

Q. Now, Diversey Avenue at the time of this occurrence was undergoing some construction, isn't that true?

A. Oh, there was some.

Q. Well, the sidewalks were being repaired, isn't that right?

A. I'm not sure. I think. I'm not sure.
Q. Well, you know that the sidewalk in front of your house had been broken through the winter. You know that, don't you?
A. Yes, I guess that's right.
Q. And the sidewalk was being repaired, wasn't it?
A. Yeah. Yeah, it was.
Q. You remember that now, don't you?
A. Yes, I do.
Q. And so as you were walking down Diversey Avenue on the south side, there were several times when you had to step around barriers, isn't that so?
A. I suppose so.
Q. Well, don't you remember that now? There were several barriers that you had to step around?
A. Well, if you say so, I guess there were.
Q. And then when you got to the end of the first block, you had to cross the street, didn't you?
A. Of course.
Q. And on that corner, there is a funeral parlor, isn't that right?
A. I think so.
Q. Now, at this time, you had not heard anybody walking behind you, had you?
A. Not then.
Q. But this was at noon, wasn't it?
A. Yes.
Q. And there are many people who live on that street, isn't that true?
A. Yes.
Q. As a matter of fact, there's a whole row of duplex apartment buildings on that side of the street, isn't that true?
A. Yes.
Q. And there are all kinds of cars parked outside of those apartment buildings on the street, isn't that true?
A. There are a lot of them.
Q. And people get out of the cars and go into the apartment buildings, isn't that true?
A. I suppose so.

Q. And after you crossed the street, you walked past the funeral parlor, isn't that true?
A. Yes.
Q. And that funeral parlor is DeStefano's, D-e S-t-e-f-a-n-o, is that correct?
A. I'm really not sure. That may be it.
Q. You've never noticed that?
A. I've noticed it, but I don't remember the name.
Q. Well, did you notice that right across from DeStefano's down the street is a large maple tree? Have you ever noticed that?
A. Not particularly.
Q. So you passed the funeral parlor and you continued walking?
A. Yes.
Q. But you tell us you didn't hear anybody behind you during that block.
A. Not then, no.
Q. But there were cars going up and down the street, weren't there?
A. Yes.
Q. Diversey's a rather busy street?
A. Yes.
Q. And this was again about noontime you tell us?
A. Yes.
Q. When you got to the end of that block, you began to cross the street again to enter the block upon which your apartment building is located, isn't that right?
A. That's right.
Q. Now, when you crossed that street, you also had a little difficulty, didn't you?
A. I think I did.
Q. And the reason you had a little difficulty is because that street is also torn up, isn't that true?
A. Well, it's not torn up. There's some repairs—there were some repairs going on.
Q. Well, it's being repaired. It isn't repaired yet, is it?
A. Not completely.
Q. It wasn't repaired yesterday, was it?

A. Not completely, no.

Q. It wasn't repaired this morning when you came down to court, was it?

A. No.

Q. So you had to make your way around that barrier there to get to the other side of the street.

A. Yeah. They've got some wooden things up so you don't walk into the holes and that sort of affair, yeah.

Q. Now, when you got to the other side of the street, the very first building that you encountered on your left was a tavern, isn't that right?

A. I think so, yes.

Q. And that's called Harry's Tavern, isn't it?

A. I suppose.

Q. And a lot of young people hang out there, don't they?

A. Yes, that I've seen.

Q. And the reason a lot of young people hang out there is because a lot of young people hang around there and live around there, isn't that true?

A. I really don't know. I know there are a lot of them there.

Q. Well, aren't there a number of colleges located in that part of the city?

A. Not too far away, yeah.

Q. And don't a lot of college students live in that area?

A. Yes, I've seen them.

Q. And don't a lot of those college students wear T-shirts?

A. Yes.

Q. And don't a lot of those college students wear long hair?

A. I suppose.

Q. And don't a lot of those college kids wear Levis?

A. Yes.

Q. And aren't some of those Levis white Levis?

A. Oh, could be.

Q. Well, you've seen a lot of them on the street like that, haven't you?

A. Yes, I guess so.

§7.18 —Use of Photographs

In the illustration in **§7.17**, the witness generally accepted the cross-examiner's suggestions concerning the street repairs and structures in the vicinity of the place at which the theft occurred.

Many witnesses, however, may tend to minimize or even to deny such facts. In that event, as suggested in **§7.07,** the cross-examiner should be prepared to present extrinsic proofs of those suggestions. In most cases, the most useful and persuasive vehicle for such proof is a photograph.

This section presents an example of the employment of a photograph in questioning a witness like Ms. Good who is unwilling to admit anything that might weaken his or her identification.

In most jurisdictions, the cross-examiner will not be able to introduce the photograph until the witness' proponent will have rested his or her case; but if, as normally happens, the witness concedes facts which qualify the photograph as an exhibit, it may be used during cross-examination without restriction if the cross-examiner promises to introduce it when the adversary rests. Not infrequently, it is possible to cause the exhibit to be received as an exhibit during cross-examination because the witness' proponent may deem it tactically unwise to present a technical objection to the offer. The illustration which follows deals only with the questions to be propounded during cross-examination and makes no reference to the tender and admission of the photograph.

Q. (BY MS. DE FENE). Now, Ms. Good, when you crossed that street, you also had a little difficulty, didn't you?

A. I don't recall any difficulty.

Q. Well, the street is torn up in that area, isn't it?

A. There are a few repairs being made, I believe, but nothing that would cause difficulty in crossing the street.

Q. Those repairs have been going on for some time, haven't they?

A. For a while.

Q. And when you crossed the street that day, did you have to walk around the workers fixing the street?

A. No. There weren't any workers.

Q. Don't they work on that street fairly constantly?

A. No, they hardly ever work on it.

Q. So it's pretty much in the same condition now, that it was in at the time your purse was stolen, is that right?

A. Pretty much.

Q. I show you now a photograph previously marked as Defense Exhibit 1 for Identification, and I ask you whether you are familiar with the street scene there depicted.
A. That's the intersection near my house.
Q. And that's the way it looked on the day your purse was stolen, isn't it?
A. I don't think all those boards were there at that time.
Q. Do you deny that this is a photograph of the intersection taken exactly 10 days after your purse was stolen?
A. It might be.
Q. And do you deny that no work whatsoever was done on that intersection during the 10 days following the theft?
A. I don't know.
Q. Well, you'd expect the records of the Department of Streets to prove it one way or the other, wouldn't you?
A. I guess so.
Q. You wouldn't argue with those records, would you?
A. No.
Q. You don't deny, then, that the wooden barriers shown in this photo were present the day your purse was stolen?
A. I really don't know.
Q. So they could have been there, isn't that right?
A. I guess so.
Q. And those barriers reach across the entire sidewalk, don't they?
A. Yes.
Q. So to cross that street, you have to walk completely outside the pedestrian crosswalk, don't you?
A. Yes.
Q. That's what you had to do this morning, isn't it?
A. Yes.
Q. And for lots of mornings before today, isn't that right?
A. Yes
Q. In fact, for many months, isn't that right?
A. I think so.

§7.19 —Event Reconstructed with Distractions

The usefulness of the techniques suggested in **§§7.08** and **7.09** is illustrated in this section. The cross-examiner here casts doubt upon the clarity of the witness' observations by reconstructing the circumstances of the theft described in **§7.16,** with emphasis upon the factors tending to distract the witness' attention from the features of her attacker.

For purposes of this example, assume that the victim, Ms. Good, and the thief were walking toward each other and that the thief grabbed the purse as they passed.

Q. (BY MS. DE FENE). Ms. Good, your apartment is located in the middle of the block, isn't it?

A. Yes.

Q. And you tell us that when you turned around you were standing in front of about the third apartment from the corner, isn't that right?

A. The third apartment building, yes.

Q. The third apartment building from the corner?

A. Yes.

Q. And directly in front of that apartment building there is construction going on right now, isn't there?

A. Yes.

Q. That is to say, construction workers are repairing the sidewalk, aren't they?

A. Yes.

Q. And that sidewalk was being repaired on the day in which you had this experience, isn't that true?

A. That's right.

Q. When you suddenly turned around, you actually turned around down on some gravel because the sidewalk was being replaced, isn't that true?

A. Yes, that's right.

Q. And when you spun around, you fell down, isn't that true?

A. He pushed me down.

Q. But you went down.

A. Yes.

Q. When you fell, the back of your head struck a piece of sidewalk that was jutting up, isn't that correct?

A. Yes.

Q. And you received a bad blow, didn't you?

A. It hurt, yes.

Q. As a matter of fact, you subsequently received some medical treatment for that blow, didn't you?

A. Yes, I did.

Q. Now, Ms. Good, when you got off the bus, it was your intention simply to go home, wasn't it?

A. Yes.

Q. You had been to work that day, is that right?

A. Yes, I had.

Q. And you performed all your normal duties?

A. Yes.

Q. And then you had ridden the bus home?

A. Yes.

Q. And you were kind of anxious to get home at the end of the workday?

A. Yes, I was.

Q. After the bus ride.

A. Yes.

Q. The bus was rather crowded, wasn't it?

A. Yes.

Q. It really wasn't a very comfortable ride back, was it?

A. Well, wasn't too bad.

Q. Now, in any event, as you were then walking along, you were thinking about going home, weren't you, and the things you were going to do when you got home?

A. Generally, yes.

Q. And you were thinking about things that had happened at work that day?

A. Well, I really don't remember what I was thinking about.

Q. In any event, you certainly weren't thinking that your purse was going to be snatched. You weren't thinking that, were you?

A. Certainly not.

Q. Now, you've already said, I believe, that there was quite a bit of traffic on Diversey Avenue, is that right?

A. Yes. At noontime there is—

Q. It was noontime? Cars were going by?

A. Yes.

Q. There were other people on the street?

A. On my side of the street, I don't remember anybody.

Q. There were people on the other side?

A. Yes, I think so.

Q. You were able to see them?

A. Yes. I generally remember people being there.

Q. So as you were walking along, you were kind of casually looking at what there might be to see on the way home, is that right?

A. Well, I was walking along.

Q. And you were observing the obstructions in the street so you wouldn't trip or fall, weren't you?

A. Yes. I had to be a little bit careful.

Q. Meanwhile, you saw a man walking toward you from a block away, is that right?

A. Yes, just vaguely at first.

Q. Now, the two of you were walking, you say, toward each other, is that right?

A. Yes.

Q. And so you were then facing each other more or less for a couple of minutes or so, is that right?

A. Yes.

Q. As you saw him coming toward you, you did not take any special note of him, did you? Any more than anyone else you would, did you?

A. No.

Q. Now, Ms. Good, you were walking down the street, then, just in the same way that you normally would walk down any street, isn't that right?

A. Yes.

Q. And as you normally walk down the street, you generally pass other people, don't you?

A. Yes, many times.

Q. Many times. And as you pass other people, you don't make any particular attempt to memorize their features, do you?

A. No.

Q. You just walk past them and they're faces in the crowd, is that about it?

A. I suppose so, unless they're familiar to me.

Q. Well, now, at the time, the man that grabbed your purse, he wasn't familiar to you, was he?

A. I'd never seen him before.

Q. And so, ultimately, the two of you approached each other until you became quite close, isn't that right?

A. Yes.

Q. And he waited, did he not, until he got quite close to you before he grabbed your purse or tried to, isn't that right?

A. Yes. He was right across from me when it happened.

Q. And right up to that time, you had no special reason to pay any particular attention to him, did you?

A. No.

§7.20 —Minimization of Time Frame

Q (BY MS. DE FENE). Now, Ms. Good, ultimately when the man was right within reaching distance of you, he reached out and he grabbed your purse, isn't that right?

A. Yes, he did.

Q. And he grabbed it quickly, did he not?

A. Just like that.

Q. Just like that. You didn't have a chance to protect yourself, did you?

A. I wasn't thinking of doing that.

Q. And he quickly grabbed it from you and pushed you, is that right?

A. Well, I don't know which happened first.

Q. It all came very quickly, didn't it?

A. It all happened at once.

Q. Now, Ms. Good, would it be a fair statement that the man seemed to you to be fairly athletic, in good control of his body, and capable of moving just as quickly as he had to move?

A. Well, he was a young man. He is a young man.

Q. Now, Ms. Good, would it be a fair statement, then, that as the man came up to you he reached out like this, grabbed your purse, shoved you, and turned away just as I've just done? Is that right?

A. I really don't know what he did because I started to fall down immediately.

Q. Now, Ms. Good, from the time that he reached out to grab your purse until the time you began to fall, that was almost a matter of seconds, wasn't it?

A. It all happened at once. He took the purse and he was gone.

Q. And this, as you say, was a man you had never seen before, is that right?

A. That's right.

§7.21 —Familiarity

The demonstration which follows portrays a cross-examination which exploits both aspects of the familiarity element which is considered in **§7.11.**

The questioner here points up both the lulling effect of the accustomed surroundings and circumstances and the distracting effect of an unanticipated and aberrant event.

Q (BY MS. DE FENE). Ms. Good, I believe that you testified that you are employed in the downtown area of the city, isn't that right?

A. Yes, it is.

Q. And you're on an early morning shift that brings you in there sometime around six in the morning and you're free sometime around noon, is that about right?

A. That's right.

Q. And whenever you go to work, you walk down the same street, Diversey Avenue, that we've been talking about, isn't that right?

A. In the morning, yes.

Q. And when you come back, you reverse your path and you come back home along that same street, is that right?

A. As a general rule, yes.

Q. And you've traveled that street, then, literally thousands of times, haven't you?

A. Yes.

Q. It's a perfectly familiar environment to you, is it not?

A. That's right.

Q. And there's nothing particularly unusual about you walking down that street, isn't that right?
A. Not at all.
Q. You've done it many times, isn't that right?
A. Yes.
Q. And you've done it many times without anything unusual happening to you there, is that right?
A. Certainly not something like this.
Q. Now, the event that you've described, that is in fact the only time, is it not, that you have been physically threatened in all the time that you've been walking down that street?
A. Yes, this is the very first time it ever happened to me. It's happened to other people, though.
Q. Pardon?
A. It's happened to other people, though.
Q. But you weren't there, were you?
A. No, I wasn't.
Q. So that this was the first time that it ever happened to you, isn't that right?
A. Yes.
Q. And the first time that you had ever seen anything like that happen, isn't that right?
A. That's right. It was terrifying.
Q. Now, Ms. Good, when this six-foot-tall man walked up to you, grabbed your purse, and shoved you down, it would be a perfectly fair statement to say that you were really quite frightened, weren't you?
A. I was terrified.
Q. You didn't know at first what was happening, isn't that right?
A. That's right.

§7.22 —Predisposition

In the following excerpt, the defense attorney establishes the victim's predisposition to identify whomever the police officer had arrested.

Q (BY MS. DE FENE). Ms. Good, about three days after your purse was snatched, you got a call from Officer Right, did you not?

A. Yes.

Q. And he told you that he would like you to come down to the police station, isn't that right?

A. Yes.

Q. Because he had somebody there he wanted you to see, isn't that right?

A. Yes. He wanted me to look at someone.

Q. And from what he said, you understood that he wanted you to tell him whether that was the person who had stolen your purse, isn't that right?

A. Yes. That's why he wanted me to come.

Q. And you went, didn't you?

A. Yes.

Q. You went right away, isn't that right?

A. Well, yes.

Q. And you went right away because of the fact that you were anxious to know if this was the person who had taken your purse, isn't that right?

A. Yes. I wanted my purse back.

Q. And if that was the person that took it, you might be able to get your purse back, isn't that right?

A. I was hoping so.

Q. You were hoping so. And, of course, there were things in the purse that you wanted, isn't that right?

A. Yes.

Q. And you wanted to see if you could get those things back, isn't that right?

A. Why, of course.

Q. So when you went down to the station, you went down there hoping that you might be able to get your things back, isn't that right?

A. Yes.

Q. And of course you could get them back that day only if the person whom Officer Right was holding was the person who had taken your purse, isn't that right?

A. Well, yes, and if he had it.

Q. And so you were hoping, were you not, that the person that Officer

Right was holding was somebody who could tell you where your purse was? Isn't that right?

A. I was hoping that, yes.

Q. You were hoping in short that the person that Officer Right was holding was the person who had snatched your purse, isn't that right?

A. Yes.

§7.23 —Prior Inconsistency

The final illustration is of a cross-examination designed to take advantage of the apparent weakness of the initial description of the attacker which Ms. Good furnished to the police.

The cross-examiner here emphasizes the omissions which marred the initial interview: no meaningful notes or record and no effort to refine the description of the attacker by sketch or by word-picture. The cross-examination ends with the suggestion that the witness simply was unable to furnish any significant details concerning the attacker. Later, during summation, the defense attorney will argue that the reason no notes or sketches were made was the apparent inability of the eyewitness to furnish sufficient detail to justify such procedures.

Q (BY MS. DE FENE). Ms. Good, about an hour or so after your purse was snatched, Officer Right came to your home, isn't that right?

A. Yes.

Q. You had called the police and Officer Right responded, isn't that right?

A. Yes.

Q. And he asked you certain questions, isn't that right?

A. Yes.

Q. He asked you what happened, isn't that right?

A. Yes.

Q. Now, Ms. Good, as you told him what was happening, was he writing down your statement at that time? Was he writing down word for word what you told him?

A. No.

Q. Did he have a tape recorder?

A. No.

Q. He had no tape recorder to record your statement?

A. No.

Q. Is there anybody in the world who heard what you told Officer Right other than you and Officer Right?

A. No one else was there.

Q. And except as you remember it and Officer Right remembers it, we have no way now of knowing what you told him, isn't that right?

A. That's right.

Q. Just your memory and his, isn't that right?

A. That's right.

Q. Ms. Good, at any time after that, were you visited by a police artist?

A. No.

Q. Did you visit a police artist?

A. No.

Q. Did anyone show you a sketch and ask you whether that sketch resembled the person who had snatched your purse?

A. No.

Q. No kind of drawing, nothing like that, is that right?

A. No, just—

Q. Did anybody ask you whether you could help to construct—

A. No.

Q. —such a sketch?

A. No.

Q. None of those things happened, isn't that right?

A. That's right.

Q. At any rate, you told them whatever you could about the appearance of your attacker, didn't you?

A. Yes.

Q. And whatever notes Officer Right made, were made after he left you, isn't that right?

A. I guess so.

Q. Do you know whether those notes say anything at all about the thief except that he was about six feet tall, with medium build and long hair?

A. I've never seen it.

Q. No further questions.

8 Expert Testimony Concerning Eyewitness Reliability

§8.01 The Role of the Expert

The psychological and psychoneurological factors which affect a witness' perception and memory are varied and complex.[1] Nonetheless, jurors place enormous stock in the testimony of eyewitnesses under the common misconception that the person who saw the event is in the best posture to relate what happened. It is the function of the trial lawyer to educate the jury about those factors which influence the perception and memory of eyewitnesses. One effective means of accomplishing this function is to present expert testimony which informs the jury of the findings of psychologists who have done research and experiments on the problem of eyewitness misidentification. The expert should be asked to explain in nontechnical terms, and by using readily understandable examples, how perception, memory, and the suggestibility of the human mind may affect the eyewitness' account. Although psychologists have been used on occasion in criminal trials to testify to the fallibility of eyewitness accounts,[2] little attention has been given to the use of such testimony in civil cases. Nonetheless, the use of experts on perception and memory in both civil and criminal cases will likely become greater as their works and findings become better known to the legal community.[3]

§8.02 Relevant Law of Evidence

The admissibility of expert testimony is largely left to the sound discretion of the trial judge. The Federal Rules of Evidence take a liberal approach to the introduction of expert testimony. The rules provide that a witness qualified as an expert because of his or her knowledge, skill, experience, training, or education may testify in the form of an opinion or otherwise if scientific, technical, or other specialized knowledge will assist the trier of fact to understand the evidence or to determine a matter of fact.[4] The rule seems to be similar in many states.[5]

---

[1] See **ch 2**.

[2] See Arnolds, Carroll & Seng, *The Admissibility of Expert Testimony on the Issue of Eyewitness Identification in Criminal Trials,* 2 N Ill UL Rev 59 (1981).

[3] See, e.g., Psychology in Legal Contexts (S. Lloyd-Bostock ed 1981); E. Loftus, Eyewitness Testimony (1979); A.D. Yarmey, The Psychology of Eyewitness Testimony (1979); B. Clifford & R. Bull, The Psychology of Person Identification (1978); see also P. Wall, Eye-Witness Identifications in Criminal Cases (1965); T. Sannito, Discrediting Eyewitness Testimony (1979). See generally the extensive bibliographies in all of the above works.

[4] Fed R Evid 702. *Cf* Barefoot v Estelle, 51 USLW 5189, 5196 (US July 6, 1983).

Nonetheless, the reported cases show a general reluctance to admit the testimony of experts on eyewitness identification. A number of the reported decisions exclude the testimony on the ground that it would invade the province of the jury.[6] However, this rationale is not appropriate in jurisdictions which follow the Federal Rules of Evidence, because the rules permit an expert's opinion to embrace an "ultimate" issue to be decided by the trier of fact.[7]

A more common explanation is that the matter is within the experience of the average juror.[8] For instance, in *United States v Fosher,*[9] the court commented that it does not take an expert to tell a juror that a person under stress is likely to make a mistake. In fact, however, there is much confusion among laypersons on just how stress will affect the reliability of an identification. Professor Elizabeth Loftus cites studies which show that many people wrongly believe that cross-racial identifications are more likely to be accurate, that many people wrongly believe that stress enhances one's ability to perceive,

---

[5] See 7 J. Wigmore, Evidence §1923 (Chadbourn rev 1978); Ibn-Tamas v United States, 407 A2d 626 (DC 1979). *Cf* Fed R Evid 403 (the court may exclude relevant evidence "if its probative value is substantially outweighed by the danger of unfair prejudice, confusion of the issues, or misleading the jury, or by considerations of undue delay, waste of time, or needless presentation of cumulative evidence"). Wigmore has urged that all opinion testimony be admissible subject only to the trial court's discretion to exclude it upon consideration of trial convenience. 7 J. Wigmore, *supra,* at §1929.

For a more detailed treatment of the issues involved in **§§8.02-8.03,** see Arnolds, Carroll & Seng, *The Admissibility of Expert Testimony on the Issue of Eyewitness Identification in Criminal Cases,* 2 N Ill UL Rev 59 (1981).

[6] United States v Brown, 540 F2d 1048, 1054 (10th Cir 1976), *cert denied,* 429 US 1100 (1977); United States v Brown, 501 F2d 146, 150 (9th Cir 1974), *revd on other grounds,* 422 US 225 (1975); United States v Fosher, 449 F Supp 76 (D Mass 1978), *affd,* 590 F2d 381 (1st Cir 1979); People v Brooks, 51 Cal App 3d 1, 7, 112 Cal Rptr 834, 837 (1974); Pankey v Commonwealth, 485 SW2d 513, 522 (Ky 1972); People v Suleski, 58 AD2d 1023, 1027, 397 NYS2d 280, 282 (1977). *But see* United States v Watson, 587 F2d 365, 369 n 6 (7th Cir 1978).

[7] Fed R Evid 704. *See* United States v Watson, 587 F2d 365, 369 n 6 (7th Cir 1978). *Cf* Barefoot v Estelle, 51 USLW 5189, 5196 (US July 6, 1983).

[8] People v Johnson, 97 Ill App 3d 1055, 423 NE2d 1206 (1981), *cert denied,* 455 US 951 (1982). *Accord* United States v Brown, 540 F2d 1048, 1054 (10th Cir 1976), *cert denied,* 429 US 1100 (1977); United States v Fosher, 449 F Supp 76, 77 (D Mass 1978), *affd,* 590 F2d 381 (1st Cir 1979); Criglow v State, 183 Ark 481, 36 SW2d 400 (1931); People v Lawson, 37 Colo App 442, 448, 551 P2d 206, 209 (1976); Dyas v United States, 376 A2d 827, 832 (DC 1977); Nelson v State, 362 So2d 1017, 1021 (Fla Dist Ct App 1978); People v Dixon, 87 Ill App 3d 814, 410 NE2d 252 (1980); Commonwealth v Middleton, 6 Mass App 902, 378 NE2d 450 (1978); Nebraska v Ammons, 208 Neb 812, 816, 305 NW2d 812, 814 (1981).

[9] 449 F Supp 76 (D Mass 1978), *affd,* 590 F2d 381 (1st Cir 1979).

and that most people wrongly believe that witnesses will remember more clearly the details of a violent crime than a nonviolent crime.[10]

A number of other decisions reject the testimony of eyewitness experts on the ground that it will not significantly aid the jury.[11] However, the Federal Rules of Evidence should be literally interpreted to allow the testimony whenever it will assist the trier of fact in evaluating or determining a fact in issue.[12]

Other decisions merely point to the availability of cross-examination and closing argument as effective alternatives to expert testimony.[13] Although jurors can be informed through direct and cross-examination of the facts which lead up to the identification, they will not thereby be informed why those facts render the identification suspect. Jurors will probably not be aware of all the complex physiological and psychological factors which influence identification; indeed, they may have serious misconceptions about what factors are conducive to an inaccurate identification. While defense counsel is free to argue during summation the inconsistencies and vagaries of the testimony that argument may well not succeed in convincing the jury if supporting scientific data are not in the record.

Counsel may request the court to instruct the jury to evaluate carefully any eyewitness testimony, but such an instruction alone will not educate the jury to those factors which make eyewitness testimony vulnerable.[14] Furthermore, the common instruction which states that

---

[10] E. Loftus, Eyewitness Testimony 171-77 (1979). See generally Note, *Did Your Eyes Deceive You? Expert Psychological Testimony on the Unreliability of Eyewitness Identification* 29 Stan L Rev 969 (1977).

[11] *E.g.*, United States v Watson, 587 F2d 365 (7th Cir 1978); United States v Fosher, 449 F Supp 76, 77 (D Mass 1978), *affd,* 590 F2d 381 (1st Cir 1979); United States v Collins, 395 F Supp 629, 637 (MD Pa), *affd,* 523 F2d 1051 (3d Cir 1975); Dyas v United States, 376 A2d 827, 832 (DC 1971); Porter v State, 94 Nev 142, 149, 576 P2d 275, 279 (1978). *See also* United States v Amaral, 488 F2d 1148, 1152 (9th Cir 1973); State v Galloway, 275 NW2d 736, 741 (Iowa 1979) (concurring opinion).

[12] Fed R Evid 702. See also J. Weinstein, Evidence ¶702.[02] (1980); Barefoot v Estelle, 51 USLW 5189, 5196 (US July 6, 1983).

[13] *E.g.*, United States v Amaral, 488 F2d 1148, 1153 (9th Cir 1973); United States v Collins, 395 F Supp 629, 636 (MD Pa), *affd,* 523 F2d 1051 (3d Cir 1975); People v Lawson, 37 Colo App 442, 448, 551 P2d 206, 209 (1976); Jones v State, 232 Ga 762, 768, 208 SE2d 850, 853 (1974); People v Johnson, 97 Ill App 3d 1055, 423 NE2d 1206 (1st Dist 1981); State v Galloway, 275 NW2d 736, 741 (Iowa 1979) (concurring opinion); State v Helterbridle, 301 NW2d 545, 547 (Minn 1980); Porter v State, 94 Nev 142, 150, 576 P2d 275, 279 (1978); State v Porraro, 404 A2d 465, 471 (RI 1979).

[14] In State v Warren, 230 Kan 385, 635 P2d 1236, 1243 (1981), the Supreme Court of Kansas held that the trial court was not required to admit the testimony of Dr. Loftus on the subject of eyewitness testimony. After considering the cases and literature on the subject, the court concluded that:

> requiring trial courts to admit this type of expert evidence is not the answer to the problem. We believe that the problem can be alleviated by a proper cautionary

jurors may take into consideration their own life experiences and common knowledge may actually aggravate error if their common knowledge is erroneous.

§8.03 —Recent Developments in Use of Experts at Trial

Despite the rationales given by the courts to exclude expert testimony on eyewitness identifications, the underlying reason for excluding such testimony would seem to be that the courts simply do not trust it[15] and do not want to see trials become bogged down with "battles of the experts."[16] Nonetheless, there have been significant advances in the past few years in the knowledge that psychologists have gained from experimentation on the issues of perception and memory.[17] This knowledge cannot simply be disregarded by the courts. The Court of Appeals for the Sixth Circuit recently issued a strong indication that expert testimony on eyewitness identification will be admitted if the expert is prepared to relate the psychological principles to the facts of the case.[18] The argument that the admission of expert testimony will be time consuming and lead to *battles of experts* could be employed in any case where expert opinions are routinely allowed. For instance, an appellate court has held that it was error for a trial judge to refuse to

---

> instruction to the jury which sets forth the factors to be considered in evaluating eyewitness testimony. Such an instruction, coupled with vigorous cross-examination and persuasive argument by defense counsel dealing realistically with the shortcomings and trouble spots of the identification process, should protect the rights of the defendant and at the same time enable the courts to avoid the problems involved in the admission of expert testimony on this subject.

See also **ch 9.**

[15] *See* United States v Fosher, 449 F Supp 76, 77 (D Mass 1978), *affd,* 590 F2d 381 (1st Cir 1979); *but cf* United States v Smith, 35 Cr L 2224 (6th Cir June 7, 1984) distinguishing *Fosher. See also* United States v Collins, 395 F Supp 629, 636 (MD Pa), *affd,* 523 F2d 1051 (3d Cir 1975); Nelson v State, 362 So2d 1017, 1021 (Fla Dist Ct App 1978); State v Brown, 17 Wash App 587, 564 P2d 342, 346 (1977). *But see* United States v Cyphers, 553 F2d 1064, 1072 (7th Cir 1977); State v Mitchell, 390 A2d 495, 501 (Me 1978) (holding that there is no general evidentiary requirement that an expert testify with "certainty"). *See also* Ibn-Tamas v United States, 407 A2d 626, 637 (DC 1979) (where the court rejected the government's argument that testimony concerning the *battered-woman syndrome* by a psychologist was not sufficiently developed, as a matter of scientific knowledge, to warrant testimony under the guise of expertise).

[16] United States v Brown, 501 F2d 146, 150 (9th Cir 1974), *revd on other grounds,* 422 US 225 (1975); Jones v State, 232 Ga 762, 765, 208 SE2d 850, 853 (1974); State v Galloway, 275 NW2d 736, 742 (Iowa 1979) (concurring opinion); State v Porraro, 404 A2d 465, 471 (RI 1979).

[17] See **ch 2.**

[18] United States v Smith, 35 Cr L 2224 (6th Cir June 7, 1984).

admit the testimony of a clinical psychologist regarding the *battered-wife syndrome,* which was offered to support a defense to a charge of murder.[19] The court held that the testimony did not invade the province of the jury and concluded, as a matter of law, that the probative value of the testimony outweighed any countervailing considerations. The court noted that "in exercising its discretion, the trial court must be guided by the principle that 'the defense should be free to introduce appropriate expert testimony' and that such evidence should be admitted if the opinion offered will be likely to aid the trier in the search for truth."[20]

Similarly, in an appeal involving a man who was convicted of distributing heroin,[21] the trial court had refused to allow a clinical psychologist to testify concerning the defendant's entrapment defense. The expert would have testified to the defendant's psychological characteristics, subnormal intelligence, and resulting susceptibility to persuasion and psychological pressure. The Third Circuit reversed, noting that:

> [I]f the expert can reach a conclusion, based on an adequate factual foundation, that the appellant, because of his alleged subnormal intelligence and psychological profile, is more susceptible and easily influenced by the urgings and inducements of other persons, such testimony *must be admitted* relevant to the issues of inducement and predispositions.[22]

Recently, the United States Supreme Court upheld the use of psychiatric testimony in a sentencing hearing before a jury to determine whether the death penalty should be imposed.[23] Two psychiatrists, in response to hypothetical questions, testified that the convicted felon would probably commit further acts of violence and represent a continuing threat to society. In an amicus curiae brief filed with the court, the American Psychiatric Association estimated that two out of three predictions of long-term future violence made by psychiatrists are wrong.[24] Nonetheless, the United States Supreme Court was uncon-

---

[19] Ibn-Tamas v United States, 407 A2d 626 (DC 1979).

[20] *Id* 632 (quoting Fennekohl v United States, 354 A2d 238, 240 (DC App 1976); Kaplan v California, 413 US 115, 121 (1973); and Jenkins v United States, 307 F2d 637, 643 (DC Cir 1962).

[21] United States v Hill, 655 F2d 512 (3d Cir 1981).

[22] *Id* 516 (emphasis added).

[23] Barefoot v Estelle, 51 USLW 5189 (US July 6, 1983).

[24] *Id* 5200 (Blackmun, J, dissenting).

vinced that the adversary process could not be trusted to sort out reliable from unreliable evidence.[25] The Court emphasized that the witnesses were subject to cross-examination[26] and that the defendant could present the opposing views of his own doctors.[27] The Court also held that the psychiatrists could testify about future dangerousness in response to hypothetical questions without having examined the defendant personally.[28]

The sole reported case in which an appellate court reversed a criminal conviction because the trial judge erred in refusing to admit the testimony of an expert on perception and memory is *State v Chapple,*[29] a decision of the Supreme Court of Arizona. The defendant was convicted of murder and transporting marijuana on the eyewitness testimony of two coconspirators who only briefly saw a man named Dee and who picked the defendant's photograph out of a lineup more than one year after the crime. Prior to that time, one of the witnesses had pointed out another man's picture as resembling Dee. The record did not disclose any follow-up to this tentative identification. Also in an earlier photographic lineup, one of the witnesses had failed to identify the defendant's photo. The defense called Dr. Elizabeth Loftus to testify about the area of experimental and clinical psychology dealing with perception and memory. While noting that the cases have uniformly affirmed trial court rulings denying admission of this type of testimony, the court nonetheless held that the trial judge abused his discretion in this case. There was a detailed offer of proof; the time involved in taking the testimony was not "undue" in comparison with the importance of the interests before the court, and the evidence did not "invade the province of the jury" because expert testimony is admissible even though "it embraces an ultimate issue."[30] The court further held that the "generality" of the testimony—the fact that Dr. Loftus would testify only to general facts applicable to the case without expressing her opinion with regard to the accuracy of the specific identification—actually favored its admissibility because it allowed the trier of fact itself to draw the ultimate inference.[31] The court also held that under the circumstances of the particular case the offered evidence was a proper subject for expert testimony. The court referred to such variables as the

---

[25] 51 USLW at 5195.

[26] *Id* 5196 n 10.

[27] *Id* 5194.

[28] *Id* 5196.

[29] 660 P2d 1208 (1983).

[30] *Id* 1219.

[31] *Id.*

delay in the identification, the stressful nature of the events, the problems of "unconscious transfer," (see **§8.09**) the assimilation of postevent information, and the question of confidence and its relationship to accuracy and concluded that it would not assume that the average person would be aware of these variables concerning identification and memory.[32] The court cautioned, however, that it did not intend to "open the gates" to a flood of expert evidence on the subject and that the rule in Arizona would continue to be that in the usual case the trial court's discretionary ruling on admissibility would not be disturbed.[33]

An expert on perception can be equally as helpful to a jury in a civil case as can an expert on accident reconstruction, automobile speeds, or ballistics. In a criminal case, the testimony of an expert may be crucial when a person is in danger of being sent to jail or death on the basis of the testimony of an eyewitness who only fleetingly saw the person or event while he or she was under great stress. For these reasons, greater discretion should be exercised by the courts in favor of admitting the testimony of eyewitness experts.

Because the courts are legitimately concerned about becoming bogged down with battles of the experts, they appear to be afraid to lay down any rule which would open the floodgates. Nonetheless, the obvious problem with leaving the question whether to admit expert testimony to the unguided discretion of the trial judge is that the result is an unguided and unequal application of the law.

There would appear to be no need to admit expert testimony where there is abundant evidence which corroborates the eyewitness testimony or where the witness knew the party. Nonetheless, where eyewitness testimony is the only evidence, and where the person being identified is a stranger, it is difficult to justify not allowing the expert to testify. The authors would therefore suggest that a workable criterion would be that where the corrobative evidence alone is sufficient to take the case to a jury, no expert testimony on the issue of eyewitness identification need be permitted; but where, except for the eyewitness testimony, the trial court would be required to direct a verdict, and in cases of personal identity where the person was not well known to the witness, the expert should be allowed to testify.

---

[32] *Id* 1221.

[33] *Id* 1224.

§8.04 Pretrial Use of Experts

Whether or not the jurisdiction allows the testimony of experts on eyewitness identification, an expert may prove helpful to the attorney in preparing his or her case for trial. An expert may be helpful to the attorney in pointing out lines of inquiry and how best to structure and to argue the case. The expertise of these resource people may also be helpful in early case preparation. Conflicting reports of witnesses may be reconciled in the light of the principles which underlie perceptual errors. Time and money may thereby be saved in avoiding unfruitful investigations. On the other hand, new areas of investigation may be opened by an expert's suggestion of possible error in the witnesses' accounts and the probable direction of that error. Therefore, attorneys should make themselves familiar with the pool of experts that is developing in this area and call upon them for help in appropriate cases, not only for testimonial purposes but also for assistance at the earliest stages of a lawsuit.

The Ninth Circuit recognized the importance of the use of experts in preparing an identification case in *United States v Barrett.*[34] The government offered into evidence the testimony of an FBI photographic expert, who compared the clothing of Barrett with that worn by the robber in a bank surveillance photograph by using a microscope and high-intensity light. The government had not notified Barrett of its intention to call a photographic expert as a witness until eight days before the trial. Barrett asked for a continuance to prepare for the expert and possibly to obtain a defense expert, but this request was denied. Although Barrett made a diligent effort to secure an expert, he was unsuccessful. Two days before the trial, the government provided the defense with the results of its expert's report. The court found that Barrett was not given adequate time to obtain an expert to assist in attacking the government's expert and that the trial court erred in not granting a continuance. The court however found the error to be harmless because the government had introduced other overwhelming evidence at trial identifying Barrett as the robber.

---

[34] 703 F2d 1076 (9th Cir 1983). In United States v Sims, 617 F2d 1371, 1375 n 3 (9th Cir 1980), the court indicated that in an appropriate criminal case a trial judge might be required to appoint a psychologist to help in the preparation of the defense, whether or not the expert would be allowed to testify in the trial itself.

§8.05 Qualifications

The Federal Rules of Evidence provide that a person may be qualified as an expert by "knowledge, skill, experience, training, or education."[35] Only rarely have courts excluded testimony on eyewitness identifications on the ground that the witness was not properly qualified as an expert.[36] Nonetheless, it is important that the witness be properly qualified to testify not only for reasons of admissibility, but also to establish the witness' credibility before the trier of fact. It is because of this latter reason that counsel will not want to accept a stipulation from opposing counsel that the witness is qualified and forego the opportunity to inform the trier of fact of the impressive background of the witness. Counsel will want to impress the trier of fact with the expert's academic credentials, his or her long experience in practical experimentations, and his or her standing among other professionals.

An example of how one goes about establishing the qualifications of an expert is given below:[37]

Q. For the record would you state your full name and spell your last name?

A. Ralph Norman Haber, H-a-b-e-r.

Q. And what is your address, Mr. Haber?

A. 3268 Summit Avenue, Highland Park.

Q. What is your occupation or profession?

A. Professor of psychology at the University of Illinois.

Q. And do you teach there?

A. I teach and do research there.

Q. And how long have you been a teacher in the field of psychology at the University of Illinois?

---

[35] Fed R Evid 702.

[36] *See* State v Brown, 17 Wash App 587, 594, 564 P2d 342, 346 (1977), where the trial court held that Dr. Elizabeth Loftus was not an expert, and the appellate court affirmed on the ground that the trial court had not abused its discretion. In People v Suleski, 58 AD2d 1023, 1027, 397 NYS2d 280, 282 (1977), the appellate court agreed that a witness who had never previously testified regarding eyewitness identification and who acknowledged that he could not testify about what was wrong with the lineup utilized in that case was not proven to be qualified as an expert.

[37] The transcript is from People v Kramm, Indictment Nos 80 CF 1261 and 80 CF 1262 (Cir Ct Du Page County, Ill) on Oct 29, 1980. The testimony is from an offer of proof made in the course of a criminal trial. The trial judge refused to allow the testimony to be introduced to the jury, holding that the subject matter was within the competence of the average juror.

A. I'm in my second year there.

Q. Prior to the two years that you taught at the University of Illinois, did you teach anywhere else?

A. Yes. I was 15 years at the University of Rochester in Rochester, New York.

Q. What did you teach there, sir?

A. Also in the psychology department as a professor.

Q. And prior to that?

A. I was six years at Yale University.

Q. And you were a teacher at Yale?

A. I was a teacher also.

Q. And in what field did you teach at Yale?

A. In all of these it has been the same, experimental psychology.

Q. Would you outline for the Court your educational background beginning with your undergraduate work?

A. My bachelor's degree is at the University of Michigan. I received that in philosophy in 1953.

I then went to Wesleyan University in Connecticut where I received a master's degree in experimental psychology.

I then went to Stanford University where I received my Ph.D. in 1967, also in experimental psychology.

The year of post doctoral training occurred in England in 1976 when I was at the Medical Research Council there.

Q. And what area did that deal, please?

A. All of these have been in visual perception, perceptional memory.

Q. Now, would you explain, please, to the Court and for the record, what psychology is in general?

A. In general it is the study of human behavior.

Q. And is experimental psychology a sub-speciality in the general area of psychology?

A. Yes. It is one part of it. Other parts would be the developmental psychology concerned with other parts of clinical psychology concerned with treatment of disease.

Experimental is learning the factors that affect behavior, doing experiments rather than treating the patients.

Q. What specifically, Professor Haber, is the area of visual perception and memory? What does that involve? Is that a further sub-speciality in the area of experimental psychology?

A. That's one part of experimental psychology. . . .
The area of vision and visual memory are concerned with how we see, how we perceive, how we observe events and particularly how we are able to remember those events and recall them later.

Q. And how long have you been actively involved in that field of psychology known as visual perception?

A. My Ph.D. is 23 years ago. I was working in it for several years before that, but since that point I have been actually employed as a professor and researcher.

Q. . . . Have you written any books in the field of visual perception and memory?

A. Yes. I've written or edited eight books covering the wide range of topics in visual perception including the standard textbook in this field that's used all through the country.

Q. Have you written any articles, scientific articles for scientific journals in the area of experimental psychology and visual perception and memory?

A. I published 95 articles in these 23 years, almost all of which probably all are in the area of visual perception and perceptional memory.

Q. Now, in the area of visual perception and memory, have you had occasion during these number of years, to perform experiments yourself dealing with these factors?

A. Almost all of those articles I published are [based on my] experiments.

Q. Any of these experiments deal with the factors that may or may not affect one's ability to accurately perceive something and later recall it?

A. Oh, many of them did. Probably half.

Q. At the university that you are now at, do any of your courses that you deal with have anything to do with eyewitness identification?

A. Many of them deal with it as part of it. I teach courses in perception. I teach courses in perception memory. I teach courses in cognizance and thinking. And in all of those, eyewitness testimony is part of the course, part of the material that I teach.

The foregoing testimony clearly establishes this witness as an expert in his field. Other questions which might have been pursued are whether the witness had ever testified in court before as an expert (this one had not) and whether the witness had ever done any work or consultation with law enforcement or governmental agencies relating to eyewitness identifications. To further impress the jury, the witness might also have been asked to estimate the number of witnesses he had tested over the years in research on eyewitness perception and memory. A typical answer might be: "Several thousand subjects." The witness might also have been asked whether he was generally familiar with the published literature on eyewitness perception and memory and whether he was a member of any professional associations.

§8.06 Substantive Testimony

The testimony of experts in the field of perception and memory generally covers those factors which influence an identification. Counsel will want to have his or her expert explain in detail those factors which are present in the identification involved in his or her case which militate against an accurate identification.

The testimony in each case will of course be distinctive because of the circumstances involved. For instance, if the case involves a cross-racial identification, the attorney will want to focus on the numerous studies which show how racial stereotypes may unconsciously affect a witness' perception.[38] Similarly, in an appropriate case, the attorney may ask the expert to explain how the sex of the witness can affect the focus of his or her attention.[39] Such testimony can make a crucial difference to the outcome of a trial.[40] Probably the best way to decide on what areas to question the expert in detail is to have the expert review all the facts involved in the identification and suggest what is important. Even where one ultimately decides not to use the expert, or where the judge disallows his or her testimony, his or her suggestion regarding weaknesses in the identification can be invaluable in developing not only cross-examination questions, but also voir dire questions and ideas for opening and closing statements.

A major consideration in using an expert is whether to limit his or her testimony to those factors which affect perception, memory, and recall in general or whether to ask his or her opinion on the *ultimate issue*

---

[38] *E.g.*, E. Loftus, Eyewitness Testimony (1979); A.D. Yarmey, The Psychology of Eyewitness Testimony 1310-31 (1979); P. Wall, Eyewitness Identification in Criminal Cases 122-25 (1965). For examples of testimony in a case involving a cross-racial identification, see **§§8.11-8.15.**

[39] See Arnolds, Carroll & Seng, *The Admissibility of Expert Testimony on the Issue of Eyewitness Identification in Criminal Trials,* 2 N Ill UL Rev 59, 80 (1981).

[40] E. Loftus, Eyewitness Testimony 204-35 (1979). See generally Levine & Lapp, *The Psychology of Criminal Identification: The Gap from Wade to Kirby,* 121 U Pa L Rev 1079 (1973).

of whether a particular identification is valid. Again the latter question could be asked directly or by means of hypothetical questions based on the facts of a particular identification. Although courts have traditionally allowed experts to give their opinions on ultimate questions,[41] the authors feel that the testimony of an expert will be of greater credibility and aid to the jury if the expert is questioned only on those factors which can influence an identification in general. No psychologist can ever state for certain whether a particular person misapprehended a person or event; at most he or she is making an informed guess. However, a psychologist can describe scientifically those factors which influence perception, memory, and recall. The jury is then left free to draw its own inference on the applicability of these factors to the particular case. The integrity of the expert is thus not compromised, and the jury is left to fulfill its ultimate function.

The transcript excerpts in **§§8.07-8.10** are from a criminal case,[42] but much of the testimony could be applicable to civil cases as well.

---

[41] *See e.g.*, Barefoot v Estelle, 51 USLW 5189 (US July 6, 1983). However, in State v Chappel, 660 P2d 1208, 1219 (1983), the Arizona Supreme Court commented that the generality of the testimony of Dr. Loftus on the accuracy of identifications in general actually favored its admissibility because it allowed the trier of fact itself to draw the ultimate inference. In People v Valentine, 53 AD2d 832, 385 NYS2d 545 (1976), the court commented that for an expert to apply the general principles relating to eyewitness vagaries to the facts of a case would invade the domain of the jury. In Hampton v State, 92 Wis 2d 450, 285 NW2d 868 (1979), the court allowed a psychologist to testify to factors which could influence an identification, but not to apply those factors to the concrete circumstances of the case. Conversely, in People v Suleski, 58 AD2d 1023, 397 NYS2d 280 (1977), the court excluded the testimony of an expert who admitted that he had no opinion to offer as an aid to the jury concerning the impropriety of the lineup in question and who could only conjecture that the lineup must have been faulty. And in United States v Thevis, 665 F2d 616 (5th Cir 1982), the court held that a trial judge did not err in excluding the testimony of Dr. Buckhout. Dr. Buckhout would not have commented specificially on the identification made by two government witnesses but instead would have testified as to the problems of eyewitness identifications in general. The court noted that "to admit such testimony would permit the proponent's witness to comment on the weight and credibility of opponent's witnesses and open the door to a barrage of marginally relevant psychological evidence." *Id* 641. *Cf* United States v Brown, 540 F2d 1048, 1054 (10th Cir 1976), where the court commented in dicta that an expert could not testify that a defendant, within the factual setting of a case, would have signed a document placed before him regardless of the truth or falsity of its contents.

Where hypothetical questions regarding the validity of eyewitness identifications were asked, the courts have generally held that the testimony would invade the province of the jury. Criglow v State, 183 Ark 481, 36 SW2d 400 (1931); Jones v State, 232 Ga 762, 208 SE2d 850 (1974); Porter v State, 94 Nev 142, 148, 576 P2d 275, 278 (1978).

[42] Testimony of Dr. Ralph Haber in People v Kramm, Indictment Nos 80 CF 1261 and 1262 (Cir Ct Du Page County, Ill) on Oct 29, 1980. The trial judge refused to allow the testimony to be introduced to the jury, holding that the subject matter was within the competence of the average juror.

§8.07 —Testimony on Memory and Perception in General

The first thing that the expert should be asked to explain is how the process of memory and perception works in general.

Q. Can eyewitness identification—the topic eyewitness identification be considered visual perception as applied to identification of peoples as opposed to other objects for example?

A. Very definitely. There's a great deal of research on that topic alone.

Q. . . . Based on your experience as a teacher and having studied through these years in the area of experimental psychology, can you explain to the Court what human memory and identification involve? Can you explain how the memory works in general first?

A. In very general terms, memory is a repository and specific things that happen to us in the course of our lives.

It is not, however, like making a video tape. We don't record everything that we see. We don't save it without loss and when we're trying to retrieve something, it is not like simply putting the tape back on the machine and playing it back, so that most of the research that is being done now and most of my own interests have been looking at the various factors that would affect how accurately would somebody perceive an event in the first place, how well would they remember them after the event and what changes might occur in those memories and what kind of changes might occur, losses that would occur at the time of trying to recall the memory.

Q. Doctor, is it fair to say that there are three stages in connection with memory and identification?

A. Yes.

Q. Would you describe, first of all in general terms, what those three areas are?

A. Most of the research has broken them down into these areas. The first being those factors concerned with the acquisition. The factors—the things that occur at the time of observation.

The second set of factors are those that occur during the retention from after the observation and until you attempt to recall it.

The third set of factors concern the recall itself, the attempt to make an identification.

Q. So there are three stages involved in memory, acquisition;

retention, which is a period of time that you've stored this information prior to being asked to recall it and in some cases make an identification?

A. Right.

Q. Are there individual factors which psychologists have learned through experimentation that affect each of the three stages?

A. Yes.[43]

§8.08 —Testimony on Individual Factors Which Influence Perception

The expert may be asked to articulate particularized influences on a person's perception. These influences should focus especially on those factors which may have been present in the case under consideration. In the following example the attorney asks the expert to focus particularly on the length of time for observation, the lighting, the presence of violence, the effect of stress, and the use of weapons.

Q. First, I'd like to talk about the acquisition stage. What, if any, effect does exposure time have on one's memory and ability to make an identification?

A. The longer you have to observe an event or observe a person, the more likely it is that the observation will be correct.

In other words, that you could make an accurate identification later.

There's a substantial number of studies that have shown the time that a person has to look at a picture or look at a scene or look at a set of events and the accuracy of identification is always easier the longer that observation is.

Q. Is that conclusion one that's accepted within the scientific community generally today?

A. Very much so.

Q. Does the frequency of exposure have any effect one way or the other on memory and later identification?

A. Very definitely. The most difficult kind of identification to make is of a person that you've just seen briefly once. The more

---

[43] Testimony of Dr. Ralph Haber in People v Kramm, Indictment Nos 80 CF 1261 and 1262 (Cir Ct Du Page County, Ill) on Oct 29, 1980. The trial judge refused to allow the testimony to be introduced to the jury.

frequently you see somebody the more accurate you're going to be able to identify them later.

Q. Have there been tests and experiments performed that you are familiar with in the area of exposure time and the frequency of exposure in relation to the accuracy and probability of making an accurate observation and identification?

A. Yes.

Q. Are you familiar with those experiments?

A. Yes, I am.

Q. In fact, have you performed some of them yourself?

A. Some of them are ones I've done.

Q. Now, what, if any, effect does the lighting have, for example, on a person's ability to make an accurate observation, later recall it and identify what one has seen?

A. We know that our ability to notice details deteriorates dramatically as light level goes down, so that if you are trying to make an identification in the dark or even in dim light, it is much more difficult. You can get general shape contour, but very difficult to get any kind of detail.

Violence and Stress

Q. What, if any, effect does the factor of violence of an event have? For example, if an event that one is witnessing is violent as opposed to a nonviolent event, is that a factor in any way?

A. Very substantial one. Contrary to what, I think most people believe, the more violent the event that you are observing, the less likely you will remember the details about it later.

There have been specific experiments that have manipulated the violence of the event that have been watched and—

Q. Are you familiar with any of those experiments?

A. Yes, I am.

Q. Can you give us an example of what type of experiments have been done in that area?

A. There have been a number. One type is where the subjects observed a simulated crime in which half the subjects saw an enactment of the time in which there were just several people shouting at each other and another one there was actual punching and hitting and knocking down. All of the other events in the enactment were identical. The subjects were then asked questions about the crime and were then asked to pick out the actors from a line-up of the participants. The accuracy of those identifications and the accuracy of the details that were remembered was much poorer when the crime was violent.

There are others. That's one experiment. There are other varieties which varied the particular way in which the experiments were done, but the same kind of result was had.

Q. And the conclusion you are indicating that psychologists have reached, is that an individual is less likely to remember individual details when he's witnessing violent activity as opposed to nonviolent activity?

A. That's a conclusion and it is strongly supported in the literature.

Q. Now, is stress a factor in one's ability to make an accurate observation?

A. That's the other side of the coin. If the witness or the observer is under stress, if the event is producing a lot of excitement, anxiety, trauma, then you find the same thing, that their ability to identify details or remember or identify faces or pick people out of a line-up is decreased. This seems to occur with a kind of narrowing of attention so much of the details just don't get picked up at all.

Weapon Focus

Q. Are you familiar with the factor known as weapon focus?

A. Yes. This is related to what I [have] just been talking about. If there's a weapon or the observer suspects that there's a weapon, then there's a very strong focus of attention on the weapon.

Q. Have experimental psychologists done any work or experiments in the area of weapon focus to determine what if any effect it has on a person's ability to perceive?

A. Yes. Specifically on this question.

Q. Could you talk about those experiments a little bit, please?

A. Same type of experiment that I just mentioned. In this case, half of the subjects observe the enactment with the criminal holding a weapon and the other half observe the same enactment in all respects except there is no weapon visible. The subjects are then later asked about the events they saw and also asked specifically to pick the criminal out of the line-up. Their accuracy is decreased both in picking them out of the line-up and also in answering general questions when there's a weapon present.

When they're asked questions about the weapon, they're very

accurate. It appears as if their attention is riveted to the weapon and they just don't have an opportunity to observe faces or other aspects of the scene.

Light Adaptation

Q. Now, Doctor, are you familiar with the term light adaptation?
A. Yes.
Q. And is that something that you've studied as a visual perception expert?
A. Yes.
Q. Have you studied that a great deal in connection with your work?
A. Yes.
Q. Now, is that also a factor which has been shown to affect a person's ability to make an accurate observation, to acquire information accurately?
A. Yes, it has.
Q. Could you explain to the Court what light adaptation involves, please?
A. Whenever you go from a room that has one light level to a room that's different, whether it is greater or less, there will be a momentary loss in ability to perceive, to see.
Q. Now, is there a physical explanation for that?
A. Yes, in terms of changes that actually occur in the photo chemicals in the eye itself.
Q. Could you describe that briefly, please?
A. The visual system is rather slow in adjusting to large illumination changes as a way of protecting the eye.

If you're in a dark room and move to a brightly lighted room, you'll experience dazzle for a number of seconds.
Q. Would you explain to the Court what you mean when you say dazzle?
A. Well, it is almost kind of a blinding and you'll close your eyes.

If you're in a dark movie theater and go out into the afternoon; if you're going to a matinee, it will take several seconds, maybe as much as 10, if it was a dark theater on a bright day, before you would be able to recognize people on the street or even be able to walk comfortably.

The effect of sunlight can be so strong that you won't be able to keep your eyes open.

Q. Now, does dazzle occur in every instance when you go from a darker place to a lighter place? Does that always happen—

A. It will always happen.

Q. —if there's a severe contrast?

A. The amount that it will occur is going to depend on the contrast. If you walk from this room outdoors, there wouldn't be a lot, but there would be a little bit because there's some change. If you're in a dark room and you go into quite a bright room, then there will be a substantial dazzle and the number of seconds that your vision will be impaired will be longer the greater the contrast.

Q. So how dark and how light the two areas are would affect how long the dazzle would occur; is that right?

A. Right.[44]

§8.09 —Testimony on Those Factors Which Influence the Retention and Retrieval of Perceptions in General

In addition to the factors noted in the excerpts in **§§8.07-8.08,** the expert may also be questioned on the phenomenon known as *unconscious transference* and its influence on identifications made from photo-spreads and lineups.

Q. Now, Doctor, I would like to talk a minute about the second phase of memory which you described as retention. Are there any post event factors which can taint or affect the information which was first stored when first observed?

A. Yes, there are.

Q. Are you familiar with the term unconscious transference?

A. Yes.

Q. Is that a term that experimental psychologists have developed to describe certain phenomena?

A. Yes.

---

[44] Testimony of Dr. Ralph Haber in People v Kramm, Indictment Nos 80 CF 1261 and 1262 (Cir Ct Du Page County, Ill) on Oct 29, 1980. The trial judge refused to allow the testimony to be introduced to the jury.

Q. Are you familiar with photo spreads and physical line-ups?

A. Yes, I am.

Q. And have experimental psychologists done a number of experiments to determine what effect, if any, photo spreads and physical line-ups have on later identification?

A. Yes.

Q. Could you explain to the Court how photo spreads and physical line-ups may affect an identification at a later time?

A. Unconscious transference, the phenomenon itself, is where an observer confuses one memory and mixes it up with another one. It is called unconscious because observers aren't aware of doing it, it is a normal part of memory.

With respect to photo spreads, one of the places where it can occur is if you examine a photo spread and pick someone out of it as a suspect and that identification is erroneous, you are more likely to pick that person again in the actual line-up even if the real criminal is in the line-up.

Q. Now, have there been any tests done that you are familiar with, by experimental psychologists, in the area of photo spreads and physical line-ups?

A. Yes.

Q. Are you familiar with experiments that have been done where they re-enact a crime scene either on a videotape or actually in person?

A. Yes.

Q. And in any of those experiments did they subsequently show subjects or show photographs and later show them physical line-ups?

A. Yes.

Q. Would you describe those experiments for the Court, please?

A. Again the experiment might be like the earlier ones that I described, the subjects see an enactment of the crime or watch a videotape of a crime and are then shown a photo spread—in most of those experiments, the actual criminal will not be on view for a long time, maybe four or five seconds—they are then shown a photo spread and are asked to pick out the criminal, and since the subjects did not see the criminal very well, in those kinds of experiments the accuracy of picking them out isn't terribly large. In most of the experiments it runs 50 percent or less.

When the subjects are then subsequently shown an actual

physical line-up in which the line-up itself are the persons that they had picked erroneously and the actual criminal, having picked the persons from the photo spread first, they're much more likely to pick them again and ignore the real criminal.

Q. How does that relate to unconscious transference, Doctor?

A. We use that term to describe what we think is happening, that the witness here is confusing the person they've identified in the photo spread with a real criminal so that by the time they get a chance to look at the physical line-up they are remembering the person they picked out of the photo spread and no longer remembering the criminal themselves.

Q. Now, are there any factors that would increase the likelihood of a misidentification in connection with a physical line-up where there's been a previous photographic spread?

A. Unconscious transference is much more likely to occur, the greater the chance that an error is made in the picking out the person from the photo spread, so the poorer the original observation—those acquisition factors you asked me about at first [see **§8.08**], the poorer those are, the less likely a correct identification will be made and that would increase the chances of an unconscious transference and so that the wrong person would be picked out of the line-up.

The second factor would be if the line-up itself was biased, was not a fair line-up.

Q. Now, have there been tests done by experimental psychologists using photo line-ups that preceded a physical line-up that you've termed biased?

A. Yes, there have.

Q. Now, when you use the term bias, would you explain to the Court what you mean by that?

A. The purpose of a photo spread or a line-up ought to be to determine whether the witness can identify the criminal uniquely.

In other words, that only a person that actually saw the criminal commit the crime ought to be able to pick them out and that anybody else looking at the photo spread—if everyone else looking at the photo spread also picked the same person out without having observed the crime, they must be doing it by on some other set of factors, some kind of bias.

So a biased line-up would be one in which people that never saw the criminal, but just knew the description of the criminal, were still able to make an identification.

Q. Based on your definition of a biased photo spread, is it fair, Doctor, to say that the more similar the photographs look, the less biased it will be?

A. Correct.

If you take the general description from the witness, then all of the photographs in the photo spread or all of the persons in the physical line-up should share those general characteristics so the only way the witness could identify the real criminal correctly would be to be able to remember the actual way the criminal looked.

Q. Now, if, for example, Doctor, you had a photo spread of eight photographs and the photographic spread was unbiased, that is to say the physical characteristics of all eight people displayed to the witness were basically the same, conformed to the description, what would be the chances of a non-observer picking out the correct suspect merely from the description having viewed the photographs?

A. If they're eight photographs, it should be one out of the eight.

In other words, each of the eight people should be picked equally often by someone who knew the general description of the criminal but in fact had never seen the criminal, that would be a fair line-up.

Q. And that would insure that the person that had actually seen whatever it is he's trying to identify, the criminal for example, would be selecting the photograph based on individual features as opposed to general characteristics?

A. Identifying the photo based upon their actually having seen that person and not simply responding to general characteristics.[45]

§8.10 —Testimony Concerning an Experiment in Relation to the Witness in *People v Kramm*

Although the testimony introduced in most cases concerns those factors which influence memory and perception in general, when the expert has performed an experiment based on the identification in question, he or she may be questioned as follows:

---

[45] Testimony of Dr. Ralph Haber in People v Kramm, Indictment Nos 80 CF 1261 and 1262 (Cir Ct Du Page County, Ill) on Oct 29, 1980. The trial judge refused to allow the testimony to be introduced to the jury.

Q. Doctor, in connection with the case of People versus Kramm, I asked you to perform a test at the University of Illinois; is that correct?

A. That's right.

Q. And I asked you to perform a test in relation to a photographic spread that had been shown to the witnesses in this particular case; is that right?

A. That's what you told me.

Q. Now, I want to show you what's been marked in this cause as Defendant's Group Exhibit No. 11 and ask you if you can keep them in that order and ask you if you can identify those photographs, please?

A. Yes. These are the ones that I—that you gave me and that I did the experiment on.

Q. Now, would you tell the Court specifically what you did in connection with that experiment?

A. I attempted to apply a standard test that's been used before to determine whether there was any bias in this set of pictures. Specifically what I wanted to know was that if the subjects, very much like the witness, viewed this set of pictures and had the same description that the witness had given in front of them, could they pick out—would they distribute their choices equally among the eight pictures.

Q. Did you perform a test such as the one you just described?

A. I did such an experiment.

Q. Would you first of all explain in general how the experiment was conducted?

A. I tested 28 subjects. These were all women in their early 20's, either students at the University of Illinois or employees. The instructions that I gave the subjects—each subject I tested individually—was that a witness had seen a crime and had given a description and that the description you furnished me, which was the description given by the witness in this case and I handed that description to my subject and I said that this was the description given.

The witness then was shown the following photo spread.

Q. The one that you have in your hand?

A. The one I have in my hand. I handed that to the subject and at this point I said that I would like you to go through this set of pictures and tell me the picture you think that most resembles the person described by the witness.

Q. Now, when you gave the photo spread to the witness, did you lay them out all in front of the witness or hand it to them?

A. I simply handed them to my subject. I permitted the subject to examine them any way they wanted. Most of the subjects flipped through them three or four times. Several of the subjects spread them out.

Q. But you handed them—

A. I simply handed them.

Q. Did you say anything to them as they went through the photographs?

A. No. Most of the subjects immediately started flipping through them. Some subjects would make descriptive comments to me and others would be silent until they would hand me—

Q. Did you interject any comments, Professor Haber?

A. No.

Q. Were there any time limitations imposed on how long each subject could view the photos?

A. None at all.

Q. Now, how many subjects did you display the photos for?

A. I tested 28 subjects.

Q. How did you come up with the figure 28?

A. I spent about a day finding subjects and as the day got to the end, I had 28.

Q. Now, you've indicated that tests similar to this have been conducted by experimental psychologists; is that correct?

A. Many. And in fact, 28 is more than a substantial number.

Q. When you say it is more than substantial enough, what do you mean by that?

A. Well, if the line-up was unbiased, I should have expected the 28 scores to spread evenly among the people, the eight pictures, and I would then apply a statistical test based on probability to determine whether the scores distributed randomly—with 28 people it would be quite easy to detect when there was a bias.

Q. Now if I understand your testimony, you read something to each witness, that is a description of the purported assailant which I provided you from the People's discovery.

A. Correct.

Actually I handed it to the subject so that they could read it themselves and the subject was allowed to keep the description so that they weren't having to remember it or—

Q. Professor Haber, let me show you what's been marked Defendant's Exhibit 27 for identification. Tell me if you can identify that card, please.

A. Yes. That's the instructions that I gave to the subject and that's what I said to them.

Q. Would you read that into the record, please?

A. Yes.

"A witness saw a man commit a crime. The witness gave this description:" and at this point I read the other one.

Q. Would you look at Defendant's 28 for identification? . . . Did the subjects have Defendant's 28 with them at the time they viewed the photographs?

A. Yes, they did.

Q. You didn't take it back?

A. I did not take it back.

Q. So they could keep it with them and refer to it from time to time as they looked through the photographs?

A. Correct.

And most of them did so.

The description is: male, white, early 20's, 5'7", 140-150 pounds. Weak, thin build: very small hips and waist, skinny. Wire-rimmed glasses. Unkempt. Unshaven or dirty face, mustache. Hair: dishwater blond or dark blond, dirty, coarse, worn over ears but above shoulders. That was the end of the description. I then continued in my instruction.

Q. Are you now reading from Defendant's 28?

A. Yes. No, 27.

Q. 27, excuse me.

A. "Here is a photo spread that the police assembled, what I'd like you to do is look at these pictures and pick out the picture that most resembles the witness' description. Take as much time as you want."

Q. And it was at that point they viewed the photographs; is that correct?

A. Right.

As a matter of fact, when I said, "Here is a photo spread that the police assembled," I handed them the pictures.

Q. Now, with respect to that photo spread, did you compile your results?

A. Yes, I did.

Q. Referring to your notes, Doctor, what were the results, if any, of your test on Defendant's Group Exhibit No. 11?

A. The 28 subjects' responses were that 16 of the 28 were 59 percent and chose picture No. 4.

Q. Did you number each of these?

A. Yes, I did.

Q. And in the order—

A. And there was a number on the bottom that was visible.

Q. Does Defendant's Exhibit 11 depict what you described as picture 4?

A. Yes.

Q. And 59 percent of the subjects that individually viewed the photographic line-up selected Defendant's 11B; is that correct?
For the record, that is a photograph of my client.

A. Six more subjects were 21 percent and picked photograph No. 1.

Q. And for the record, what you're describing as photograph 1 is Defendant's Group Exhibit 11A for identification.

A. The remaining six subjects spread pretty much one per picture. So that 59 percent picked one picture of your client; 21 percent picked a second and the combining 80 percent picked two out of the eight pictures.

Q. Did you reach any conclusions with respect to that photo spread?

A. Yes. In terms of a statistical test, the chances of these results having occurred by random selection among the eight is infinitesimal so that has to be a biased line-up.
In other words, there's something that's making my subjects, who never viewed the criminal, pick one of these pictures much more [frequently] than [they would] by chance.[46]

---

[46] Testimony of Dr. Ralph Haber in People v Kramm, Indictment Nos 80 CF 1261 and 1262 (Cir Ct Du Page County, Ill) on Oct 29, 1980. The trial judge refused to allow the testimony to be introduced to the jury.

§8.11 Substantive Testimony in a Case Involving a Cross-Racial Identification

If the case in question involves a cross-racial identification, the expert's testimony should be tailored to that fact. The following testimony was given by Dr. Robert Buckhout in a rape case.[47] The victim was a white woman who wore glasses. The assailant was a black man whose face she saw only fleetingly some minutes before the actual attack.

After the crime, the witness called the police. The police immediately apprehended the defendant and exhibited him, handcuffed between two police officers, in the street outside the victim's window. The victim later picked out the defendant in a line-up at the police station.

§8.12 —Testimony Concerning the Scene of the Crime

Dr. Buckhout, in the case described in **§8.11,** was first asked to identify those factors that in general influence an identification. The doctor noted that the identification can be affected by the circumstances at the scene of the crime itself. These circumstances can include such factors as lighting and the length of time for observations.

Q. What do you mean by an "insignificant observation?"

THE WITNESS: An example of this would be the case in which a customer is standing in a bank next to a person in the other line where the person in the other line eventually robs the teller.

He may well have looked over in that direction but was unaware at that time that that person was anybody worth remembering.

Later on, when everybody's locked in the bank, he may be asked to give an identification or a description of the person who was next to him in the line; and yet, *it was insignificant then and made significant after the fact.*

This after-the-fact-focus on that type of situation usually results in rather poor descriptions.

Q. Are there any other factors within this original situational setting that affect eye-witness identification?

---

[47] Testimony in People v Johnson, Indictment No 77 C 1300 (Cir Ct Cook County, Ill) on April 14, 1978. The testimony of Dr. Buckhout was not allowed to be heard by the jury. The defendant was convicted, and the conviction was affirmed on appeal. People v Johnson, 97 Ill App 3d 1055, 423 NE2d 1206, *cert denied,* 455 US 951 (1982).

A. Yes, the shortness of the time of observation.

Q. Could you relate what you mean when you say that?

A. As a general rule of thumb, we have employed research techniques that involve controlling the amount of time that the fact is exposed, "face time;" and the shorter the face time, the less accurate is the intake of information, even though—even up to the extreme of having no face showing.

Q. What happens when you have no face showing?

A. We have done this recently, once again, controlling a film in such a way that while the general features of the person committing the crime were visible, his face, in fact, never showed; and yet, we were able to find people willing to give a description and also to attempt an identification later on.

Q. And the description included a facial description?

A. It included a facial description, presumably, on the basis of their imagination.[48]

§8.13 —Characteristics of the Witness Which May Affect the Identification

Dr. Buckhout (see **§8.11**) was then asked to identify those specific characteristics of the witness which might have affected the validity of the identification.

Q. Now, I think the second general category you listed was the witness herself or himself.

A. Yes.

The factors we've been able to identify there, some of them are fairly familiar factors dealing with the physical condition of the witness concerning the functioning of the eye and the brain, whether the person is sober, and so on.

The factor we've studied is the wearing of glasses, which as many as half of the people in the United States wear; and we find that just the wearing of glasses, even when they're worn at the time the observation is made, produces some inaccuracies in the eyewitness reports that we get.

Q. Is there any explanation for that that you've been able to—

---

[48] Testimony of Dr. Robert Buckhout in People v Johnson, Indictment No 77 C 1300 (Cir Ct Cook County, Ill) on Apr 14, 1978 (emphasis added).

A. As a general rule, we have found that people are not up-to-date in keeping their prescriptions up-to-date; and this seems to contribute to it, yes.

Q. Would stress or fear have any effect on—

A. Yes.

Stress, in particular, we have taken pains to study since we have a bit of a clash between our research and what a lot of people think.

Two things happen in stress: the person is very well able to describe verbally an event, give verbal labels, and to give a reasonably-good story as to a sequence of events.

Their ability to remember details that were seen, however, is less under stress than it is under normal circumstances.

We've confirmed this with a fairly elaborate program of study on military observers who are otherwise good—very good observers but under stress broke down and tended to rely on their imaginations.

Q. As opposed to what they actually saw?

A. Yes.

Q. When studying stress, did you ever study the eye movements under stress?

A. Yes.

We have a device which can measure eye movements; and as a way of explaining the breakdown in performance, we find that eye movements under stress are simply inefficient, ineffective.

The person is not nearly as likely to scan the entire scene but to jerk and move around in a jumpy kind of fashion; and this in and of itself degrades the amount and quality of information coming in.

Q. Is there any research on whether persons under stress tend to focus on whatever is causing the stress as opposed to something else?

A. To the extent that we knew from military research, they would tend to focus on methods of escape, such as, the handle to eject oneself from an aircraft, focusing on a stick and missing key signals coming in on the instruments.

We have some evidence from animal research only that would indicate a tendency of an animal, at least, to roll his eyes back.

We've never created that much stress in a laboratory setting to be able to control it, but we do generalize from that understanding that a gaze directly in the eye, for example, from one animal to an attacking animal is considered by animal researchers to be a source of threat and thereafter is avoided.

Whether that carries over into human action, we can only conjecture.

Q. Does the physical condition of the witness have any effect, their actual physical condition on the day of the observation, does that have any effect on their ability to observe and accurately recall?

A. Yes.

We have limited understanding because of—my background is not in medicine and, you know, I synthesize what I've been told about other drugs; but, in general, just the category of a person who uses drugs and who is currently on them does tend to produce some inaccuracy in our session; that is, they state they're on drugs. We measure their performance, and it's a little bit less accurate than those who are not.[49]

§8.14 —Testimony Concerning Cross-Racial Identifications

With the testimony in **§§8.11-8.13** as background, Dr. Buckhout was then asked about the problems inherent in cross-racial identifications.

Q. Are there any other factors under the witness category?

A. Yes.

A considerable amount of our work is social psychology in this area, and we've attempted to isolate the fact that people report stereotyped judgments to us.

Stereotypes seem to come from two sources. One is ordinary experiences, that is, the fact that a person has certain types of experience has led us to show that card players, for example, will frequently miss a rigged deck because they're so expecting a certain type of stimulus coming at them, they don't look very carefully. They take a very quick scan, and they'll miss a change in the color of the ace of spades, for example.

We've tried to point out that in this case, familiarity may breed a certain amount of smoothness in a fair deck; but if the deck has changed in any way, they frequently do not catch it, whereas, inexperienced players are very quick to catch them.

The area bias, we have an older history of experiments to fall

[49] Testimony of Dr. Robert Buckhout in People v Johnson, Indictment No 77 C 1300 (Cir Ct Cook County, Ill) on Apr 14, 1978.

back on that have been done in the past showing that biased observers tend to—in quick scenes that are very much like crime scenes, they tend to distort the information in the direction of their biases.

We have some experiments with pictures in which a white man and black man are arguing, and it takes a very long look to see who has the weapon. The usual quick look that's taken causes the prejudiced witness to say that it's in the hands of the black man when, as you can imagine in this type of research, it's always nearly in the hands of the white man.

Q. Is there any literature or have you personally studied interracial identifications and the reliability of those kinds of identifications?

A. Yes.

We have recently published some work on the same crime in both black and white literature.

We had a black perpetrator and a white perpetrator commit exactly the same crime. We choreographed it so the actions were identical. The only change was in the race of the perpetrator.

We then took groups of witnesses who were either black or white and asked them to see the crime, give a report, and later make an identification.

In both cases, we found that when a person goes across race, they—they were less accurate in recognizing the person who committed the attack.

Blacks tended to miss whites, and whites tended to miss blacks.[50]

§8.15 —Testimony Concerning Suggestive Police Procedures

After the testimony excerpted in **§§8.12-8.14,** Dr. Buckhout was asked about the methods used by the police to secure an identification of the defendant by the victim.

Q. Moving on to the testing procedure itself, could you tell us a little bit about what your research tells you within that broad category?

A. First of all is the problem of filling in which, in any kind of gathering of a report after the fact, is as much a part of the social climate as anything else.

We have the facts; and one of the things that we find is that in

---

[50] Testimony of Dr. Robert Buckhout in People v Johnson, Indictment No 77 C 1300 (Cir Ct Cook County, Ill) on Apr 14, 1978.

asking repeatedly for a story, the person tends to give a more detailed story the second and third and fourth times around.

Q. Are their stories the second, third, and fourth time around more accurate?

A. They tend to be more complete in the sense that details could be imagined and thought up; but, they also tend to pay a price in that they will put things into that story that should have been there but were not, in fact.

We have arranged our films in such a way that when they are asked to give a more complete story, they tend to put details in the environment, such as, open windows which, in fact, were not there.

Perhaps the best example of this, a colleague of mine found that people who witnessed an accident on film, when asked to describe the scene, tended to put broken glass, even though those happened to be films provided by the Ford Motor Company, and they never use windshields.

The speed of the crash, in particular, was so high that the witnesses tended, after many tellings, to add details, many of which were not there.

Q. So, they become more complete but not necessarily more accurate?

A. Yes; and at that point, they have an opportunity to compare notes with themselves and other people, and the details improve.

We've allowed this to happen on some of our studies, and we deliberately allowed witnesses to get together to talk in order to get a more coherent idea of what happened; but then, later on in identification, when all tested separately in a line-up, there was no improvement at all in memory; and we found no way that we can find to improve their memory of the face so far.

Q. What about the testing procedure, itself? How might that affect an identification?

A. We, essentially, created a set of rules for good testing, and then go in intending to violate them.

We deliberately, for example, will avoid giving an unbiased test by having somebody who is showing the line-up or showing the photos smile when a certain photo comes up, something as simple as that.

Obviously, if he said, "This is the one," this is pretty heavy bias; but even if he just smiles on a certain picture, that picture will tend to be picked.

This is particularly so in the case where we have set up a situation where all of the pictures are of innocent men. We do this largely to counter and deal with one of the problems that we find with witnesses, their immense cooperativeness, their tendency to say "yes," and to make an identification of a photo array assuming that the person must be in there somewhere.

This is both a danger and an aid. You get more identifications; but when, of course, they're all innocent, they can be guided by the simplest things.

In another instance, we tilted a photograph. In another instance, we have simply made one person stand out because of a peculiar walk or stance, and that person, though innocent, will tend to be picked by the witness who is essentially under some degree of pressure to be cooperative and make an identification.

Q. Without anybody saying anything?

A. Without anybody saying anything, correct.

Q. How often do they tend to make an identification irrespective of what they may or may not have seen?

Are there any figures on that?

A. Whether they're right or wrong, we're finding in our work something like eighty percent of witnesses will make an identification.

The British who have studied real line-ups in the field report seventy percent.

We don't have too much data beyond that in the United States; but, at least, the British have reported a very similar tendency for people to make some kind of identification whether right or wrong.

It's hard in the real world to figure out whether it's right or wrong because one would have to trace the case but—

Q. You can control that?

A. Yes, we can control that because in many instances, our line-ups are composed of people who may look like the description but were, in fact, innocent.

Q. Have you studied the effect of an unfair test on subsequent fair tests?

A. I have assisted and reviewed a paper recently that went to that matter particularly. I've done some of it, but this one did it better.

A photograph of an innocent person was shown in an array on one instance. Later on, when the line-up was conducted—one of several line-ups—the person whose photo, although innocent, had appeared in the first array tended to be picked by a majority of the witnesses in the case.

The belief of the researcher in this case is that the person then is remembering the test, and he has assumed that the rules have changed, that he's being tested on consistencies rather than on the memory of the crime.

Q. So, if I understand correctly, what they're doing the second time is reporting what they did the first time and not necessarily what they saw at the time of the crime.

A. Yes, our rule of thumb that we've derived from this work is that the first test must be the best test. Any subsequent test is likely to be affected by the first one, and particularly in that type of sequence where they've seen the face before.

It's like taking a multiple choice test in which somebody's given you the answers, and this tends to produce close to one hundred percent recognition of the test picture.

Q. But not necessarily the actual perpetrator?

A. In the real sense, we would never know at that point. We don't know where it comes from.

Q. You've dealt briefly with the relation to people of authority—the witness' relationship to people of authority.

Does that have any effect on the outcome of the test?

A. The variations that we've done simply are whether the line-up or photo test is conducted by a person in uniform or a person in ordinary clothing or somebody who's the average age of the person being tested.

The single effect that the uniform has is more identifications, again, whether right or wrong.

The tendency is to encourage more cooperation and more identifications. In the case of our innocent-man-line-ups, this means, of course, more mistaken identifications.

And so, that it is a source of unreliability in this type of testing, that can possibly be avoided by using somebody who's a little bit less identified, particularly with the investigation.

We have made specific recommendations of this to police agencies to get somebody involved to run line-ups who essentially has no stake in the outcome and doesn't know the answer.

Q. Now, there are a couple of factors within your list that I haven't touched on yet; but, would it be basically correct that the more of these factors which you have mentioned, the more of them that exist within any given case, the less reliable the identification becomes?

A. There are sources of unreliability; and it's in my judgment, they do compound, they do add up.

Q. There may be other factors to consider?

A. There may be other factors to consider, yes.[51]

§8.16 Treatise Corroboration

In reaching his or her conclusions, the expert may rely not only on his or her own observations and experiments, but also on the treatises and experiments of others working in the field. In preparing for his or her testimony, the expert will no doubt examine all sorts of studies and reports. Under the Federal Rules of Evidence, if facts or data are the type reasonably relied upon by experts in the field, they need not be admissible in evidence.[52] Judge Weinstein has concluded that a liberal interpretation of this rule works well in practice because:

> In non-jury cases the judge is fully capable of discounting the probative force of the expert's opinion by considering the source of his data. And, in jury cases, when the matter is brought to the jurors' attention by a proper instruction, they show a full sensitivity to the problem—in fact often discounting the expert's opinion too much when it is based on hearsay or secondary evidence of documents or the like. We ought not assume the jurors are less intelligent or alert than lawyers or judges. And we ought not inhibit experts from giving us as much aid as they can.[53]

Also under the Federal Rules of Evidence the expert need not disclose the underlying facts and data for his or her opinions unless the court requires otherwise.[54] Nonetheless, as the transcript recorded in **§§8.07-8.10** illustrates, a disclosure of the methodology used to form an opinion will frequently bolster the expert's testimony and should be inquired into by counsel. In any event, if the facts and data are not disclosed on direct examination, they may properly be explored during cross-examination.[55]

---

[51] Testimony of Dr. Robert Buckhout in People v Johnson, Indictment No 77 C 1300 (Cir Ct Cook County, Ill) on Apr 14, 1978.

[52] Fed R Evid 703.

[53] Weinstein & Berger, Weinstein's Evidence §703[03], 703-18 to 19 (1981).

[54] Fed R Evid 705.

[55] *Id.*

Under Rule 803(18) of the Federal Rules of Evidence, learned treatises, periodicals, and pamphlets are an exception to the rule against hearsay and may be read into evidence to the extent relied upon by an expert witness on direct examination or called to his or her attention on cross-examination. Thus, once it has been established by expert testimony or judicial notice that a text is authoritative, the direct examiner may have it read into evidence if his or her witness relied on it, and the cross-examiner may do the same if the text is called to the attention of the opposing expert. If one's expert has relied on portions of, for example, Elizabeth Loftus' book, *Eyewitness Testimony*,[56] the text can be read to the jury. Should an opposing expert disagree with Loftus, the portion of the work wherein she disagrees with him or her can be read into evidence, too, if it is called to the expert's attention first.

The following simulation is an example of how an attorney can corroborate an expert's testimony by the use of a treatise:

Q. Doctor, you have testified that the fact that a witness gives a good verbal description of a person does not necessarily facilitate his or her ability to recognize that person in a face-to-face encounter. Is that correct?

A. Yes.

Q. Doctor, did you rely upon the research or work of anyone else to reach that conclusion?

A. Yes, I relied particularly upon a discussion by A. Daniel Yarmey in his recent book entitled *The Psychology of Eyewitness Testimony*, published in 1979.

Q. Is that book in general use and circulation in your field?

A. Yes.

Q. Is it considered to be authoritative?

A. Yes, it is.

Q. Doctor, I show you Dr. Yarmey's book entitled *The Psychology of Eyewitness Testimony* and ask you to read to the jury his conclusions on the link between language and recognition memory for faces?

A. After discussing a number of experiments, Dr. Yarmey notes on page 139 that:

> It can be concluded that accuracy of facial recognition is decidedly more dependent upon visual encoding than upon verbal processes of memory. In addition, observers' ability to verbally describe faces

---

[56] E. Loftus, Eyewitness Testimony (1979).

is not predictive of their ability to recognize these faces (Goldstein, Johnson, and Chance, 1977).

On cross-examination, counsel will want to show that this conclusion is not universally accepted.

Q. Doctor, you referred in your testimony to Dr. Yarmey's conclusions on the relationship between language and recognition memory for faces. Is that not correct?

A. Yes, it is correct.

Q. Doctor, you will acknowledge that Dr. Yarmey frankly admits the existence of studies which have reached different conclusions. Is that not correct?

A. That is correct.

Q. And he specifically cites a recent study by McKelvie that shows a link between language and recognition memory for faces. Is that not correct?

A. Yes, it is correct.

Q. Doctor, you would therefore acknowledge that there are differing views among those working in the field on the relationship between verbal descriptions and the accuracy of facial recognition. Is that not correct?

A. Well, yes, it is.

§8.17 Offer of Proof

As shown in **§§8.02** and **8.03,** the admission of expert testimony on the issue of perception and memory is largely discretionary with the trial judge. It is therefore extremely important that the attorney wishing to offer such testimony make a proper offer of proof. In most instances, this offer should be made in an in camera hearing, by calling the expert to testify to those matters which could be properly elicited from him or her at trial. For the reasons stated below, it is suggested that this in camera hearing be held, when at all possible, in advance of trial.

The importance of a proper offer of proof cannot be overemphasized. Most obvious is the need to preserve the record for appeal in the event the trial judge holds the evidence to be inadmissible. However, owing to the great discretion given to trial judges in admitting such testimony, the possibility of a court of appeals reversing the decision of a trial judge on an admissibility question is not strong.[57]

[57] *But see e.g.*, Ibn-Tamas v United States, 407 A2d 626 (DC 1979); United States v Hill, 655 F2d 512 (3d Cir 1981).

However, the offer of proof is also important from another standpoint. In a criminal case, the expert's testimony may also be relevant to an argument on a motion to suppress an identification secured under suggestive circumstances.[58] For this reason, the offer of proof might best be made at the same time as the hearing on the motion to suppress. The expert's testimony can thus be used to bolster the argument on suppression. If the trial judge refuses to suppress the identification, then the testimony of the expert at the suppression hearing may serve as the offer of proof at trial. If the trial judge refuses to admit this evidence, the record is available for argument on appeal on both the issue of suppression and the issue of admissibility.

§8.18 Exclusion Techniques

One who is opposing the admissibility of the testimony of an expert on perception and memory has many objections to raise. Rarely will he or she succeed in excluding the testimony on the ground that the witness is not an expert—at least when the witness has the proper educational and practice credentials. Depending upon the jurisdiction, he or she may argue that the evidence will invade the province of the jury. He or she may be more successful in arguing that the testimony will only confuse the jury and therefore not significantly advance the truth-finding function of the trial.[59] He or she will argue that the jury can use its own experience in judging the credibility of the witness and that counsel has the means through cross-examination and closing argument to alert the jurors to any weaknesses in the witness' testimony. Especially where the witness' identification is corroborated by other reliable evidence, he or she should succeed in convincing the trial judge that the evidence will simply be too time consuming in light of the limited potential helpfulness for the finder of fact.[60]

§8.19 Cross-Examination of the Expert

The *do's and don't's* of cross-examining an expert witness are well

---

[58] See **§2.11.**

[59] United States v Fosher, 449 F Supp 76, 77 (D Mass 1978), *affd,* 590 F2d 381 (1st Cir 1979); United States v Collins, 395 F Supp 629, 637 (MD Pa), *affd,* 523 F2d 1051 (3d Cir 1975); Porter v State, 94 Nev 142, 148, 576 P2d 275, 278 (1978). *See also* United States v Amaral, 488 F2d 1148, 1152 (9th Cir 1973); State v Galloway, 275 NW2d 736, 741 (Iowa 1979) (concurring opinion).

[60] See Arnolds, Carroll & Seng, *The Admissibility of Expert Testimony on the Issue of Eyewitness Identification in Criminal Trials,* 2 N Ill UL Rev 59, 84 (1981).

known—even if they are not well followed.[61] They can probably all be summed up under the familiar admonition that there is no substitute for good preparation.[62] Ask only questions to which you know the answer and do not allow the witness to explain.[63] The effective cross-examiner will have become familiar with the relevant authorities and treatises in the field and will seldom waive cross-examination. But rather than provide a half-hearted effort which merely gives the witness the opportunity to reiterate and reinforce the appearance of expertise and the opinions expressed on direct examination, counsel should force the opposing expert to make admissions that help the cross-examiner's own case.

While it is rare that a cross-examiner will succeed in impeaching the expert's qualifications, it is often possible to show that many of those qualifications are irrelevant to the case at hand. Also, the cross-examination can point out that the witness' testimony was based not on his or her own work and experiments, but simply on treatises and reports of others. If the expert personally conducted the experiments, counsel may want to inquire into the precise methodology utilized, if it is believed to be vulnerable to attack.[64] The cross-examiner can then focus on the conditions under which the experiments were conducted and show that they differed from the conditions surrounding the disputed identification. It also may be effective to stress the statistical nature of the expert's generalizations[65] and point out the lack of any objective basis for concluding that the generalizations about, for example, cross-racial identification (see **§§8.11-8.15**) apply to the

---

[61] See R.E. Keeton, Trial Tactics and Methods 155-65 (2d ed 1973); Goldstein & Lane, Goldstein Trial Technique §§14.24-.27, 16.01-.57 (2d ed 1969); Wellman, The Art of Cross-Examination ch 5 (1923).

[62] J. McElhaney, Effective Litigation 27 (1974).

[63] *Cf* J. Jeans, Trial Advocacy §13.41 (1975).

[64] See Metroff & Kilman, *On Evaluating Scientific Research: The Contribution of the Psychology of Science,* 8 Tech Forecasting & Soc Change 163-75 (1975); B. Kantowitz & H. Roediger, Experimental Psychology: Understanding Psychological Research 14 (1978).

[65] Experimentalists normally do not believe that test results warrant making serious life decisions unless the mathematical analysis indicates that there are no more than five chances in 100 that they may be wrong. Some decisions may require that the odds be even more favorable. See R. Hyman, The Nature of Psychological Inquiry 72 (1964). For a more readable discussion of how statistical inferences interact with real life decisions, see B. Kantowitz & H. Roediger, Experimental Psychology: Understanding Psychological Research 14 (1978). For a thorough mathematical analysis of the procedure, see Q. McNemar, Psychological Statistics (4th ed 1969). The experimental method, which employs controlled factors and statistical analysis, is at the heart of modern science, both theoretical and applied, and it is frequently employed to support life-and-death decisions, such as in cancer treatment.

particular identification in the case at bar. That is, since the findings of experimental psychologists show only that certain characteristics are found with a certain statistical frequency in a particular population and do not establish that the eyewitness in the present case shares these characteristics, *that witness* may be able to identify persons of a different race very well.

The cross-examiner may force the expert to acknowledge the experiments or writings which have reached contrary conclusions to his or her own. Under the Federal Rules of Evidence, these experiments or reports, once they are established as reliable authority by the witness or otherwise, can be admitted into evidence (but not as exhibits) and read to the trier of fact.[66]

Certainly the cross-examiner can get some favorable admissions from the expert which can then be used in argument to the jury. The most effective procedure is simply to call to the expert's attention all the factors involved in the identification which argue in favor of its reliability; for example, that the parties were of the same race, the witness was wearing his or her glasses, it was daylight, the photo-spread contained 100 photographs, etc.

Usually the expert will not have performed any laboratory experiments simulating the conditions of the identification in dispute, and that fact can be brought out. The witness who has testified only to general principles of perception, memory, and recall can be made to admit that he or she has no expert opinion about whether this particular witness was mistaken.

Of course, the cross-examiner can bring out that the expert is being paid, and if the expert is one who lectures at trial technique seminars on subjects such as *persuasion in the courtroom,* a little research can go a long way. Many jurisdictions would permit questions like, "Doctor, isn't it true that just a month ago you told a group of lawyers there's no such thing as an unbiased expert?" or "Doctor, didn't you give a speech last week on how to pick a biased jury?"

§8.20 —Example of Cross-Examination of an Expert

The following is a simulated cross-examination of an expert similar to the expert who testified in **§§8.07-8.10.**

Q. You are not a medical doctor, are you?

---

[66] Fed R Evid 803(18).

A. No.

Q. You are a doctor of philosophy, aren't you?

A. Yes, in psychology.

Q. You can get a doctor of philosophy in physical education, can't you?

A. Yes.

Q. You can get one in home economics, too, right?

A. I'm not sure. Perhaps.

Q. Well, you don't open people up and take out a perception or a memory and put it under a microscope to study, do you?

A. Of course not.

Q. The things you told us about can't be studied that way, can they?

A. No.

Q. You told us about statistical probability; you psychologists use that a lot, don't you?

A. Yes, it is a research tool.

Q. As a matter of fact, it is your *main* tool at arriving at your conclusions?

A. It is a very important one.

Q. But broadly speaking, statistical probability tells you what happens lots of times—but does not tell you what in fact happened *this* time, isn't that a fair statement?

A. Broadly, yes.

Q. It suggests what might have happened, but does not tell you what in fact did happen?

A. Yes.

Q. So when we get down to an actual case, such as we have here, we are pretty much on our own?

A. I don't know how you mean that.

Q. Well, in the final analysis you give us a lot of maybe's but the jury has to figure out what *did* happen?

A. I can shed light on the degree of likelihood that something occurred.

Q. Well, closer to the point, there is no scientific evidence that says that *this specific witness,* Mr. Henderson, did not clearly see and remember accurately his attacker's face just because a gun was used?

A. It can't go that far, but—

Q. You do agree then that it is entirely consistent with your science that Mr. Henderson clearly saw and remembered accurately the face of his attacker?

A. Of course. But I am speaking of the probability of that happening when the gun was present.

Q. So the answer to my question is that it is consistent with all the psychological research you spoke of that Mr. Henderson accurately saw and recalled the face of his attacker?

A. It is a possibility that is consistent with the research.

Q. It is the jury's job to determine what happened in fact, isn't it?

A. I believe that's their function.

Q. It is *not* their function to determine, say, what happens in six out of ten other cases, is it?

A. I suppose not.

Q. And you can tell us what happens in six out of ten cases but you can't tell us who belongs among the six wrong and who belongs among the four right?

A. Well, sometimes we can do better than six in ten.

Q. And the same goes for stress, doesn't it?

A. What do you mean?

Q. Well, you told us that stress interferes with many peoples' accurate perception but it does not with others in a particular situation, isn't that what you told us?

A. Yes.

Q. So there is no scientific proof that Mr. Henderson in fact was too upset to perceive and recall accurately the face of his attacker just because the situation was stressful?

A. No, I cannot say how Mr. Henderson actually performed. I can just illuminate the difficulties.

Q. He may have seen and recalled very accurately?

A. He may have.

Q. By the way, with regard to that photo display you described, the photo of the defendant is quite a good likeness of the defendant in person, is it not?

A. Yes, it is.

Q. And Mr. Henderson's verbal description before he saw the photo of the defendant fits the defendant quite well, doesn't it?

A. Yes.

Q. In fact, it fit the defendant better than any of the others pictured in the photo-spread, did it not?

A. Yes, but that's the point—

Q. Well, you admit the photo fit the description of the attacker?

A. Yes, but so might other possible photos.

Q. But my question is about *this* photo—it did fit the description, did it not?

A. Yes.

Q. And that is the photo of the defendant, is it not?

A. Yes.

Q. And the defendant fits the description of the attacker?

A. Yes.

Q. So Mr. Henderson, bias and all, might be very accurate in his identification of the defendant as his attacker, right?

A. He could be.

Q. Your psychology doesn't say that's out of the question, does it?

A. Not out of the question.

Q. By the way, you tell us that we are more likely to be accurate in our perception and recall of the face of someone of our own race, didn't you?

A. Yes.

Q. And both the defendant and Mr. Henderson are white, aren't they?

A. Yes.

Q. Light helps in the perception of facial details, doesn't it?

A. Yes.

Q. So when Mr. Henderson tells us it was still light, he has something going for himself, doesn't he?

A. Better than if it were dark.

Q. And Mr. Henderson had his glasses on, didn't he?

A. I don't know if I was told.

Q. If he did, it would help?

A. Of course.

Q. You don't need psychology to know that, do you?

A. I suppose not.

Q. Doctor, you've never been allowed to testify to these psychological generalizations in a court before, have you?

A. I have never testified before.

Q. One thing finally, Doctor, you weren't present when Mr. Henderson was attacked, were you?

A. No.

Q. But Mr. Henderson was there, wasn't he?

A. Yes.

Q. You did not see the attacker, did you?

A. No.

Q. Mr. Henderson saw the attacker, did he not?

A. Yes.

Q. No further questions.

9 Jury Instructions

§9.01 In General

The lesson from the most recent cases in the United States is that the courts, while paying lip service to the fallibility problems inherent in eyewitness testimony, are quite willing to let the jury evaluate and weigh the evidence and decide the credibility of eyewitness accounts. The Supreme Court has not rigorously adhered to *Wade*[1] and *Stovall*,[2] and

[1] United States v Wade, 388 US 218 (1967) (Supreme Court held that a postindictment lineup is a critical stage of the prosecution so that an accused is entitled to have counsel present). The efficacy of *Wade* was diluted in Kirby v Illinois, 406 US 682 (1972) (Supreme Court held that counsel is not required at line-ups which occur prior to the institution of formal criminal proceedings).

[2] Stovall v Denno, 388 US 293 (1967) (Supreme Court held that identification evidence which was secured by means which are so suggestive and conducive to mistaken identification as to deny due process of law must be suppressed). The efficacy of *Stovall* was diluted in Manson v Brathwaite, 432 US 98 (1977) (Supreme Court held that identifications secured by suggestive means may be admissible if they are deemed reliable).

most recently, the Court has emphasized that evaluating the reliability of eyewitness testimony is primarily the function of the jury.[3] Therefore, the possibility of suppressing an eyewitness' statement because it is unreliable or tainted by illegal police practices is remote at best. In addition, American courts have refused to require corroboration of eyewitness testimony, and therefore a jury can base its verdict on the account of only one eyewitness without further support.[4] While the rules of evidence clearly allow such testimony, the courts have shown a general reluctance to open the gates and allow experts to testify to the fallibility of memory, perception, and recall.[5] In all of these instances the courts, either explicitly or by implication, state that the unreliability of eyewitness evidence is best brought out by effective cross-examination and by closing argument and by instructions given to the jury by the court.

The question therefore to be discussed in this chapter is how counsel can best insure that the jury is properly instructed about the pitfalls inherent in eyewitness testimony. Detailed jury instructions on the fallibility of eyewitness accounts are clearly not a substitute for vigorous cross-examination, the use of expert testimony, or an effective closing argument. Nonetheless, the importance of proper jury instruction should not be overlooked. An instruction cautioning the jury about the problems inherent in perception, memory, and recall can be a valuable adjunct to cross-examination, expert testimony, and closing argument.

§9.02 The Role of Jury Instructions

Under modern practice, it is the role of the jury to resolve disputed questions of fact. It is the role of the trial judge to instruct the jury properly on the law. However, in actual practice the relationship between judge and jury is not so clean-cut. In the postrevolutionary period, jurors frequently were left to resolve not only the facts but also to decide the law of the case.[6] Today, of course, judges play a much more active role in trials; nonetheless, both state and federal constitu-

---

[3] Watkins v Sowders, 449 US 341, 347 (1981).

[4] United States v Holley, 502 F2d 273, 274 (4th Cir 1974); United States v Telfaire, 469 F2d 552, 554 (DC Cir 1972).

[5] See **ch 8**.

[6] See R. L. McBride, The Art of Instructing the Jury 10 (1969).

Indeed, as late as 1830, Justice Baldwin instructed a jury: "[Y]ou have the power to decide on the law as well as the facts of the case, and are not bound to find according to our opinion of the law. . . ." United States v Wilson, 28 F Cas 699, 712 (CCEDPA 1830) (No 16730).

tional restraints limit judges and carve out some juror responsibilities which may not be breached.[7]

If jurors are going to fulfill their responsibilities, they need careful guidance from the court. There are no schools to train jurors, and there are no courses on how to be an effective juror. For most jurors, sitting on a jury is their first experience with a real trial and their first contact with *the law.* Therefore, the average juror will have no prior knowledge of the procedures used in the courts or the rules under which evidence is admitted. It is thus a primary function of the judge, and also of counsel, to make sure that throughout the trial the jurors fully understand what is taking place.

There has been much criticism of the jury system in recent years, from Chief Justice Warren Burger of the United States Supreme Court on down. Critics argue that jury trials are costly and time consuming. They argue that, especially in complex cases, the average juror simply does not have the technical ability to sift through all the evidence and render a *scientifically* established verdict. However, the fact remains that the jury system does function well. If injustices result, it is all too often the fault of the judge or of counsel for having failed to present the case in a clear and intelligible manner.

The problem of instructing the jury does not begin only after the presentation of the evidence and summation by counsel. It begins with the first questions asked in selecting the jurors. It is therefore crucial that counsel and the judge focus from the beginning on instructing the jury as to how to handle the law and the facts in the case under consideration. Particularly in an eyewitness case, it is too late to let the jury hear all the evidence and then, only after the jurors have formed at least some preliminary opinion as to the credibility and weight to be given the eyewitness testimony, to tell them to be careful. Counsel should be prepared throughout the trial, whether by means of formal objections or by positive requests, to suggest to the court certain admonitions to be given to the jurors to help them in evaluating the case.

The judge and counsel should be at least generally aware of the recent studies done on the jury system, and especially of the recent study on jury instructions by Elwork, Sales, and Alfini.[8] The results of this study emphasize the importance of clarity in jury instructions. Words and

---

[7] US Const amend VII, provides in pretinent part that in civil cases, "no fact tried by a jury, shall be otherwise reexamined in any Court of the United States, than according to the rules of the common law."

[8] A. Elwork, B. D. Sales, & J. J. Alfini, Making Jury Instructions Understandable (1982).

phrases commonly used by lawyers and judges to capsulize legal concepts all too often go right over the heads of jurors.[9] When evaluated against the study done by Elwork, Sales, and Alfini, it is possible that even the special instructions adopted by progressive courts on eyewitness evidence may be deficient on the ground of clarity.

§9.03 Arguments for Special Instructions in Eyewitness Cases

Virtually every court routinely instructs the jury on the credibility of witnesses. Most credibility instructions are general and are applicable to all types of cases. A typical credibility instruction will state:

> It is for you to determine the weight and credit to be given the testimony of each witness. You have a right to use that knowledge and experience which you possess in common with men in general in considering the testimony of each witness. You also may take the following factors into consideration when weighing a witness's testimony:
>
> a) The witness's ability and opportunity to observe and know the things about which he had testified;
> b) The clarity and accuracy of the witness's memory;
> c) The witness's manner and conduct while testifying;
> d) Any interest the witness may have in the result of the trial;
> e) The reasonableness of the witness's testimony when considered in light of all the evidence in the case; and
> f) Any bias, interest, prejudice or motive the witness may have. . . .[10]

---

[9] The importance of clarity in jury instructions is also emphasized by R. L. McBride, *supra* note 6, at 36-37:

> It is the business—and the principle business—of the trial judge to reduce the language of the reviewing courts to simple and concise English. It is the responsibility of the trial judge to take high sounding and general pronouncements of law and translate them into the language of the layman.

On the importance of clarity in legal writing in general, see R. L. Goldfarb & J. C. Raymond, Clear Understandings (1982). Of course, the classic work which debunks *legalese* is F. Rodell, Woe Unto You, Lawyers (1939).

[10] This instruction is taken from State v Warren, 230 Kan 385, 635 P2d 1236, 1245 (1981). It is similar to most recommended pattern instructions. See, e.g., E. J. Devitt & C. B. Blackmar, Federal Jury Practice and Instructions §17.01 (1977); Book of Approved Jury Instructions 2.20 (Committee on Standard Jury Instruction, Civil, of the Superior Court of Los Angeles County, Cal 1977); Illinois Pattern Jury Instructions: Civil §2.01 (2d ed 1971); New York Pattern Jury Instructions, Civil 1:41 (1974).

This instruction probably would not pass the test of clarity offered by A. Elwork, B.

This instruction, however, is not sufficient in a case involving the uncorroborated testimony of a single eyewitness. By telling the jurors to use their own knowledge and life experiences, the court may actually be aggravating error if the life experiences of the jurors are erroneous. Obviously most persons are aware that people often err in their perception of events and that memory plays tricks with the passage of time. However, many persons wrongly believe that cross-racial identifications are more likely to be accurate, that stress enhances one's ability to perceive, and that witnesses will remember more clearly the details of a violent crime than a nonviolent crime.[11] The common credibility instruction may thus actually aggravate error.

Moreover, the general credibility instruction does not educate the jury to those factors which make eyewitness testimony vulnerable. The Court of Appeals for the District of Columbia has emphasized that because eyewitness cases present special problems of reliability, the court's instructions should plainly focus the minds of the jurors on the issue of identity.[12] Judge Bazelon has gone even further and has urged that the jurors not only be apprised of the existence of the problem, but also be given sufficient information in the instructions to enable them clearly to evaluate the impact of the eyewitness testimony.[13]

In *State v Warren,*[14] the Supreme Court of Kansas, noting that trial judges are required to test the reliability of eyewitness testimony for *admissibility* purposes by using the five factors mentioned in *Neil v Biggers,*[15] reasoned that:

> If these five factors should be considered in determining the admissibility of the testimony, it would seem even more appropriate to require the jury to consider the same factors in weighing the credibility of the eyewitness identification testimony. Otherwise the jury might reasonably conclude that the admission of the

---

D. Sales & J. J. Alfini, Making Jury Instructions Understandable (1982). These authors suggest that the word *believability* be substituted for *credibility* and *importance* for *weight.* Instead of telling the jury to use "that knowledge and experience which you possess in common with men in general," the court should tell the jury to use "your own common sense as reasonable men and women." *Id* 290-91.

[11] E. Loftus, Eyewitness Testimony 171-77 (1979).

[12] United States v Telfaire, 469 F2d 552, 555-56 (DC Cir 1972).

[13] *Id* 559 (Bazelon, CJ, concurring).

[14] 230 Kan 385, 635 P2d 1236, 1244 (1981).

[15] 409 US 188, 199, 200 (1972). The five factors mentioned by the Court are: (1) the opportunity of the witness to view the defendant at the time of the crime, (2) the witness' degree of attention, (3) the accuracy of the witness' prior description of the criminal, (4) the level of certainty demonstrated by the witness at the confrontation, and (5) the length of time between the crime and the confrontation.

> evidence by the trial court vouched for its reliability. We think it clear that, in order to prevent potential injustice, some standards must be provided the jury so that the credibility of eyewitness identification testimony can be intelligently and fairly weighed. The giving of such an instruction will take only a couple of minutes in trial time and will be well worth it, if some future injustices can be avoided.[16]

It is not unusual for trial courts to instruct jurors on special precautions which they should take in evaluating the credibility of accomplices,[17] informers,[18] or immunized witnesses.[19] Given the reliability problems inherent in eyewitness cases, a similar special instruction should be given whenever a witness' perception or memory is seriously called into question.[20]

§9.04 Suggested Special Instructions in Eyewitness Cases

Those courts which have given special eyewitness instructions have differed in the specificity required for those instructions. The focal point for any discussion on eyewitness instructions is the model suggested by the Court of Appeals for the District of Columbia, the so-called *Telfaire* instruction:

> One of the most important issues in this case is the identification of the defendant as the perpetrator of the crime. The Government has the burden of providing identity, beyond a reasonable doubt. It is not essential that the witness himself be free from doubt as to the correctness of his statement. However, you, the jury, must be satisfied beyond a reasonable doubt of the accuracy of the identification of the defendant before you may convict him. If you are not convinced beyond a reasonable doubt that the defendant was the person who committed the crime, you must find the defendant not guilty.

---

[16] 635 P2d at 1244.

[17] See E. J. Devitt & C. B. Blackmar, *supra* note 10, at §17.06.

[18] See *id* §17.03.

[19] See *id* §17.04.

[20] *See* People v Whalen, No 234 (NY App Div June 16, 1983), where the court noted that because in a case where a defendant offers an alibi defense the trial judge will instruct the jurors on the possible bias in the testimony by the defendant's family or friends, "out of a sense of fairness, attention should [likewise] be drawn to the possible unreliability of identification testimony."

Identification testimony is an expression of belief or impression by the witness. Its value depends on the opportunity the witness had to observe the offender at the time of the offense and to make a reliable identification later.

In appraising the identification testimony of a witness, you should consider the following:

(1) Are you convinced that the witness had the capacity and an adequate opportunity to observe the offender?

Whether the witness had an adequate opportunity to observe the offender at the time of the offense will be affected by such matters as how long or short a time was available, how far or close the witness was, how good were lighting conditions, whether the witness had had occasion to see or know the person in the past.

[In general, a witness bases any identification he makes on his perception through the use of his senses. Usually the witness identifies an offender by the sense of sight—but this is not necessarily so, and he may use other senses].*

(2) Are you satisfied that the identification made by the witness subsequent to the offense was the product of his own recollection? You may take into account both the strength of the identification, and the circumstance under which the identification was made.

If the identification by the witness may have been influenced by the circumstances under which the defendant was presented to him for identification, you should scrutinize the identification with great care. You may also consider the length of time that lapsed between the occurrence of the crime and the next opportunity of the witness to see defendant, as a factor bearing on the reliability of the identification.

[You may also take into account that an identification made by picking the defendant out of a group of similar individuals is generally more reliable than one which results from the presentation of the defendant alone to the witness.]

[(3) You may take into account any occasions in which the witness failed to make an identification of defendant, or made an identification that was inconsistent with his identification at trial].

(4) Finally, you must consider the credibility of each identification witness in the same way as any other witness, consider whether he is truthful, and consider whether he had the capacity and

---

*Sentence in brackets ([]) to be used only if appropriate. Instructions to be inserted or modified as appropriate to the proof and contentions. [Footnote by court.]

> opportunity to make a reliable observation on the matter covered in his testimony.
>
> I again emphasize that the burden of proof on the prosecutor extends to every element of the crime charged, and this specifically includes the burden of providing beyond a reasonable doubt the identity of the defendant as the perpetrator of the crime with which he stands charged. If after examining the testimony, you have a reasonable doubt as to the accuracy of the identification, you must find the defendant not guilty.[21]

In a concurring opinion, Judge Bazelon argued that the *Telfaire* instruction was still too general and that in a case involving a cross-racial identification the court should further include the admonition that:

> In this case the identifying witness is of a different race than the defendant. In the experience of many it is more difficult to identify members of a different race than members of one's own. If this is also your own experience, you may consider it in evaluating the witness's testimony. You must also consider, of course, whether there are other factors present in this case which overcome any such difficulty of identification. For example, you may conclude that the witness has had sufficient contacts with members of the defendant's race that he would not have greater difficulty in making a reliable identification.[22]

Believing that elaboration on the specific circumstances surrounding an identification is best left to oral argument, the Seventh Circuit has recommended an abbreviated *Telfaire* instruction:

> The reliability of eyewitness identification has been raised as an issue in this case and deserves your attention. Identification testimony is an expression of belief or impression by the witness. Its value depends upon the opportunity the witness has to observe the offender at the time of the offense and later to make a reliable identification, and upon the influences and circumstances under which the witness made the identification.

---

[21] United States v Telfaire, 469 F2d 552, 558-59 (DC Cir 1972). See also E. J. Devitt & C. B. Blackmar, Federal Jury Practice and Instructions §15.19 (1977).

[22] United States v Telfaire, 469 F2d 552, 561 (DC Cir 1972) (Bazelon, CJ, concurring). In a separate concurring opinion, Judge Leventhal cautioned that before discerning a generalization on interracial identifications ready for inclusion in a model instruction, appellate judges should explore the wording of the instruction with trial judges and lawyers in a manner more like a legislative committee than a decision in an adversarial proceeding. *Id* 563.

> You must consider the credibility of each identification witness in the same way as any other witness. Consider whether he is truthful, and consider whether he had the capacity and opportunity to make a reliable observation on the matter covered in his testimony.
>
> The government has the burden of proving beyond a reasonable doubt that the defendant was the person who committed the crime.[23]

The Supreme Court of Kansas has approved a more detailed instruction which lists the five reliability factors enunciated by the United States Supreme Court in *Neil v Biggers:*[24]

> (1) One of the questions in this case is the identification of the Defendant as the one who committed the crime charged. The prosecution has the burden of proving beyond a reasonable doubt not only that the crime was committed, but that the Defendant was the person who committed it.
>
> (2) In considering whether the prosecution has proved beyond a reasonable doubt that the Defendant was the person who committed the offense, you should consider the following:
>
> (3) The witness's opportunity to observe the criminal act and the person or persons committing them, including the length of time available for observation; the amount of time between the aforementioned observation and any subsequent identification; the witness's state of mind at the time of the offense; whether a weapon was involved; whether the witness had occasion to see or know the Defendant before the incident and any other circumstances affecting the witness's opportunity to observe the person or persons committing the offense.
>
> (4) The identification made by the witness after the offense must be the product of his own memory. You may take into consideration any subsequent identification, the circumstances surrounding the identification, the state of mind of the witness at the time, and other circumstances bearing on the reliability of the identification. You may also consider the length of time that elapsed between the occurrence of the crime and the time the witness saw the Defendant as a factor bearing on the reliability of the identification.
>
> (5) You may take into account any occasions on which the witness

---

[23] Federal Criminal Jury Instruction No 3.06 (Committee on Federal Criminal Jury Instructions of the Seventh Circuit 1980).

[24] 409 US 188, 199, 200 (1972).

failed to make an identification of Defendant or made an identification that was inconsistent with his identification at trial and all other circumstances which you found affected the identification.[25]

These instructions, while differing in detail as to those factors which should be articulated by the courts, agree in their central thesis—that eyewitness testimony should be carefully scrutinized by the trier of fact and should not necessarily be taken at face value.

§9.05 Arguments against Special Instructions in Eyewitness Cases

A number of arguments can be advanced with varying degrees of success against a trial court's giving detailed instructions to jurors concerning the fallibility of eyewitness identifications. The more abstract argument concerns the proper role of the judge and the jury. It is primarily the function of the jury to resolve disputed questions of fact. How much credence should be given to any particular evidence is to be determined by the jury. Therefore, a judge can be accused of invading the province of the jury when he or she singles out eyewitness testimony and tells the jury to consider it with special skepticism.

However, while jurors do have the responsibility of resolving disputed questions of fact, judges have traditionally instructed jurors on how best to evaluate those facts. Judges caution jurors to be wary of the biases of certain witnesses. Jurors are routinely instructed on the special credibility problems inherent in the testimony of such persons as accomplices, informers, and immunized witnesses.[26] Consequently, there seems to be no structural argument that stands in the way of a special eyewitness instruction.

A more pragmatic argument against detailed instructions is that they load the dice against the proffered eyewitness testimony. In many cases, especially in situations where wrongs have been committed in private such as in cases of rape and sexual assault, the only credible evidence is the testimony of an eyewitness. It would be very difficult for the prosecution ever to win such a case if the jury were specifically instructed to be skeptical about eyewitness testimony. It can be argued that jurors will naturally be aware that people err in their perceptions and that over time memory plays tricks, and consequently, the common

---

[25] State v Warren, 230 Kan 385, 635 P2d 1236, 1244-45 (1981).

[26] See E. J. Devitt & C. B. Blackmar, Federal Jury Practice and Instructions §§17.03, 17.04, 17.05 (1977). *See also* People v Whalen, No 234 (NY App Div, June 16, 1983).

sense of the jurors will be sufficient protection against an erroneous verdict.

However, this argument ignores the special reservations appellate courts have expressed with regard to eyewitness cases. It also ignores the findings of psychologists and other experts on the inherent unreliability of eyewitness testimony. It therefore seems reasonable that if psychologists and judges are both in agreement about the dangers of error in eyewitness testimony, this fact should be communicated by the trial judge to the jury.

A final argument which could be advanced is that there is no absolute agreement among the experts on what factors produce error in eyewitness cases. Therefore, once a judge goes beyond the general cautions contained in most credibility instructions, he or she runs the risk of stating as a matter of law that which cannot be firmly established in fact. For instance, not all cross-racial identifications are equally suspect.

This argument does merit caution. The Seventh Circuit has recognized that specific questions concerning reliability should be resolved through oral argument, not through a detailed jury instruction.[27] Nonetheless, the factors enunciated in the *Telfaire* instruction[28] and the five *Neil v Biggers* factors[29] which the Kansas Supreme Court[30] incorporated into an instruction are not matters upon which one can learnedly argue. Therefore, on balance, the better practice would seem to favor such instructions.

§9.06 Eyewitness Instructions in the Federal Courts

First Circuit: The United States Court of Appeals for the First Circuit has not yet considered whether a special eyewitness instruction is appropriate.

Second Circuit: The Second Circuit has left the decision whether to give a special eyewitness instruction to the sound discretion of the trial judge.[31] The court has held that a trial judge did not err in failing to give the instruction where the testimony was "so equivocal as to make

---

[27] See Federal Criminal Jury Instruction No 3.06 (Committee on Federal Criminal Jury Instructions of the Seventh Circuit 1980).

[28] United States v Telfaire, 469 F2d 552, 558-59 (DC Cir 1972). See **§9.04.**

[29] 409 US 188, 199, 200 (1972). See **§9.03.**

[30] State v Warren, 230 Kan 385, 635 P2d 1236, 1244 (1981). See **§9.03.**

[31] United States v Evans, 484 F2d 1178 (2d Cir 1974).

its fallibility self-evident."[32] The court has also held that a trial judge did not err in refusing to give a special instruction in a case not involving a "dubious identification."[33]

Third Circuit: The Third Circuit has held that a special instruction is mandatory "in any case raising the question whether the defendant was in fact the criminal actor."[34] However, a trial judge has no responsibility to give the instruction unless a specific request is made by counsel.[35]

Fourth Circuit: The Fourth Circuit has held that the *Telfaire* instruction,[36] or its substantial equivalent, is required "where there is an identification by a single witness with no other corroborating circumstantial evidence."[37] However, the instruction is not required to be given when not requested by counsel, where other independent evidence, whether direct, circumstantial, or both, which is corroborative, is presented.[38]

Fifth Circuit: The Fifth Circuit has held that no special instruction is necessary to emphasize the fallibility of eyewitness testimony.[39] However, the court has stated that it might be the "better practice" for trial judges to give one.[40]

Sixth Circuit: The Sixth Circuit has held that the *Telfaire* instruction[41] may be used at the discretion of the trial judge to deal "realistically with the shortcomings and trouble spots of the identification process."[42]

---

[32] United States v Gentile, 530 F2d 461, 469 (2d Cir 1976), *cert denied,* 426 US 936 (1976) (upon request, the trial judge had said he would give the jury a cautionary instruction but then failed to do so).

[33] United States v Montelbano, 605 F2d 56 (2d Cir 1979).

[34] United States v Barber, 442 F2d 517, 528 (3d Cir 1971), *cert denied,* 404 US 958 (1971). The court held that the jury should be instructed that the identification testimony may be treated by the jury as a statement of fact by the witness: if the witness had the opportunity to observe the accused; if the witness is positive in his or her identification; if the witness' identification testimony is not weakened by prior failure to identify or by prior inconsistent identification; and if, after cross-examination, his or her testimony remains positive and unqualified. However, in the absence of any of these four factors, the court should admonish the jury that the witness' testimony "must be received with caution and scrutinized with care." *Id.*

[35] United States v Wilford, 493 F2d 730 (3d Cir 1974), *cert denied,* 419 US 851 (1974).

[36] See **§9.04.**

[37] United States v Holley, 502 F2d 273 (4th Cir 1974).

[38] United States v Revels, 575 F2d 74 (4th Cir 1978).

[39] United States v Banks, 485 F2d 545 (5th Cir 1973), *cert denied,* 416 US 987 (1973).

[40] United States v Rhodes, 569 F2d 384, 389 (5th Cir 1978), *cert denied,* 439 US 844 (1978).

[41] See **§9.04.**

[42] United States v Scott, 578 F2d 1186, 1191 (6th Cir 1978) *cert denied,* 439 US 870 (1978). *See also* United States v Boyd, 620 F2d 129 (6th Cir 1980), *cert denied,* 449 US 855 (1980).

Seventh Circuit: The Seventh Circuit has stated that it will "view with grave concern the failure to give" its suggested equivalent of the *Telfaire* instruction[43] where "the crucial issue involved is the defendant's identification, and where an instruction specifically bringing the identity issue to the jury's attention is requested by counsel and tendered to the court."[44]

Eighth Circuit: The Eighth Circuit, like the Seventh Circuit, "will view with grave concern the failure to give specific and detailed instructions . . . where identification of the defendant is based solely or substantially on eyewitness testimony."[45] The court has found it to be reversible error for a trial court to fail to give a *Telfaire* instruction[46] upon proper request where the identification by the eyewitness is the sole basis for the conviction and the possibility for misidentification exists.[47]

Ninth Circuit: The Ninth Circuit has held that general credibility and burden of proof instructions are sufficient to apprise jurors of their duty carefully to evaluate the evidence.[48]

Tenth Circuit: The Tenth Circuit has held that it is discretionary with the trial judge whether to give a special instruction, especially in cases where there is corroborating evidence.[49]

Eleventh Circuit: The Eleventh Circuit will presumably follow existing precedents from the Fifth Circuit.

DC Circuit: The United States Court of Appeals for the District of Columbia, while noting that the *Telfaire* instruction[50] is not compulsory, has stated that "a failure to use this model, with appropriate adapta-

---

[43] See **§9.04.**

[44] United States v Hodges, 515 F2d 650, 653 (7th Cir 1975). *But see* United States v Fleming, 594 F2d 598, 606 (7th Cir 1979), *cert denied,* 442 US 931 (1979) (failure to give special instruction not reversible error when the instruction was not requested by counsel).

[45] United States v Dodge, 538 F2d 770, 784 (8th Cir 1976), *cert denied,* 429 US 1099 (1976). It is not reversible error, however, where the instruction was not requested by the defense, United States v Rivers, 693 F2d 52, 55 (8th Cir 1982); United States v Cripler, 533 F2d 1055 (8th Cir 1976), *cert denied,* 429 US 844 (1976), or to delete portions of the *Telfaire* instruction relating to facts supported by corroborating circumstantial evidence. Durns v United States, 562 F2d 542, 550 (8th Cir 1977), *cert denied,* 434 US 959 (1977).

[46] See **§9.04.**

[47] United States v Greene, 591 F2d 471, 477 (8th Cir 1979). *But see* United States v Cain, 616 F2d 1056 (8th Cir 1980), where identification was strongly corroborated by the testimony of another witness.

[48] United States v Sambrano, 505 F2d 284, 287 (9th Cir 1974). *See also* People of Guam v Dela Rosa, 644 F2d 1257, 1261 (9th Cir 1980); United States v Masterson, 529 F2d 30, 32 (9th Cir 1976), *cert denied,* 426 US 908 (1976).

[49] United States v Cueto, 628 F2d 1273, 1276 (10th Cir 1980).

[50] See **§9.04.**

tions, would constitute a risk in future cases that should not be ignored unless there is strong reason in the particular case."[51]

§9.07 Eyewitness Instructions in Selected State Courts

Alabama: An Alabama appellate court has held that a special eyewitness instruction "which deals realistically with the shortcomings and trouble spots of the identification process should be given where the principle has not been covered by the court's oral charge."[52] However, a special instruction can be refused if it is only an "abstract statement of legal principle and is not phrased as requested charges are required to be phrased, that is, hypothesized on a belief from the evidence."[53]

Alaska: Whether or not a particular instruction should be given is in the discretion of the trial court.[54]

Arizona: If requested, the trial court must instruct the jury that "it must be satisfied beyond a reasonable doubt that the in-court identification was independent of the previous pretrial identification or if not derived from an independent source, it must find from other evidence in the case that the defendent is the guilty person beyond a reasonable doubt."[55] However, because the Arizona Constitution prohibits a judge from commenting on the evidence, the more specific *Telfaire* instruction[56] has been rejected.[57]

Arkansas: Trial judges give basic reasonable doubt and credibility instructions, and the Arkansas Constitution has been construed to forbid the judges to go further in commenting on the evidence.[58]

California: California decisions require that special identification instructions be given, but the failure to do so may not be prejudicial if

---

[51] United States v Telfaire, 469 F2d 552, 557 (DC Cir 1972). *See also* United States v Butler, 636 F2d 727 (DC Cir 1972).

[52] Brooks v State, 380 So 2d 1012, 1014 (Ala Crim App 1980), *cert denied,* 397 So 2d 189 (Ala 1980).

[53] Vincent v State, 399 So 2d 923, 927 (Ala Crim App 1981).

[54] Dayton v State, 598 P2d 67 (Alaska 1979).

[55] State v Dessureault, 104 Ariz 380, 453 P2d 951, 955 (1969). *See also* State v Schilleman, 125 Ariz 294, 609 P2d 564 (1980); State v Stow, 109 Ariz 282, 508 P2d 1144 (1973).

[56] See **§9.04.**

[57] State v Valencia, 118 Ariz 136, 575 P2d 335 (Ct App 1977).

[58] Conley v State, 270 Ark 886, 607 SW2d 328, 330 (1980).

the jury was nonetheless generally instructed on burden of proof and credibility.[59]

Colorado: A special instruction need not be given if the jury was given a general instruction on credibility.[60]

Connecticut: A special instruction should be given when "the identification [is] dubious, [or] present[s] any special difficulties."[61]

District of Columbia: The better practice is for a trial court to give a special eyewitness instruction, but it need not be given unless requested by counsel.[62]

Florida: The appellate decisions in Florida are in conflict whether a special instruction must be given if identification is in issue and if such an instruction is requested.[63]

Georgia: Trial judges in Georgia are not required to instruct the jury on "the possible dangers of mistaken identification."[64]

Hawaii: It is discretionary with the trial court whether or not to give a special identification instruction.[65]

Idaho: A trial court may refuse a cautionary instruction on identification because the subject is adequately covered in the general burden of proof instruction.[66]

Illinois: In 1948, the Illinois Supreme Court held that it was reversible error for a trial court to refuse an instruction covering the question of identification in a case where the defendant was identified by only one of four eyewitnesses to the crime.[67] Nonetheless, the Illinois Judicial Conference Committee on Pattern Jury Instructions recommends that no instruction be given on the circumstances of an identification because the subject is adequately covered by the general instruction that

---

[59] People v Hall, 28 Cal 3d 143, 167 Cal Rptr 844, 616 P2d 826 (1980). *See also* People v Guzman, 47 Cal App 3d 380, 121 Cal Rptr 69 (1975).

[60] People v Palumbo, 192 Colo 7, 555 P2d 521 (1976); People v Martinez, 652 P2d 174 (Colo Ct App 1981); People v Reynolds, 68 Colo App 258, 559 P2d 714 (1976).

[61] State v Maturo, 188 Conn 591, 452 A2d 642 (1982). *See also* State v Harden, 175 Conn 315, 398 A2d 1169 (1980).

[62] Wilkerson v United States, 427 A2d 923 (DC 1981); Smith v United States, 343 A2d 40 (DC 1975). The District of Columbia courts do require a special instruction on the corroboration of a child complainant's testimony in sex offender cases, even if not specifically requested by counsel. Fitzgerald v United States, 443 A2d 1295, 1303 (DC 1982).

[63] *See, e.g.,* Freeman v State, 371 So 2d 114 (Fla Dist Ct App 1979) (instruction required); Cruz v State, 310 So 2d 360 (Fla Dist Ct App 1975) (instruction not required).

[64] Burke v State, 161 Ga App 407, 288 SE2d 276 (1982).

[65] State v Pahio, 58 Hawaii 323, 568 P2d 1200 (1977); State v Padilla, 57 Hawaii 150, 552 P2d 357 (1976).

[66] State v Oldham, 92 Idaho 124, 438 P2d 275, 285 (1968).

[67] People v Ricili, 400 Ill 309, 79 NE2d 509 (1948).

the jury is the sole judge of credibility.[68] An Illinois appellate court has held that the factors surrounding the circumstances of an identification are better discussed in closing argument than in the court's instructions.[69]

Indiana: The Indiana Supreme Court has held that "the trial court should not single out the testimony of any witness and attack its credibility or indicate an opinion as to the weight that should be accorded to it."[70]

Iowa: No specific cautionary instruction need be given because trial courts should give a "general instruction . . . applicable to all witnesses alike."[71]

Kansas: A cautionary instruction, if requested, must be given "in any criminal action in which eyewitness identification is a critical part of the prosecution's case and there is a serious doubt about the reliability of the identification."[72] However, it does not have to be given in a case where there was never a waiver or doubt in the minds of the witnesses concerning the defendant's identity, even though there may be some minor discrepancies in the witnesses' description of the robber.[73]

Kentucky: Special instruction in eyewitness cases is not required.[74]

Louisiana: It is prejudicial error for a trial court to refuse to give a special instruction on identification where the only defense is mistaken identification.[75] However, a general credibility instruction which asks the jury to look at the witness' ability to observe and the conditions under which the observation was made is sufficient.[76]

---

[68] Illinois Pattern Jury Instruction—Criminal ¶3.15 (1981). Ill S Ct Rule 451(a), Ill Rev Stat (1981) ch 110A, §451(a), states that the decision to give a nonpattern instruction is within the sound discretion of the trial court.

[69] People v White, 58 Ill App 3d 226, 374 NE2d 250 (1978). *See also* People v Hefner, 70 Ill App 3d 693, 388 NE2d 1059 (1979).

[70] Beasley v State, 370 NE2d 360, 363 (Ind 1977). In Stanley v State, 435 NE2d 54 (Ind Ct App 1982), the court stated that "credibility instructions should be general and apply equally to all witnesses." *Cf* Pearson v State, 441 NE2d 468 (Ind 1982) (holding it was not error to refuse a cautionary instruction on hypnotically refreshed testimony because singling out the credibility of one witness is improper).

[71] State v Wright, 274 NW2d 307, 314 (Iowa 1979).

[72] State v Warren, 230 Kan 385, 635 P2d 1236, 1244 (1981). The exact instruction recommended in *Warren* is not required so long as the "substance of the instruction" is given. State v Werner, 8 Kan App 2d 364, 657 P2d 1136, 1138 (1983).

[73] State v Shephard, 232 Kan 614, 657 P2d 1112, 1116 (1983).

[74] Brock v Commonwealth, 627 SW2d 42 (Ky Ct App 1981), *cert denied,* 102 S Ct 2302 (1982); Jones v Commonwealth, 556 SW2d 918 (Ky Ct App 1977).

[75] State v Hills, 129 So 2d 12 (La 1961).

[76] State v Artis, 391 So 2d 847 (La 1980).

Maryland: A general instruction which treats permissible inferences, credibility, and weight of evidence is sufficient.[77]

Massachusetts: A defendant who fairly raises the issue of mistaken identification is entitled to a *Telfaire* instruction,[78] which may be modified or embellished as required.[79]

Michigan: Although Michigan has a recommended identification instruction, it is not to be given where the witness had a good opportunity for positive identification, is positive in his or her identification, and his or her identification is not weakened by a prior inconsistent identification or by a prior failure to identify. Its use in those circumstances would only confuse the jury.[80]

Minnesota: When requested by counsel, the trial judge "should instruct on the factors the jury should consider in evaluating an identification and caution against automatic acceptance of such evidence."[81] However, it is not error for the trial judge to refuse a cautionary instruction when the eyewitness' testimony was unequivocal and convincing[82] or when there was sufficient corroborating evidence.[83]

Mississippi: The trial court can give general instructions on burden of proof and reasonable doubt,[84] but the trial judge cannot "comment on the testimony or charge the jury as to the weight of the evidence."[85]

Missouri: The Missouri Supreme Court has held that no special instruction on the theory of misidentification is required because the subject is adequately covered in the Missouri Approved Instructions—

---

[77] England v State, 274 Md 264, 334 A2d 98 (1975).

[78] See **§9.04.**

[79] Commonwealth v Bowden, 379 Mass 472, 399 NE2d 482 (1980); Commonwealth v Rodriguez, 378 Mass 296, 391 NE2d 889 (1979). In Commonwealth v Conceicao, 388 Mass 255, 446 NE2d 383, 389-90 (1983), the court rejected an argument that the defendant was denied effective assistance of counsel because an extensive instruction on identification was not requested, when counsel focused heavily on the possibility of misidentification in cross-examination and in closing argument and when the judge's instruction clearly alerted the jury to the issue of misidentification. *Cf* Commonwealth v Avery, 14 Mass App 137, 437 NE2d 242 (1982) (cautionary instruction allowed in discretion of trial judge when child testifies so long as jury not given any indication of whom the judge believes).

[80] People v Dyson, 106 Mich App 90, 307 NW2d 739 (1981); People v Whitmore, 88 Mich App 177, 272 NW2d 346 (1978). *See also* People v Gardner, 402 Mich 460, 265 NW2d 1 (1978).

[81] State v Burch, 284 Minn 300, 170 NW2d 543 (1969). *Accord* State v Christian, 244 NW2d 284 (Minn 1976).

[82] State v Bishop, 289 Minn 188, 183 NW2d 536 (1971).

[83] State v Richie, 292 Minn 413, 195 NW2d 570 (1972).

[84] Miller v State, 399 So 2d 1338 (Miss 1981).

[85] Ragan v State, 318 So 2d 879 (Miss 1981).

although these instructions do not specifically refer to mistaken identification.[86]

Montana: An eyewitness instruction may be required "when there is only a single eyewitness' unsubstantiated testimony which identifies the offender," but not when there is corroborating testimony.[87]

Nevada: General instructions on credibility and burden of proof are sufficient.[88]

New Hampshire: The New Hampshire Supreme Court will view with grave concern the failure to give the *Telfaire* instruction[89] upon proper request when the identification is based solely or substantially on eyewitness testimony.[90]

New Jersey: Trial courts should give the New Jersey model eyewitness instruction when doubts are raised about the accuracy of an identification.[91]

New Mexico: No error for a trial judge to refuse a cautionary instruction because the general credibility and reasonable doubt instructions are sufficient to cover identification problems.[92]

New York: Although an eyewitness instruction is not required if the trial judge gives an accurate credibility and burden of proof instruction, the New York Court of Appeals has held that the better practice is to give an expanded charge when it is requested by the defendant.[93]

North Carolina: A specific cautionary instruction must be given, even if not requested by counsel, if the evidence strongly suggests the

---

[86] State v Quinn, 594 SW2d 599, 604-05 (Mo 1980). *See also* State v White, 617 SW2d 596 (Mo Ct App 1981).

[87] State v Hart, 625 P2d 21, 31 (Mont 1981), *cert denied,* 454 US 827 (1981); State v Strain, 618 P2d 331, 336 (Mont 1980).

[88] Langford v State, 95 Nev 631, 600 P2d 231 (1979). *But see* May v State, 89 Nev 277, 510 P2d 1368 (1973) (a special cautionary instruction should be given in a rape case if the evidence does not clearly point to the defendant's guilt and the victim's testimony is not corroborated).

[89] See **§9.04.**

[90] State v Burke, 448 A2d 962, 966 (NH 1982).

[91] State v Green, 86 NJ 281, 430 A2d 914, 919-21 (1981) (failure to give instruction is reversible error even though it was not formally requested by counsel, but where counsel objected to the court's instruction). *See also* State v Carter, 91 NJ 86, 449 A2d 1280, 1304 (1982) (requirement for special instruction met when the trial court refused the defendant's request to instruct specifically on the witness' state of mind and opportunity to observe but did tell the jury that "the identification testimony is to be received by you with great caution").

[92] State v Mazurek, 88 NM 56, 537 P2d 51 (Ct App 1975).

[93] People v Whalen, No 234 (NY App Div June 16, 1983).

likelihood of irreparable misidentification.[94] However, a specific instruction dealing with interracial identifications is not required.[95]

Ohio: It rests in the sound discretion of the trial judge whether to give a *Telfaire* instruction.[96] However, an appellate court has ruled that in a case involving conflicting and confusing identification testimony, it was reversible error for the trial court to refuse to give an instruction which specifically directed "the jury's attention to the very nature of, and the potential problems of reliability inherent in, eyewitness testimony itself."[97]

Oklahoma: It is prejudicial error for a trial judge to refuse to give a cautionary instruction when requested in a case "where eyewitness testimony is far from positive."[98]

Oregon: A cautionary instruction may be given if requested; however, the *Telfaire* instruction[99] is considered to be "prolix, it tends to overemphasize the issue, and it contains elements that amount to comments on the evidence."[100]

Pennsylvania: A defendant is entitled to a cautionary instruction in a case where the opportunity for a positive identification was not good.[101]

Rhode Island: The Rhode Island Supreme Court has expressed a concern about the potential hazards in the use of eyewitness testimony and has approved of cautioning the jury on the weaknesses in identification evidence.[102] However, in a civil damage action where the plaintiff had been injured and suffered amnesia for from five to seven months, the supreme court felt that the trial judge improperly instructed the jury to consider "whether [someone] has the memory to recall

---

[94] State v Kinard, 54 NC App 443, 283 SE2d 540, 543 (1981). *See also* State v Marten, 53 NC App 297, 280 SE2d 778 (1981) (no error not to give instruction when the identification is supported by corroborating evidence).

[95] State v Allen, 301 NC 489, 272 SE2d 116, 119-20 (1980).

[96] State v Guster, 66 Ohio St 2d 266, 421 NE2d 157, 161 (1981). For the *Telfaire* instruction itself, see **§9.04.**

[97] State v Dale, 3 Ohio App 3d 431, 445 NE2d 1137, 1140-41 (1982).

[98] Driskell v State, 659 P2d 343, 360 (Okla Crim App 1983). *See also* Hall v State, 565 P2d 57 (Okla Crim App 1977); Melot v State, 375 P2d 343 (Okla Crim App 1962).

[99] See **§9.04.**

[100] State v Classen, 31 Or App 683, 571 P2d 527, 533 (1977). The recommended instruction is set forth in State v Calia, 15 Or App 110, 514 P2d 1354, 1356 (1973), *cert denied,* 417 US 917 (1974). *See also* State v Rovles, 41 Or App 653, 598 P2d 1249, 1252 (1979).

[101] Commonwealth v Kloiber, 378 Pa 412, 106 A2d 820 (1954), *cert denied,* 348 US 875 (1954); Commonwealth v Mouzon, 456 Pa 230, 318 A2d 703 (1974); Commonwealth v McKnight, 307 Pa Super 213, 453 A2d 1 (1982). The instruction must be requested. Commonwealth v Jackson, 248 Pa Super 420, 375 A2d 168 (1977).

[102] State v Lewis, 115 RI 217, 341 A2d 744, 749 (1975).

accurately."[103] The court felt that under the circumstances the trial judge had invaded the province of the jury by conveying to them his impression of the plaintiff's credibility.[104]

South Carolina: An instruction must be given which will "adequately [focus] the attention of the jury on the necessity for a finding that the testimony identified defendant as the offender beyond a reasonable doubt," but nothing can be stated "in respect to matters of fact," and therefore the *Telfaire* model is not proper.[105]

Texas: A special cautionary instruction is not allowed in Texas. The trial judge may not "single out" facts concerning a witness' identification and "magnify them before the jury," because to do so would amount to an impermissible "comment on the weight of the evidence."[106]

Utah: It is within the discretion of the trial judge whether to give a cautionary instruction.[107]

Vermont: An instruction on identification is "preferable."[108]

Virginia: A special instruction would "overemphasize" the question of identification; hence, a general reasonable doubt instruction is sufficient.[109]

Washington: General burden of proof and credibility instructions are sufficient; a special cautionary instruction would invade the province of the jury.[110]

West Virginia: A *Telfaire* instruction[111] may be appropriate if the identification testimony is uncorroborated.[112]

Wisconsin: A general instruction stating that the identification of the defendant must be proved beyond a reasonable doubt is sufficient.[113]

---

[103] Valente v HP Hood & Sons, 108 RI 558, 277 A2d 505, 507 (1971).

[104] *Id.*

[105] State v Robinson, 262 SE2d 729, 731-32 (1980). For the *Telfaire* instruction, see **§9.04.**

[106] Wilson v State, 581 SW2d 661, 664-65 (Tex Crim App 1979).

[107] State v Malmrose, 649 P2d 56, 61 (Utah 1982) (defense did not object at trial to the court's instructions).

[108] State v Roy, 140 Vt 219, 436 A2d 1090, 1095 (1981); State v Kasper, 137 Vt 184, 404 A2d 85, 100 (1979).

[109] Evans v Richmond, 210 Va 403, 171 SE2d 247, 250 (1969).

[110] State v Edwards, 23 Wash App 893, 600 P2d 566 (1979).

[111] See **§9.04.**

[112] State v Gravely, 299 SE2d 375, 386 (W Va 1982). A cautionary instruction is required in a rape case where the victims' testimony is uncorroborated. State v Ray, 298 SE2d 921, 924 (W Va 1982); State v Payne, 280 SE2d 72, 77 (W Va 1981).

[113] Hampton v State, 92 Wis 2d 450, 285 NW2d 868 (1979).

Wyoming: A special eyewitness instruction did not have to be given in a case where the defendant did not object and when basic credibility and burden of proof instructions were given.[114]

§9.08 Theory of the Case

Criminal defendants[115] and all civil litigants[116] have a clear right to jury instructions explaining each one's theory of the particular case. Notwithstanding the obvious importance of such an instruction, it is requested by criminal defendants with surprising infrequency. Where eyewitness testimony is challenged in a criminal case, delivery of a theory instruction can do much to offset the refusal to give a *Telfaire* instruction[117] and to reinforce the principles which otherwise might be weakened by the equivocal language of the Seventh Circuit's variation of *Telfaire.*[118]

If the defense rests without presenting evidence, relying upon the application of the *reasonable doubt* doctrine, the defense's theory instruction would deal exclusively with that issue. In a more complex case, the defense's theory in respect to the eyewitness identification may be stated as an integral part of a broader instruction embracing other consistent or alternative defense theories, such as the extortion of a confession, alibi, or title to stolen property. It should be remembered, however, that a theory instruction, like all instructions, must be tendered in reasonably concise and intelligible terms.[119]

A hypothetical tender based on the testimony shown in **§6.08**[120] might resemble the following:

> It is the theory of the defendant that Ms. Good's identification of him as the offender is insufficient to prove his guilt beyond a reasonable doubt. The defendant relies upon the circumstances under which that identification was made, including the fact that Ms. Good's initial report to the investigating policemen made no

---

[114] Campbell v State, 589 P2d 358, 368 (Wyo 1979).

[115] *See* United States v Musgrave, 444 F2d 755, 764-65 (5th Cir 1971); United States v Leach, 427 F2d 1107, 1112 (1st Cir 1970) and cases there cited.

[116] *See* Brown v Addressograph-Multigraph Corp, 300 F2d 280 (6th Cir 1970).

[117] United States v Telfaire, 469 F2d 552 (DC Cir 1972), discussed in **§9.04.**

[118] Federal Criminal Jury Instruction No 3.06 (Committee on Federal Criminal Jury Instructions of the Seventh Circuit 1980), discussed in **§9.04.**

[119] United States v American Radiator etc, 433 F2d 174 (3d Cir 1970).

[120] This fact scenario is based upon the problem "State v. Lawrence," *Problems and Cases in Trial Advocacy, Law School Edition,* 2nd Ed. (1981), which is published by the National Institute for Trial Advocacy (NITA). Adapted and reproduced with the permission of NITA.

> mention of the defendant's identifying features such as his tattoo, scar, and even his age. The defendant also points out that the showing to Ms. Good by the investigating police of two photographs of the defendant, rather than a group of photographs of several different individuals, might have influenced Ms. Good and affected her subsequent personal identification of the defendant. He also relies upon the fact that at the lineup, the defendant was the only person wearing white pants, and he contends that this was another suggestive factor which might have produced a mistaken identification.
>
> You should keep the defendant's theory in mind when you consider the evidence during your deliberations. If, in the light of all the evidence, and in view of the defendant's theory, you have a reasonable doubt of the defendant's guilt, your verdict should be not guilty.

The theory instruction may, and as a tactical matter normally should, embrace all significant elements of the defense's position. The only restriction is that it must have an arguable basis in the evidence.[121] Depending upon the facts of the case, it may be expanded to embrace factors such as the sudden change of ambient light intensity which resulted from Ms. Good's leaving the bus and the likelihood that during the attack Ms. Good was concentrating on her purse at least as much as upon the features of her attacker. An important distinction, therefore, must be made between those two contentions. The change of light intensity is an undisputed factual proposition expressly conceded by Ms. Good. It may therefore properly be referred to within the tendered instruction as a *fact.* Her concentration on the purse during the attack, however, is only a defense conjecture based upon the belief that it is *likely* that Ms. Good would have behaved in that manner. That element of the defense theory, therefore, should be described in terms appropriate to the case—e.g., "The defendant further contends that, in the circumstances, it is probable that, notwithstanding her denial, Ms. Good naturally would have focused at least a substantial part of her attention on the purse which she was attempting to save from her attacker, rather than on the attacker's facial features."

The importance of observing the distinction between fact and contention in the formulation of the instruction derives from the court's right to refuse any tendered instruction which places the court in the position of advocate. Clearly, for example, an instruction making reference to the *fact* that Ms. Good's attention was diverted from her

---

[121] Womack v United States, 336 F2d 959 (DC Cir 1964); *Cf* United States v Williams, 604 F2d 277 (6th Cir 1979); *see* United States v Brake, 596 F2d 337 (8th Cir 1979).

attacker to her purse would, if delivered, place the court in the position of ruling that Ms. Good's denial of that suggestion is not credible and would justify refusal of the instruction.

The defense's summation, of course, should make proper reference to the theory instruction, just as to other significant instructions approved by the court in the instruction conference.[122]

§9.09 Requesting Special Eyewitness Instructions

The role of counsel in seeing that the jury is properly instructed is crucial. The cases are virtually uniform in holding that it is the responsibility of counsel to request a special cautionary instruction, and if a proper request is not made the issue is waived for appeal purposes.[123] Counsel must also be certain that his or her requested instructions are made part of the official court record. If an instruction conference is held with the judge in chambers, counsel must make sure that his or her requests and objections are noted and recorded by the court reporter. Frequently, this requires counsel to make a detailed statement on the record when the parties return to the courtroom. Although some jurisdictions may review instructions even if only a general objection is noted,[124] to be safe, counsel should be as specific as possible.

Counsel should have the proposed instructions typed and in good form prior to the opening of the trial. The local rules of many courts require that the instructions be submitted with the final pretrial order. Although some courts may be more liberal and tailor a general instruction to meet the requirements of the case,[125] the general rule is that if any part of a submitted instruction is erroneous the trial judge may properly reject the entire instruction. Therefore, counsel should prepare alternative instructions and get a specific ruling on each alternative. Thus, counsel might want to prepare a detailed *Telfaire* instruction,[126] a more specific instruction on cross-racial identifications,

---

[122] See **§10.06.**

[123] A rare example where a court has stated that in special circumstances a cautionary instruction should be given even if no request is made is State v Allen, 301 NC 489, 272 SE2d 116, 119-20 (1980). *See also* People v Hall, 82 AD2d 838, 439 NYS2d 661 (1981); People v Gardner, 402 Mich 460, 265 NW2d 1, 8 (1978).

[124] *See, e.g.,* State v Gardner 86 NJ 281, 430 A2d 914 (1981).

[125] *See, e.g.,* People v Hall, 28 Cal 3d 143, 167 Cal Rptr 844, 616 P2d 826, 835 (1980); People v Guzman, 47 Cal App 3d 380, 121 Cal Rptr 69, 73 (1975).

[126] United States v Telfaire, 469 F2d 552, 558 (DC Cir 1972). See **§9.04.**

if that is appropriate,[127] and a more general instruction such as that recommended in the Seventh Circuit.[128] Whichever instruction ultimately is accepted, counsel is protected.

Especially in eyewitness cases, cautionary instructions should not be reserved until the end of the trial. Most of the commentators agree that the jury should be instructed at the voir dire on the problems inherent in eyewitness cases.[129] Hence the *Telfaire* instruction or an appropriate substitute should be read to the jury at the commencement of the trial. This alerts the jurors to the problem and insures that they will carefully scrutinize a witness' testimony at the time it is being offered.

Counsel may also request a cautionary instruction at the time a witness testifies. This may be especially helpful in a case where the witness has previously viewed the defendant in a suggestive photospread or lineup. A trial judge may well refuse a general credibility instruction at the time the witness is testifying for fear that the instruction will unduly prejudice the jury against the witness; however, the judge should not refuse a special instruction which deals with a specific problem in the witness' testimony. Such an instruction is necessary to insure that the jury places the testimony in the proper context and perspective.

§9.10 General and Special Verdicts

At common law, verdicts returned by juries could be either general or special. The Federal Rules of Civil Procedure and the practice in many states continue the distinction.[130]

A general verdict is a conclusory determination of what, if anything, a plaintiff is entitled to recover. Except by implication by the result, a general verdict does not disclose the basis for the resolution of each subsidiary factual issue.

A special verdict requires the jury to resolve specific factual issues.

---

[127] United States v Telfaire, 469 F2d 552, 561 (DC Cir 1972) (Bazelon, CJ, concurring). See **§9.04.**

[128] Federal Criminal Jury Instruction No 3.06 (Committee on Federal Criminal Jury Instructions of the Seventh Circuit 1980). See **§9.04.**

[129] Note, *Eyewitness Identification Testimony and the Need for Cautionary Jury Instructions in Criminal Cases,* 60 Wash ULQ 1387 (1983). See also A. Elwork, B. D. Sales & J. J. Alfini, Making Jury Instructions Understandable 21-24 (1982); McBride, The Art of Instructing the Jury 42 et seq (1969).

Many commentators also state that the better practice, especially in cases involving complex instructions, is to give the jurors written copies of the instructions. E.g., A. Elwork, *et al, supra,* at 18-20.

[130] Fed R Civ P 49.

These resolutions are then turned over to the trial judge who applies the law and renders a judgment. The federal rules provide that parties waive their right to a jury on issues which are omitted in the special verdict form unless counsel makes a timely objection. As to omitted issues, the court may make a finding or the issue is deemed to have been resolved in accordance with the judgment.[131]

The federal rules also allow a general verdict to be accompanied by answers to interrogatories on one or more issues of fact. If the answers are consistent with each other but conflict with the general verdict, the trial court may enter judgment in accordance with the answers, notwithstanding the general verdict, or the court may send the matter back to the jury for further consideration or order a new trial. If the answers are inconsistent with each other and likewise conflict with the general verdict, the judge must send the matter back to the jury or order a new trial.[132]

The Federal Rules of Criminal Procedure refer only to general verdicts and do not provide for interrogatories or special verdicts.[133] In rare cases, courts have allowed special interrogatories over the objection of counsel.[134] However, the concern is that in a criminal case, unless the questions are very carefully drafted, they will lead the jury in a step-by-step progression to a verdict of guilty.[135] A further concern is that they may prevent a jury from acquitting a defendant for the perfectly proper reason that the jurors have no sympathy for the government's position.[136]

A case whose sole issue is the accuracy of eyewitness testimony does not lend itself well to a special verdict. An interrogatory to the jury in such a case would do nothing more than to restate the only issue which the jury must decide in order to reach a general verdict. In that situation, it seems far preferable to tender a jury instruction delineating the relationship between the credibility of the eyewitness and the disposition of the case.

If, on the other hand, evidence has been introduced which could justify a verdict for the proponent even though the eyewitness were not

---

[131] *Id* 49(a).

[132] *Id* 49(b).

[133] Fed R Crim P 31.

[134] *See* United States v Palmeri, 630 F2d 192, 202 (3d Cir 1980), *cert denied,* 450 US 967, 983 (1981). *But see* United States v Wilson, 629 F2d 439 (6th Cir 1980); United States v Spock, 416 F2d 165 (1st Cir 1969).

[135] United States v Palmeri, 630 F2d 192, 202 (3d Cir 1980), *cert denied,* 450 US 967 (1981).

[136] United States v Wilson, 629 F2d 439, 443 (6th Cir 1980).

believed, a special interrogatory is technically improper. The purpose of such an interrogatory is to assure that the general verdict is not the product of mistake, sympathy, or other improper influence. For that reason, the procedure is proper only if the special verdict presents a question of fact which must be answered in order to decide the case, so that some possible answer to the question could impeach a general verdict. If the jury properly could find for the proponent even though the eyewitness were not believed, a special verdict testing the jury's evaluation of the eyewitness would serve no legally acceptable purpose, since a general verdict for the proponent could stand even though the special verdict might show that the eyewitness was not believed.

It seems unlikely, therefore, that a special interrogatory can be useful in resolution of the issue of the accuracy of eyewitness testimony.

10 Summations

§10.01 The Right to Argue

In sharp distinction from the law's treatment of the opening statement,[1] the summation is generally held to be a right rather than a mere privilege. A New York statute which granted trial judges the right to forbid summations in criminal cases was ruled unconstitutional by the Supreme Court, which found it to be a denial of Sixth Amendment rights as applied to a defendant who had waived a jury.[2] That holding, of course, applies a fortiori to jury trials, as is evident from the language of the opinion:

> In a criminal trial, which is in the end basically a factfinding process, no aspect of [partisan] advocacy could be more important than the opportunity finally to marshal the evidence for each side before submission of the case to judgment.[3]

Although this case has facial application only to criminal litigation, the authors find no precedent for prohibition of summations in civil trials as well. Typical of the views expressed in authoritative treatises is the following sweeping comment: "Counsel for each side, in both civil and criminal cases, has the right to argue his case at the close of all the evidence, in both jury and nonjury cases."[4]

Waiver of the right to present final argument seems an improbable tactic when challenged eyewitness testimony will be a significant factor in the outcome. Most such cases are criminal prosecutions, in which it generally is held that the prosecutor has an affirmative duty to present

---

[1] See **§5.06.**

[2] Herring v New York, 422 US 853 (1975).

[3] *Id* 862.

[4] Hunter, Federal Trial Handbook §86.1 (1974).

a summation.[5] Although the defense has the right to waive argument, such waiver normally is viewed as undesirable in eyewitness contests. Lacking defense guidance, the jury may well fail to appreciate the significance of the factors which cast doubt on that testimony. In civil cases, a plaintiff is free to waive argument, and mutual waivers occur somewhat more frequently than in criminal trials. In the authors' view, a mutual waiver may be desirable in some cases from the standpoint of the party who vouches for the challenged witness. The opposing party, however, should not lightly surrender the opportunity to highlight the infirmities of that testimony, a process which normally requires that the jury be led rather than left to feel its way unguided on a critical exploration beneath the surface of that testimony.

§10.02 The Trial as Prologue

Delivery of summations by the opposing lawyers generally is regarded as the climax of the trial. The arguments deal, however, with events which occurred in the sight and hearing of the jurors, who are likely to have made their own evaluations of the evidence. They also have had ample opportunity to have formed a personalized image of each of the contending lawyers, based upon the lawyers' conduct during the previous phases of the trial. In all probability, the jurors will be unwilling to be guided by a lawyer's arguments during summation, unless the lawyer's previous actions have instilled a receptive attitude.

Such an attitude is unlikely to be engendered by a lawyer whose trial performance lacks coherence. The lawyer must proceed in accordance with a unifying case theory, and the jury must be made aware of that theory long prior to the commencement of the summation—ideally at the earliest possible stage of the trial and certainly no later than during the opening statement. Subsequent direct and cross-examination, and even objections and motions, should appear to the jury to adhere to that unifying theory.

As stated by one commentator, "Everything you say and do in the presence of the jury throughout the trial is a part of your argument, whether you want it to be or not."[6]

---

[5] *See, e.g.*, Fed R Crim P 29.1. Any different procedure would shift the burden to the defense.

[6] B. Palmer, Courtroom Strategies 272 (1959).

§10.03 The Advocate's Objective

The lawyer commencing summation must bear in mind that the jury has heard the eyewitness under both direct and cross-examination and is familiar with the respective theories of the contending parties. Most members of the jury, in all probability, have formed at least tentative impressions with respect to both the accuracy of the witness' observations and the reliability of the lawyer's interpretations of trial developments.

If those impressions are unanimous, or nearly so, summation may well be an exercise in futility. That matter, however, can be determined, if at all, only after the fact. The conscientious lawyer must proceed as though a significant number of the jurors would cast ballots on each side of the case if they were required to vote before hearing the arguments. The argument, therefore, must be directed to an audience which the speaker presumes to have approached the recital with mixed views on the merits of the case.

The jurors' reactions to the points made during summation may reasonably be presumed to be analogous to their reactions to evidentiary developments which reinforce or contradict their earlier tentative impressions: receptivity toward assertions which reinforce their opinions and resistance to those suggestions which contradict those opinions.[7]

The lawyer, accordingly, should frame arguments which serve several complementary purposes. He or she tries to reinforce the sense of self-assurance of the friendly juror and to furnish that juror with ammunition for use during the deliberations. At the same time, the lawyer attempts to weaken the adverse juror's confidence and sense of commitment and to provide such a juror with a comforting analysis of the factors which tended to cause such a mistaken view: erring witnesses, misleading tactics, natural sympathies, and trial developments which may have been confusing but which the lawyer now will interpret properly.

The thoughtful trial tactician does not indulge the naive assumption that the jurors have obeyed the judge's command that, in defiance of every known principle of psychology and basic human nature, they must form no opinion until they have heard the summations and instructions. The classic psychological absurdity—"Go sit in a corner and do *not* think about elephants!"—is unfeasable under the best of circumstances. It becomes completely preposterous if a motion picture of a pachydermal

---

[7] See **§5.01.**

stampede, in full color and sound, is projected on the wall at which the subject of the command is forced to stare.

In eyewitness litigation, and in other cases as well, the lawyer should approach summation with a very different assumption: that the jurors have formed opinions, but that those opinions are diverse, tentative to some degree, and subject to modification during the ultimate deliberation which will produce the verdict.

§10.04 Creating a Receptive Climate

This book deals only with those principles of persuasion which have special importance as applied to eyewitness litigation. Among the most significant of these is that the jury is much more likely to empathize with a witness than with a lawyer, for obvious reasons. It follows that an ad hominem attack on the witness is a last resort.

Awareness of the jury's probable tendency to identify with the witness should also cause the lawyer to hesitate to resort to the use of humor in most contexts. Even though the witticisms are not directed against the witness, a laughing lawyer contrasts poorly with the obvious, often plodding sincerity of the mistaken eyewitness. Such sallies also frequently detract from the aura of significance which must appear if the jurors are to avoid surrendering to their natural desires to return to their private activities by rendering a quick verdict at the expense of adequate consideration of the issues. Such a verdict almost always will favor the witness rather than the joking lawyer if the positions of the two are in conflict.

The attitude of the lawyer must be one of sincerity, confidence in the rectitude of his or her cause, and an awareness (but an awareness devoid of awe) of the seriousness of the situation. The lawyer's communicated sense of serious purpose, however, must never descend to pomposity; that attitude, no less surely than unseemly humor at the other end of the scale, will contrast poorly with the jury's image of an honest witness in a forbidding environment.

In attempting to cast doubt on the testimony of such a witness, lawyers must walk a narrow line. In order to avoid the appearance of pomposity and invidious comparison with the witness under attack, they must speak in normal, conversational terms. At the same time, they must maintain a position of leadership, carrying the jury with them as they appear to take charge of the courtroom, filling a role similar to that of classroom teachers without ever looking down or talking down toward those whom they would instruct. Wherever logically possible, the lawyer should attempt to create an image of collective wisdom and freedom from egotism by using the pronoun *we* rather than *I*.

Whether as proponent or opponent of the eyewitness, the lawyer's proper posture is clearly defined: toward the witness and the victim, particularly where they are the same, sympathy; toward the jury, courtesy, informative leadership, and thoughtful analysis; and toward the person accused by the contested testimony, a sense of shared nightmare, if that person is the client, or an attitude bordering on indulgence toward a false denial to be expected in all such cases as a matter of obvious self-interest, if the accused is the opponent.

§10.05 The Structure of the Argument

In framing the summation, the lawyer challenging an eyewitness would do well to embrace the caveat directed by Hippocrates to the medical profession: "Primum non nocere!" (The first consideration is to avoid doing harm.) A lengthy catalogue of blunders in both the courtroom and the operating theatre bears witness to the fact that within both professions that maxim frequently is aspirational rather than functional.

As previously demonstrated, delivery of a summation probably is indispensable to a well-conducted eyewitness contest. The realistic objective, however, is less to win the case than to avoid losing it.

The framing of a summation in eyewitness litigation should be governed by certain principles whose application seems specially forceful in cases of that type. The next group of sections consider the tactical significance of some of those principles.

§10.06 —Brevity

The lawyer planning a summation in eyewitness litigation must resist the temptation toward grandiloquence. The jurors' initial attitude may be one of sanguine expectation based on television programs; but even if initially receptive, the jurors are basically weary of the case when final argument begins. They will resent any apparent (and perhaps further) wasting of time. They will sit through an inappropriate or inept summation, often with no apparent displeasure, because they may see no alternative to supine acceptance; but their attention quickly gives way to boredom and resentment if they are subjected to a badly conceived argument.

The first structural consideration, accordingly, should be brevity. One specialist in communication techniques who has devoted substantial study to courtroom dynamics has concluded that summations tend to lose effectiveness after 20 minutes and become counterproductive if they last longer than 30 minutes.[8]

§10.07 —Succinct Review of Facts

The principle of brevity adumbrates a second consideration which merits special attention in eyewitness contests. Resolution of a question of eyewitness credibility involves, in most cases, a fairly straightforward and clearly defined issue. The facts bearing on that issue may be complex and subtle, but the jury heard those facts once and will not take kindly to being required to hear them again in any unnecessary detail. The summation, therefore, should touch only upon the truly significant facts bearing on the accuracy of the witness' perception, interpretation, retention, and explication. If other evidentiary details become significant in the course of the jury's deliberations, those details are almost certain to be within the unaided memory of at least one of the twelve jurors. To the extent that such questions are likely to arise, therefore, the jury itself probably will furnish the answers from its own membership.

For all these reasons, therefore, a detailed review of the facts is almost never desirable as a part of the summation when the central issue is the reliability of eyewitness testimony. Such wasting of time is completely antithetical to effective summation. The time limitation placed on the arguments by the judge is likely to be misleading; a much tighter constraint is imposed by the jury's willingness to concentrate on those arguments.

An effective summation in an eyewitness contest, therefore, is one which is focused on the reasons for testimonial conflicts, the factors which tend to make the testimony reliable or unreliable, and an explanation of those relevant trial events whose importance probably was not appreciated fully by the jurors—in short, an *analysis,* not a chronicle. In Professor Jeans' words, "Argument is not the time to tell them the *what* of the case, but rather the *why* of the case."[9]

§10.08 —Graphic Terminology

Another significant structural element derives from the uses to which language is put in everyday life. As one commentator has observed,

---

[8] J. Rasicot, Jury Selection, Body Language and the Visual Trial 138 (1983).

[9] J. Jeans, Trial Advocacy 381 (1975).

people "in general do not judge things. Rather they judge the names the things are called."[10] Commentators on trial practice seem generally agreed that graphic terminology should be employed whenever possible to reflect the lawyer's interpretation of the matter thus described.[11] The eyewitness' proponent will refer to the "identification" by the witness and the "facts" which the witness provided to buttress that identification. The opponent, on the other hand, anticipating the *Telfaire* instruction,[12] will refer to the witness' "opinion", "impression", or even "guess".

§10.09 —Reference to Instructions

Mention of *United States v Telfaire*[13] suggests a third element of effective summation: the exploitation of the court's instructions to the jury. Counsel have, of course, the right to comment on those instructions as long as the inferences presented are legally acceptable.[14] The jury, unaware that the instructions were painstakingly composed by counsel, are likely to be impressed favorably by the judge's apparent endorsement of counsel's position. Thus, it is proper for the attorney to preface the outline of his or her case theory by stating: "The court has, as required by law, made its own analysis of this case from a legal standpoint and is, I believe, prepared to define for you our theory of this case in these terms: that the witness is simply mistaken, as indicated by [specifics of the case]."[15] That approach carries substantially greater force than a simple statement of one's position and theory.

§10.10 —Coherence

A fourth component with special significance in eyewitness cases is the element of coherence. A proper appreciation of its significance requires a review of the overall trial dynamic.

The traditional view of the trial lawyer's relationship with the jury may properly be analogized to the enforcement of a contract. The basic contract was made during jury selection, when the veniremen agreed

---

[10] B. Palmer, Courtroom Strategies 181 (1959).

[11] Rasicot, Jury Selection, Body Language and the Visual Trial 138 (1983); B. Palmer, *supra* note 10, at 181-83; McElhaney, Effective Litigation 123 (1974).

[12] United States v Telfaire, 469 F2d 552 (DC Cir 1972). See **§9.04.**

[13] 469 F2d 552 (DC Cir 1972).

[14] Hunter, Federal Trial Handbook §86.11 (1974).

[15] The *theory of the case* instruction is treated in **§9.08.**

that if the case were or were not proved in accordance with the requisite legal standard, they would reach a verdict in accordance with that proof. In consideration of that promise, they were accepted as jurors.

The two mutually exclusive contracts were refined during opening statements when each lawyer disclosed the manner in which he or she proposed to perform the contract obligation. Each lawyer promised to prove certain facts, perhaps even naming the witnesses and exhibits by which the proofs would be made.

The evidence phase, of course, was the lawyers' attempted performance of their respective contractual undertakings. Each in turn produced, or failed to produce, the evidence promised during the opening statement.

Finally, during the summation, if the evidence has developed reasonably in accordance with the planned strategy, the lawyer should be able to tell the jury, with sufficient deference and euphemism to remove any possible taint of effrontery, that he or she has fulfilled the contract obligation and is entitled to expect the same from the jurors. The barely hidden message here is a challenge to the jurors' integrity. The lawyer's promise has been kept, and the jurors can do no less in turn. It is for that reason that summations often include a reminder of the content of the lawyer's opening statement and a claim that the promise then made has been fulfilled.

That procedure, of course, creates the opportunity for mild but effective imposture, as the reader doubtless will have noticed, because the refinement of the contract is only unilateral. In delivering the opening statement, the lawyer did *not* say that the promised evidence would be sufficient from a legal standpoint to create the legally required degree of certainty or doubt. Indeed, the lawyer could not properly have said any such thing, regardless of the cogency of the promised evidence, because a proposition of law may not properly be expressed within an opening statement. The unarticulated message of that opening, however, is quite unmistakable. The lawyer is saying, from the jury's perspective, that the evidence promised during the opening statement will, if actually produced during the trial, satisfy the legal standard by which the jurors previously promised to be bound and will entitle the client to a favorable verdict. The jurors, however, are unable to reopen the negotiations and may well consider themselves obligated to accept the refined contract.

That concept has forceful application in eyewitness litigation. The skillful proponent includes within the opening statement every fact tending to lend credibility to the eyewitness' story. The opponent likewise provides for the jury all the elements which tend to cast doubt on that story. If both parties adopt the contract approach, the decision is likely to favor the one who can most realistically claim to have fulfilled the promise made during the opening statement. If only one of them pursues that theory, however, that party would seem to have a clear advantage, provided the evidence justifies the initial claims.

A routine factual setting may provide an example of the operation of the contract technique. Assume a criminal case such as *People v Pure*[16] in which the defendant is charged with purse snatching based on the testimony of the victim. During cross-examination, the victim conceded that the theft occurred at twilight, that she had no prior acquaintance with the defendant, and that she was able to view him only as he quickly grabbed the purse before running away from her. Such testimony may well be believed by the jury; the authors are aware of many criminal convictions based on evidence no stronger than that.

The defendant's prospects for acquittal, however, will be brightened substantially if, during summation, his lawyer can remind the jury, vividly and forcefully, that each member swore to acquit on reasonable doubt of guilt; that in reliance on that sworn promise, defense accepted them as jurors; that the lawyer in turn promised to prove twilight conditions, lack of antecedent acquaintanceship, and fleeting observational opportunity—not merely one fact, but an entire series of facts demonstrating reasonable doubt; that the defense kept its promise, and proved every one of those facts; and that the time has come to place the matter into the hands of the jury. In discharge of a solemn duty to the client and to the cause of justice, and with real confidence that the jurors will do so, the lawyer calls upon them to fulfill their pledge, just as he or she is proud to say that the defense redeemed completely the pledge made to them.

Properly employed, that technique effectively transforms a criminal defendant into a contract plaintiff—a far more comfortable posture!

§10.11 —Structural Logic

An effective summation technique used by many skilled lawyers involves presenting the jury with an analysis of the case which suggests that all the evidence, on both sides, rests upon a single overriding principle. The argument focuses the jury's attention upon that principle, which is intended to guide their evaluation of the evidence, the

---

[16] This hypothetical is set forth more fully in **ch 6.** The fact scenario is based upon the problem "State v. Lawrence," *Problems and Cases in Trial Advocacy, Law School Edition*, 2nd Ed. (1981), which is published by the National Institute for Trial Advocacy (NITA). Adapted and reproduced with the permission of NITA.

arguments, and even the instructions of the court—all the elements which enter into their ultimate decision. The indispensable prerequisite to the employment of that technique, of course, is that the lawyer must come forward with a principle that is both forceful and airtight, since it must support the entire structure of the case. One writer has referred to arguments thus structured as *inverted pyramids.*[17]

Simple and effective basing points are available to counsel on both sides of the controversy. The proponent of the eyewitness can point to the social disaster that would be caused by disdain for eyewitness observations; in many situations, by circumstance or by malevolent design of the actor, no other source of information is available. The opponent can invoke the simple and impregnable proposition that anyone can be mistaken. Subsequent sections of this chapter present illustrations of the arguments suggested here.

§10.12 Categories of Variables

As previously noted,[18] jurors are likely to overrate the inherent reliability of eyewitness testimony. Everyone will acknowledge readily, however, that reliability will vary with the circumstances of each case.

Those obvious propositions determine the thrust of a proper summation in eyewitness litigation. The party who seeks to disparage the reliability of such testimony has a more challenging task than does the party who asks the jury to accept it. The challenger must therefore, if possible, focus upon the specific facts of the case which weaken the testimony, rather than be burdened with the resistance with which the jury would be likely to react to an undifferentiated attack on the reliability of all such testimony.

Although the witness' sponsor might prefer to rely upon a more general approach, the opponent's emphasis on specifics forces the sponsor to respond in kind, since failure to do so probably would forfeit the case. In many cases the sponsor, who normally will be the plaintiff and therefore entitled to argue first, will initiate the discussion of the case-specific reliability factors, anticipating the probable attack of the opponent.

Each party, therefore, must be prepared to demonstrate the significance of the particular facts which bear upon the likelihood that the individual witness would have been able accurately to have acquired the

---

[17] B. Palmer, Courtroom Strategies 180 (1959).

[18] *See, e.g.,* **§§1.03** and **8.01.**

relevant information, to have stored it in memory without compromise, and to have recalled it clearly while on the witness stand.[19]

Within this chapter are listed the factors most likely to bear upon the reliability of such testimony in any given case.[20] It is suggested that reliance upon such a checklist can simplify the problem of framing the summation.

For reasons which will become clear, this chapter also assigns the factors to discrete categories. The classifications are not offered as an academic exercise, but as a practical device which will impart added force to summations in eyewitness cases.

The relevant factors may be personal to the witness or they may arise from considerations related to the event. Significant subgroupings exist within each of those categories. The personalized factors may be classified as either physical or emotional. The facts peculiar to the event will likewise fall into two groupings: environmental factors determined by the place where the event occurred, and influences exerted by the actions of the participants.

§10.13 Significance of Classification

The forcefulness of a summation will be intensified if the lawyer is able to point out at least one factor within each category which is favorable to his or her position. In that situation, the lawyer can offer the following analysis:

> The judge will, I believe, instruct you that in evaluating the reliability of [the eyewitness'] testimony, you should consider all relevant matters including your own knowledge and experience.
>
> Now, we all know that sometimes when people observe things, their impressions are highly accurate and reliable. Other times, they are mistaken in what they tell us, even though they are trying hard in all good faith to tell the complete truth.
>
> And we all know, from our normal experiences in life, why that happens. There are really four tests of reliability; four things that we would want to know in our own private affairs before deciding how likely it is that a person such as [the eyewitness] actually saw exactly what he[21] claims that he saw. The first two questions relate to the person himself: Was there anything about his physical make-up that would affect his observations? And second, how likely

---

[19] See **§§8.07-8.10.**

[20] See **§§10.14-10.26.**

[21] Use the gender of the eyewitness.

> is it that most people in that same emotional or psychological situation would have made an accurate and reliable observation of the things that he claims to have seen and would have remembered it well enough to tell it accurately?
>
> The second two questions relate to the event itself. First, was there something about the appearance or actions of the people he saw which would have made it easy or hard to identify them later? And second, what about the place where it happened? Was there something about the scene which would likely have affected his ability to see or to concentrate?
>
> Those, then, are the four questions that each of us instinctively asks when it becomes important—really important—to know whether we can put complete trust in the story of a person who comes to us and tells us what he saw at an earlier time. Four questions: What was his physical condition; what was his emotional or psychological situation; how fast-moving was the event; and finally, what were the conditions at the scene—the environmental influences, some might say—that would have affected his ability to observe? Those are the four basic questions which determine the reliability of any eyewitness testimony such as you have heard in this case. Let's answer those questions, one by one.
>
> First: What was [the eyewitness'] physical condition? Well, as you heard. . . .

From that point, the lawyer would proceed to select a factor from each of the categories and to explain the manner in which that element supports his or her theory of the case. The lawyer will conclude that portion of the argument by stating that his or her position, whether endorsing or denigrating the witness' story, is supported by every accepted test of reliability.

The argument can be adapted, with somewhat diminished impact, to cases in which the facts will not justify invocation of tests embracing all four categories. In that situation, the prefatory reference to the jurors' normal experiences in life should be modified. In place of the four tests of reliability, the lawyer would argue: "There are at least three [or two] questions that we would want to ask in that situation." The lawyer would conclude by saying, "I urge you to ask those same questions in this case. The answers to all three make it clear that the witness should be believed [or is mistaken]."

§10.14 Distribution of Factors

Several of the tests of reliability may be said to encompass facts which are relevant to more than one of the four categories described in **§10.13.** The assailant who bursts suddenly upon the scene, discharges a firearm, and runs away has erected two discrete barriers to subsequent identification. The startling quality of the acts creates a psychological obstacle to perception, while the same quick movements create a physical obstruction to observation.

It therefore becomes possible for the lawyer to categorize, for purposes of summation, the same basic fact—sudden and dramatic action—as either emotional or physical obstruction. The lawyer may properly elect to treat both categories as applicable, assigning the unexpected nature of the event as a matter which required psychological adjustment precedent to meaningful perception, and treating the offender's motion as a physical impediment to observation.

The lawyer often is free, within reason, to make arbitrary assignments of facts to one or more of the relevant categories. An effort should be made to avoid obvious duplication of argument, but frequently it will be possible credibly to treat all four questions as answered by elements of the case which do not present four discrete facts.

Mindful of the essentially arbitrary quality of many of the category assignments, the reader may now proceed to a consideration of the individual factors which most frequently affect the reliability of eyewitness testimony, whether by enhancement or debasement.

§10.15 —Physical Condition: A Note of Caution

Discretion, diffidence, and sympathy, both in fact and in appearance, are necessary qualities for the lawyer who must address the problem of witness infirmities. From time to time, a uniformly youthful jury may be impaneled in a case involving an elderly eyewitness, but it cannot be assumed that these jurors will react favorably to a denigration of the perceptive powers of older persons. To the contrary, poignant family or other relationships with the elderly may cause them to feel active resentment if the topic is presented in an insensitive manner. The same may be said of any form of physical infirmity.

Primum non nocere![22] Do not harm the witness, your client or yourself. The issue must be raised, but raised without gratuitous offense. Careful advance consideration must be given to any argument which points up

---

[22] The first consideration is to avoid doing harm. See **§10.05.**

physical infirmity. The unreliability of an aged person as an eyewitness can be urged with gentleness.

> [The eyewitness'] wealth of experience commands respect from all of us. I pray that I shall some day possess his[23] dignity and worthiness as a person. People such as he see many things to which I am blind. Their strength of vision is the capacity for insight, deeper perspectives, qualities at least as important and valuable as the routine ability to take accurate account of harsh and literal reality. We lack his years and the special talents that his years have brought to him. We normally see only what is actually, physically before our eyes. The trial of a lawsuit, however, is one of the few occasions on which our type of vision is more useful than his.

In many situations, there may be no words which will make the advocate's point without giving offense. In those situations, the infirmities of the witness generally are obvious to all concerned and should not be mentioned during summation other than in the most oblique terms.

§10.16 —Physical Condition of the Witness

The physical condition of the witness is significant only to the extent that it reflects upon his or her powers of observation. Almost any physical infirmity, however, is potentially relevant under special circumstances. A person gifted with exceptional visual acuity may be adversely affected as a witness by confinement in a wheelchair, if his or her view of the event required an agile turn to follow the action.

Elements of physical condition most likely to be relevant include the general state of health, visual acuity, and age.

General State of Health

Almost any illness tends to interfere with observation. If the witness had a cold, it is probable that one or more of the customary symptoms—sneezing, coughing, nasal discharge, fever—amounted to a meaningful distraction. If the witness had a headache, his or her power of concentration probably was impaired. Conversely, perfect health may be emphasized as a positive factor.

---

[23] Use the gender of the eyewitness. If more than one, use the plural pronoun.

Visual Acquity

If the witness wears glasses, any irregularity such as failure to use them, breakage, or outdated prescription is a matter worthy of note if the observational opportunity was marginal. The lawyer must remember, however, that in all probability some of the jurors wear glasses and may resent any suggestion that seems to reflect adversely on their own general fitness as observers. The issue should be avoided, as a matter of common sense, if the witness' claimed observation is one which probably could have been made regardless of any problem with glasses. If the issue is to be raised, the lawyer should wear glasses during the trial, even though the lens may be nonprescription, in order to lend an air of authority and inoffensiveness to the discussion of the problem.

Weather conditions can have a strong collateral impact on eyeglass wearers, since rainwater may distort the lens image and cold may produce a steaming effect when the wearer enters a warm building.

On the positive side, the proponent should emphasize the witness' ability to drive a car, to operate machinery, and to pursue hobbies which require reasonable vision.

Age

As previously emphasized,[24] age is a sensitive consideration, but one likely to be accepted by the jurors as a limiting factor in perception if presented with restraint and dignity. The presence of a juror of the same age as the witness need not preclude proper reference to that limitation. Indeed, it is a matter which can be turned to the advantage of the challenger by an argument which notes with deference that there is a member of this jury who is far better able than the lawyer to describe the difficulties which attend efforts by persons such as the witness to recall past events with clarity, or to make accurate observations, or to perform whatever function might have been relevant to the jury's evaluation of the testimony offered by that witness. This line of argument must, of course, be adapted to the special circumstances of the witness, the juror, and the case itself.

The suggestion that infirmity attends age may be most tenable and acceptable in those cases involving a substantial lapse of time between the event and the identification. An elderly juror who does not experience memory problems is likely to count himself or herself fortunate and to agree that most of his or her contemporaries are affected in some degree.

The recommended format for the proponent's summation is similar

---

[24] See **§10.15.**

to that suggested in the case of a challenge to visual acuity. Any evidence demonstrating current competence in business or family matters, and hobbies and interests such as bridge or chess which require concentration and memory, should be presented as proof of mental alertness.

§10.17 —Psychological Influences on Witness

This section and the following sections do not address any problem arising from the possible personal eccentricities of the witnesses whom the reader is likely to encounter. The very breadth of such an undertaking is a sufficient barrier to inclusion of such a discussion, which is completely beyond the scope of this volume.

These sections consider quite a different concept: those influences commonly encountered by a person who observes an event of the type likely to become the subject of litigation. Such events are likely to be startling and confusing at first view, and as a result initial impressions may be misleading. Jurors are likely to accept that proposition if presented with a reasonable argument drawing their attention to the circumstances of the event and the probable impact of those circumstances upon the observer.

Other psychological influences are far more subtle, and their acceptance by the jury probably is dependent in most cases upon the introduction of expert testimony. An example is the potential suggestive effect of an improper photographic lineup upon a subsequent personal encounter with the person depicted in one of the photographs.[25]

Any tenable argument based upon psychological influences may be presented in most situations without concern for the probability of resentment on the part of the jury, since no indignity or disrespect is involved. Such arguments, therefore, are generally less controversial and demanding than those based on physical disabilities.

In presenting these points, the witness' adversary can invite the jurors to draw upon their personal experiences in analogous situations. The driver of an automobile is relatively alert to the possibility of trouble, but most drivers have narrowly missed being struck by ineptly driven vehicles which they could not have described in meaningful detail a moment later; and many have seen scrapes and collisions between other cars while registering only a vague impression of the manner in which the accident occurred. In short, they were thinking of other things, and events proceeded while they adjusted mentally to an unanticipated situation.

---

[25] See **§§8.10** and **8.15**.

The proponent of the witness, on the other hand, is likely to minimize the adjustment time required by the witness, to point out that the people involved in the incident moved much more slowly than do automobiles, and to appeal to the self-esteem of the jurors by asking them whether they, in circumstances similar to those confronting the witness, would be able to make reliable observations.

These sections present the specific elements most likely to require consideration by counsel, in a sequence designed to accommodate the analysis of the underlying event as it appeared to those who were on the scene.

§10.18 —Contemporaneous Significance

Immediately prior to the event, did the witness have any reason to focus attention on the person or object which he or she described during the trial? It is only after the dawning of such awareness that useful observations are likely to be made. The party adverse to the witness may profitably ask the jurors whether they can recall people who sat next to them for an hour on public transportation if there was no special reason to take note of that person. Even a mild awareness is unlikely to produce a useful impression for later recall. The jurors might be reminded of the occasions on which, after eating in a restaurant, they were unable to remember which waiter had served them when it was time to call for dessert or to pay the bill.

The witness' proponent should emphasize any facts which attracted attention to the subject before the event occurred. Lacking such facts, attention should be drawn to any details which the witness was able to furnish immediately after the event as indicative of reliable contemporaneous observations.

§10.19 —Surprise

This element is related to in some degree but discrete from the question of contemporaneous significance, and it should receive separate consideration from counsel. Immediately before the event, was the witness expecting anything unusual to occur? If so, he or she may have been giving close attention to the scene, so that the events registered meaningfully on his or her consciousness as they unfolded. If not, however, then the event was probably a startling one, and useful observations were possible only after a period of emotional adjustment. It is for that reason that a hunter or bird watcher is able to react more quickly and reliably to the appearance of the target than would a casual stroller who encountered the same animal. Illustrations similar to that one will be useful to the party benefited by the relevant facts. The argument supports the testimony of a police officer waiting for a burglar after receiving an advance tip. It weakens the testimony of a casual passerby observing the same event.

§10.20 —Excitement

This concept embraces a broad range of feelings, from joy to terror to depression. Any highly emotional state is an impediment to observation. Don Jose's murder of Carmen will be observed by an opera patron with much greater clarity than will a similar event which occurs under grimmer circumstances in a tavern.

Excitement must be distinguished from surprise and prior awareness. Even if a noisy encounter of several minutes' duration precedes the tavern killing, and even though an opera patron may be watching *Carmen* for the first time, the completely sober tavern customer will be unable to match the opera goer in reliability of observation. The reason is simply that the operagoer relatively is calm, while the spectator at a tavern killing is in a state of tense excitement. The murder witness' concentration is directed inward, rather than focused upon the event.

Examples such as the foregoing are available to either party. Their usefulness is determined by the evidentiary indications of the witness' probable reaction to the stimulus of the event. The jurors should be invited to consider, from their own experiences, the clarity of their observations of a startling event in real life, compared to their ability to observe a similar event as portrayed theatrically.

§10.21 —Exposure Time

The notion that duration of observation will affect the reliability of recollection is too obvious to require comment. The important consideration, however, is to determine what was exposed. A victim may have confronted an armed robber for several minutes, but he or she certainly did not spend that period in rapt study of the robber's features. During the encounter, the victim also watched the weapon, probably with substantial attention born of concern that it might be used. The victim looked at his or her possessions while surrendering them. For at least a part of that period, the robber was at the victim's side or rear, precluding useful observation.

Another fact to be considered in this context, and bearing a peripheral relationship to the element of fear, is that the victim or observer concerned for his or her own safety will be reluctant to give the appearance of studious attention to detail, because the offender's reaction to such apparent storing of facts may well be the perceived necessity to resort to further violence to prevent those observations from being used to identify or denounce the perpetrator at a later time.

The witness is very likely to overestimate the time frame involved in the encounter. Challenging him or her during cross-examination to use the words *start* and *stop,* or some similar device, to reproduce the time frame frequently is self-defeating; the witness may consciously exaggerate the period of exposure. Counsel should consider an alternative; using the details of the encounter as disclosed by the witness' testimony, the lawyer may perform a one-person reenactment before the jury during summation, inviting the jurors to time the reenactment by the courtroom clock. The lawyer, of course, will have adequate opportunity to rehearse and time that performance before summations commence. In almost all cases, a reenactment by counsel which appears to give the witness every benefit of the doubt will tend to show that the exposure time was much shorter than the testimonial estimate. Conversely, if the witness has provided an unrealistically short estimate, the proponent may use the same technique to demonstrate that the time frame probably exceeded the witness' estimate. The proponent must be careful, however, to avoid the appearance of discrediting the witness.

§10.22 —Familiarity

The proposition that an identification is more likely to be accurate if the eyewitness had a prior familiarity with the person, thing, or scene which he observed probably will seem obvious to most jurors. Less obvious, however, is a basic weakness which affects one's observations of familiar objects: The tendency to see what one expects to see. The intellectual tension between those two concepts enables the resourceful lawyer to derive benefit from almost any set of circumstances surrounding an identification.

The person who is hailed on a public sidewalk by a stranger who tentatively misidentifies him or her as a friend or relative is likely to attach no special significance to the event. It is quite commonplace—so much so, indeed, that almost any juror is prepared to accept it as an unremarkable event. Under thoughtful analysis during summation, however, that routine occurrence becomes the starting point for a presentation designed to cast doubt upon eyewitness identifications made under a broad range of circumstances. The scope of that attack frequently may be expanded to embrace the entire structure of the lawyer's case theory.

It is suggested that the lawyer commence by describing for the jury a typical misidentification during a street encounter, culminating in a conversation between the parties during which it becomes clear that mistaken identification has occurred. The lawyer should emphasize the frequency with which such events occur; probably some of the jurors have themselves had that experience.

The lawyer then may profitably proceed to argue in the following vein:

> If you had not actually spoken to that stranger, you would have felt obligated to swear under oath, if the issue had arisen in court at some later time, that you had seen your friend or relative at a place at which he or she simply had not, in fact, been present. You would not have been a liar, or a perjurer, any more than [the eyewitness] is a liar or a perjurer. You would have been a mistaken witness, but an honest one, and the jury deciding the fate of your friend or relative may well have accepted your story and wrongly condemned him or her. Your friend or relative, in short, would have experienced the same nightmare which now confronts [the client].

From that point, the course of the lawyer's argument is dictated by the presence or absence of an antecedent acquaintanceship between the client and the eyewitness. If the parties were strangers to each other, the lawyer would proceed to argue that such misidentifications, occurring between people who have known each other for years and in some cases for all their lives, points up the inherent fallibility of the psychological process of identification. If such mistakes can occur under those ideal circumstances, the lawyer argues, how very much more likely it is that a mistake would occur in the identification of a total stranger.

If, on the other hand, the parties were acquainted, the lawyer should of course adopt a very different line of argument. After setting up the nightmare scenario, the lawyer should point out that the mistaken identifications simply reflect the human tendency, shared by all to some degree, to believe that we have seen what we expected to see, even though we in fact have observed something or someone quite different. As a corollary to that tendency, when we see someone who seems vaguely to resemble a person whom we know, we tend to believe that person to be an acquaintance rather than a stranger who resembles an acquaintance. The psychological basis for that predisposition is presented in **§§2.06** through **§2.09.** The concept of perceptual constancy expressed in **§2.09** is of particular relevance here.

Arguments which point up the weakness of identifications of prior acquaintances are, of course, much more challenging to the lawyer than are arguments designed simply to stress the likelihood of misidentification of strangers. The lawyer's burden is eased considerably if the argument can be based upon expert testimony. Even where such testimony has been excluded, however, it frequently is possible for the lawyer to present fairly esoteric psychological concepts as matters of common knowledge. That technique is described in **§10.31.**

An illustrative argument designed to weaken eyewitness testimony concerning the identification of a prior acquaintance is presented within **§10.32.**

§10.23 —Special Qualification as Observer

The tendency of many jurors to grant uncritical acceptance to the testimony of an eyewitness frequently is intensified if the witness lays claim to special qualifications derived from professional activities.

In some contexts, such reliance is appropriate. Where a layperson observes a jet plane flying by, a military pilot may see an F-86-D at 10,000 feet on a northwest heading at 400 knots. Where that same pilot sees a typewriter, a secretary may discern a Xerox Model 8000 word processor.

Observations such as those, however, properly are to be evaluated in terms of familiarity, rather than expertise as an observer.

Observational expertise per se, as distinguished from specialized recognition, is a talent frequently claimed by law enforcement officers at all levels and frequently accepted by the jury. In other cases which have come to the attention of the authors, testimonial claims of special talent have been made by a bank teller, a military officer, and, on at least one lamentable and unreported occasion, a Boy Scout.

There is no empirical basis for most of those contentions. Individuals undoubtedly vary in their ability to make and recount observations, but such variations are much more likely to be caused by disparities in natural gifts than by training.

People can, of course, be trained to look for personalized identifying characteristics which might escape the attention of the uninitiated. Just as is true of ability to identify aircraft or office equipment, however, the ability to individualize earlobes, foreheads, or other features reflects a limited and narrowly focused skill intended for use in controlled conditions, rather than exceptional proficiency as an observer of people or objects in unstructured situations.

Such training, although theoretically available, is quite uncommon because the course is lengthy and expensive, because its applicability to police activities is relatively limited, and because the skill is lost quickly unless constantly exercised.

The testimony of a forensic psychologist would be of assistance in dispelling the notion that police officers acquire special qualifications as eyewitnesses. Introduction of such testimony, however, may be resisted on the ground of lack of relevance, since the police eyewitness ordinarily does not overtly claim exceptional observational skills, relying instead on a popular mystique which is likely to cause many jurors simply to assume that police are, by virtue of their positions and training, exceptionally reliable eyewitnesses. The relevance of the proffered expert testimony frequently is not established until the stage of summation. At that stage, the proponent of the eyewitness is likely to make his or her first overt claim that the eyewitness was a person possessed of unusual talent as an observer, by telling the jury that the eyewitness testimony came from a police officer or detective or federal agent who is specially qualified by training and experience to observe and report accurately and precisely. That argument is effective because it exploits the presuppositions of many jurors.

Several responses are available to the lawyer opposing the eyewitness. The first and most obvious is to object that the proponent's argument is not based on the evidence and to point out forcefully that there is no evidence that the witness had any special training of the type which the proponent has suggested.

It is probable that the proponent of the eyewitness will be the party with the burden of proof, entitled for that reason both to open and to close the summations. If the claim of special talent is made during the final summation, the opponent will have no formal opportunity to respond. In that situation, an objection should be as elaborate and as informative to the jury as circumstances will permit. The eyewitness' opponent may also consider a request to reopen the proofs for the purpose of introducing evidence refuting the proponent's claim. Such a request is unlikely to be granted, but the effect of the jury's hearing that request may be quite salutary. Joined with a motion for mistrial, the request also may serve a useful record purpose in the event of an appeal.

Some lawyers opposing police eyewitnesses approach the problem in a very different manner. These lawyers undertake affirmatively to rebut the unspoken claim of special qualification *before* the claim is made, reasoning that an objection during final argument is of limited utility and that the jury may well assume that police observations are distinctively reliable even if no overt claim is made by the proponent. Such lawyers frequently expand their cross-examinations to include two additional distinctive areas if the eyewitness is a police officer. The cross-examination explores all the routine details of which the witness did not take notice at the scene of the claimed identification and further attempts to show that the witness has had little if any special training in distinguishing one person from another. Both these areas of inquiry pose special problems, which are considered in **§§7.16-7.23.**

Because the police officer eyewitness normally testifies on behalf of the party carrying the burden of proof, the opponent probably will be limited to a single summation which is sandwiched between the opening and rebuttal summations by the proponent. If the proponent's opening summation contained a claim that the eyewitness identification acquires special reliability because of the witness' official status, the opponent has no practical alternative but to meet the issue head-on. If the proponent has made no such claim, that failure is more likely to have its base in tactics than in reticence: The proponent probably has made a conscious election to reserve the point for rebuttal, thereby precluding effective refutation.

The authors recommend that the opponent address the issue during summation in either situation. Illustrative arguments on behalf of the opponent of a police eyewitness, designed for the case in which the opponent has not presented expert testimony and in which the proponent's opening address has not raised the issue, are presented in **§§10.33-10.35.** With minor modifications, they can be adapted to any case involving police officers as eyewitnesses.

§10.24 —Motion and Rapid Developments

It is easier to hit a stationary target than one which is moving, because the stationary target can more readily be subjected to precise focus. Otherwise stated, it is more clearly visible than is the moving target. It is easier to see.

Much the same thing is true if the observer is moving. A physicist would be likely to suggest that Einstein proved it meaningless to inquire, as between observer and target, which of the two is in motion. Unless each is stationary with respect to the other, the view of each is subject to the vibration and, usually more important, the continuing change of angle, distance, and perspective which motion necessarily creates.

If a witness identifies a person who was in motion when observed, it may be helpful for the opponent to simulate that motion during summation. If the path of the subject was perpendicular to the gaze of the observer, the jury often will be able to see that the image will progress from front quarter to side to rear quarter, changing constantly.

Perhaps more to the point, the summation should point out that as a matter of human nature, an observer who takes an interest in a moving person, does not simply look at that person but also looks to see *where that person is going,* instinctively devoting some attention to a determination whether anything lies in the target's path and to an attempt to anticipate the destination. The observer's attention, in short, is diluted. The jurors may confidently be invited to conduct their own experiments in that regard.

The observer's attention is even more distracted if it is the observer who is in motion. In that circumstance, the observer must be concerned for possible obstructions in his or her own path, and that concern in most situations will take precedence over any interest in the target.

If the subject of the observation is directly in front of and moving toward the observer, these considerations are minimized. In any other situation, however, they are very real, and the reality may be made clear to the jurors through a thoughtful summation.

The simple fact of motion, however, normally is less significant than the speed involved and the number of people or objects which are moving simultaneously. If a number of possible observational targets are in motion, the attention of the observer is attracted by all of them. The observer will almost certainly direct some attention to as many moving elements as he or she sees, for each of them may create a new area of interest or exert some effect upon the observer's target, the observer, or both.

In a fast-moving situation, therefore, with developments unfolding simultaneously or following each other quickly, observation is always distracted and diffused. The witness who claims to have observed many things admits inadvertently to a failure to have concentrated on any of them. The witness who failed to take note of significant developments, on the other hand, may give the appearance of inattentiveness.

Fast-moving action, therefore, invites jury arguments based both on emotional impact and on impairment of observational opportunity. Emotionally, a rapidly unfolding situation generates surprise and excitement, elements which are considered in **§§10.19** and **10.20.** In terms of observational opportunity, such activity challenges the observer with constantly shifting angles and distances, even as the multiple targets create distraction. In delivering the summation, therefore, the lawyer properly may treat a fast-moving scenario as relevant to two discrete aspects of the eyewitness problem, perhaps selecting separate actions for emphasis within each category.

Conversely, the compression of the time frame of a relatively uncomplicated event such as a robbery, as suggested in the treatment of exposure time in **§10.21,** may in many cases justify an argument based on the rapid action component of the problem. The relationship of the psychological impact of exposure time to the physical distractions and obstructions created by a fast-moving situation is obvious. The party challenging the eyewitness is well advised to bring as many problem categories as possible within the framework of the summation; and fast-moving action presents the lawyer with an additional opportunity for allocation of elements to categories in accordance with the requirements imposed by the case.

§10.25 —The Scene

The elements of the scene which must be considered by the lawyer in framing the summation are obstructions, illumination, distraction, and distance.

Obstructions: How clear was the witness' field of view? Could interference have resulted from structural elements, vehicular or pedestrian traffic, precipitation, or other influences? Were the witness and the subject on the same level, or did the witness have to look up or down at the subject? If the witness had to look down, was the subject wearing a hat whose brim might have blocked much of the view of his or her face?

Illumination: What lighting was available, natural or artificial, and what was its level of intensity? Was the lighting the same at the locations of both the subject and the observer, or was one standing in brighter light than the other? In such a situation, as most jurors know, it is difficult for the person in the brighter area to see clearly into the darker area. Had the witness recently left a place where the lighting intensity was different?[26]

Distractions: Aside from the event described by the witness, did anything occur at the time which might have served to dilute the witness' attention? Consider such things as entertainment, actions of companions or others, loud noises, and minor annoyances.

Distance: The obvious significance of this element sometimes masks its more subtle components. Both the maximum and minimum distances should be measured, and appropriate reference points established within the courtroom, so that the lawyer will be able, during summation, to walk confidently to the predetermined point and announce: "I am now 30 feet from [the nearest juror]." That tactic lends added realism to the argument. If the distances are great, the lawyer

---

[26] This problem is considered in **§§2.15** and **8.08.**

should point or walk to the farthest available position in the courtroom, and invite the jury to note that this distance from them is only a specified fraction of the distance that separated the witness from the subject.

The portion of the summation which contends that the evidence describing the scene itself supports or contradicts the eyewitness testimony is presumed by the jury to deal with concrete physical facts rather than with philosophical or psychological concepts. In many cases, the jury may have inspected the scene under court supervision. If not, photographs and diagrams may have been received in evidence, and if the case is truly significant, tabletop models may have been made available.

The questions related to the scene, in short, are expected and assumed to be focused on clearly established facts. A verdict based on those facts, therefore, is one which a juror can present with a smaller degree of internal anguish and uncertainty than would be true of a verdict based on more abstract concepts.

For that reason, the facts related to the impact of the scene upon the eyewitness are likely to be viewed as determinative by jurors considering contested eyewitness testimony. Unfortunately, those facts have a tendency to be misleading in many such cases.

In the presentation of that element of the summation, the lawyer should bear in mind two concepts. First, the scene itself is almost never neutral; instead, it enlists on the side of the more resourceful advocate. A distance of 30 feet may be much or little, depending upon one's viewpoint. The impact of a 50-watt lightbulb in a stairwell at night is a matter subject to argument and persuasion. An open highway intersection on a clear day can invite recklessness or assure that oncoming traffic will be seen and avoided, depending upon whose vehicle is being observed.

The second principle is a paraphrase of Heraclitus: You cannot step into the same scene twice. The intersection which appears accident-proof at 10 in the morning can resemble a demolition derby track during the evening rush hour. A street which presented no impediment to a view of intersecting traffic in March can resemble a rain forest in July. The crime scene which offers no challenge to an eyewitness when viewed by the jury during the day can be impenetrably dark at night, but jurors normally visit crime scenes only during court business hours.

Infrequently, but often enough to be disturbing, manufactured alterations will occur between the time of the event and the commencement of the trial. The jurors should not be presumed to be aware of the change. A proper summation, supported by models and diagrams in evidence, will enable the jurors to evaluate the eyewitness' story in accordance with the conditions which existed at the time of the event.

From time to time, the summation must not only refer to but must improve upon the physical facts laid before the jurors. Improvement upon facts is required, for example, when the jurors have viewed the scene in bright sunlight although the event occurred during a rainstorm. In such a situation, the witnesses probably will agree that rain was falling during the event, although the intensity of that rain is likely to be a matter of dispute. It will be the lawyer's job to point out vividly for the jury the difference that rain can make when an event is viewed from the eyewitness' position. A similar situation is presented by every disparity between conditions at the time of the event and conditions at the time of the jury's viewing. The summation in such a case presents the challenge of persuading the jury to disregard what it has seen with its own eyes in favor of the imagery conjured up during the summation.

Even if the jury has not been taken to the scene, the lawyer must assume that one or more of them will go there out of curiosity during the trial or will be familiar with it before the trial begins. If anything has changed since the time of the event, the lawyer should introduce evidence of that change and remind the jury of that evidence during the summation.

Nature itself sometimes will lend support to a summation. If the weather is clear at the time of the summation but was dark and stormy on the preceding day, the lawyer should draw the jury's attention to the contrast as reflecting the difference that a change in weather can make.

It is not only weather and traffic conditions that can cause the jury's mental image of the scene to be inaccurate. The lawyer's challenge is to give the jury a realistic picture of the circumstances under which the eyewitness' observations were made. If uncertainties remain, the lawyer seeks to become the beneficiary of any doubts. The best chance of achieving that indulgence lies in creating the impression that the lawyer has done everything possible to give the jurors the relevant information and sincerely wants them to have all the facts because the facts favor his or her client.

§10.26 Analysis of Tactics

The credibility of an eyewitness is raised as a contested issue more often in criminal litigation than in any other class of case. Typically, the disputed witness testifies on behalf of the prosecution and provides the essential link between the defendant and the offense. Even when the question occurs in a civil context, however, such a witness is more likely to appear for the plaintiff than for the defendant.

For that reason, the proponent of the witness normally presents the opening summation. The emphasis which he or she places upon that testimony will vary according to the impression made by the witness and the strength of the corroborating evidence. Almost always, however, the lawyer will make the point that the witness is a stranger to the transaction with no incentive to falsify.

The defendant's argument frequently is the more difficult undertaking. The defense attorney assumes the ultimate burden in the case—the discrediting of the eyewitness—while attempting to avoid the appearance of carrying that burden, which legally falls on his opponent. The defense attorney must present every reason that would justify the jury in disregarding the eyewitness testimony and must demonstrate the equivocal character of the evidence offered to corroborate that witness.

Above all, the defense attorney should emphasize the proposition that the witness is mistaken rather than deliberately lying. The reason for that argument is that if no bias or other reason for lying has been shown, the lawyer must avoid a jury attitude which would produce a verdict for the plaintiff on the simplistic basis that the eyewitness was not lying.

In reply, the plaintiff denigrates the defendant's attack and urges that no meaningful basis has been shown to justify the jury in disregarding the sworn testimony of the eyewitness. Plaintiff's lawyer thus attempts to create an atmosphere in which the defendant appears to be burdened with the obligation to disprove that testimony. Finally, plaintiff again adverts to every circumstance which tends to corroborate the eyewitness and offers an expression of gratitude and respect for persons, such as that witness, who are willing to come forward in situations such as that which has been shown to this jury. Without such persons, the lawyer suggests, the streets would become the property of malefactors who could perform their misdeeds with impunity. Such hyperbole is not uncommon at that stage.

§10.27 Illustrative Extracts: Inverted Pyramid

The examples which follow are designed to illustrate the employment of the inverted pyramid technique[27] in a criminal case involving a single eyewitness whose accusation is supported by equivocal corroborating circumstances.

The strategy exemplified within the three following sections is readily

---

[27] See **§10.11.**

translatable to civil litigation and to cases involving multiple and conflicting witnesses. In the interest of enhanced clarity, these extracts include not only the apex of the pyramid but also those portions of the respective counsels' arguments which directly focus upon or resonate with the principles offered to the jury by the opposing lawyers as the keys to the case.

§10.28 —Prosecutor's Initial Argument

Denigration of Defense Theory

Against all of that evidence, the defense has offered nothing but a nit-picking attack on [eyewitness]. You've heard suggestions that [eyewitness] shouldn't be believed because she wears glasses, and because she has a tendency to become excited when she's assaulted on the street by a strong-arm robber and her purse is stolen, and because she doesn't pull out a stopwatch when she's being robbed.

Stimulation of Jury Identification with Eyewitness

Well, ladies and gentlemen, I believe the court will instruct you that in making your decision, you are entitled to rely on your experience in the affairs of life. That's just another way of saying that you don't have to check your brains at the jury room door. The thing that makes you most valuable as jurors is the fact that you have experienced life in this community, that you know your way around silly and misleading arguments, and that you know generally how people act and what they can do.

Lots of us wear glasses. That doesn't mean that we should have no recourse if we're robbed on the street, or that we shouldn't be believed when we tell what happened. And of course we become excited when we're victimized by strong-arm robbers such as [defendant]. That doesn't mean that strong-arm robbers can avoid justice by simply making their victims become excited. And yes, none of us is likely to pull out a stopwatch when we're being robbed. Like [eyewitness], we're too busy trying to save our lives.

Inverted Pyramid Thesis

There is really a very basic point to this case that seems to have been overlooked by the defense. It is simply this: Nobody is going to commit a crime in the presence of witnesses if he can help it. Of course, we have only one witness. If the defendant had been more cautious, or had found a purse lying on a park bench next to its owner, we probably wouldn't have any witness at all. That's what strong-arm robbers and sneak thieves trade on. They can pick their spots and wait for a situation in which nobody is present except the victim. The rest of us can only hope that we won't be the victim.

Vindication of Eyewitness

But there's one other thing we can do. When we become victims, we can take the time and trouble necessary to assure that the criminal will be brought to justice. By doing so, we make it a little less likely that the same thing will happen to one of our fellow citizens. That's what [eyewitness] has done in this case, and she deserves the thanks of all of us. Certainly, she deserves something better than she has received in this case from the defense.

§10.29 —Defense Arguments

Inverted Pyramid Thesis

The key to this case, simply, is the fact that anybody can be mistaken. And that is indeed a fact. Good and sincere people can be just as mistaken as anyone else. We all know that; it's something that became clear to us when we were very young, and it's proved over and over again every day.[28]

Witness' Character Placed in Proper Context

A sincerely mistaken witness, such as we have in this case, is in many ways more troublesome than a cynical liar. This jury would have little trouble recognizing a liar. But for that very reason, you[29] can defend yourself against an outright liar much more easily than

---

[28] An appropriate illustration to serve as a bridge from the general principle to the facts of the case might be the description of the mistaken approach to the stranger suggested in **§10.22.**

[29] The second person pronoun here is technically incorrect but is designed subliminally to cause the jurors to identify with the plight of the defendant.

you can defend yourself against the honest but misguided opinion of a person such as [Eyewitness].

Issue Definition Understating Witness' Position

Let's remember why we're here. The issue before us is not whether [Eyewitness] is an honest person, or a sincere person, or whether she really believes what she is saying. The issue is whether [Defendant][30] is guilty of attempted murder. And that is a very different issue indeed, because the law which you swore to uphold says that he is not guilty of attempted murder if you have any reasonable doubt of his guilt.

It's as simple as that. The issue is not whether [Eyewitness] is certain that [Defendant] is guilty, but whether *you* are certain of that, beyond all reasonable doubt. And if [Eyewitness] is as decent a person as she appears to be, I am sure she would be the first to agree that she, like anyone else, *can* be mistaken and that you should examine all the circumstances very carefully to see whether there is any reason to doubt the complete accuracy of her opinion.[31]

Sympathy for Eyewitness Turned to Defendant's Advantage

Any decent person would insist on a very careful examination of the circumstances, because no decent person wants to be responsible for a mistaken conviction. We all know of such cases. And for every such case, there is likely to be a sincerely mistaken witness who never again will feel at peace. For every such case, there are 12 honorable people who share a sense of torment. [Eyewitness], a decent person as we all know, would not want to be responsible for inflicting that torment on you. And whether or not she knows our system of justice well enough to realize the fact, she has to rely on you to protect her from that nightmare, just as [Defendant] has to rely on you to extract him from the nightmare in which he is living right now.

---

[30] It is important for the defense that the jury think of the defendant as a fellow human being rather than as an abstract entity. Therefore, the defense attorney should be careful to call the defendant by name, and in many cases, use of the first name may be more appropriate than a formal designation by surname.

[31] The word *opinion* is chosen deliberately. See **§10.08.**

§10.30 —Prosecution Rebuttal Arguments

Issue Definition Emphasizing the Witness' Position

> There has been nothing said here by the defense that could not be said in any case in which a citizen like [eyewitness] comes forward to tell what she saw and to offer her time and to sacrifice her convenience because she believes in doing the right thing. You have been given no reason to doubt [Mr. or Ms. Eyewitness] that wouldn't apply to anyone else in the same position. In all probability, no jury ever will be offered a more reliable witness than [Eyewitness]. If you do as the defendant asks, you will be saying, for all practical purposes, that anybody who commits a crime in the presence of only one witness does not have to worry about being convicted.

Empathy toward Eyewitness Turned to Plaintiff's Advantage

> Are you going to tell [Eyewitness] that you don't believe her and that she has wasted her time? Are you going to tell other people who see crimes committed in the future that they might as well walk on, refuse to get involved, and spare themselves not only time and inconvenience, but humiliation as well? Defense counsel spoke of nightmares. I ask you to consider the nightmare in which we all live right now as we walk the streets, and I ask you to avoid making that nightmare any worse.

§10.31 The Illusion of Science and Expertise

In arriving at their verdict, the jurors are entitled, and indeed are obligated, to draw upon their common sense and experience in the affairs of life. Guided by that principle, many skilled lawyers routinely argue the inferences from the evidence in terms of what seems reasonable in the light of the jurors' common experience, urging them to evaluate the evidence in the light of the probabilities established by their knowledge of human nature.

When dealing with eyewitness testimony, that type of argument offers significant opportunities to bring to the attention of the jury information which normally could be derived only from expert testimony. A court, after all, is hardly in a position to rule, as a matter of judicial notice, that a facially reasonable proposition is or is not a part of the general knowledge of the human race.

It is normally quite impossible for the lawyer to offer common sense as a substitute for scientific evidence. The lawyer who attempts to persuade a jury that, as a matter of common sense, trace metal detection technique is superior to neutron activation analysis in a given application would forfeit all claim to credibility as a reasonable person and would invite a justified objection that his or her remarks constituted unqualified testimony rather than argument.

In presenting arguments which focus on the strengths and infirmities of eyewitness testimony, however, the lawyer has much greater latitude for invasion of the expert's realm. When expert testimony on the issue is excluded, the customary rationale is that such evidence is unnecessary because the matter is within the competence of the average juror.[32] It would be grossly inconsistent with that position to preclude reference to the jurors' supposed common knowledge on the ground that the supposedly superfluous expert testimony had not been introduced.

Lawyers' expressed views on this topic, if properly presented, may receive special deference from the jury because they are perceived as the possessors of special qualifications, born of experience in recurrent encounters with the eyewitness problem. When they speak of things that *we all know,* the jury may place a weighty interpretation upon the pronoun *we.* The demands of the dual role of advocate and expert, however, probably will necessitate a serious compromise of the principle of brevity endorsed in **§10.06.**

The illustrative arguments which follow are intended to demonstrate the manner in which a lawyer may compensate for inability to present expert testimony, by treating scientific principles as matters of common knowledge during summation.

§10.32 Illustration: Attack on Identification of Acquaintance

The effect of the eyewitness' prior familiarity with the identified person or object upon the presumptive reliability of that identification is considered in **§10.22.** It is there suggested that in an eyewitness context, the greatest challenge to the advocate's power of persuasion is presented by the attempt to argue, without support from expert testimony, the unreliability of an unimpeached eyewitness' identification of a prior acquaintance.

This section presents a sample argument designed to meet that situation. The lawyer invites the jurors to draw upon their own

---

[32] See **§8.02.**

experiences as emblematic of certain basic truths which are presented as matters of common knowledge, although the same information would have been an appropriate subject of expert testimony.

Now, what really happened here? The answer to that question turns on facts known to all of us, but which we frequently tend to overlook.

[Eyewitness] got up on that witness stand and told you that on the day in question, he saw [client] at the bank. And beyond question, he believes that he did indeed see [client] at that time and place. But that is an important point: Whenever somebody tells you, as [eyewitness] did, about the thing or event or person that he saw at an earlier time, he is telling you what he or she *believes.* That belief may or may not be well founded. One thing, however, is absolutely certain and beyond question: anyone can be mistaken. Anyone. The best-trained, most alert, most competent observer in the world can be mistaken. And with all respect to [eyewitness], who is a sincere and honest man, he is not the world's best and he doesn't claim to be.

I would be less than honest if I didn't tell you[33] that, in general, an eyewitness is more likely to be correct if, like [eyewitness], he is talking about someone he knows than if he is talking about someone he has never seen before.[34] That fact is well known by people who have devoted their professional lives to a study of eyewitness problems. But there is a basic weakness to that type of identification, too, and it is one which you know as well as the professionals, as well as I.

The first thing we ought to think about is the way we, all of us, you, I, [client], [eyewitness], or anyone else, go about identifying someone we know. If we say that we saw an acquaintance—let's call him Joe—on the street, what we mean is simply that we caught sight of someone whom we believed to be Joe. Obviously, we didn't make a list of his individual features or tell *why* we thought it was Joe. We simply form the *conclusion* that the person we saw was Joe.

And that is important. We do not say "That man has a nose just

---

[33] The substance of this statement is a concession to the adversary, who therefore is most unlikely to object. The mood, however, is that of a teacher who *tells* the jury about the psychology of identification. The word *admit* should never be used in this context.

[34] The contrast drawn is between recognition of an acquaintance and identification of a total stranger. The scope of the concession is thereby minimized. "The better acquainted a witness is with a subject, the more likely it is that the witness' identification will be accurate" would be a logically equivalent sentence, but far more damaging to the speaker.

like Joe's, and a mouth just like Joe's, and a head shaped like Joe's, and he is about Joe's height and build," before concluding that it is Joe. We don't *say* those things; but subconsciously, that is exactly the process we have to go through in forming our opinion that the person we saw on the street was Joe.

Sometimes, we form an opinion that the person we saw was Joe, even though we did not observe his face or other identifying features in any real detail. We don't get much of a look at the person in many cases—perhaps nothing more than a kind of one-quarter view from the rear side, as [eyewitness] had when he believed that he saw [client]. But in some circumstances, for various reasons, we are likely to believe that we saw Joe, which is another way of saying that we form an *opinion* that we saw Joe, even though we didn't get a clear look at the man. [The Court will tell you, I believe, that][35] a statement of identification such as [eyewitness] made on the stand concerning [client] is actually nothing more than an opinion; and that is exactly the process by which such opinions are formed.

Now, that is not to say anything against [eyewitness]. He did what we all do in that situation: he formed his opinion, and like most of us who haven't considered the problem seriously, he believes what he said on the stand. He believes his opinion is correct, because he doesn't really believe that it is an opinion. In short, he is confusing opinion with fact.

All of you were selected as jurors because the lawyers on both sides of the case trusted your judgment. Your *judgment.* Your ability to pass *judgment* on a situation, to look carefully and critically at the things witnesses say from the stand in order to determine how likely it is that they are mistaken.

The Court will tell you, I believe, that the thing that makes you valuable as jurors is your critical judgment, your experience in the affairs of life, and that you should use that judgment and experience in passing on the facts of this case. The Judge also will tell you, I believe, that you are not required to believe anything merely because a witness has said it, if you believe, based on your judgment and experience, that the witness is mistaken.

And that, really, is your job as jurors: not to serve as rubber stamps for anyone, not to accept statements as true, but to make

---

[35] This phrase is appropriate if the court has approved a *Telfaire*-type instruction described in **§9.04.** If the instruction has been refused, a substitute may be used for the bracketed phrase. For example: "When we stop to think about it, we all know as well as any psychologist that. . . ."

a searching inquiry as to *whether* they are true. And that searching inquiry is specially important as applied to a sincere, honest, but mistaken witness such as [eyewitness]. Most outright liars really do not present much of a challenge to jurors such as yourselves. For many reasons, they are fairly easily detected. You can almost smell them. The jury system really proves its worth when it passes judgment on the story of a witness who is not a liar; who is sincere, and honest, and doing his best, and who is simply but tragically mistaken. In that situation—in *this* situation—the American jury comes into its own.

And so I ask you to pass careful, searching judgment on [eyewitness'] story. And I believe that you will do exactly that. I believe that you will not simply take his statement at face value, assuming that he must be right because he is an honest man identifying a person who was already known to him. And when I tell you that I don't believe that you will make that simplistic assumption, I am not just being polite. I genuinely believe that you won't. I will go farther: I think that one of the very few points upon which [opposing lawyer] and I would agree is that you will not make that simplistic assumption. You won't do it, because you said you wouldn't. You said you would do your job, and we believe you. That job requires you to approach the story of every witness, and especially [eyewitness], with skepticism rather than trust, with doubt rather than gullibility. And you will do that. You said you would.

Well, then, what do we know as people, all of us, from our experiences in the affairs of life? As applied to [eyewitness'] story, we know that there is a strong tendency to see what we expect to see, to see the familiar rather than the unfamiliar. It is one of the most basic principles of human behavior. *Occam's Razor* is the term used, I believe, by philosophers to describe this tendency to see what we expect to see.[36]

---

[36] An esoteric reference of this type is not appropriate in addressing all juries. If the lawyer believes that one or more members of the jury will appreciate the reference—or would take false pride in pretending so to do—its articulation will establish a bond with those jurors, while reinforcing the lawyer's posture as a knowledgeable commentator on the phenomenology of identification. It is equally important, however, not to lose rapport with the jury by giving the impression of pompous pedantry. In deciding whether to employ a reference of this type, as with every element of the summation, the lawyer must be mindful of the composition of the jury.

The reference itself is to a general philosophical principle and thus is not properly objectionable as overt interjection of technical information which is not based on evidence.

Let me illustrate. Suppose you, in your own normal activities, walk past the work station of a fellow employee. You see a person's back. You don't get much of a view, but you know that this is the place where your acquaintance—let's call him Al—is supposed to be working. The person you see appears to be working there and is not obviously dissimilar to Al. Under those circumstances, you would probably do what we all do under such circumstances. You would assume that you had seen Al.

That is the kind of assumption we all make, routinely, as we go about our daily activities. We assume that we have seen Al, because we expected to see him. And if someone asks us later whether we saw Al at work, we answer "Yes." Because, you see, we forget the specifics of what we saw. Our answer to the question of whether we saw Al, is based entirely on our conclusion, our opinion, that we saw Al. We forget that all we saw was a man's back, or a partial side view that didn't really register. We remember, mistakenly but firmly, that we saw Al. We are sure that we saw Al. We formed our opinion that it was Al from all the circumstances, just as on other occasions we might form the opinion that we had seen an acquaintance by taking a quick look at a person from the front. The human mind, in short, is not a precision tool.

And that is why it is that we have all seen and probably even participated in a mistaken identification of a friend or relative. We are all familiar with that type of incident: The man named Bill who is greeted with a friendly cry of "Hi, Harry!," the familiar and pleasant "Hello" that is met with a blank stare, the rueful "Sorry, wrong guy." These are things that happen to perfectly competent and normal people, day in and day out, mistaken identifications of people whom they confuse with friends and relatives whom they have known for years, perhaps for their entire lives.

But those are the *known* mistakes, the *proven* misidentifications, the wrong opinion on identity which gets straightened out on the spot, before it has a chance to become fixed in anyone's mind. Those are the errors which are cleared up by a face-to-face conversation with the person wrongly identified, before we walk away convinced that we saw our friend Harry when we actually saw a stranger named Bill.

How much more often does it happen, though, that we do *not* pause to say "Hi, Harry!" Perhaps we are busy and go on our way without special greeting. Perhaps we simply smile, or wave, and receive an acknowledgement which confirms, in our own minds, that we saw our friend Harry. But how many times have you received a smile, a wave, or a hello from a stranger? Was that stranger simply being friendly toward the world as a whole, or were you mistaken for someone he or she knew?

One thing is certain. On every one of the occasions on which a man named Bill, or Pete, or Joe, or Ernie is greeted with a "Hi, Harry!", if no greeting had been spoken on the spot and if the person making the mistake had simply gone on his or her way or smiled and received a polite smile and nod in return—on every such occasion, that mistaken party would have walked away believing that he or she had seen Harry. And if the issue had arisen in court later, that mistaken person, if required to testify, would have felt morally obligated to swear that Harry had been present at that time and place. That testimony, like that of [eyewitness] in this case, would have been honest in the sense that the witness would have believed what he or she was saying; but it would have been tragically mistaken and false.

And it can happen to any of us. Like [eyewitness], we are not precision machinery. Any one of us can easily make a mistaken identification and plunge an innocent person into the kind of nightmare that [client] is living through this very minute. Any one of us, for that matter, can be the object of that type of sincere but mistaken identification, and if that happens, the nightmare is ours.

You will never have occasion to perform a more significant civic service than is open to you in this case: to take a sympathetic but realistic view of the eyewitness testimony presented in this case; to reject it as an unworthy basis for condemning any human being; and thereby to do your bit to make it less likely that some other person will be sitting through this same nightmare next week, or next month, or next year.

§10.33 Illustrations: Denial of Police Expertise

The predisposition on the part of many jurors to attach special credibility to eyewitness testimony given by law enforcement officers is considered in **§10.18.** As there noted, that prevalent attitude poses special problems for the opponent, who frequently is placed in the position of defending against unarticulated claims.

The party opposing the police eyewitness will, in most situations, be limited to a single summation address sandwiched between opening and rebuttal summations delivered on behalf of the party sponsoring the witness. To some degree, the opponent's approach to the problem must be tailored to meet the tactics employed by the witness' sponsor, as described in §10.23. Essentially, however, the opponent's argument is based upon the proposition that the jurors' own experiences have taught them that police are not gifted with exceptional talents in any area relevant to credibility as eyewitnesses.

In this situation, lawyers walk a narrow line. They must evaluate the probable impression upon the jury made by the police witness. Thus guided, they must elect between two lines of argument.

§10.34 —Lack of Expertise in Particular Police Officer

One of these follows the path of least resistance, but it is available only if the lawyer is prepared to point to some articulable deficiency in the police witness' performance. In that situation, the lawyer may decide not to challenge the assumption that police in general are well-qualified observers, but only to contend that this endemic occupational attribute has not yet rubbed off on the witness in question:

> It may be that police officers are better-trained and more reliable observers than the rest of us. I would like to think so, and I am sure you would, too, because we are all dependent upon them for our safety, and it would be comforting to believe that they have special skills which enable them to provide that protection.
>
> There has been a lot of debate about whether police are any better than the rest of us at identifying people whom they observe under stressful conditions. It is an interesting question and an important one, in a way, but it is not one that we have to consider in deciding this case. Whatever your opinion may be about the skill level of the police as a group, there is one point on which every intelligent person is agreed: all police are not equally competent, and therefore no opinion, good or bad, is valid if it is applied to *all* police. Regardless what other police officers may have been able to do in that same situation, it is clear from Officer [Eyewitness'] testimony that when it comes to identifying people seen under pressure, Officer [Eyewitness] is certainly no better than anyone else.

The opponent then proceeds to expand upon that contention by pointing out the specific shortcoming demonstrated by the evidence. It is usually more effective to show compassion than disdain. It may be possible, for example, to argue that the witness' duty assignments within the police department do not lend themselves to the development of observational powers. In yet other situations, it may be wise to attribute the witness' shortcoming to factors such as exceptional stress or distraction, thus avoiding all adverse comment upon the officer's capability. The choice will depend upon the lawyer's reading of the interaction between the police officer and the jury.

§10.35 —Lack of Expertise in General

Normally, the evidence presents no basis for the contention that the police officer's performance as an observer was deficient in some meaningful particular. As suggested in **§10.23,** the cross-examiner may have drawn attention to several routine matters which the witness failed to note or no longer recalls. Such references, however, do not reflect adversely upon the witness' competence as an observer; if the jury believes that to be the purpose of the questioning, the cross-examiner may be scorned as a nit-picker. The jury must be made to understand that the purpose of the questioning was only to dispel the Superman aura with which police often attempt to clothe themselves in judicial proceedings:

> Now, some of you properly may be wondering why I went to the trouble, in cross-examining Officer [Eyewitness], to show that he did not recall or even note whether there were any pictures on the wall in that room, or whether the defendant was wearing a charm on a gold neck chain. What do those things have to do with the real issues in this case?
>
> Now, of course, with the advantage of hindsight, we know that the picture and the charm are not important to the case. But when Officer [Eyewitness] first encountered the defendant, there was no reason to believe that the chain, and the charm, and the picture were any more or less important than the things that the officer does claim to remember: the color of the defendant's shirt, for example, and the fact that his golf equipment was leaning against the closet door.
>
> We know now what facts are important and what facts are not. But Officer [Eyewitness] had no way of knowing that when he first saw the Defendant. He had no more reason to notice the shirt and the golf bag than he had to ignore the chain, the charm, and the picture.
>
> There is nothing inherently wrong with Officer [Eyewitness'] selection of things to remember. Anyone might have done the same thing. If we had been there, we might have noticed the chain, the charm, and the picture, while paying no attention to the golf bag and the color of the shirt. Or, as in the case of Officer [Eyewitness],

we might have reversed that, paying attention to the shirt and golf bag while ignoring the chain, charm, and picture. It is a random matter, the question of which details we happen to remember. No system to it.

But that is exactly the point. Officer [Eyewitness] behaved exactly as we would have behaved in his place. He noticed some things and did not notice others, and the selection was random, haphazard, and without structure or system. He did not have some form of unique photographic grasp of all the details. He noticed *some* of those details, just as anyone might in the same situation.

And that is important. It is important because if those questions had not been asked, some of us might have assumed that Officer [Eyewitness] has some special power of observation and identification simply because he is a police officer. We might have assumed that police are specially qualified by training and experience to observe and report more accurately than the rest of us.

And that is exactly what it would have been: an assumption. Something that we accept without proof, without evidence.

From this point, the lawyer may proceed to offset the myth that police are exceptionally skilled observers by invoking the lawyer's own illusion of expertise suggested by **§10.31.** Two points may be made, with emphasis determined by the facts of the case. The first is that there is no evidence to support the notion that police have any special qualifications as witnesses. The second is that as a matter of common knowledge, police work does not hone such skills. The two arguments are complementary and may, in most cases, be blended to good effect.

The following argument illustrates the exploitation of both these points, building on the proposition that attribution of special powers to police is based only on assumptions:

[Argument continues from previous point of interruption] An assumption. Something that we accept without proof, without evidence.

But that assumption, or any assumption, is completely out of place as an influence on your verdict. That is exactly what you swore you would not do: assume facts. There are only two proper, legitimate sources for facts that might influence your verdict. One is the evidence in the case, and the other is your knowledge and experience in the affairs of life. We ought to consider both of those sources right now, I think, because neither of them has any place for assumptions.

Now, first, the evidence. Was there anything in this evidence, any proof whatever, which showed that Officer [Eyewitness] is any more skilled an observer than you, than I, or than anyone else? Nobody testified that he could do any such thing. And indeed, nobody even testified that police generally are better observers than other people. There wasn't one psychologist, or physician, or scientist of any kind who testified that police as a group are any better at this sort of thing than anyone else. There was not one expert of any kind who told you about any experiments or tests comparing police officers with average citizens, which showed that police officers are any better at identifying or remembering people, or objects, or scenes, or anything else, any better than carpenters, or bicycle salespeople, or homemakers, or bus drivers. There is no reason, believe me, no reason for you to assume that police officers as a group have ever been proved any better than anyone else at identifying and remembering. They have not been proved any better in tests, and they have not been proved any better in this courtroom.

There is no better place in the world than this courthouse to learn for yourselves that police are no better than the rest of us when it comes to identifications such as the one involved in this case.

Well, then, what about our common knowledge and experience in the affairs of life? You have every bit as much right to draw on that as upon evidence in arriving at your verdict. Does our common knowledge and experience in the affairs of life tell us that police officers' identifications are more accurate than those of other people?

Well, that is certainly not a matter of common knowledge around here. In this building, where people work with that sort of problem all the time, there is very certainly no reason to believe that such a statement could be made without provoking a very serious argument.

But more to the point, what we have to work with in the jury system is, as I said, common knowledge and experience. *Knowledge. Experience.* Things that we *know,* that have happened to us. Not things that we assume, or things that we guess, or things that we tend vaguely to believe, but things that we *know.*

Very well. What do we know—*know*—about whether police officers can identify more accurately than the rest of us? We all know police officers. We see them all the time, doing all sorts of things. Think about what you see them doing. Does it involve any more reason to concentrate on faces, or to memorize features of people passing by, than would be true of a teacher, or a mail carrier, or a gas station attendant, or just anybody?

And yes, of course, Officer [Eyewitness'] encounter with the thief was not just some casual glance at a stray person passing by. It was a look at someone he would have reason to try to remember so that he could make the arrest. Of course, it is not the same thing as seeing someone casually walk by on the street.

But—and here is the whole point—Officer [Eyewitness] is no better than a teacher, or mail carrier, or gas station attendant at identifying thieves whom they see fleetingly, unless he acquired that skill *before* he saw the thief. He does not suddenly become a better observer than anyone else, simply because he sees a crime committed. That would be nonsense. If he is a better observer, it is because he somehow acquired that skill before he had to use it, just as with any other skill. One does not become an expert by suddenly being required to do something.

Of course, there is a difference between passing someone casually on the street and seeing that person commit a crime. But that is a difference that has nothing to do with the occupation of the observer. There is no reason for you to put any more trust in the observations made by Officer [Eyewitness] than if those same observations had been made by anyone else.

Remember the testimony concerning Officer [Eyewitness'] training as a police officer. He spent 16 weeks in a training academy. While there, he spent a lot of time on physical workouts, getting into shape. He spent a lot of time learning about the municipal code, and the criminal code, and the traffic code. He had to learn how to write traffic tickets so that they would stand up in court, so that the proper violation number would be included together with all sorts of other details. He had to learn marksmanship and weapons safety. He had to learn a little psychology and diplomacy to be used in dealing with all sorts of people. He had to learn about crime investigations, and fingerprinting, and court procedure, and the organization of the police department, and something of the law of evidence. It was a pretty full 16 weeks. If he had spent that entire 16 weeks in learning how to identify people reliably, there would be a serious question whether that would be sufficient. But in fact, he spent practically none of that time in mastering that complex and challenging skill.

And even that minimal training was years ago. What do we remember now of the techniques in physics and chemistry experiments that we mastered in high school? Even if officer [Eyewitness] had remembered, on the night he saw the thief, every detail of the two hours that he spent learning visual identification and description, it would not have done him any good. But in point of fact, he probably remembered none of it.

Since he left the training academy, he has . . . [the argument here is adapted to the specific facts of the case, with emphasis on showing that the officer has had little or no occasion to practice or be tested in identification of people whom he sees fleetingly on a one-time basis].

You have heard Officer [Eyewitness] tell you that it is a part of his job to become familiar with the people who live on his beat, to keep an eye on unexpected strangers, and so forth. But here, you can *really* draw upon your common knowledge and experience. Isn't there every difference in the world between becoming generally familiar with a group of people over a long period of time and identifying a person at whom Officer [Eyewitness] got a short and confused look one time in his entire life? Did you hear one word suggesting that he had ever been tested on his knowledge of the people who live in his area, on his ability to identify them? I am sure he believes he can do it, but did you hear one word of testimony that he ever has proved to anyone that he could do that? And if he could, it would have little or nothing to do with his ability to identify a stranger in the circumstances involved here. We have all come to recognize hundreds of people whom we encounter regularly. We may not know their names, but we know we have seen them before. Hundreds of people. Does that give us any special claim of talent in identifying a person we have seen only once in our lives, and that once in dim light, running, for a very few seconds?

Once again, there is no reason, no reason shown by the evidence in this case or by your knowledge and experience, to consider Officer [Eyewitness] a more skilled observer than anyone else, or to put any more confidence in his observations than we would in those of anyone else. The fact that he is a police officer is important only because it entitles him to make arrests. For purpose of passing judgment on his identifications, the fact that he is a police officer is completely beside the point.

§10.36 Sample Summations

The following summations by Stanley Staat, Prosecutor, and Diane

DeFene, Defense Counsel, are designed to illustrate typical effective arguments on both sides of an eyewitness controversy.

The summations here depicted deal with the hypothetical case entitled *People of the State of Columbia v Paul Pure.* The purse-snatching scenario upon which these summations are based is the same as that which has been presented in earlier chapters,[37] except that the second identification has been eliminated in order better to focus upon the summation strategy involved in a straightforward eyewitness contest.

§10.37 —Prosecutor's Initial Summation

MR. STAAT: Ladies and gentlemen, the point has come in this trial where the attorneys again have an opportunity to address you in what is known as closing argument or summation and to tell you what we believe the evidence in this case has proved.

I remind you again, as the Judge has reminded you at other times in the trial, that what I say now and what Ms. DeFene will say after I have spoken to you is not, of course, evidence in the case; and so if your recollection differs from mine, then of course you are to accept your recollection of the facts.

You will remember, ladies and gentlemen, that when you were selected as jurors in this case you agreed that if the evidence proved the defendant guilty beyond a reasonable doubt that you would return a verdict in favor of the State and indeed find the defendant guilty beyond a reasonable doubt.

You will further remember that in my opening statement I told you what I believed the evidence in this case would prove. I told you that I believed Joan Good, the complaining witness, would testify from the stand and that she would positively identify the defendant in this case, Paul Pure, sitting over there, as the man who on the date alleged in the indictment, May 4, 1983, took her purse from her against her will and without her permission and with the intention of permanently depriving Ms. Good of her property.

In fact, Ms. Good did testify here today and she did positively identify Paul Pure as the man who took her purse; and she told you that she did not give him permission to take her purse, and she told you that he took it and ran away, from which evidence you can and

---

[37] See **§§4.08-4.14, 5.05, 5.06, 6.02, 6.07, 6.08, 6.11, and 7.16-7.23.** This fact scenario is based upon the problem "State v. Lawrence," *Problems and Cases in Trial Advocacy, Law School Edition,* 2nd Ed. (1981), which is published by the National Institute for Trial Advocacy (NITA). Adapted and reproduced with the permission of NITA.

must infer that he intended permanently to deprive her of her purse and of the contents of the purse.

Now, she told you how it was that she was able to identify Paul Pure. She told you that she heard him approaching her from some distance away on a well-lighted street and that she turned around when she first heard him and that when she turned around he was facing her and she was facing him—in other words, they were face to face—and as he approached her on that street, she could see him.

She further told you that when Mr. Pure reached her he grabbed her purse and pushed her over and that she fell backwards and was looking up at him and that for some period of time he was looking down at her and that this occurred underneath the light of a mercury vapor street light and that while she was looking up at him and he was looking down at her, they were again face to face and she had an opportunity to observe him and to see his face.

Ms. Good called the police after she returned home, and she gave the police officer a description, and the description she gave the police officer was of a person of medium build with a beard and long hair and white pants and a black T-shirt; and certainly the description that she gave the police officer matches the description of the defendant here, who, as you can see, is of medium build and has long hair and a beard.

Now, he is wearing different clothes today than he was wearing that day out on the street, of course; but, nevertheless, that description does match the appearance of Mr. Pure.

More than that, ladies and gentlemen, we do not have here simply one identification, an identification that occurred here in court. We have another identification which occurred at the police station three days after Mr. Pure took Ms. Good's purse.

If you will remember the testimony both of Ms. Good and of Officer Right, Ms. Good was shown photographs of the defendant, Paul Pure; and she positively identified those photographs as being photographs of the man who took her purse, and that identification was at a time just a few days after the incident when the image of his face was certainly clearly imprinted in her mind.

But we do not have only two identifications in this case. We have a third identification. The third identification occurred when Ms. Good picked the defendant out of a lineup in which there were present four other men, and Ms. Good positively identified Paul Pure in that lineup as the man who took her purse.

Ladies and gentlemen, in this case, we have, then, three positive identifications; a positive identification from a lineup, a positive identification of a photograph, and a positive identification here in court.

Now, you will remember, ladies and gentlemen, that after Ms. Good answered the questions I asked her, she was cross-examined, cross-examined in what can be described as an extremely competent manner by Diane DeFene. You will remember that that cross-examination lasted at least twice as long as the direct examination.

And cross-examination, ladies and gentlemen, has been rightfully called one of the most basic safeguards of our liberty and one of the principal ways of arriving at the truth. But did that cross-examination do anything, ladies and gentlemen, to shake the testimony of Joan Good? It did not.

At the end of the cross-examination, she was as positive in her identification of Paul Pure as her assailant as she was at the beginning of the direct examination. In other words, she withstood the cross-examination without in any way changing her testimony or becoming hesitant about her testimony or indicating in any way that she was less than positive that Paul Pure was the perpetrator of this crime.

And I ask you, ladies and gentlemen, has there been any suggestion in this trial of any reason why Ms. Good would come in here and lie, commit perjury? Has there been any evidence that there was any animosity between Ms. Good and Paul Pure? Has there been any motivation, in other words, shown to you that would even suggest a reason why Ms. Good would come into this courtroom and say that Paul Pure was the person who took her purse if Paul Pure was not the person who took her purse or if she wasn't sure that Paul Pure was the person who took her purse?

There has been no suggestion of any reason why she should do that, and the reason there has been no suggestion of any such reason is that there is no reason why she would do that.

The only reason Ms. Good came into this court to testify that Paul Pure took her purse was because Paul Pure did take her purse. She sat on that witness stand and she testified under oath that that is what happened. She withstood cross-examination unshaken; and the facts in this case, the evidence in this case, proves beyond a reasonable doubt that Paul Pure committed the crime alleged in the indictment.

Therefore, ladies and gentlemen, the People of the State of

Columbia request that you return a guilty verdict in favor of the state and against Mr. Pure.

Thank you.

§10.38 —Defense Summation

MS. DE FENE: Ladies and gentlemen, when this case began, I told you that it was Paul Pure's position that he was not guilty of this offense, that he was not the person who took Ms. Good's purse, that he was not present at the time that purse was taken, and that Ms. Good in identifying him simply is mistaken.

Now, the Court here in judging this case has, as it is required to do, made an evaluation of the positions of the parties and is I believe prepared to define for you just what the issues are in this case; and I believe that the Court will tell you that it is the defense theory that Ms. Good is simply mistaken.

Now, I want to emphasize that word *mistaken* because Mr. Staat has told you essentially that the choice before you is either to say that Paul Pure stole Ms. Good's purse or that Ms. Good came into this courtroom to commit perjury.

Those are not the choices at all, and I think everybody in this courtroom knows that those are not the choices.

Ms. Good is not committing perjury. Ms. Good is making a mistake, and it is a serious and tragic mistake.

You were asked really why would Ms. Good say these things if they were not true. For the same reason that any other person would make a statement, believing that statement to be true, when in point of fact that statement is not true. She is mistaken.

You were told at the start of this case, and you will be told again by the Judge, that the issue in this case simply stated is this: Does this evidence prove beyond all reasonable doubt that Paul Pure stole Ms. Good's purse? Beyond reasonable doubt, beyond any doubt that is based upon a reason.

You heard this evidence. You heard a story of a woman caught in frightening and startling circumstances quickly pushed to the ground, her head injured, frightened for what might happen to her next, a confrontation with her assailant that took no more than four seconds, and then he vanished into the darkness.

Can any reasonable person not have a reasonable doubt of her ability to identify that person?

Mr. Staat points out to you that there was a period of time, as he puts it, not a period of time to be measured in terms of one or two seconds but a period of time from his perspective, during which Ms. Good's assailant was looking down at her; but the assailant, whoever he was, was looking down at a woman who had just fallen heavily to the ground, who was as stunned, as frightened, as confused as any of us would be in that situation. He was looking down with arc lights behind him and in the shadow of trees and leaves. There can be no less satisfactory view of another person than that.

Now, Mr. Staat takes considerable satisfaction in the proposition that he told you that Ms. Good would positively identify the defendant, and indeed Ms. Good proceeded to do exactly that; but I would remind you, Mr. Staat was not the only person who told you that. I made that same prediction in my opening statement to you at the beginning of this case.

It was very clear that Ms. Good would in fact positively identify the defendant and that she would stand by her story. There was never a question of that; and of course that is her opinion, that the person who took her purse is the person who is seated in this courtroom today.

Of course that is her opinion. That is her sincere opinion, but that is not what we are here to decide. The question is not whether Ms. Good sincerely believes that she accused the right person. The question is whether this evidence proves beyond reasonable doubt that Paul Pure is that person.

The question is not whether Ms. Good is committing perjury. She is not committing perjury. She has a mistaken opinion. Her opinion as to the identity of the person who assaulted her that night is mistaken, and that is something very different from perjury; and in telling you as he did that the question before you was whether Paul Pure is guilty of purse snatching or Ms. Good is guilty of perjury, the prosecutor could not have painted a more misleading picture of what this case is about, and I would hope that when he thinks it over he might in time come to blush for what he did and to apologize for it because that is not the issue at all. The issue is whether this evidence proves the defendant's guilt beyond all reasonable doubt.

The desperation really that underlies this case is I think fairly patent from the comfort that the prosecutor takes in what he refers to as three identifications. Three. Not merely two. He finds three.

The first identification that he finds is that of the display of two photographs, not one but two, two photographs of the same person shown to Ms. Good with the question: "Is this the man who stole your purse?" That was the question, wasn't it? "Is this the man who stole your purse?" Not, "Have you ever seen this man before?," not simply showing her the picture and saying essentially, "Any comment?" No.

"Is this the man who stole your purse?" And she sees a picture of a man with a beard and long hair, and that was everything that she possibly could have seen that night.

What does she say? The least she could say is that it looked like him. It was just eminently predictable that any person in her position would have said it looks like him; and then having gazed at that picture, she is then taken to a lineup. And the prosecutor finds considerable comfort in that lineup; but in that lineup in which the witness was asked to point out the person wearing white pants and a beard who had stolen her purse, the defendant was the only person in that lineup with white pants and a beard and, more than that, before entering that lineup she had seen the photographs only minutes before.

Was there any question as to what the outcome of that lineup would be, and can any reasonable person have failed to have a reasonable doubt of that procedure?

After all, had there been any real confidence in Ms. Good's ability to identify the perpetrator, is there any question that she could have been shown a series of photographs instead of only two? Is there any question but that the lineup that was shown to her might have contained more than one person with a beard?

Anyone who was not wearing a beard was completely and automatically excluded from any possible consideration as the offender. Any person in that lineup who was not wearing a beard could not possibly have been the offender, which meant that if there were six people in the lineup, five could not possibly have been the offender.

Would you like to be identified in a lineup of that type? Would you? It would be absolutely no different, no different whatever from the situation in which the suspect in a lineup is the only person of his or her own race, no different whatsoever.

But the prosecutor says there is a third identification. If those two are not good enough for you, and they would not be good enough for any thoughtful person, there is a third one, he says. She identified him right here in court.

True. Of course, she sat here while the parties were introduced to you. Everybody in this courtroom knew before the trial commenced that the defendant was Paul Pure, that he was seated in the chair right next to me. He was pointed out with clarity to everybody in the room in order that we might know whether anyone here had any acquaintanceship with him.

And even if a person had not gone through that experience, simply to enter the courtroom and observe where the parties were seated would have been very adequate as a basis for instinctively knowing who was the defendant; and at the tables, again Paul Pure was the only person with a beard.

Come on, we would all have fainted I think if she, having identified him on that previous occasion, had gone on the stand and said "I don't know whether the person is in the courtroom."

That identification is just as worthless as the other two; and, again, I believe that the prosecutor is aware of that.

I mentioned before that the Judge yet has some things to say to you. When I finish my argument and when the prosecutor finishes his answer to it, the Judge will then undertake to instruct you as to what the law of this case is, the governing law; and it is then that I believe she will tell you, as I suggested before, what our theory of this case is and repeat to you the basic proposition that the defendant is presumed innocent and that he is to be acquitted unless, guided by that presumption of innocence, you find him guilty beyond all reasonable doubt.

But I think the Judge will tell you something else, too. I think the Judge will tell you that you are not required to believe anything to be a fact merely because a witness testifies that it is a fact if, in all the circumstances, you consider that that witness may have been mistaken.

Ms. Good is mistaken. Not merely in the sense that anybody can be mistaken, and anybody can. The best witness in the world can be mistaken; but Miss Good simply, flatly did not have an adequate opportunity to enable her to say with any genuine certainty, with any genuine conviction, with any assurance who was the person who stole her purse.

The prosecutor takes considerable pride in the proposition that the description she gave matches that of the defendant. Well, of course it does; and that is because that description is so vague that it would take into its scope absolutely anybody who was approximately six feet tall, who is neither unusually fat nor unusually thin, and who is wearing a beard. It is the kind of description that really can't miss as to a very significant portion of the entire human race.

You will note that in that description there was not even a specification of the hair color of the attacker, not even the hair color. Can you believe that was because Ms. Good wasn't asked? Of course she was asked. The reason that the hair color is not there is because she was unable to furnish it; and that is perfectly understandable given the speed with which the event occurred, given the poor lighting conditions and given the fact that she was looking at her attacker with the light behind the attacker and his features were accordingly blurred and darkened by that rear lighting.

The description matches that of the defendant and just about everybody else with a beard. No age, no approximate age. Can you believe that she wasn't asked the approximate age of her attacker? Can you consider that?

But the description doesn't include the approximate age of the thief, and its not included because of the fact that she simply was unable to furnish it; and that, too, is understandable. That is perfectly understandable.

If you stay around this courthouse long enough, you find a large number of cases in which a person is placed in jeopardy of losing his or her liberty, his or her fundamental rights as a human being based upon the story of an eyewitness; and if you stay around here long enough, the stories that you have heard of the tragedies that have occurred in consequence of eyewitness mistakes would all start to become very, very real to you indeed.

Think, please, how very fallible is our capacity to identify a stranger. How many times have you heard of or perhaps even participated in a street scene in which one person walks up to another and says, "Hi, Bill," or some other name, identifying, like Ms. Good, in her own mind someone well known to her, an acquaintance, a relative, someone she has known all her life, and it turns out that she has approached the wrong person?

There are 12 of you in this jury. I am certain that it must have happened to at least one. It is a very common event.

I am talking now about people whom we have known all our lives, people whom we approach in unstructured, unhurried circumstances, and we make a mistake as to who they are.

Contrast that with the situation we have here; a man attacks a defenseless woman on the street. Despicable crime, no question about it; but it is not a situation in which compounding one tragedy with another tragedy will help anything.

The simple fact of the matter is that she was dealing with a stranger. There is no less reliable identification than that of a person whom one has never seen before. There is no less reliable identification than that of a person who is observed under fleeting and hurried circumstances, in fast motion, in a quickly unfolding situation, a situation in which the individual making the identification feels a very real, a very justified threat to herself.

In a situation such as that, one does not memorize features; and in a situation such as that, it would be an impossibility if one were to try to do it.

Ladies and gentlemen, I say again the question before you is not whether Ms. Good sincerely believes the opinion that she has offered here. The question is, rather, whether you believe that there is no reasonable doubt but that Paul Pure stole her purse.

I urge to you that in these circumstances the mark of a reasonable person is to have a reasonable doubt. No person, no reasonable person, can leave this courtroom with a moral certainty that Ms. Good is correct, only that she *believes* that she is correct. But we are not here to decide what she believes. We are here to decide what happened; and with all respect to Ms. Good, with genuine sympathy for what happened to her, I urge you that the question before you can only be answered with a finding of not guilty.

Let me remind you this case turns in its entirety upon Ms. Good's statement that the man whom she saw three days after the event is the same man who stole her purse. It turns upon her ability to make a more precise identification three days later than she was capable of making two hours after the event. It is the classic case of the mistaken eyewitness.

We would have doubts here, all of us, I think justified doubts, if this had not been the only time in her life that Ms. Good ever saw her assailant. We would have doubts here I think, justified doubts, if Ms. Good had been able to observe her assailant three or four times as long as was in fact the case. We would have doubts, justifiable, reasonable doubts, if in fact Ms. Good had not been knocked to the ground and forced to adjust to that, to overcome the confusion that goes with such an unfortunate event, to be obsessed with the possible need for self-protection. Without all of the circumstances that intruded here, that doubt clearly would be present.

I urge to you, ladies and gentlemen, the proposition that Ms. Good's opinion is not one which justifies a finding of guilt beyond reasonable doubt. I do not ask that you call Ms. Good a liar. I ask only that you say that she is mistaken in order that the unfortunate event that occurred to her not be compounded with the total tragedy that will ensue if her mistaken opinion is endorsed by this jury.

I urge your verdict of not guilty. It is the only proper, justified verdict that the evidence in this case will support.

Thank you.

§10.39 —Prosecutor's Rebuttal

MR. STAAT: Ladies and gentlemen, defense counsel really has said one thing to you: Maybe Ms. Good is mistaken. She has pointed out to you all the theoretical possibilities. She has suggested various things that occurred that might have made Ms. Good mistaken.

Now, the Court does not require you to play God, to erase all theoretical possibilities. In our human affairs, we have to deal in a very practical way. We know people sometimes make mistakes, but we also know that people do not make mistakes. We know that people are usually correct, especially when something that occurs is of great importance to them, something that burns itself upon their memories.

So put aside all of these theoretical possibilities that defense counsel would have you disturb yourself with and just think again of the testimony of Ms. Good.

She is not an hysterical person. She is not a frivolous person. You saw her on the stand. She is fully aware of the consequences of her convictions in this matter. She understands her responsibilities.

She looked at Mr. Pure and she said, "That is the man. I will never forget the face." That is what she said.

Do you believe she was mistaken? Do you believe that person said to herself, "I think that is the man. I will convict that man just on my vague feeling?"

That is not the woman you saw on the stand. You saw a woman self-possessed, a woman who was certain. She pointed to the defendant and she said, "That is the man who attacked me."

Ladies and gentlemen, in the affairs of human beings, all we can do is to make decisions when we have no reasonable doubt.

On the evening of that attack, defense counsel was not there, I was not there, you were not there. Ms. Good was there; and there was one other person there, and that was the defendant. And how do we know that? Because Ms. Good looked that man in the face under very adequate lighting. As she said, she remembered that face. She saw that face in a lineup and she said, "That is the man."

She came into this courtroom, looked at him, fully aware of the consequences of her identification, and she said, "That is the man. I will never forget the face."

Ladies and gentlemen, there is only one question for you really to determine here, and that is whether Ms. Good is correct in her identification. There is no reason in the real world of things that really happen for you to have any reasonable doubt that she was correct.

I ask you to do your duty and to return the verdict as required by the evidence, a finding of guilty.

Thank you.

11 Hypnosis

§11.01 Hypnosis as an Aid to Recall

In the last 15 years or more great interest has developed in the use of hypnosis in criminal investigations and prosecutions, as well as in civil cases. The procedure is thought to shake loose and make available perceptions the witness originally had at the time of the prior events but which now escape his or her memory. This understanding of hypnosis, however, is based on a static view of memory and can be misleading unless the dynamic nature of the memory process is kept in mind and provision is made for this creative process. As a recent federal appellate court has observed:

> The use of hypnosis in criminal investigation is based on an implicit theory of memory: the brain stores all the information received by the body's senses, and forgetting is simply the inability to retrieve stored information. Hypnosis is a method of eliminating retrieval difficulties to give the hypnotized person access to the stored information. Many memory theorists believe, to the contrary, that

> what appears to be recall is actually a constructive process in which information received after an event is integrated by the mind into the memory representation of that event. According to this view, what appears to be a witness's recollection of the event itself may in fact be a composite made up of original recall, information learned from earlier and later events, suggestions received during hypnosis, and the witness's unconscious filling-in of missing details to make the story complete or logical or to fulfill the perceived desires of the hypnotist or someone else. Whether hypnosis actually improves memory remains an open question among scientists.[1]

Nonetheless, hypnosis continues to be used by police, attorneys, and prosecutors, and in one fashion or another such use is sanctioned by many courts. Problems associated with its use are discussed in this chapter. The testimony of an eyewitness may be significantly influenced by hypnotic enhancement.

§11.02 The Nature of Hypnosis

The term *hypnosis* derives from a Greek word meaning *sleep,* reflecting the sleeplike state many understand the hypnotized person to be experiencing.[2] Physiologically, however, the condition differs markedly from the state of sleep. The brain activity, respiration, and heart rate of the hypnotized subject are not at all like that of the same subject when asleep.[3] There appears to be no general agreement as to the underlying nature of the hypnotic state. There is, however, agreement as to observable characteristics of the subject who is hypnotized.[4]

1. The subject loses initiative and lacks the desire to make and carry out plans of his or her own
2. The subject may experience vivid memories of events or details of events which in fact never occurred; subjects remain highly convinced of the reality of the events and the accuracy of their

---

[1] United States v Valdez, 722 F2d 1196, 1200 (5th Cir 1984).

[2] 9 Orne, *Macropaedia,* Encyclopaedia Britannica 133, 135 (1979); see also Pavlov, *The Identity of Inhibition with Sleep and Hypnosis,* 17 Sci Monthly 603 (1923).

[3] See A. Yarmey, The Psychology of Eyewitness Testimony 176 (1979).

[4] E. Hilgard, The Experience of Hypnosis 6 (1968); Hilgard, *Evidence for a Developmental-Interactive Theory of Hypnotic Susceptibility,* in Hypnosis: Research Developments and Perspectives 387 (E Fromm & R. Shor eds 1972). Supported by Diamond, *Inherent Problems in the Use of Pretrial Hypnosis on a Prospective Witness,* 68 Cal L Rev 313 (1980).

memories in the posthypnotic period, especially if encouraged by the hypnotist

3. In the hypnotized subject, selective attention and selective inattention go beyond the usual range
4. Severe distortions of reality can be uncritically accepted by such subjects
5. The subject is highly susceptible to suggestion, which may be intentionally or unwittingly supplied by the hypnotist or anyone present
6. The suggestions that a subject in hypnosis will accept are not limited to specific acts or perceptions; the subject will readily adopt a suggested role and carry on complex activities corresponding to that role
7. While amnesia for what occurred during the hypnotic state is not an essential aspect of hypnosis, it is a very common phenomenon and can be furthered through suggestion by the hypnotist that the subject not recall on awakening what happened during the session

It is now believed that almost everyone is susceptible to being hypnotized.[5] Perhaps excluded are those who are incapable of extended concentration, such as young children and *scatterbrained* adults. Susceptibility is not reserved for the weak-willed, impressionable, and gullible. Generally, well-adjusted people are good subjects.[6] In addition, no difference has been demonstrated between the sexes or among the races as to a predisposition to being hypnotized. Research does, however, suggest some differences in susceptibility. Liberal arts graduates and grade school children through junior high are more susceptible than others. It is suggested that an active imagination is the common factor.[7] One researcher lists the following as the characteristics of the *highly* susceptible subject:

1. A penchant for the extraordinary and unique
2. Readiness to accept the hypnotist as a teacher and guide
3. Good ability to concentrate[8]

---

[5] D. Cheek & L. LeCron, Clinical Hypnotherapy 20 (1968); Ladd, *Legal Aspects of Hypnotism,* 11 Yale LJ 173, 175 (1902).

[6] D. Cheek & L. LeCron, *supra* note 5, at 7, 21.

[7] Diamond & Taft, *The Role played by Ego Permissiveness and Imagery in Hypnotic Responsivity,* 23 Intl J Clinical & Experimental Hypnosis 130 (1975).

[8] Hilgard, *Imaginative Involvement: Some Characteristics of the Highly Hypnotizable and the Non-Hypnotizable,* cited in Spector & Foster, *Admissibility of Hypnotic Statements: Is the Law of Evidence Susceptible?,* 38 Ohio St LJ 567, 576 (1977). It still remains uncertain whether

Participants in competitive team sports (e.g., baseball, football, hockey, or basketball) are less susceptible to hypnotic suggestion than those who engage in *loner* sports activities (e.g., swimming, pole vaulting, running, or skiing).

There exists a body of opinion which holds that the hypnotic experience or state is not a phenomenon radically distinct from other normal experiences. This view is based on a belief that the condition is actually a state within the normal range of human concentration and relaxed, focused attention.[9] The theory was tested with a mixed group of subjects, some hypnotized (verification made) and others only feigning to be. The whole group was put to the task of recalling details of an event. The result reported is that *all* participants in the experiment did dramatically better than they had in previous tests in which hypnosis was not introduced—including the nonhypnotized who threw themselves into the task.[10] Such results fuel the skepticism of some members of the scientific community.

Susceptibility to hypnotic suggestion must be distinguished from the *depth* of an hypnotic state. Once hypnotized, the subject becomes more and more susceptible to suggestion as the depth of the state increases and the subject detaches himself or herself from the surrounding realities.[11] At a preliminary stage, a subject may remain fully aware of his or her surroundings and be oriented to time and place. In a deep hypnotic state, the subject can begin to hallucinate: to see, feel, and hear things and persons not present. The subject can be led to inhabit another time and place and behave in a manner appropriate to that setting. One writer acknowledges six levels of hypnotic condition.[12] Not every subject is capable of being brought to the deeper states.

As noted, there is no consensus among students of the phenomenon as to the underlying nature of the hypnotic process. Several models have been suggested.[13] One model sees it as a regression to an earlier evolutionary stage of development. There is a physiological model

---

a truly resistant subject can be hypnotized against his or her will. Some research suggests such a subject can be hypnotized. However, note the critique of these studies in 9 Orne, *supra* note 2. The danger is that a subject, otherwise unwilling, may be manipulated so as to be unconsciously willing at the moment of hypnosis.

[9] C. My, *The door in the Wall,* 7 Human Behavior 43 (1978).

[10] Reported in E. Loftus, Eyewitness Testimony 107 (1979); see also Orne in Psychology 150 (G. Lindzey & F. Aronson eds 1975); see also O'Connell, Shor & Orne, *Hypnotic Age Regression: An Empirical and Methodological Analysis,* 76 J Of Abnormal Psychology, monograph No 3, pt 2 (1970).

[11] 9 Orne, *supra* note 2, at 138. Spector & Foster, *supra* note 8, at 574.

[12] H. Crasilneck & J. Hall, Clinical Hypnosis: Principles and Application 46 (1975).

[13] 9 Orne, *supra* note 2.

which sees it as the product of certain localized brain activity or inhibition. There is a biochemical theory which views it as the result of the production of chemical substances which affect the nervous system. A reductionist model sees it merely as a form of learning and conditioning. There is a psychoanalytic model which sees it as a regression to a child-parent relationship. The phenonemon is rich enough to offer support to almost any theory.

§11.03 Hypnosis in Historical Perspective

Trancelike behavior suggestive of hypnosis is reported to have existed in all the ancient civilizations, specifically ancient Greece, China, Egypt, Meso-America, and Africa.[14] It is known in the primitive religions of today as a part of ritual and faith healing. Some of the behavior, however, may have been more drug related.

In more recent times, interest in hypnosis dates back to Franz Anton Mesmer (1734-1815), an Austrian physician practicing in France.[15] He did not use the term *hypnotism;* that word was to be coined later by a Scottish physician, James Braid, who appears to be the first to use the term when describing its efficacy in preparing a patient for surgery. Mesmer called his unorthodox method of healing *animal magnetism.* He believed a subtle fluid emanated from the practitioner into the sufferer who was *mesmerized.* At first, he and his followers identified this flow as something physical. Later, they were to view it as a personal *force.* Mesmer surrounded the hypnotic session with considerable drama. His activities aroused the French scientific community, and a royal commission was appointed to investigate the phenomenon. The famous French chemist Lavoisier and the American statesman and scientist Benjamin Franklin served on the commission examining Mesmer's activities. The commission reviewed his claims and pronounced Mesmer's *magnetism* to be quackery. The panel concluded that the beneficial reactions of Mesmer's clients were rooted in their imagination. Subsequent to this pronouncement, interest in the hypnotic process declined in Europe.

However, interest did not totally die. A disciple of Mesmer, Chastenet de Puységur, discovered that he could obtain the same results with patients by simply talking to them, without need for the more bizarre props. His technique was much like that in use today.

In the 1840s, several physicians in England began using the Mesmer

---

[14] 9 Orne, *Macropaedia,* Encyclopaedia Britannica 133, 134 (1979). This article provides a examination of the history of hypnosis discussed in this section.

[15] See also H. Crasilneck & J. Hall, Clinical Hypnosis: Principles and Application 5-11 (1975).

trance as an anesthetic device before and during serious surgery, including amputations. Whatever might be the nature of the phenomenon, it generally was effective for this medical purpose. A Scottish physician, James Braid, who was finding the technique very helpful, chose to call it *hypnotism* rather than *magnetism* in order to divert the opprobrium attached to Mesmer's activities following condemnation by the French scientific commission. Moreover, Braid viewed the phenomenon not as a tangible force emanating from the practitioner, but as a narrow focusing of the attention of the subject effected by the hypnotist. He saw it as a form of *monoideism,* or single-mindedness.

Toward the end of the nineteenth century, two French medical professors at competing universities debated the nature of hypnotism. Professor Bernheim at the University of Strasbourg, who practiced at a clinic in nearby Nancy, viewed hypnosis as a universal psychological phenomenon based on suggestion. At the Sorbonne in Paris, Jean-Martin Charcot viewed the phenomenon as a pathological condition, a concomitant of hysteria. Sigmund Freud, then a practicing physician in Vienna and yet to develop his theories of the unconscious, became interested in the procedure for its practical applications to the complaints of some patients which had no apparent physical causes. Freud traveled to France to study the procedures at Paris and Nancy. His observations there eventually led him to a psychoanalytic interpretation of the phenomenon.

The two world wars gave significant impetus to the use and study of hypnosis in medical circles. It was found very useful in the treatment of combat neuroses. An American, Morton Prince, suggested that hypnosis was similar to a neurotic disorder known as *dissociation.* As the term suggests, in dissociation the contents of the mind are thought to become disconnected and the normal association between perceptions and thoughts and meanings is broken up. Another American, psychologist Clark Hull, subjected the phenomenon to controlled laboratory study. He concluded that Bernheim was correct: hypnosis is a form of hypersuggestibility.

Throughout history, along with the medical study and use of hypnosis and the unreflective applications of it in religious contexts, there has always been the entertainer, the stage hypnotist. The entertainer thrills audiences by appearing to call upon superhuman powers. Literature has portrayed the hypnotist as a villain utilizing satanic power for evil purposes. All this encouraged a public view of hypnosis as either trickery or demonic.[16]

---

[16] Diamond, *Inherent Problems in the Use of Pretrial Hypnosis on a Prospective Witness,* 68 Cal L. Rev 313, 320 (1980).

Present theories can be reduced to two broad approaches to hypnosis. One theory views the phenomenon as some form of altered consciousness, a partial sleep, perhaps associated with a physiological condition in which a few selected centers of neural activity function. The majority of Soviet psychiatrists view it in this manner, as do some American theorists.[17] The other view stresses the interpersonal dynamic between hypnotist and subject.

Since the 1950s, the healing professions have accepted hypnosis as a valid therapeutic technique, whatever might be the reasons for its success. The British Medical Association officially endorsed it in 1955, and the Council on Mental Health of the American Medical Association did likewise in 1958.[18] By the 1970s, it had been approved as a therapeutic method by medical, psychological and psychiatric, and dental groups worldwide.

While the availability of modern anesthetic drugs has displaced hypnotism in major surgery, it continues to be used in managing pain and the fear of pain in other medical and dental settings. It is used in psychosomatic medicine to reduce blood pressure and functional disorders. Its use in psychotherapy is guarded, especially when used to revive past traumatic events suspected of having caused the psychological disturbance under treatment.[19] The present ability of the client to handle the repressed event must be properly gauged. Knowledgeable assistance must be available should the revived experience begin to overwhelm the patient. For this reason, psychologists and psychiatrists are concerned about persons without clinical training in the detection and treatment of mental disorders engaging in hypnotic induction. The American Society of Clinical Hypnosis (embracing members representing the professions of medicine, osteopathy, dentistry, and psychology) established a code of ethics, effective November 16, 1983, reflecting this concern.[20] The society was striving "to establish guidelines and to conduct a continuing program to ensure the ethical use of hypnosis. . . ."[21] Among the provisions of this code are the following:

> 1. A member of [the society] shall not support the practice of

---

[17] Orne, *supra* note 14, at 135.

[18] 168 JAMA 186-87 (1958).

[19] 9 Orne, *supra* note 14, at 139.

[20] The American Society of Clinical Hypnosis (ASCH) Code of Ethics, adopted pursuant to art XI, §D(7) and art IV, §E(2) of the Bylaws, November 16, 1983.

[21] *Id* intro.

> hypnosis by lay persons. In particular, a member of [the society] shall not teach hypnotic techniques to lay persons. Lectures informing lay persons about hypnosis are not prohibited so long as such lectures do not include demonstrations or didactic material teaching hypnotic induction.
>
> (a) A "lay person" is an individual who lacks clinical training in a therapeutic or scientific profession recognized by [the society].
>
> (b) "Clinical" means the ability to diagnose, prescribe and carry out treatment for a medical, dental or psychological disorder.
>
> 2. Members of the [society] shall only use hypnosis within their respective areas of professional competence.
>
> 3. No member of the [society] shall use hypnosis for entertainment purposes.[22]

The code also provides that the primary concern of each member must be the welfare of the subject, and therefore the professional must keep contact with the subject to determine what need for care might become apparent subsequently and to provide that care.

§11.04 Contemporary Forensic Uses of Hypnosis

Despite the concern of the mental health specialists noted in **§11.03,** an increasing number of law enforcement officers are being trained in the rather simple technique of hypnosis.[23] The police and other investigative bodies are using the technique to enhance the memory of witnesses and victims in furtherance of their investigations. The practice is not reserved to large metropolitan police forces. Even small communities have trained an officer or two to induce hypnosis, and federal investigative agencies make use of it.

Law enforcement groups without hypnotists on their staffs frequently enroll the services of a cooperative psychologist or psychiatrist or general practitioner. One observer believes that the interest among investigative bodies has been stirred by some writers on the subject who have been given to extravagant claims as to the usefulness and reliability

---

[22] The American Society of Clinical Hypnosis, *supra* note 20.

[23] Monrose, *Justice with Glazed Eyes: The Growing Use of Hypnotism in Law Enforcement,* Juris Dr 54 (Oct/Nov 1978) cited and discussed in Diamond, *Inherent Problems in the Use of Pretrial Hypnosis on a Prospective Witness,* 68 Cal L Rev 313 (1980).

of the process.[24] One of the writings makes a strong case for hypnosis as a truth-finding device. The author states that under deep hypnotic trance a subject cannot lie. If questioned properly, he or she "therefore invariably responds with the correct answer."[25] However, this opinion is not widely shared by the scientific community.

A case invariably cited by those promoting the use of hypnosis by police agencies is the 1976 Chowchilla kidnapping.[26] In that case, a school bus filled with children was abducted along with the driver. The bus was driven into a trench and covered with earth, with the children and the driver inside. When found, the driver and the children were unable to identify or describe adequately their three abductors. In fact, they could not supply any useful information. The Federal Bureau of Investigation brought in a hypnotist who hypnotized the driver. The driver was then able to recall all but one digit of the kidnappers' license plate number. With this lead, the police quickly picked up the trail of the abductors, who were apprehended and successfully prosecuted.

In the Chowchilla case, the hypnotist was a medical person. However, a lay hypnotist—i.e., a police officer or a stage entertainer with no broad clinical background—apparently may be made an effective hypnotist with a minimum of training. The concern over this skill of inducing a hypnotic state being possessed and used by one without a clinical background is noted in **§11.03.** However, the authenticity of a hypnotic state need not depend on the medical or psychological training of the practitioner.

Other investigative uses of hypnosis by the police or prosecution has been in the interrogation of suspects. In *Rex v Booher,*[27] a Canadian case, the police were interested in locating a gun, the suspected murder weapon. The prosecution made use of a medical hypnotist, a Dr. Langsner, to interrogate the suspect. The interrogation, carried on while the subject was hypnotized, led to the discovery of the gun. It also led to the confession of the suspect.

An analogous situation arose in *Leyra v Denno,*[28] an American case. While the United States Supreme Court roundly condemned the use of hypnosis by law enforcement agents, with or without the consent of the subject, in order to elicit inculpating statements, a psychiatrist close to

---

[24] Diamond, *supra* note 23, at 314.

[25] *Id* 313, quoting W. Bryan, Legal Aspects of Hypnosis (1962).

[26] Time Magazine, Law Section 56 (Sept 13, 1976).

[27] 4 DLR 795 (1928).

[28] 347 US 556 (1954); also see discussion in Levy, *Hypnosis and Legal Immutability,* 46 J Crim L Criminology & Police Sci 333, 342 n61 (1955).

the forensic scene suspects that the practice continues.[29] Fifteen years after *Leyra,* a lawyer-hypnotist published a book for law enforcement personnel in which he explains how to hypnotize a suspect without the suspect being aware of what is happening.[30]

The use of hypnosis has expanded in civil cases as well.[31] In one case involving the crash of a helicopter, a passenger of the unfortunate flight was hypnotized four years after the event in an effort to obtain details surrounding the last moments before the crash.[32] At trial, the defense unsuccessfully moved to exclude any matters recalled after the passenger underwent this hypnosis.

The criminal defense bar has also found the technique useful in searching out details that tend to exculpate the accused. In one reported case, a defense attorney needed to know the activities of the client on a particular evening.[33] Unfortunately, the defendant, charged with murder, could not recall his whereabouts that evening because of his intoxication throughout the relevant time. The attorney sought a court order allowing the assistance of a hypnotist while he interviewed the client in jail. The order was granted. In contrast, in the famous Sam Sheppard case, attorney F. Lee Bailey was unsuccessful in persuading the Ohio Supreme Court to order an hypnotic examination of his client in a posttrial bid for freedom.[34] Sirhan Sirhan, the convicted assassin of Robert Kennedy, was hypnotized by a psychiatrist in a pretrial attempt to elicit information helpful to the defense.[35]

§11.05 Hypnosis for Trial Use

In order to treat in orderly fashion the legal issues surrounding evidence which has been obtained with the assistance of hypnosis, it is necessary to separate the various possible hypnosis-related issues. The following should be distinguished.

1. Hypnosis asserted as a criminal defense or, by the prosecution, as a form of duress and force
2. In-court testimony of a witness while under hypnosis

---

[29] Diamond, *supra* note 23, at 315 n7(b).

[30] M. Teitelbaum, Hypnosis Induction Technics 168 (1968).

[31] Dilloff, 4 Ohio NUL Rev 1, 17 (1977).

[32] Wyller v Fairchild Hiller Corp, 503 F2d 506 (9th Cir 1974); *see also* United States v Awkward, 597 F2d 667, 670 (9th Cir 1979).

[33] Cornell v Superior Court, 52 Cal App 2d 99, 338 P2d 447 (1959).

[34] State *ex rel* Sheppard v Koblentz, 174 Ohio St 120, 187 NE 2d 40 (1962).

[35] Diamond, *supra* note 23, at 315 n7(c).

3. In-court testimony of a witness as to matters to which memory was restored during pretrial hypnosis
4. In-court evidence of an out-of-court statement made by a witness (or defendant) while hypnotized
5. Expert opinion on the scientific status of hypnosis and the reliability of recollections enhanced by it

In two early California cases,[36] the defendants asserted that they were under the influence of hypnosis at the time of the offenses charged and that therefore their actions were not voluntary. The courts in both cases held that there was insufficient evidence of hypnosis or that it played the responsible role in the crime. The same skepticism about the controlling force of hypnosis has inured to the benefit of defendants who have been accused of using hypnosis as a form of force upon their victims. In one case, a defendant was accused of hypnotizing a victim who then went to her bank, withdrew savings, and gave them to the accused.[37] The review court found there was insufficient evidence of *force* in hypnosis. In a seduction case, the prosecution charged that the defendant had used hypnosis to have forcible intercourse with the victim against her will.[38] He was accused of having then used the same hypnosis to cause his victim to forget the event! The court was skeptical that one who had been a virgin prior to the alleged hypnosis (as the victim claimed) would unwillingly submit under its influence. However, in a similar case another court found that the combination of flattery, lovemaking, and hypnotism was enough to overcome a finding of voluntary surrender by the victim.[39]

From time to time, a party seeks to offer a witness who would testify while under the influence of hypnosis. Sometimes the procedure is proposed as a means of putting a nervous witness at ease and facilitating the testimony. At other times, it is meant to jog the memory of the witness as he or she sits on the stand so that full details will be forthcoming. Perhaps it is meant to provide greater credibility, given the popular view that all the truth comes out under hypnosis. In one instance, the defendant was hypnotized in front of the jury and in that

---

[36] People v Worthington, 105 Cal 166, 38 P 689 (1894); People v Marsh, 17 Cal App 2d 284, 338 P2d 495 (1959); On this issue see also M. Reiter, Antisocial or Criminal Acts and Hypnosis: a Case Study (1958); Erickson, *An Experimental Investigation of the Possible Antisocial Use of Hypnosis*, 2 Psychiatry 391 (1939).

[37] Louis v State, 24 Ala App 120, 130 So 904 (1930).

[38] Austin v Baker, 90 AD 351, 85 NYS 465 (4th Dept), *retried*, 110 AD 510, 96 NYS 814 (1906).

[39] State v Donovan, 128 Iowa 44, 102 NW 791 (1905).

condition was subjected to direct and cross-examination. A charge of first degree murder was reduced to manslaughter as a result, and the defendant pled guilty.[40]

The more common use of hypnosis in preparation for trial is to revive the recollections of a witness who will testify at a later date, when the hypnotic state will have terminated. In such cases, the hypnosis may be induced merely to implant the suggestion that the witness will recall all details of a certain event once he or she is *awakened.* The recollections then appear in the posthypnotic stage under influence of the previous hypnotic suggestion. The recollections may, of course, appear during the hypnotic state itself. The objective of the hypnotic enhancement takes two forms: to restore any crucial details that have been forgotten of an event that is generally recalled; and to restore the memory of an event for which the subject has presently no recollection at all. The legal problems associated with allowing an hypnotically prepared witness to testify on matters restored by the hypnosis should be distinguished from allowing a defendant to take the stand when he or she has admittedly utilized hypnosis to aid in preparing his or her testimony. The problems relating to witnesses who have had their memories jogged by hypnosis turn on the reliability of such recollections, given present scientific knowledge.

Out-of-court statements offered for the truth of what is asserted in them are subject to the hearsay rule even when offered by the speaker who is now a witness on the stand. There are, of course, exceptions. When it is suggested that a witness has recently fabricated his or her present testimony, the witness may offer evidence of a prior consistent statement in rebuttal of the suggestion.[41] Defense counsel from time to time have offered in evidence the exculpating statements of their clients made under hypnosis.[42] The thrust of their argument has been basically that the defendant was so deeply hypnotized that he or she could not but be speaking the truth. Statements of the defendant are sometimes offered through the hypnotist who witnessed them. There are also instances of attempts to introduce tape recordings made during the hypnotic session. In like manner, the prosecution has attempted to

---

[40] An unreported 1962 Ohio case, State v Nebb, no 39,540 (Ohio Com DL, Franklin CS May 28, 1962) discussed by Dilloff, 4 Ohio NUL Rev 1, 12 (1977). See also Diamond, *Inherent Problems in the Use of Pretrial Hypnosis on a Prospective Witness,* 68 Cal L Rev 313, 328 (1980).

[41] Fed R Evid 801 (d)(1). For a complete discussion of the hearsay rule and all its ramifications, see Binder, Hearsay Handbook (Shepard's/McGraw-Hill 2d ed 1983).

[42] People v Ebanks, 117 Cal 652, 49 P 1049 (1897); People v Hiser, 267 Cal App2d 47, 72 Cal Rptr 906 (1968); People v Pusch, 77 ND 860, 46 NW2d 508 (1950); State v Harris, 241 Or 224, 405 P2d 492 (1965).

introduce admissions made by defendants during hypnotic interviews.[43] The rationale has been the same: hypnosis guarantees truth.

Finally, there is the issue of the expert opinion. Does hypnosis provide a body of scientific knowledge subject to expertise? If so, who is an expert? Should general testimony on the reliability of the procedure be allowed? Should the expert be allowed to give an opinion as to the truthfulness and accuracy of a specific witness' recollections? The use of experts is discussed in **§11.09.**

§11.06 Legal Status: Admissibility of Hypnotically Enhanced Testimony

While there have been a number of instances where a judge has allowed a defendant to testify in court while under hypnosis, the overwhelming weight of the cases runs against admissibility of such testimony.[44] In one variation, the judge allowed the defendant to be hypnotized in the presence of the jury. The defendant was given a posthypnotic suggestion that on awakening he would recall all the facts of the case and was then taken out of the trance and allowed to testify in a posthypnotic state.[45]

For the most part, case law revolves about in-court testimony of a witness as to matters to which memory was restored during pretrial hypnosis, perhaps during the investigative stage. The courts are divided on its admissibility. Rulings appear to fall into three categories:

1. The testimony is admissible and is challengeable only as to weight
2. The testimony is admitted only on a showing that certain safeguards were observed
3. The testimony is per se inadmissible

Courts that regularly allow the testimony regard the reservations that exist in scientific circles as to the reliability of the hypnosis procedure as going only to the weight of credibility to be given the testimony.[46] The revived memory is treated as a species of present recollection refreshed as to past events and is challenged with the usual tools of cross-examination. A rebuttal expert may or may not be allowed to testify as to the reliability of the process. In this view, the traditional

---

[43] People v Lyra, 302 NY 353, 98 NE2D 553 (1951).

[44] Dilloff, 4 Ohio NUL Rev 1, at 11 (1977).

[45] *Id.*

[46] United States v Valdez, 722 F2d 1196, 1198 (5th Cir 1984).

safeguards of cross-examination and cautionary instructions suffice to enable the jury to give appropriate weight to the testimony they have heard from the previously hypnotized witness. If the statements of that witness prior to being hypnotized are available, they can be compared with the posthypnotic testimony.

Other courts view with greater skepticism the ability of a jury to evaluate properly the credibility of posthypnotic testimony. In these jurisdictions, the judge, as a matter of law, must rule on the admissibility of the profferred testimony after an initial hearing in which the profferer of the testimony has the burden of demonstrating that he or she has employed procedural safeguards in procuring the testimony so as to preclude confabulation in the revived memories.[47] Unless the court is satisfied such safeguards were employed, the evidence is excluded. Even if allowed, the testimony remains subject to challenge as to credibility.

A number of jurisdictions have adopted the safeguards set out in a 1981 New Jersey case, *State v Hurd.*[48] The *Hurd* court took the position that hypnotically induced testimony may be admissible if the proponent can show that the use of hypnosis in that particular case was a reasonably reliable means of restoring memory comparable to normal recall in its accuracy. It is recognized that normal recall is also subject to error. However, the hypnotically induced testimony is viewed as the product of an unconventional process, the scientific basis for which must be established by the proponent. The reliability of results depends on the sufficiently scientific procedure observed. The minimal requirements of the procedure acceptable to *Hurd* are:

1. A psychiatrist or psychologist experienced in use of hypnosis must conduct the session
2. The professional conducting the session should be independent of and not regularly employed by the prosecutor, investigator, or defense
3. Any information given to the hypnotist by law enforcement personnel or defense prior to the hypnotic session must be recorded, either in writing or in another suitable form
4. Before inducing hypnosis, the hypnotist should obtain from the subject a detailed description of facts as the subject remembers them
5. All contacts between the hypnotist and subject must be recorded

---

[47] *Id* 1199.

[48] 86 NJ 525, 432 A2d 86 (1981).

6. Only the hypnotist and the subject should be present during any phase of the hypnotic session

Courts following *Hurd* require that the procedure used to refresh the memory of the hypnotized witness must meet the standards of *Frye v United States,*[49] before the information adduced will be admissible. Proof that that standard has been met in a particular case must be established by clear and convincing evidence. In the *Hurd* case, the prosecution failed to meet its burden in that the police officer was present during the hypnosis of the victim and asked specific leading questions during the session.

Illinois recently, in turning down a defense appeal that the court adopt a per se inadmissible rule, followed the approach of *Hurd* in spirit if not in significant detail.[50] The Illinois Appellate Court required that the trial court determine if adequate safeguards were used in procuring the revived recollections. However, it rejected the requirement that the proponent show that the procedure met the *Frye* test of scientific acceptability. In rejecting this requirement of *Hurd,* the court argued:

> [The *Frye*] test is not applicable to the admission of hypnotically enhanced testimony because that standard is concerned with the admission of expert opinion deduced from the results of a scientific technique and not the admissibility of eyewitness testimony. Secondly, that standard would single out hypnotically refreshed testimony and impose a requirement that the scientific community agree as to its accuracy in aiding recall, whereas a similar standard is not imposed on ordinary eyewitness testimony not refreshed through hypnosis.[51]

The court was obviously leaning toward the view that the disabilities of the hypnosis procedure go more to the weight of the evidence than to its admissibility. Nonetheless, it required that the trial court find that certain safeguards were observed:

1. That the hypnotist was competent (a detective with one week of training in hypnosis in police school was found not competent; he had used hypnosis in only two actual interviews previously)
2. That the procedure was not fraught with suggestive influences
3. That witness identification of a suspect be corroborated with

---

[49] 293 F 1013, 1014 (DC Cir 1923).

[50] People v Gibson, 452 NE2d 1368 (Ill App Ct 1983).

[51] *Id* 1373.

other substantial evidence unknown to the witness when the identification was made

4. That the evidence show that, at the time of the occurrence, the witness had an ample opportunity to observe the suspect

The court further interpreted the *competency* requirement to include the requirement that the hypnotist be independent of and not closely associated with either the prosecution or defense. It went on to "discourage the practice of allowing police personnel and the Assistant State's Attorney to be present during the interview."[52]

The Federal Bureau of Investigation (FBI) has developed its own guidelines for the hypnotic interview of witnesses.[53] These require the subject's written permission to hypnotize him or her. General practitioners and dentists qualified in hypnosis are permitted to conduct the interviews. The hypnotist need not, however, work independently of the agency. A specially trained FBI agent serves as the *hypnosis coordinator* and is required to participate in the hypnotic session. While he or she may not personally induce the hypnotic state, the agent is an intermediary between the hypnotist and the subject. While the hypnotic session itself is to be recorded, apparently not all communication between the subject and hypnotist need be. In addition, the hypnotist and the hypnosis coordinator apparently have access to unrecorded information before meeting the subject. Finally, the subject's prehypnotic recollections are not recorded for future comparison.

Breaking entirely with this approach, some courts have concluded that a witness who has been hypnotized prior to trial cannot be "redeemed" by whatever safeguards.[54] They hold that such a witness is incompetent to testify to events recalled under hypnosis or by posthypnotic suggestion. The basis of this view is the persuasion that hypnosis fatally taints subsequent testimony and renders it invincibly deceptive to the witness himself or herself, to experts of whatever experience, and certainly to a lay jury or finder of fact.

A voice regularly cited by the courts sharing this view (including, recently, the Fifth Circuit) puts it this strongly:

> I believe that once a potential witness has been hypnotized for the

---

[52] *Id* 1374.

[53] United States v Valdez, 722 F2d 1196, 1199 (3d Cir 1984).

[54] State *ex rel* Collins v Superior Court, 132 Ariz 180, 644 P2d 1266 (1982); People v Shirley, 31 Cal 3d 18, 181 Cal Rptr 243, 641 P2d 775, 797 (1982); Collins v State, 52 Md App 186, 447 A2d 1272 (1982); People v Tait, 99 Mich App 19, 297 NW2d 853 (1980); Commonwealth v Nazarovitch, 496 Pa 97, 436 A2d 170 (1981); State v Martin, No 49494-1 (Wash Sup Ct 1984), 35 Cr L 2245 (1984).

> purpose of enhancing memory his recollections have been so contaminated that he is rendered effectively incompetent to testify. Hypnotized persons, being extremely suggestible, graft onto their memories fantasies or suggestions deliberately or unwittingly communicated by the hypnotist. After hypnosis the subject cannot differentiate between a true recollection and a fantasy or a suggested detail. Neither can any expert or the trier of fact. This risk is so great, in my view, that the use of hypnosis by police on a potential witness is tantamount to the destruction or fabrication of evidence.[55]

The psychiatrist writer goes on to state that even should the trier of fact be fully informed on the effects of hypnosis by experts, the jury or judge "will not be able to sort out reality from witness fantasy and weigh this testimony properly."[56] That writer thus has no faith in the traditional safeguards of cross-examination, expert testimony, or procedural guidelines. He argues that if the nature and effects of hypnosis were fully understood by the legal community, testimony by a previously hypnotized witness would never be admitted into evidence.

§11.07 —Scientific Arguments against Admissibility

The arguments marshalled in favor of a per se rule prohibiting the use of hynotically enhanced testimony go somewhat as follows:

First, the hypnotist, for all his or her skill and responsibility, can never avoid implanting suggestions. The suggested cues are as often as not nonverbal. "The attitude, demeanor, and expectations of the hypnotist, his tone of voice, and his body language may all communicate suggestive messages to the subject. Especially powerful as an agent of suggestion is the context and purpose of the hypnotic session. Most hypnotic subjects aim to please."[57]

Second, the hypnotized subject on awakening cannot separate which of the thoughts, feelings, and memories he or she is experiencing are his or her own and which were implanted during the hypnotic session. Even if these thoughts, feelings, and memories are bizarre and

---

[55] Diamond, *Inherent Problems in the Use of Pretrial Hypnosis on a Prospective Witness,* 68 Cal L Rev 313, 314 (1980), cited in State v Mena, 128 Ariz 226, 624 P2d 1274, 1277 (1981); United States v Valdez, 722 F2d 1196, 1200 (5th Cir 1984).

[56] Diamond, *supra* note 53, at 314.

[57] Diamond, *Inherent Problems in the Use of Pretrial Hypnosis on a Prospective Witness,* 68 Cal L Rev 313, at 333 (1980).

uncharacteristic of the subject, the subject will seek a logical reason for their presence, of which he or she is convinced and as to which he or she is convincing to others. The strength of the subject's belief is very persuasive and withstands the most vigorous cross-examination. The subject can be the classic sincere but mistaken witness.

Third, it is very common for subjects to be totally unaware that they were hypnotized. Even deeply hypnotized subjects will later deny that the hypnosis worked, claiming that they merely pretended to go along with the procedure. Objective evidence is sometimes available to contradict this misconception.

Fourth, the hypnotized person no longer has the power to restrict his or her memory to actual facts. Out of an unconscious desire to meet the hypnotist's perhaps unspoken desires and expectations, the subject will fill in missing details with fantasy and confabulation, mixing facts from different contexts and imaginings. "The hypnotically recalled memory is apt to be a mosaic of 1) appropriate actual events, 2) entirely irrelevant actual events, 3) pure fantasy, 4) fantasized details supplied to make a logical whole."[58] The degree of confidence of the subject in the accuracy of the recovered memories is no guarantee of accuracy.

Fifth, upon awakening, the witness is not in possession of *present recollections refreshed.* He or she is in fact still under the influence of suggestions made during hypnosis. The influence may last indefinitely. This fact is especially so regarding the source of present memories. Many people have had the experience of having vivid memories of an event they believe to have occurred in childhood and which they witnessed, only to discover that it occurred before they were born. Somewhere in such a person's past, a parent or older brother or sister told of the event and perhaps showed a picture of it. Through time, the person has forgotten the source and has nourished the memory as having been one of his or her own experience. A similar mechanism appears in hypnosis. Something learned in hypnosis carries over into the posthypnotic period, but the fact that it was learned under hypnosis is forgotten. It now appears to the subject as his or her very own memory of a witnessed event. Such a belief can be quite unshakeable. It occurs spontaneously or under suggestion by the hypnotist. This *source amnesia* can be triggered even by remarks before or after hypnosis.

Sixth, even a skilled hypnotist cannot consistently detect faked hypnotism. This ability has been subjected to rigorous experimentation. The procedure therefore cannot be relied upon as a truth-finding process.

---

[58] *Id* 335.

Seventh, richness of detail in a revived memory, while very persuasive to the listener, is no guarantee of accuracy or absence of fabrication. Under hypnosis, subjects can give the impression that past, experienced events are unveiling before their eyes and can describe events and things with amazing detail. However, experiments show that a subject can be hypnotized and instructed to move into the future, perhaps 10 years hence, and into unfamiliar surroundings, and the hypnotized subject will proceed to describe the unseen persons, places, and events with the same detail, fluency, and air of conviction which characterized his or her alleged memory of past events. The confabulation occurring in this age progression technique suggests that the same thing is happening in age regression, when the subject is taken back to the scene of the crime, so to speak. At least it is a highly disturbing possibility.

Eighth, independent corroboration of some of the hypnotically adduced memories does not assure reliability as to the rest. The reason is that the hypnotist may have unwittingly supplied cues to the subject as to facts the hypnotist already knew to be established, or the subject may have come by the information from another source but because of the nature of the hypnotic experience now believes them to have first come to light during the the session and out of his or her own recall.

Ninth, recording the hypnotic interview is not an adequate safeguard for detecting improper suggestion. If the recording is in the form of a transcript, there is no way of detecting the suggestion that is communicated through tone of voice and body language. However, even a videotape or audio record is insufficient. Influences before and after the hypnotic experience but which become integrated with the hypnotic experience would be missed.

> The only adequate record of the hypnotic experience would be a videotape of everything that transpired before, during, and after the sessions. Yet that, in itself, would be a powerful distorting factor for the knowledge that one is being recorded can alter one's attitudes and behavior. Therefore the confidence expressed by some courts in the protection offered by stenographic, audio, or video recordings of the hypnotic session is not justified.[59]

Tenth, hypnosis adds significantly to a witness's confidence in his or her recollections and renders him or her measurably more persuasive to a jury. A witness who was tentative about an identification from a photograph or line-up may become quite certain after hypnosis. The very nature of hypnosis rests upon suggestion and suspension of critical

---

[59] *Id* 339.

judgment. The subject told under hypnosis that he or she will recall every detail on waking experiences supreme confidence as to his or her recollections in the posthypnotic stage. Such a witness thus has an advantage over the usual witness who readily admits the possibility if not the probability of being in error.

Eleventh, there is no possibility of expert opinion testimony as to the truth or falsity of enhanced memories. An expert can only inform the court as to the probabilities of the effect of the hypnosis. When the expert advances to offering an opinion as to the substantive truth of the recollection, he or she is no longer speaking as an expert since there is no scientific way of determining that fact. The expert can add little or nothing to the jury's own insight into that issue after explaining the hypnotic procedure and the conditions under which it was employed in the instant case.

Twelfth, admittedly fallible but nevertheless admissible eyewitness testimony is not on the same footing as hypnotically enhanced testimony. The distortions of normal eyewitness observations that *may* occur can be made understandable to the trier of fact. The inevitable distortions of hypnotically enhanced memory escape detection even by experts. The insidiousness and pervasiveness of the hypnotic influence cannot be adequately conveyed to a jury by experts during a trial. It is naive and irresponsible to expect an *informed* jury properly to appraise the credibility of posthypnotic testimony.

The foregoing arguments are substantially the published views of Dr. Bernard Diamond, a preeminent scholar and practitioner in legal psychiatry. An equally authoritative voice in the field of hypnosis and its legal application is that of Dr. Martin Orne. While sharing most of Dr. Diamond's views, Dr. Orne continues to be more sanguine about the possibility of safeguarding the integrity of the pretrial hypnotic interview and successfully informing the jury as to the pitfalls of hypnosis, thereby justifying the admissibility of posthypnotic testimony when certain conditions have been fulfilled. Dr. Orne's suggestions were influential in the *Hurd* guidelines.[60]

§11.08 —Legal Arguments against Admissibility

The legal arguments made in favor of a per se ban on testimony as to all matters relating to events revived under hypnosis, from the time

---

[60] State v Hurd, 86 NJ 525, 432 A2d 86, 96 (1981), discussed in **§11.06.**

of the hypnotic interview forward, are those of due process and the Sixth Amendment right to confrontation.[61]

It is argued that since hypnosis does not meet the *Frye v United States*[62] test of scientific acceptability as a reliable method of procuring accurate recall while inducing an abnormal confidence in such accuracy in the witness, it is a violation of basic fairness to expose a fact-finder to the testimony of such a witness. In addition, since hypnosis has the effect of producing such abnormal and unwarranted confidence in an otherwise fallible eyewitness by replacing his or her original, tentative memory with an artificially unshakable hypnotic memory, the defendant is denied confrontation with the original perception and recollection. Since cross-examination of such a witness would be an exercise in futility and would, in all probability, be counterproductive, examination of the witness is effectively defeated.

Out-of-court statements made by witnesses (or defendants) while hypnotized are universally inadmissible.[63] The argument that there is a presumption of truth about such statements is rejected for the same reasons that statements supported by the polygraph or *truth serum* are rejected. The reliability of the statements so produced or tested is questionable. Therefore, these out-of-court statements are treated as any other out-of-court statements offered to prove the truth of the matter asserted. They are subject to the hearsay rule and its exceptions. However, in a few jurisdictions they may be used as the basis of an expert opinion on some other issue—e.g., the defendant's mental condition at the time of the offense.[64]

§11.09 —Expert Testimony

Finally, there is the role of the expert testifying at trial on the issue of hypnotically obtained statements. This role is potentially twofold. The expert may be called to testify as to the scientific status of the procedure, explaining the nature of the technique, its effects, uses, and reliability as a truth-seeking process. Such evidence is generally admissible and, indeed, may be required before a previously hypnotized witness is allowed to testify. Second, the expert witness may be called for an expert opinion as to the reliability of a particular witness' revived recollections. Case law has gone both ways as to admissibility on this

---

[61] *See e.g.*, People v Shirley, 641 P2d 775, 797 (Cal 1982); State v Mack, 292 NW2d 764, 770 (Minn 1980).

[62] 293 F 1013 (1923), discussed in **§11.06.**

[63] People v Shirley, 31 Cal 3d 18, 181 Cal Rptr 243, 641 P2d 775, 783 (1982).

[64] *Id.* See also Diamond, *Inherent Problems in the Use of Hypnosis on a Prospective Witness*, 68 Cal L Rev 313, at 315 n 7(d) (1980). *But see* Jones v State, 542 P2d 316 (Okla 1975).

issue.[65] The trend has been to exclude opinion as to the reliability of a defendants' enhanced recollections while being more receptive to such opinion testimony when offered in regard to prosecution witnesses.[66]

Exactly who is an expert on these issues? It has been noted that some courts require more than mere facility with hypnotic technique to render one competent to conduct a pretrial hypnotic interview of a witness who is to testify later.[67] These courts require broader professional training for this role. Dr. Bernard Diamond would argue that even more stringent qualifications are needed in one offering an opinion on the issues described here.[68] His own view is that hypnosis is a scientifically proven tool for therapeutic and diagnostic purposes but has no scientific standing as a guarantor of accurate recall. Furthermore, there are no experts on the issue of which specific recollections are trustworthy. Even psychologists and psychiatrists skilled in the therapeutic and diagnostic uses of hypnosis may be extremely naive in their appraisal of the process' ability to promote reliable recall. Such practitioners are concerned with the meaning assigned a recalled event, the *emotional* content of the recollection, and not its truth value. The clinicians' appreciation of hypnosis for their particular purposes may not equip them to respond to the question in which the court is interested: its truth-testing capabilities. In this regard, Dr. Diamond has observed:

> I have found that, with very few exceptions, such so-called experts may be highly skilled in the therapeutic and diagnostic use of hypnosis, yet be totally unaware of its shortcomings in the context of the legal situation. Usually, they are familiar with the literature of hypnotherapy but often lack knowledge of the extensive experimental work of Hilgard, Orne, and the many other researchers who have made important scientific contributions to this field. Law enforcement-oriented author-hypnotists, police staff psychologists, and policeman-hypnotists especially tend to be ignorant of the extensive body of scientific knowledge that has accumulated through research on hypnosis. Many policeman-hypnotists have taken only short courses in hypnotic technique but have read avidly and uncritically articles and books on its use in

---

[65] L. Taylor, Eyewitness Identification 90 (1982).

[66] *Id.*

[67] See **§11.06.**

[68] Diamond, *Inherent Problems in the Use of Pretrial Hypnosis on a Prospective Witness,* 68 Cal L Rev 313 (1980). See **§11.07.**

criminal investigation, and have become highly skilled in inducing the hypnotic state and interrogating subjects. They have no difficulty in qualifying as experts. Yet their lack of scientific background and of familiarity with the research literature causes them to assert palpably false or misleading positions concerning hypnosis. In the cases in which I participated, the hypnotists who had professional training in psychology or medicine were similarly deficient in real knowledge about hypnosis even though there were skilled in its use. The very nature of the hypnotic experience makes it peculiarly difficult for either the subject, the hypnotist, or the observer to remain objective and emotionally detached. Here, more than in any other field of expertise, the claim of being an impartial expert is likely to be fallacious.[69]

---

[69] Diamond, *supra* note 66, at 341.

Cases

A

B

C

D

People v Kramm, Indictment Nos 80 CF 1261, 80 CF 1262 (Cir Ct DuPage County, Ill Oct 29, 1980) **§8.05**

People v Lawson, 37 Colo App 442, 551 P2d 206 (1976) **§8.02**

People v Lee, 44 Ill 2d 161, 254 NE2d 469 (1970) **§3.15**

People v Levine, 99 Ill App 3d 141, 426 NE2d 215 (1981) **§3.15**

People v Lyra, 302 NY 353, 98 NE2d 553 (1951) **§11.05**

People v Malloy, 240 NE2d 37, 22 NY2d 559 (1968) **§6.09**

People v Mamon, 67 Ill 2d 564, 367 NE2d 1313 (1977), *cert denied,* 435 US 937 (1978) **§3.15**

People v Marsh, 17 Cal App 2d 284, 338 P2d 495 (1959) **§11.05**

People v Martinez, 652 P2d 174 (Colo Ct App 1981) **§9.07**

People v McCoy, 78 Ill App 3d 157, 397 NE2d 79 (1979) **§3.15**

People v Owens, 54 Ill 2d 286, 296 NE2d 728 (1973) **§3.15**

People v Palumbo, 192 Colo 7, 555 P2d 521 (1976) **§9.07**

People v Petterson, 266 NYS2d 884 (NY 1966) **§6.09**

People v Poor, 178 Cal Rptr 375 (1978) **§3.15**

People v Pusch, 77 ND 860, 46 NW2d 508 (1950) **§11.05**

People v Reynolds, 68 Colo App 258, 559 P2d 714 (1976) **§9.07**

People v Ricili, 400 Ill 309, 79 NE2d 509 (1948) **§9.07**

People v Rodriquez, 137 Cal Rptr 594 (Cal Ct App 1977) **§3.15**

People v Rogers, 81 Ill 2d 571, 44 Ill Dec 254, 411 NE2d 223 (1980) **§6.09**

People v Shirley, 31 Cal 3d 18, 641 P2d 775, 181 Cal Rptr 243 (1982) **§§11.06, 11.08**

People v Simpson, 39 Ill App 3d 318, 349 NE2d 441 (1976) **§6.09**

People v Suleski, 58 AD2d 1023, 397 NYS2d 280 (1977) **§§1.04, 8.02, 8.05, 8.06**

People v Sweeny, 57 Ill App 3d 897, 373 NE2d 663 (1978) **§3.08**

People v Tait, 99 Mich App 19, 297 NW2d 853 (1980) **§11.06**

People v Taylor, No 77-4604 (Cir Ct of Cook County, Ill, Sept 6, 1977) **§3.04**

People v Valentine, 53 AD2d 832, 385 NYS2d 545 (1976) **§§8.06-8.10**

People v Watson, 36 Ill 2d 228, 221 NE2d 645 (1966) **§3.10**

People v Whalen, No 234 (NY App Div, June 16, 1983) **§§9.03, 9.04, 9.07**

People v White, 58 Ill App 3d 226, 374 NE2d 250 (1978) **§9.07**

State v Dale, 3 Ohio App 3d 431, 445 NE2d 1137 (1982) **§9.07**

State v Degraffenreid, 447 SW2d 57 (Mo 1972) **§6.09**

State v Dessureault, 104 Ariz 380, 453 P2d 951 (1969) **§9.07**

State v Donovan, 128 Iowa 44, 102 NW 791 (1905) **§11.05**

State v Edwards, 600 P2d 566 (Wash Ct App 1979) **§9.07**

State v Gardner, 86 NJ 281, 430 A2d 914 (1981) **§9.08**

State v Gordon, 441 A2d 119 (Conn 1981), *cert denied,* 455 US 989 (1982) **§3.15**

State v Gravely, 299 SE2d 375 (W Va 1982) **§9.07**

State v Grien, 86 NJ 281, 430 A2d 914 (1981) **§9.07**

State v Guster, 66 Ohio St 2d 266, 421 NE2d 157 (1981) **§9.07**

State v Hall, 93 NJ 552, 461 A2d 1153 (1983) **§3.09**

State v Harden, 175 Conn 315, 398 A2d 1169 (1980) **§9.07**

State v Harris, 241 Or 224, 405 P2d 492 (1965) **§11.05**

State v Hart, 625 P2d 21 (Mont), *cert denied,* 454 US 827 (1981) **§9.07**

State v Heald, 120 NH 319, 414 A2d 1288 (1980) **§3.15**

State v Henderson, 116 Ariz 310, 569 P2d 252 (1977) **§3.15**

State v Hills, 129 So 2d 12 (La 1961) **§9.07**

State v Holterbridle, 301 NW2d 545 (Minn 1980) **§8.02**

State v Howze, 66 Ohio App 2d 41, 420 NE2d 131 (1979) **§3.15**

State v Hurd, 86 NJ 525, 432 A2d 86 (1981) **§§11.06, 11.07**

State v Kasper, 137 Vt 184, 404 A2d 85 (1979) **§9.07**

State v Kinard, 54 NC App 443, 283 SE2d 540 (1981) **§9.07**

State v Lewis, 341 A2d 744 (RI 1975) **§9.07**

State v Mack, 292 NW2d 764 (Minn 1980) **§11.08**

State v Malmrose, 649 P2d 56 (Utah 1982) **§9.07**

State v Marten, 53 NC App 297, 280 SE2d 778 (1981) **§9.07**

State v Martin, No 49494-1 35 Cr L 2245 (Wash Sup Ct 1984) **§11.06**

State v Maturo, 188 Conn 591, 452 A2d 642 (1982) **§9.07**

State v Mazurek, 88 NM 56, 537 P2d 51 (Ct App 1975) **§9.07**

State v McGee, 350 So 2d 370 (La 1977) **§3.08**

State v Mena, 128 Ariz 226, 624 P2d 1274 (1981) **§11.06**

State v Mitchell, 390 A2d 495 (Me 1978) **§8.02**

State v Nebb, unreported 1962 Ohio Case **§11.05**

State v Oldham, 92 Idaho 124, 438 P2d 275 (1968) **§9.07**

State v Padilla, 552 P2d 357 (Hawaii 1976) **§9.07**

State v Pahio, 568 P2d 1200 (Hawaii 1977) **§9.07**

United States v Barber, 442 F2d 517 (3d Cir), *cert denied,* 404 US 958 (1971) **§9.06**

United States v Barnes, 416 F Supp 1176 (WDNY 1976) **§3.15**

United States v Barrett, 703 F2d 1076 (9th Cir 1983) **§§3.06, 8.03**

United States v Bierey, 588 F2d 620 (8th Cir 1978), *cert denied,* 439 US 935 (1979) **§3.08**

United States v Bowie, 515 F2d 3 (7th Cir 1975) **§3.15**

United States v Boyd, 620 F2d 129 (6th Cir), *cert denied,* 449 US 855 (1980) **§9.06**

United States v Brake, 596 F2d 337 (8th Cir 1979) **§9.08**

United States v Brown, 501 F2d 146 (9th Cir 1974), *revd on other grounds,* 422 US 225 (1975) **§§1.04, 8.02**

United States v Brown, 540 F2d 1048 (10th Cir 1976), *cert denied,* 429 US 1100 (1977) **§§1.04, 8.02, 8.06**

United States v Butler, 636 F2d 727 (DC Cir 1972) **§9.06**

United States v Cain, 616 F2d 1056 (8th Cir 1980) **§9.06**

United States v Callahan, 434 F Supp 1203 (D Minn 1977) **§3.08**

United States v Collins, 395 F Supp 629 (MD Pa), *affd,* 523 F2d 1051 (3d Cir 1975) **§§8.02, 8.18**

United States v Crews, 445 US 463 (1980) **§§1.05, 3.13**

United States v Cripler, 533 F2d 1055 (8th Cir), *cert denied,* 429 US 844 (1976) **§9.06**

United States v Crouch, 478 F Supp 867 (ED Cal 1979) **§3.08**

United States v Cueto, 611 F2d 1056 (5th Cir 1980) **§§3.15, 9.06**

United States v Cyphers, 553 F2d 1064 (7th Cir 1977) **§8.02**

United States v Daniels, 506 F2d 791 (3d Cir 1974) **§3.08**

United States v Dinitz, 424 US 600 (1976) **§§5.02, 5.07**

United States v Dodge, 538 F2d 770 (8th Cir), *cert denied,* 429 US 1099 (1976) **§9.06**

United States v Escobedo, 430 F2d 14 (7th Cir 1970) **§5.07**

United States v Evans, 484 F2d 1178 (2d Cir 1974) **§9.06**

United States v Fleming, 594 F2d 598 (7th Cir), *cert denied,* 442 US 931 (1979) **§9.06**

United States v Fosher, 590 F2d 381 (1st Cir 1979) **§§1.04, 3.10, 8.02, 8.18**

United States v Freeman, 514 F2d 1184 (10th Cir 1975) **§5.07**

United States v Gentile, 530 F2d 461 (2d Cir), *cert denied,* 426 US 936 (1976) **§9.06**

United States v Greene, 591 F2d 471 (8th Cir 1979) **§9.06**

United States v Harding, 525 F2d 24 (7th Cir 1975) **§6.11**

United States v Hearst, 412 F Supp 893 (ND Cal 1976), *affd,*

563 F2d 1331 (9th Cir 1977) **§1.04**
United States v Hershenow, 680 F2d 847 (1st Cir 1982) **§5.07**
United States v Hill, 655 F2d 512 (3d Cir 1981) **§8.02**
United States v Hodges, 515 F2d 650 (7th Cir 1975) **§9.06**
United States v Holley, 502 F2d 273 (4th Cir 1974) **§§1.05, 9.01, 9.06**
United States v Kimbrovich, 528 F2d 1242 (7th Cir 1976) **§3.15**
United States v Leach, 427 F2d 1107 (1st Cir 1970) **§9.08**
United States v Masterson, 529 F2d 30 (9th Cir), *cert denied,* 426 US 908 (1976) **§9.06**
United States v McNeil, 434 F2d 502 (DC Cir 1970) **§1.04**
United States v Montelbano, 605 F2d 56 (2d Cir 1979) **§9.06**
United States v Musgrave, 444 F2d 755 (5th Cir 1971) **§9.08**
United States v Palmeri, 630 F2d 192 (3d Cir 1980), *cert denied,* 450 US 967 (1981) **§9.10**
United States v Penick, 496 F2d 1105 (7th Cir), *cert denied,* 419 US 897 (1974) **§3.10**
United States v Porter, 430 F Supp 208 (WDNY 1977) **§3.15**
United States v Revels, 575 F2d 74 (4th Cir 1978) **§9.06**
United States v Rhodes, 569 F2d 384 (5th Cir), *cert denied,* 439 US 844 (1978) **§9.06**
United States v Rich, 580 F2d 929 (9th Cir 1978) **§3.08**
United States v Rivers, 693 F2d 52 (8th Cir 1982) **§9.06**
United States v Salovitz, 701 F2d 17 (2d Cir 1983) **§5.07**
United States v Sambrano, 505 F2d 284 (9th Cir 1974) **§9.06**
United States v Scott, 578 F2d 1186 (6th Cir), *cert denied,* 439 US 870 (1978) **§9.06**
United States v Sims, 617 F2d 1371 (9th Cir 1980) **§§3.10, 8.04**
United States v Singleton, 702 F2d 1159 (DC Cir 1983) **§3.15**
United States v Smallwood, 473 F2d 98 (DC Cir 1972) **§3.07**
United States v Smith, 521 F2d 957 (DC Cir 1975) **§6.09**
United States v Spock, 416 F2d 165 (1st Cir 1969) **§9.10**
United States v Telfaire, 469 F2d 552 (DC Cir 1972) **§§1.05, 4.05, 9.01, 9.03, 9.04, 9.06, 9.07**
United States v Thevis, 665 F2d 616 (5th Cir 1982) **§8.06**
United States v Tolliver, 569 F2d 724 (2d Cir 1978) **§3.08**
United States v Valdez, 722 F2d 1196 (5th Cir 1984) **§§11.01, 11.06**
United States v Wade, 388 US 218 (1967) **§§1.05, 3.07, 3.08, 3.12, 3.19, 9.01**
United States v Watson, 587 F2d 365 (7th Cir 1978) **§§1.04, 8.02**
United States v Wilford, 493 F2d 730 (3d Cir), *cert denied,* 419 US 851 (1974) **§9.06**

V

W

Index

A

E

L

R

T

U

V

W